Unholy Kingdom

Unholy Kingdom

Religion, Corruption and Violence in Saudi Arabia

Malise Ruthven

VERSO
London • New York

This updated English-language edition first published by Verso 2025
Originally published as *L'Arabie des Saoud*
© La Fabrique éditions 2019
© Malise Ruthven 2019, 2025

All rights reserved

The moral rights of the author have been asserted

1 3 5 7 9 10 8 6 4 2

Verso
UK: 6 Meard Street, London W1F 0EG
US: 207 East 32nd Street, New York, NY 10016
versobooks.com

Verso is the imprint of New Left Books

ISBN-13: 978-1-83976-010-5
ISBN-13: 978-1-83976-012-9 (UK EBK)
ISBN-13: 978-1-83976-013-6 (US EBK)

British Library Cataloguing in Publication Data
A catalogue record for this book is available from the British Library

Library of Congress Cataloging-in-Publication Data

Names: Ruthven, Malise, author.
Title: Unholy kingdom : religion, corruption and violence in Saudi Arabia / Malise Ruthven.
Other titles: Religion, corruption and violence in Saudi Arabia
Description: Updated English-language edition. | London ; New York : Verso, 2025. | Originally published in English in 2020. | Includes bibliographical references and index.
Identifiers: LCCN 2024038189 (print) | LCCN 2024038190 (ebook) | ISBN 9781839760105 | ISBN 9781839760136 (ebk)
Subjects: LCSH: Āl Saʻūd, Muḥammad bin Salmān bin ʻAbd al-ʼAzīz, Crown Prince of Saudi Arabia, 1985- | Āl Saʻūd, House of. | State crimes--Saudi Arabia. | Islam and state--Saudi Arabia. | Wahhābȳyah--Saudi Arabia. | Saudi Arabia--History--1932- | Saudi Arabia--Politics and government--1932-
Classification: LCC DS244.52 .R85 2025 (print) | LCC DS244.52 (ebook) | DDC 322/.109538--dc23/eng/20241114
LC record available at https://lccn.loc.gov/2024038189
LC ebook record available at https://lccn.loc.gov/2024038190

Typeset in Fournier by MJ & N Gavan, Truro, Cornwall
Printed and bound by CPI Group (UK) Ltd, Croydon CR0 4YY

To my grandson Zephyr, who has challenged our addiction to fossil fuels, and to friends among the Huwaitat who made me welcome in their goat-hair tents during my teens

Contents

Maps	viii
Al Saud Dynasty	x
1. Murder in Istanbul	1
2. The Wahhabi Mission	45
3. Ibn Saud: Founder of a Kingdom	67
4. Petroleum and Patriarchy	94
5. Managing the Ulama and Mismanaging the Hajj	116
6. Conflicting Currents	140
7. A Sectarian Outreach	159
8. Arms and Benefits	196
9. Family Values	230
10. Terraforming Arabia	263
Acknowledgements	335
Notes	336
Index	355

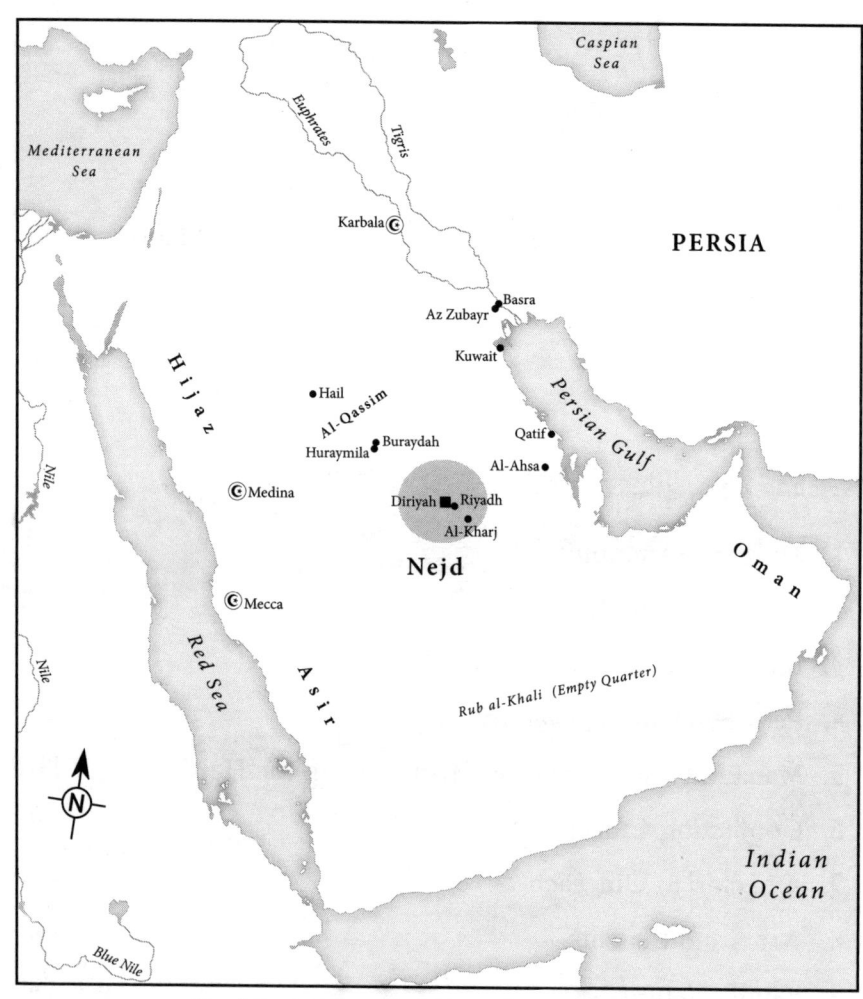

Arabia in the eighteenth century CE

- 🟤 Saudi family hinterland
- ■ Saudi capital
- • Town
- Ⓒ Holy city

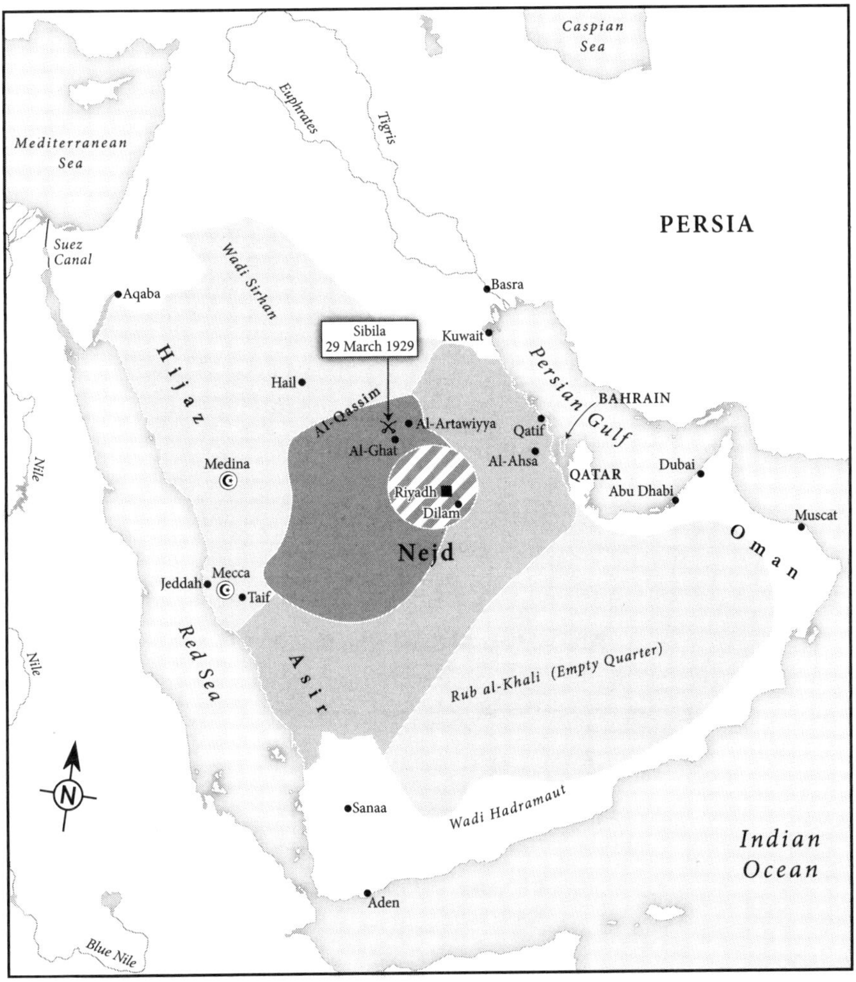

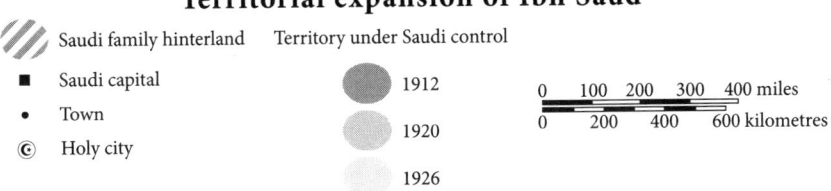

Territorial expansion of Ibn Saud

- ▨ Saudi family hinterland
- ■ Saudi capital
- • Town
- Ⓒ Holy city

Territory under Saudi control
- 1912
- 1920
- 1926

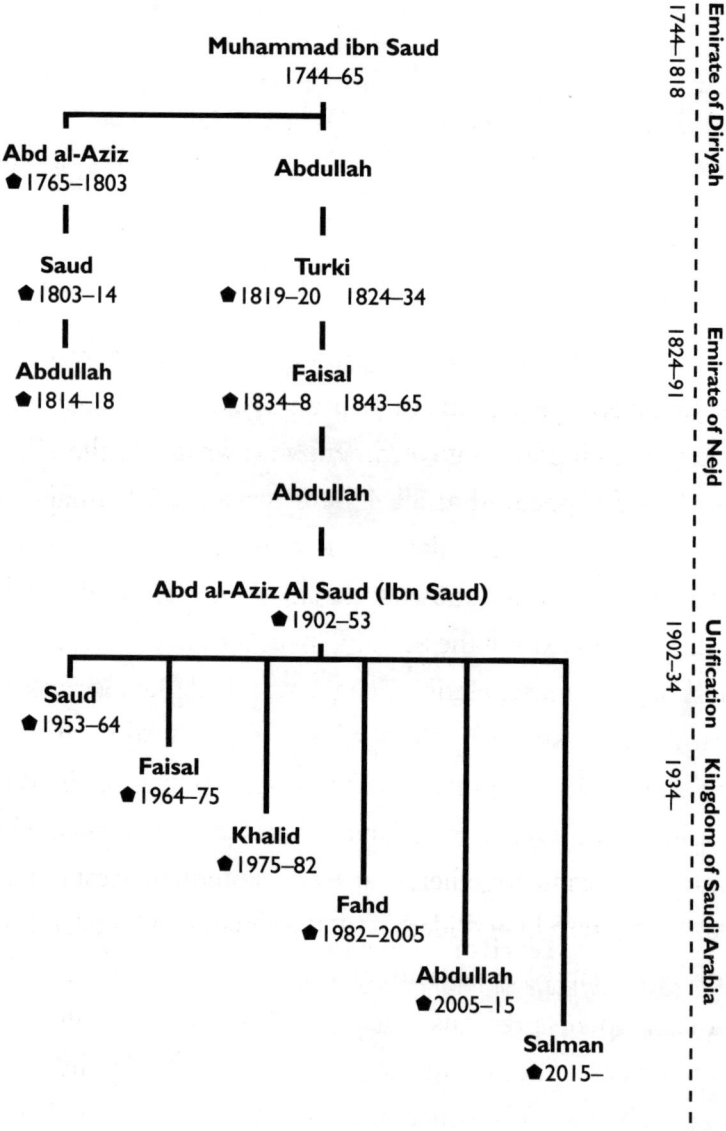

1
Murder in Istanbul

The official Saudi story kept changing. At first there was the denial that Jamal Khashoggi, the high-profile Saudi journalist and recent critic of the kingdom's government who wrote for the *Washington Post*, had disappeared at all. There were CCTV images of him entering the Saudi consulate in Istanbul, and then blurred images surfaced on YouTube showing a man of similar build and wearing similar clothes exiting the building from a back entrance. However, Khashoggi's fiancée, Hatice Cengiz, wrecked that charade from the start. A thirty-six-year-old academic working for a doctorate in Gulf studies, she had met Khashoggi at a conference in May 2018. Despite the difference in age and Khashoggi's complicated marital history, they came together, sharing a common interest in seeking to balance Western liberal ideas with their mainstream Islamic beliefs.[1] In order to marry her Khashoggi needed documentary proof that the divorce from his previous wife in Saudi Arabia was valid. When he had first visited the consulate, he had been treated politely and told to return in a week to collect the document. On this second visit he had not been especially worried. However, he did not want to hand over his phones to the security men in the consulate, so he left them with Hatice. Unfortunately for the Saudis, the phones contained the number of one of his high-level contacts, Yasin Aktay, an advisor to Recep Tayyip Erdogan, the Turkish president.

So the story of Khashoggi's brutal killing emerged via a cascade of disclosures emanating from Turkish intelligence that began to appear in the press. Thanks to the incompetence of the Saudis, who had failed to 'de-bug' the consulate, Turkish intelligence had an audio record of every brutal stage. The killing was done by a hit squad or 'Rapid Intervention Force' sent from the Saudi capital Riyadh. The commander was Maher Abdulaziz Mutreb, forty-seven, a brigadier general who six months previously had been photographed in the entourage of Crown Prince Mohammed bin Salman, known as MBS, on a visit to Texas.[2] The squad had arrived in two batches, three of them staying in the Wyndham Grand Hotel and twelve in the Mövenpick Hotel close to the consulate where they had booked suites and rooms for three days.[3] Jonathan Rugman, a television reporter, has left a detailed account of the murder based on the Turkish audio record.

As Rugman relates, the dominant voice is that of Mutreb, followed by Dr Salah al-Tubaigy, a forensic pathologist whose presence suggests that killing was seen as a likely outcome, if not the actual intention. At first Mutreb tries to persuade Khashoggi to return with the group to Saudi Arabia, falsely claiming there is an Interpol warrant for his arrest. Mutreb proffers a phone, and orders Khashoggi to call his son Salah in Riyadh. When Khashoggi refuses, tools are laid out on a table: syringes, scissors and a Taser stun gun. Security men are ordered to subdue him while he struggles. 'Keep pushing', says a voice captured on audio. 'Push here. Don't remove your hand.' Khashoggi is apparently sedated and then suffocated with a plastic bag. 'It is over, it is over, it is over', says the voice. There are sounds of human panting and the shifting of plastic sheets as the victim's clothes are removed. Then sounds of a saw cutting into the body, a process that takes around half an hour. Tubaigy, the pathologist, is heard shouting, 'Why are you standing around like that?' while he evidently works on the corpse. According to the CIA, which accessed the audio, the murder took place in the consul general's office, but the adjacent briefing room may also have been used. Here, according to Rugman, gold-framed portraits of three Saudi rulers hang above the diplomat's desk, 'silent witnesses to the killing … In the centre, Ibn Saud, Saudi Arabia's first king; on the right his son, King Salman, and on the left his grandson Crown Prince Mohammed bin Salman.'

After eventually admitting that Khashoggi had been killed, the Saudis continued to dispute the Turkish version. They claimed that an argument had taken place in the consulate which had got out of hand, implying that the death had been unintentional. An announcement carried on Saudi state television said discussions between Khashoggi and officials had quickly turned violent, ending in Khashoggi's death, after which those responsible had tried to cover it up. Eleven of the supposed 'rogue operatives' had been arrested and were facing capital charges in Saudi Arabia. The Turkish president and media, however, were not buying this story. Rumours about the shouts and noises recorded on 'bugs' in the consulate were already circulating when Erdogan announced in a highly anticipated speech that the murder had been deliberate and premeditated. While this was hardly news, Erdogan provided some interesting details – stating, for example, that hours before Khashoggi arrived for his appointment the consulate's security cameras had been disconnected. Later, in March 2019, new, more gruesome, details emerged in a television documentary aired on the Qatari-based channel Al Jazeera. Rather than being dissolved in acid – as suggested in one of the possible scenarios – the dismembered journalist's body was taken in bags to the Saudi consul general's residence and burned in a tandoori oven over a period of three days. A worker engaged in constructing the oven to the consul's specifications said it had been built to withstand temperatures of 1,000 degrees Celsius – hot enough to melt metal. To explain the smell of incineration, the killers' accomplices had ordered thirty-two portions of barbecue meat from a local restaurant. The tandoori story, however, was only one of several theories advanced to account for the fact that no body or traces of Khashoggi's blood or DNA have ever been found. Before they were allowed access to the consulate, Turkish police learned that Saudi officials had explored a park north of Istanbul as well as farmland 100 kilometres to the south, but no traces of human remains were found. Turkish police put the lack of any evidence in the consulate down to successive Saudi efforts over a two-week period, with 'wipers' including Khaled Yahya al-Zahrani, a toxicologist, and Ahmad Abdal Aziz al-Junaibi, a chemist, sent specially to clean up the interior. When Turkish investigators were finally allowed to enter the diplomatic building on 15 October, almost two weeks after Khashoggi's disappearance, they found it had already been disinfected and wiped clean. As Rugman points out,

> While the Saudi government has continued to deny authorizing the murder of Jamal Khashoggi, the obstruction of justice afterwards was so deliberate and so extensive that it adds up to as great, if not a greater case for state culpability. If the state did not order the operation, then why cover it up?[4]

One plausible destiny for the unfortunate journalist's remains could have been the Kingdom of Saudi Arabia. A Turkish TV channel obtained security footage showing luggage being transferred from a van into the Saudi consul's residence. In one of the recordings released by the Turkish authorities Khashoggi is referred to as a sacrificial animal (*thabiha*). A senior police officer told Rugman that the police had come to the conclusion that the van was carrying dismembered body parts: no other conclusion could be reached because 'every other line of inquiry had been exhausted'.[5] This conclusion was supported by Turkey's defence minister, Hulusi Akar, who suggested that diplomatic practice, if not formal immunity, had enabled the Saudi officials to leave without having their luggage examined (although only two of the fifteen suspects were travelling on diplomatic passports). A senior British lawyer, Baroness Helena Kennedy QC, who assisted the United Nations investigation, told Rugman there was every likelihood the body had been flown out of Turkey in one of the two private jets that left on 2 October. The theory is consistent with the macabre anecdote that Khashoggi's hand is now used as a trophy on bin Salman's yacht *Serene* (see Chapter 10).

The massive clean-up, widely reported in the press, clearly pointed to Saudi state complicity. 'We have significant signs that this was not something which happened instantaneously, but was planned', said the Turkish president. Responding to these new disclosures the Saudis changed their story yet again. After speaking to Erdogan by phone, Mohammed bin Salman, the young crown prince and country's de facto ruler, broke his silence on the killing. He called Khashoggi's death 'a heinous crime'. Saudi media released pictures of him shaking hands with Khashoggi's son Salah, a gesture greeted with a storm of adverse comment on social media outside the kingdom. The images showed the crown prince taking a defiant stand against rumours that he might be pushed aside over the case.

This was far from being the first time that the Saudis had been accused of extra-judicial killings. As Madawi al-Rasheed, Saudi Arabia's leading English-language historian, points out, 'People go missing so frequently in Saudi Arabia – dissidents, journalists, princes – with barely a mention in the press – that the scale of the outcry over Khashoggi's disappearance must have come as something of a surprise to the crown prince.'⁶ Any surprise he felt, however, must reflect a certain parochialism of outlook. Unlike some of his princely peers, MBS was not educated – even partly – in the United States. He may not have anticipated that the dispatch of Khashoggi – botched or otherwise – would create an international furore. As a US resident and regular columnist for the *Washington Post*, the victim had numerous American friends and was very well known in media circles. He had bought a home in the Washington suburb of McLean and was applying for US citizenship. As well as being a journalist with regular access to the media, he had been accepted as a fellow of the Woodrow Wilson International Center for Scholars, a highly respected institution. I myself had met him at a meeting of the Council on Foreign Relations in New York back in 2004: a pleasant, quietly spoken man dressed in traditional Saudi attire, who seemed less inclined to push himself forward than some of his more loquacious peers.

Apart from the scandal of Khashoggi's murder there was also an issue about warnings. Under a July 2015 directive signed by James R. Clapper, who served as President Obama's director of the National Intelligence overseeing the National Security Agency (NSA), US intelligence has a duty to warn 'US and non-US persons of impending threats of intentional killing, serious bodily injury, or kidnapping'.⁷ According to John R. Schindler, a former intelligence analyst, 'America's big ear' – as the NSA is known – had 'intercepted Saudi communications that indicated Riyadh had something unpleasant in store for Khashoggi' at least a day before he went to the Saudi consulate in Istanbul, though what exactly might be planned was 'not clear from the intercepts'. 'It needs to be asked', wrote Schindler, 'what, if anything, the White House did with this Top Secret warning.' In the event, fifty-five congressmen wrote to Dan Coates, Clapper's successor as NSA director, asking him to clarify what the intelligence community knew about the risks facing Khashoggi prior to his disappearance.

What now seems clear is just how ruthless and reckless the Saudis had become under the crown prince's rule. 'We've never seen it on a scale like this', Bruce Riedel, a former CIA analyst now with the Brookings Institution, told the *New York Times*. 'A dissident like Jamal Khashoggi in the past wouldn't have been considered worth the effort.'[8] According to *Middle East Eye* – a Qatari-funded news site based in London – the crown prince had at his disposal a death squad, known as *firqat al-namir* ('leopard squad'), recruited from different branches of the Saudi security forces whose operatives are unflinchingly loyal to him. Unnamed US officials who spoke to the *New York Times* referred to it as a Rapid Intervention Force. According to an intelligence source cited by *Middle East Eye*, the squad's mission was to 'covertly assassinate Saudi dissidents inside the kingdom and on foreign soil in a way that goes unnoticed by the media, the international community and politicians'. The reasoning appeared to be that disappearances, deaths by illness or from accidents such as house fires or car crashes in one of the world's most accident-prone countries would invite less attention than arresting critics, which produced pressures from allied governments or human rights organizations. One dissenting cleric, Sheikh Suliman Abdul Rahman al-Thuniyan – president of the Mecca public court – is said to have been injected with a deadly virus when he visited hospital for a routine check-up. The same source claimed that the death of Prince Mansour bin Muqrin, deputy governor of Asir province and son of the former crown prince Muqrin, in a helicopter crash in 2017 was not an accident as claimed by his family, but an assassination by the squad. Meshal Saad al-Bostani – a Saudi air force lieutenant and one of the team who visited Turkey – is said to have shot down the prince's helicopter when he was fleeing to Yemen. Bostani was reported to have died in a car crash after returning to Saudi Arabia – but this was disputed by the intelligence source who claimed he had been poisoned.

The leopard or tiger squad was named after Major General Ahmed al-Assiri, deputy head of Saudi intelligence who is widely known as the Leopard (or Tiger) of the South. While the intelligence source was unable to state who issued commands to the squad, two of the men sacked after the Khashoggi killing came to light – General Assiri and Saud al-Qahtani – were said to be part of its 'command structure'. In October 2018, the *Daily Sabah*, a news outlet close to the Turkish president, published the names and pictures of the fifteen-member Saudi hit squad, apparently taken at the airport passport control. In addition to al-Bostani and Maher Abdulaziz Mutreb, a diplomat often photographed with MBS in Madrid, Paris, Boston and New York, the list included Salah Mohammed al-Tubaigy, the 'bone-saw man' who headed the Saudi Council of Forensics, Abd al-Aziz al-Hasawi, a personal bodyguard, and Thaer al-Harbi, a member of the Saudi Royal Guard, as well as Mustafa Mohammed al-Madani, a man of similar build to Khashoggi's who was filmed leaving the consulate wearing Khashoggi's clothes. Turkish intelligence is said to have intercepted at least fourteen phone calls between Mutreb and the crown prince's office on 2 October, the day of the killing, while he spoke to Badr al-Asaker, head of his private office, on several occasions after the murder. These and other details, including gruesome accounts of the tortures to which Khashoggi had been subjected before being killed and dismembered, were carefully leaked by Turkish intelligence to maximize the Saudi government's embarrassment as it struggled to make its story fit the facts as they came to be disclosed.

Further disclosures about the hit team came from American sources. In June 2021, the *New York Times* ran a story with the headline 'Saudi operatives who killed Khashoggi received paramilitary training in the US'. It provided details of Tier 1, a security company based in Arkansas, owned by a private equity firm named Cerberus Capital Management, that provided training, including surveillance and close-combat methods, to protect Saudi leaders. A senior executive of Cerberus, Louis Bremer, confirmed his company's role in the training in written answers to questions from US lawmakers during nomination proceedings, subsequently withdrawn, for a Pentagon post during the Trump administration. In a document he supplied to the newspaper Mr Bremer acknowledged that four members of the Khashoggi hit squad (who were not named) had received Tier 1 group training in 2017 and that two of them had participated in a previous iteration of the training, from October 2014 until January 2015. 'The training provided was unrelated to their subsequent heinous acts' said Mr Bremer, but as the report concluded: 'the fact that the government approved high-level military training for operatives who went on to carry out the grisly killing of a journalist shows how intensely intertwined the United States has become with an autocratic nation even as its agents commit horrific human rights abuses'.[9]

As following chapters will show, human rights count for little when there are vast economic interests at stake. In 2016, MBS – by then already in charge of economic policy – announced plans to implement 'Vision 2030', a formidable project aimed at weaning the kingdom off hydrocarbons at a time when the price of oil hovered at less than $60 a barrel, driven down by the fracking revolution in the US and falling global demand. Oil won't sustain the Saudi economy for ever, and MBS's programme – developed with considerable input from leading US consultancy firms McKinsey and the Boston Consultancy Group – is aimed at curbing public spending and diversifying the economy. The plans include investing in Islamic tourism and in a revamped financial district in Riyadh, as well as expanding revenue streams generally and increasing job opportunities for young Saudis. Blue-collar foreign workers are to be replaced by Saudi nationals in areas such as mobile phone technology and engineering. The consultants recommended the provision of more entertainment for youth and greater employment of women, a strategy that al-Rasheed sees as a 'top-down initiative to make the crown prince the centre of the decision making process with no regard to the people's interest or their opinions', with McKinsey accused of monitoring young Saudis who objected to or criticized the crown prince's reforms.[10] As the *Economist* noted, Saudis had tended to lack the technical skills needed for the crown prince's programme of reforms: 'Schools stuff young heads with religion, but neglect more practical subjects such as math and science.'[11]

As well as Saudi oil money, MBS looked to foreign investors to finance his plan. The vehicle for MBS's plan is a public investment fund (PIF) that has already invested tens of billions of dollars at home and abroad, in companies ranging from Uber to Magic Leap, and in ventures with Blackstone and SoftBank, with the aim of doubling its assets under management to $600 billion by 2020. According to the *Financial Times*, since MBS took it over in 2015, the PIF has 'morphed into the most powerful force in the Arab world's biggest economy'. One Saudi analyst told the paper it 'was one of the first departments targeted by Prince Mohammed', 'a one-man investment vehicle' driving the most important 'political, personal, economic and social agenda in the country'.[12]

A central part of the plan is to sell off 5 per cent of Saudi Aramco, the world's largest corporation, worth possibly $2 trillion, dwarfing Apple, Google, Amazon or ExxonMobil, and listing it on a foreign stock exchange in the world's biggest ever initial public offering: Hong Kong, Singapore and London were among the contenders for the listing. Oil revenue – until recently Aramco's profits were taxed at 85 per cent by the Saudi government – would be replaced by a vast sovereign wealth fund, to be invested in property and businesses abroad as well as at home, much as Qatar has done already. The as yet relatively small Saudi fund began its overseas adventures in 2016 with a $3.5 billion investment in Uber.

The public profile of the PIF was raised by the Future Investment Initiative conference held in October 2017 and widely dubbed 'Davos in the Desert' after the World Economic Forum in Switzerland. It was attended by some 3,000 economists and businesspeople from ninety countries, including Christine Lagarde, the managing director of the International Monetary Fund, US Treasury Secretary Steven Mnuchin, BlackRock CEO Larry Fink, and Japanese business magnate Masayoshi Son, CEO of SoftBank. In what was described as Saudi Arabia's 'coming out party' with the charismatic young prince seeking to woo bankers and investors for Vision 2030, MBS swept like a rock star through the crowd, pausing for handshakes or posing for selfies as some of the world's most powerful financiers 'clamored for their moment with the Saudi heir-apparent'.[13] Plans he announced included a $1 billion investment in Virgin Galactic, the private space project of British financier Richard Branson, who would sit on the board of Neom, the futurist city inspired by Singapore that the prince intends to build at Tabuk on the Red Sea Coast. In a symbolic gesture, Prince Mohammed announced that he had granted Saudi citizenship to Sophia, a 'social humanoid robot' developed by the Hong Kong–based company Hanson Robotics. Announcing that his country was finally lifting its ban on women driving, he told the conference that Saudi Arabia was returning to a more 'moderate' form of Islam, one that would be 'open to all religions of the world'. 'Honestly' he told the conference 'we won't waste 30 years of our life dealing with any extremist ideas.'[14]

One year later the killing of Khashoggi had put some of these plans in jeopardy. By 15 October, less than two weeks after the journalist's disappearance, most of the big investors had decided not to attend the 2018 Future Investment Initiative conference scheduled for 23–5 October. As the stories leaked out from Istanbul, the swell of non-attendees grew. The list of last-minute drop-outs read like a who's who of the world's most powerful capitalists and media moguls: they included James Dimon of JPMorganChase, Bill Ford of the Ford Motor Company, Dara Khosrowshahi, chief executive of Uber, Blackstone CEO Stephen Schwarzman, Siemens boss Joe Kaeser, Blackrock CEO Larry Fink, MasterCard CEO Ajay Banga, Viacom CEO Bob Bakish, Thrive CEO Arianna Huffington of the Huffington Post, World Bank President Jim Yong Kim, Patrick Soon-Shiong, owner of the *Los Angeles Times*, *Economist* editor Zanny Minton Beddoes, who had previously given the prince a highly flattering interview, and Andrew Ross Sorkin of the *New York Times*.[15] The Bill and Melinda Gates Foundation pulled its funding from the crown prince's MiSK Foundation, a non-profit aimed at helping young entrepreneurs. As David Callahan of the trade journal *Inside Philanthropy* put it: 'I would imagine they really didn't want to pull the plug … But obviously, the optics are really bad: the world's biggest charitable foundation in bed with a guy who kills political dissidents.'[16] The US trade secretary Steven Mnuchin pulled out of the conference at the very last minute, opting instead for a 'private meeting' with the prince. One of the few international 'big boys' who bucked the general trend was McKinsey, which had been hired to advise on austerity measures resulting in the 2015 fall in oil prices. Despite damaging claims in the *New York Times* that the firm had been complicit in tracking dissidents who were then imprisoned by the Saudi government, McKinsey persisted in attending the conference despite the international scandal. With some 600 projects in the kingdom between 2011 and 2016, it preferred to take the view that issues of human or civil rights were best tackled 'from within'. As two investigative reporters Walt Bogdanich and Michael Forsythe commented:

> At a time when democracies and their basic values are increasingly under attack, the iconic American company has helped raise the stature of authoritarian and corrupt governments across the globe, sometimes in ways that counter American interests.[17]

McKinsey was far from alone in overcoming any distaste its executive might have felt in association with an international pariah. In 2017, the *Financial Times* disclosed that the former British prime minister David Cameron, later Britain's foreign secretary, was employed by Greensill Capital, a firm specializing in supply chain financing, to lobby not only his former conservative colleagues in the British government but also the de facto ruler of Saudi Arabia. Following investigations prompted by the collapse of the company in March 2021, it emerged that only two months after Khashoggi's death Cameron and the Australian financier Lex Greensill had 'bonded' with the crown prince in a tent under the starry Arabian sky, with the former prime minister and his Saudi host sharing their common experience as students of law at university.

The response of President Trump was just as ambivalent and morally ambiguous as that of McKinsey and Cameron. He set great store on the value of the US–Saudi relationship. His visit to Riyadh, in May 2017, was his first to a foreign capital. He was accompanied by his son-in-law Jared Kushner, who formed a strong personal bond with Mohammed bin Salman, then deputy crown prince. Kushner, an Orthodox Jew, is a close family friend of Israeli Prime Minister Benjamin Netanyahu, and the Kushners are known to have contributed heavily to Israeli non-profits supporting Jewish settlements in the Palestinian territories of the West Bank. In addition to this, Mike Pence, the vice president, was a fundamentalist Christian believing that Jewish settlements, though illegal under international law, were a prerequisite for the Second Coming of Christ.

It is thought that in the course of their conversation the two young men – Kushner being thirty-seven and MBS thirty-three – decided they could short-circuit the usual diplomatic process and forge a peace between Palestinians and Israelis that would outflank the leverage that regional actors, such as the Iranians and their Hezbollah allies in Lebanon, have over the Palestinian peace process. As will be shown in Chapter 9, this was not really a new policy, built as it was on the anti-Iranian demarche of former vice president Dick Cheney and Prince Bandar bin Sultan, former Saudi ambassador to the US, during the administration of George W. Bush, but it held the prospect of giving new traction to the de facto alliance between Israel and the Saudi kingdom. Although Kushner had no knowledge of the region apart from his family's support for Israeli settlements, his friendship with MBS made him an influential actor. Some American officials were in no doubt that the Saudis and their Emirati allies were treating him as a 'useful idiot' in their designs against Iran. But Kushner and his friends in the White House could also see the advantage in having a friend in the Saudi court at a time of growing, if unacknowledged, alignment between Israel and the Arab monarchies. As Martin Indyk, a former US diplomat, explained to the *New York Times*: 'The relationship between Jared Kushner and Mohammed bin Salman constitutes the foundation of the Trump policy not just toward Saudi Arabia but toward the region.' The administration's reliance on the Saudis in the Israeli–Arab peace process, its support for the kingdom's feud with Qatar, an American ally, and its backing of the Saudi-led intervention in Yemen, he said, all grew out of what he called 'that bromance'.[18]

As the MBS–Kushner relationship came under growing public scrutiny in the aftermath of the Khashoggi affair, revelations about the Al Saud–Kushner 'bromance' took an even more sinister turn. It appeared that Kushner might be less interested in brokering Middle East peace than in having the Saudis rescue his own family's finances in exchange for helping them acquire nuclear capability. Thanks to a disastrous investment in a New York property with the apocalyptic address of 666 Fifth Avenue, the property business Kushner shared with his father Charles (a convicted felon and disbarred lawyer) was in dire straits. Kushner Jr looked to the Qatari sovereign wealth fund, but they turned him down. He was rescued instead by Brookfield Asset Management, a company that owns Westinghouse Electric, a nuclear services business aiming to sell nuclear reactors to the Saudi kingdom. Shortly after his rebuff by the Qataris, Kushner, as Trump's senior foreign policy advisor, with a special remit for the Middle East, provided critical US support for the diplomatic assault on Qatar, led by Saudi Arabia and the United Arab Emirates (UAE), which culminated in the blockade of the Gulf state. According to reports at the time, Kushner was instrumental in undermining efforts by Secretary of State Rex Tillerson (a seasoned oil-man with knowledge of the area) to bring an end to the standoff before Trump's peremptory dismissal of Tillerson in March 2018. While the Saudis claim they want the nuclear plants for electricity generation, they insist on producing their own nuclear fuel rather than buying it more cheaply abroad. As the *New York Times* columnist Nicholas Kristof commented, 'producing fuel is a standard way for rogue countries to divert fuel for secret nuclear weapons programs, and the Saudi resistance to safeguards against proliferation bolsters suspicions that the real goal is warheads.'[19]

The Khashoggi killing clearly embarrassed the Trump administration, not least because the victim was well known in Washington and had many friends on Capitol Hill and in the US media. After talking on the phone to both the king and the crown prince, Trump had bought into the story that the killing had been the work of rogue actors. Here the role of Kushner appears to have been pivotal, according to the *New York Times*. Although officials had tried to restrict his communications with MBS in accordance with protocols that members of the National Security Council should participate in all calls with foreign leaders, the two men, who are on first-name terms, continued to talk and text each other using WhatsApp. With the US intelligence agencies concluding that the killing may have been ordered by Prince Mohammed, Mr Kushner became the prince's most important defender inside the White House, citing 'people familiar with its internal deliberations'.[20]

In a rare example of making a public disclosure of intelligence findings, the director of the CIA, Gina Haspel, concluded after reviewing the audio tapes with her team that MBS's tight grip on decision-making made the 'rogue actor' story highly improbable. But she balked at pointing the finger directly at the crown prince. In January 2019, she told the Senate Intelligence Committee that Khashoggi had been the victim of 'premeditated murder', but declined to state whether the crown prince was personally responsible.[21]

The CIA's conclusions were not confined to the audio tapes, in which the crown prince's fixer, Saud al-Qahtani, could be heard exchanging insults with Khashoggi on a Skype call and telling his men to 'bring me the head of the dog'.[22] According to leaks to the *Washington Post*, the CIA had been monitoring other calls, including one from the crown prince's brother Khalid bin Salman – at that time the Saudi ambassador in Washington. In one such call – denied by the embassy – the crown prince's brother had given Khashoggi assurances that it would be safe for him to retrieve his divorce papers from the Saudi consulate in Istanbul.

Confronted with mounting evidence of the crown prince's involvement, Trump's response was vacillating: 'maybe he did, or maybe he didn't'. 'Will anyone really know?' he asked in an interview on his favourite TV channel Fox News. But when it came to the CIA tapes, he balked at listening to the recording: 'it's a suffering tape, it's a terrible tape', he said. As Mark Landler, the *New York Times* White House correspondent, commented, Trump's reluctance to hear the tapes or acknowledge evidence of the crown prince's involvement, his acceptance of his denial in several phone calls, was a

> vivid illustration of how deeply Mr Trump had invested in the 33-year-old heir who has become the fulcrum of the administration's strategy in the Middle East – from Iran to the Israeli-Palestinian peace process – as well as a prolific shopper for American military weapons, even if most of those contracts have not paid off yet.[23]

Trump's response put him at odds with his own intelligence agencies, as well as with senators and congressmen on both sides of the political divide. Direct complicity on the part of the prince has never been fully established, though there is an abundance of clues. During his campaign for the US presidency, the Democratic candidate Joe Biden vowed to make Saudi Arabia 'pay the price' by ending weapons sales because of its war in Yemen 'and make them in fact the pariah that they are' for Khashoggi's murder.[24] After becoming president in January 2021, Biden authorized the release of the CIA assessment previously leaked to the *Wall Street Journal* and *New York Times* indicating the prince's possible complicity. While there were no unambiguous references to Khashoggi in calls between Mutreb in Istanbul and al-Qahtani in Riyadh, the phrase 'tell your boss' made shortly after the killing, which appeared in a Saudi-commissioned report, was regarded by the Americans as signalling 'mission accomplished'. While John Bolton, President Trump's hawkish national security advisor, insisted that the audio tape of the murder 'does not in any way link the crown prince to the killing', Riedel thought that 'a phone call like that is about as close to a smoking gun as you are going to get'.[25]

In contrast to Bolton's denial, no less a figure than Senator Bob Corker, Republican chair of the Senate Foreign Relations Committee, told the Senate it was his belief that the crown prince had ordered the killing. He 'has done nothing to show ownership over what has happened and that is an affront – not just to the American people, but it's an affront to the world'.[26]

Despite the strong consensus in Washington, based on intelligence findings, that MBS was responsible for the murder, President Trump insisted on standing by the crown prince. Kushner – as well as Trump's claim that arms sales worth $110 billion were at stake – appears to have been the key to this support. In February 2019, the White House defied a congressional deadline for a report from President Trump about who directed the killing, sidestepping pressure to acknowledge the intelligence findings about Prince Mohammed's role. Not long after the deadline expired, Kushner flew to Riyadh for his first face-to-face meeting with Prince Mohammed since Mr Khashoggi's death. As the *New York Times* noted, 'Both Mr. Trump and Jared Kushner are expected to go back into the business of selling real estate investments when they leave the White House.'[27]

Trump retained his commitment to the prince in the face of later revelations that came ever closer to a proverbial 'smoking gun' directly linking the prince with the murder. On 7 February 2019, the *New York Times* reported that the National Security Agency and other intelligence organizations had uncovered a conversation in which Prince Mohammed had told one of his top aides more than a year before Khashoggi's murder that if the self-exiled journalist could not be lured by inducements to Saudi Arabia he should be brought back by force. In a conversation with one of his aides,

Turki al-Dakhil, MBS had allegedly said that if force failed to enable his return to the kingdom they would go after Khashoggi 'with a bullet'.[28] Reports from the US intelligence agencies were backed up by the initial findings of Agnes Callamard, the United Nations special rapporteur on extra-judicial killings and summary executions, who having listened to 'parts of the chilling and gruesome audio material obtained and retained by the Turkish intelligence agency' said the Saudi dissident was the victim of a 'brutal, premeditated killing planned and perpetrated by officials of the state of Saudi Arabia'.[29] In June 2019 she produced her detailed report on the murder of Jamal Khashoggi. 'There is credible evidence warranting further investigation of high-level Saudi officials' individual liability, including the crown prince's', she wrote in a 100-page report, issued after a five-month investigation.

> Evidence points to the 15-person mission to execute Mr. Khashoggi requiring significant government coordination, resources and finances ... Every expert consulted finds it inconceivable that an operation of this scale could be implemented without the crown prince being aware, at a minimum, that some sort of mission of a criminal nature, directed at Mr. Khashoggi, was being launched.[30]

The killing, she pronounced, constituted an 'extrajudicial killing for which the state of the Kingdom of Saudi Arabia is responsible'. It might also have constituted an 'act of torture' banned under international treaties to which the kingdom had been a signatory. The attempted kidnapping of Khashoggi would also have constituted a violation under international law. Saudi Arabia's purported trial of eleven officials it identified as linked to the killing, with proceedings conducted in secret, did not meet international standards. Its investigation was not conducted in good faith and may have amounted to obstruction of justice. Callamard's report also cited evidence that Saudi officials had hindered the work of Turkish investigators, including having the murder scene forensically cleaned before it could be examined. She called on the international community to impose targeted sanctions on officials said to have been involved in the murder, including the Saudi crown prince. The sanctions should focus on the prince's personal assets abroad, 'until and unless evidence has been produced that he bears no responsibility for the execution of Mr Khashoggi'.[31]

On leaving her post in the spring of 2021 to take up her new job as secretary general of Amnesty International, Callamard revealed that she had received what she and her colleagues took to be 'death threats' from an unnamed Saudi official at a meeting at the United Nations in Geneva in January 2020. She claimed the official had told her UN colleagues that she would be 'taken care of' if the organization did not rein her in.[32]

The murder of Khashoggi was a singular event, a tragedy for his family and friends. But it was also more than that: like the murder of the Archduke Franz Ferdinand in Sarajevo, Bosnia, in June 1914, it came at a point where the alignment of competing powers and popular forces were balanced so precariously that a singular event could generate a global catastrophe. As two scholars, Tarek Cherkaoui and Michael Arnold, point out in their essay *Chronicle of a Death Foretold*, the 'botched operation' took place against the backcloth of the popular insurgencies known as the Arab Spring, with the Saudis and their primary allies, the UAE, combatting the forces of change.[33] As they point out, Riyadh's engagement was based on its 'intrinsic fear' of the democratic progress that was achieved in Arab countries such as Tunisia. They were terrified that the democratic current would spread to other countries, particularly Egypt, the Arab world's most populous state, and they sought to undermine it with a combination of money and force.[34]

The Saudis and Emiratis were behind the coup that brought General Abd al-Fattah al-Sisi, a former military attaché in Riyadh, to power in July 2013 after overthrowing the Muslim Brotherhood government of Mohamed Morsi, killing some 900 demonstrators when they broke up the sit-in at the Rabiya al-Adawiya Mosque, the most brutal massacre in Egypt's modern history. For all his ineptitude and blinkered religiosity, Morsi (who died in custody in June 2019) is the only Egyptian president to have been elected in a relatively transparent manner. With a $15 billion aid package and promises of more to come, the Saudis provided the Egyptian military with the financial lifeline that enabled them to pursue a policy of repression that makes the Mubarak regime look positively benign by comparison.

As Cherkaoui and Arnold argue, 'The near obsession of the Saudis to quash the Arab uprisings is not surprising per se, given the autocratic nature of the regime. What is shocking, however, is the use of the Arab Spring as a key determinant for Saudi state identity in the twenty-first century.'[35]

As will be shown in subsequent chapters of this book, Saudi identity is a complex mix of Salafi-Wahhabism – a sectarian Islamic cult based on strict observance of certain behaviours in dress, deportment, gender separation, prayer observance and so forth – alongside recognition, not to say worship, of the Al Saud family as guardians and promoters of the cult. The relationship between Wahhabi-Salafism and power, however, is far from stable. Wahhabi divines who have their own scholastic and collegiate tradition were often resistant to the introduction of new ideas into the kingdom and to many aspects of the rampant programme of modernization undertaken in the wake of the petrodollar bonanza after 1970. The 1979 seizure of the Grand Mosque in Mecca, outlined in Chapter 5, was the most conspicuous example of this resistance.

As will be shown in Chapter 8, not all members of the Al Saud family are personally religious in the Wahhabi-Salafi sense. Before the rise of MBS, the most high-profile member of the family was Prince Bandar bin Sultan (b. 1949), an accomplished diplomat and jetsetter whose parties in Washington were legendary and whose preference for Western-style clothes and general demeanour appear very different from that of the Wahhabi-Salafists (see Chapter 8). In an age of social media, the lifestyle of Saudi princes can no longer be hidden. Saudi Arabia has one of the world's highest rates of 'internet penetration' with 25 million 'active social media accounts', comprising 25 per cent of the population, as well as 23 million YouTube visitors (71 per cent) and 22 million Facebook users (66 per cent), along with Instagram (17.96 million or 45 per cent) and Twitter (17.29 million or 52 per cent) users.[36]

It also has the world's highest level of Twitter users, with the regime's security services charged with 'infiltrating it to gather data of Saudi critics, activists and dissidents'.[37] The trick, as the family appears to have understood, has been adapting the traditionalist Wahhabi ideology of the religious establishment into a personality cult based on the dynamic young MBS.

On 19 October, less than three weeks after the Khashoggi murder, when the whole world was pointing its finger at the Saudi prince, Sheikh Abdulrahman al-Sudais, imam of the Grand Mosque in Mecca and the kingdom's highest religious authority, delivered his Friday sermon from a written script previously approved by the Saudi security apparatus. Friday sermons from the podium where the Prophet Muhammad is supposed to have given his final sermon are broadcast live on cable networks and social media sites, to be watched with reverence by millions of Muslims all over the world. As Khaled Abou el-Fadl, a leading authority on Islamic culture and law, points out, 'these sermons carry a great deal of moral and religious authority'.[38] In his sermon, Imam Sudais referenced a famous hadith (saying or 'tradition') attributed to the Prophet Muhammad, according to which once in every century God sends a great renovator or interpreter (*mujtahid*) to reclaim or reinvigorate the faith in order to address the unique challenges of the era.

> The path of reform and modernization in this blessed land ... through the care and attention from its young, ambitious, divinely inspired reformer crown prince, continues to blaze forward guided by his vision of innovation and insightful modernism, despite all the failed pressures and threats.[39]

Invoking the debate that followed the Khashoggi murder, Imam Sudais warned Muslims against believing 'ill-intended media rumors and innuendos' that sought to cast doubt on the great Muslim leader. The conspiracies against the crown prince, he said, were aimed at destroying Islam and the Muslims, warning that 'all threats against his modernizing reforms are bound not only to fail, but will threaten international security, peace and stability'. In praising the prince, Imam Sudais used the word *muhaddath*, 'uniquely and singularly gifted', an honorific the Prophet is supposed to have attached to Umar ibn al-Khattab, his esteemed Companion who became the second caliph of Islam. One can see this as an implicit challenge to the claims of Abu Bakr al-Baghdadi, the so-called caliph of ISIS, who proclaimed himself caliph – or 'deputy' of the Prophet – in July 2014.

The significance of the imam's sermon in the holiest shrine of Islam cannot be underestimated. Abou el-Fadl points out the worldwide response to the sermon was far from complimentary: the reaction of scholars on social media was mainly 'disdain and outrage', while Arabic-language comedies and talk shows on YouTube reacted with mockery and contempt. A negative response, however, could paradoxically serve the prince's aim of underpinning his image with religious authority. Authoritarian leaders know that one way to garner support is to generate opposition by creating the sense that the society they lead faces threats that are both internal and external. Adolf Hitler achieved this, famously, by eliding two entirely contradictory elements – international capital (which many working-class Germans saw as responsible for their troubles, such as the Great Depression of 1929 and its attendant hyperinflation) and the 'Jewish Bolsheviks' of communism. The supposed international Jewish conspiracy outlined by documents such as the *Protocols of the Elders of Zion* was the element common to both. The Saudis tend to elide the threat they perceive from Shia Iran with the Muslim Brotherhood, an organization of Sunni reformers that occupies a broad spectrum of political stances, from full if grudging acceptance of democratic pluralism (as held by the Brotherhood-linked Ennahda party in Tunisia) to the militant jihadism of Sayyid Qutb and his followers. As MBS stated in a television interview with CBS in March 2018, he regards Iran's Supreme Leader Ayatollah Ali Khamenei as an existential threat to his country who 'wants to create his own project in the Middle East, much like Hitler. Many countries in Europe did not see how dangerous Hitler was until what happened, happened. I don't want to see the same events happening in the Middle East.'[40]

While there have been alliances of convenience between militant Sunnis and Shias – for example the Shiite Hezbollah movement in Lebanon supported the radical Islamist Hamas government in Gaza – there are also significant differences, not least in a distinctly Sunni trajectory – informed by Wahhabi-Salafism – in which the militants of organizations such as ISIS tend to be radically anti-Shiite in their views. Yet in the lengthy interview he gave to *Time* magazine in April 2018, MBS glossed over any such differences, seeing radically different factions – the Houthis fighting the Saudi-backed government in Yemen, al-Qaeda in the Arabian Peninsula – as 'terrorists' driven by ideological militancy rather than by sectarian, tribal or regional interests. If Saudi Arabia had not intervened in Yemen, he said,

> You would see Yemen divided between two terrorist groups: the Houthis, the new Hezbollah in the north, and al-Qaeda in the south, they are trying to take advantage of what's happening there and they are trying to grow in 2015. So you will see Yemen split between those two terrorist groups … [A]ll the extremist organizations in Saudi Arabia, we treat them as terrorist organizations, like the Muslim Brotherhood. They are very dangerous, and they are classified in Saudi Arabia, Egypt, UAE and a lot of countries in the Middle East as a terrorist organization. So the person, he doesn't get from normal to terrorist. He gets from normal to a little bit conservative, to a little bit extreme then more extreme 'til he's ready to turn into a terrorist. And the Muslim Brotherhood network, it's part of this movement. So if you see Osama bin Laden, he used to be in the Muslim Brotherhood … If you see Baghdadi the leader of ISIS, he used to be from the Muslim Brotherhood. Actually if you see any terrorist, you will find that he used to be from the Muslim Brotherhood. And you know what's the biggest danger? They're not in the Middle East because they know that the Middle East is taking good strategy against them in Saudi Arabia, Egypt, UAE, Jordan, and a lot of countries. Their main target is to radicalize Muslim communities in Europe. They hope that Europe in 30 years will turn to a Muslim Brotherhood continent, and they want to control the Muslims, in Europe by manipulating the Muslim Brotherhood. So this will be much more dangerous than the Cold War, than ISIS, than Al Qaeda, than whatever we've seen in the last hundred years of history.[41]

As will be seen below (p. 37), the crown prince and his mentor Mohamed bin Zayed's demonization of the Brotherhood as having linkages to Iran that are problematic – to say the least – is a relatively new modulation of the Saudi discourse. But as a manifestation of Saudi feeling, the demonization does not have to be unpopular in a country where half the population is twenty-five or younger. Tweets such as 'I pledge allegiance to my Lord, his Royal Highness the Crown Prince Mohammed bin Salman, to listen and to obey', though re-circulated by Saudi media, may reflect reality in a country where more than 90 per cent of eighteen- to twenty-four-year-olds are avid internet users: there is much less noise to the contrary. There is also another reason that the rise of MBS has been widely applauded by younger people: he has promised social and economic change, as well as an end to the filial gerontocracy that has endured for more than half a century. In a country where 40 per cent of people between the ages of twenty and twenty-four are unemployed, where 40 per cent of Saudis live in relative poverty and at least 60 per cent can't afford to buy homes because of the princely grip on real estate (see Chapter 9), prospects for reform under a dynamic new leader who could rule for decades seem exciting.

As in the past, the regime's religious legitimacy is premised on the king's role as Guardian of the Two Holy Shrines of Mecca and Medina, as well as defender of Sunni Islam in the face of a 'foreign' Shiite threat emanating from Iran. The new 'twist of irony', as Cherkaoui and Arnold point out, is that Iran is now 'invoked in connection to the amorphous threat of "political Islam" caricatured in the form of the Muslim Brotherhood'. As shown in Chapter 3, the formation of the Saudi state in the eighteenth century CE and its subsequent revivals in the nineteenth and twentieth centuries were premised on the radical anti-Shiism of the Wahhabi-Salafi discourse. Talmiz Ahmad, an Indian Muslim diplomat and his country's former ambassador to Riyadh, points out that 'animosity for the Shia and the conviction that they are not Muslim lies at the heart of Salafist doctrine'.[42] In confounding the existential threat to Saudi Arabia allegedly posed by Iran with the various ramifications of the Muslim Brotherhood, it is MBS, rather than Khamenei, who most resembles Hitler.

After his appointment as crown prince in October 2017, MBS declared to media throughout the world that he wanted to restore the 'moderate' Islam that prevailed in the kingdom prior to the 1979 Iranian revolution. To protect itself from the challenge of the Iranian revolution, went his argument, the kingdom had adopted a more restrictive interpretation of the faith than had been applied previously. The prince's implication was that the Shiite revolution was responsible for the limits on religious activity, social behaviour and cultural expression in the kingdom. This evidently suited his purpose of situating Saudi chauvinism in an anti-Shiite, anti-Iranian mould while appealing to a rising generation of Saudis who found the prevailing social mores too restrictive.

In an essay challenging these claims, the Catholic scholar Chiara Pellegrino points out that while the kingdom may have responded to the Iranian revolution by 'reactivating the anti-Shi'ite component inherent in Wahhabism' MBS's claims do not stand up at all. She points out, for example, that the origins of the Sahwa movement, a potentially explosive combination of Wahhabi exclusivism and the political activism of the Muslim Brotherhood, were introduced in the kingdom in the 1960s during the 'Arab Cold War' when republican nationalists led by Nasser's Egypt and supported by the Soviet Union were lined up against the mainly monarchist countries of the Islamic bloc led by King Faisal of Saudi Arabia and supported by the United States. The University of Medina, established in 1961 with the aim of 'Wahhabizing' the Hijaz region (see Chapter 2), hired important members of the Muslim Brotherhood, including Muhammad Qutb – younger brother of Sayyid Qutb, its leading ideologue – Abdullah Azzam, ideologist of the jihad against the Soviet occupation of

Afghanistan, as well as the fundamentalist scholar Muhammad Nasir al-Din al-Albani (1914–99) who demanded stricter adherence to Wahhabi norms and texts.

While MBS's claims about the religious situation in Saudi Arabia prior to his birth in 1985 might be explained by the fact that he had yet to be born, no such excuse can apply since his ascension to power. In the autumn of 2017 dozens of preachers, activists and intellectuals were arrested on charges of plotting against the government with the kingdom's enemies (the Muslim Brotherhood and Qatar in particular). Far from being the old-school reactionaries who were resisting the prince's modernizing reforms, many had adopted 'neo-Sahwa' or liberal currents of thought. Among them was Salman al-Awdah (b. 1956), a famous preacher with 14 million followers on Twitter who made himself unpopular with the government for supporting the Arab Spring. In 2011 the government had already suspended his popular television programme and forbidden dissemination of his book *Questions of the Revolution* that challenged the official doctrine of 'unconditional obedience to the ruler'. His outlook, as Pellegrino describes it, is a hybrid of Western political thought with Islamic tradition:

> The preacher borrowed from the West the notion of peaceful revolution understood as a search for political change through a collective action that manifests itself in certain political, social, psychological and economic conditions; he Westernized the Islamic notion of shura (consultation), claiming that the entire Islamic community, not just a selected few as happens today in Saudi Arabia, should access such mechanism; he believes that the application of the sharia is appropriate, but cannot be forced.[43]

More radically, al-Awdah theorizes the idea of a state founded on a civil contract between the ruler and the society, in which the separation of powers – executive, legislative and judicial – leave no room for theocracy. In 2017 he was arrested and held in solitary confinement for refusing to comply with an order by Saudi authorities to tweet a specific text in support of the UAE–Saudi blockade of Qatar. At a legal hearing in September 2018 prosecutors applied for him to be *sentenced to death*. Held in solitary confinement since 2017, al-Awdah has been in progressively declining health. In December 2020 his son Abdullah, who teaches in the United States, urged the then president-elect Joe Biden to press the Saudis to release political prisoners, including his father, when he came into office.

> My father's physical and mental decline has accelerated over three years of abuse and isolation. During the first three to five months of his detention, in Dhahban prison in Jeddah, guards shackled his feet with chains and blindfolded him while moving him between interrogation rooms and his cell. Interrogators deprived him of sleep and medication for many days in succession, he told our family during visits.
>
> On one occasion, the guards threw a plastic bag of food at him without removing his handcuffs. He was forced to open the bag and remove the food with his mouth, causing considerable damage to his teeth. Following this prolonged mistreatment, in January 2018, he was hospitalized for a few days for dangerously high blood pressure.[44]

Other victims of the emerging MBS dictatorship include Abdullah al-Hamid (b. 1950), co-founder of an association of political and civil rights who advocates peaceful jihad (non-violent public protests including hunger strikes and civil disobedience, currently banned in the kingdom) as a public and expanded form of *nasiha* – the advice clerics give privately to the sovereign, as well as the preacher Safar al-Hawali, a former associate of al-Awdah who has been arrested along with members of his family. While Hawali aspires to return to the original ideal of the first Saudi state and is closely faithful to the teaching of the founder Muhammad ibn Abd al-Wahhab, al-Awdah aspires towards a modern Muslim polity, with a constitution and a representative government.

While detaining or silencing critical voices from the clerical establishment, MBS has privileged a small group of more pliable clerics who support his agenda. Stéphane Lacroix, France's leading observer of Saudi affairs, argues that these religious figures have little social credibility. 'The discourse they produce is meant to be seductive to Western ears: they denounce terrorism, call for religious tolerance, defend the social measures taken by MBS.' As Lacroix observes, 'If religious reform is only a push from above and not the result of genuine social debate, it is easily reversible.'[45]

Along with al-Sudais, Muhammad bin Abdul-Karim al-Issa, a former justice minister, is the most prominent of these figures, having been appointed head of the Muslim World League. Under his watch the League that formerly acted as a leading global disseminator of hard-line Wahhabism moderated its stance, organizing conferences that promoted religious pluralism and presenting MBS as a 'tolerant leader bent on fostering inter-faith dialogue'. Issa has rejected the use of violence, including violence directed at Israel, and has denounced Holocaust deniers. In January 2020 he visited Auschwitz on the seventy-fifth anniversary of its liberation, joining with rabbis and leaders of the American Jewish Committee in offering prayers. 'My appointment', he told *Le Monde*, 'did not please the ultra-conservatives, but that doesn't bother me. All religious institutions must modernize their speech to make it compatible with the times. Most Islamic concepts are not embedded in sacred texts but are interpretations.'

It is against this background of the Saudi state imposing its authority on Islamic discourse that the Khashoggi murder must be seen. Unlike most Saudi clerics and intellectuals whose oppression or resistance would be unlikely to make much impression outside of the kingdom or specialist circles, the journalist had excellent Western connections while being well established inside the country. Far from being known as a 'dissident' he had worked as a foreign correspondent for a number of Arab newspapers in Afghanistan, Algeria, Bosnia and Sudan and had 'close ties' with the Saudi intelligence services through Prince Turki al-Faisal, a former Saudi intelligence chief and ambassador to London and Washington, for whom he became the principle spokesman and media advisor. However, Khashoggi's reformist views in favour of ideas of democratic Islamism espoused by figures such as Rachid al-Ghannouchi – leader of Tunisia's Ennahda party – soured his relations with Prince Turki. Whereas the former Saudi intelligence chief regarded the Muslim Brotherhood as a terrorist cult, 'Khashoggi saw the Islamist movement as the best hope for change in the Arab world'.[46] After the murder, Ghannouchi, as Tunisia's opposition leader, publicly lamented the 'heinous death' of the 'media martyr' (incurring the rage of President Essebsi who wanted to preserve 'fraternal relations' between Tunisia and the Saudi kingdom). Prince Turki by contrast challenged the CIA's claims of the crown prince's involvement, insisting that the storm surrounding them was an 'unfair attempt to criminalize the crown prince on the part of the media'.[47] His attitude suggests that the climate of panic now gripping the House of Saud overrode any considerations of personal loyalty. As in any Mafia-type system of organized crime, sticking by 'family' transcended considerations of truth or justice.

Khashoggi was neither dissident nor radical. Though he appeared as cultivated, enlightened and modest (when I met him briefly in New York in 2004), he had shared his former protector's paranoia about the Shia and Iran, and he endorsed the Saudi narrative on the civil war in Syria. As late as 2016, he supported the execution of the Shiite dissident Sheikh Nimr al-Nimr, stating, 'We target only terrorists or dissidents that call for violence. We do not execute political criminals.'[48] After the Battle of Qusayr in June 2013, a key event that began to turn the tide in favour of the Assad regime in Syria, Khashoggi wrote,

> With the resulting enlistment of hundreds of Iraqi Shiite volunteers in the war overtly championed by Iran, the [Shia] Crescent is liable to evolve into a political axis stretching from Tehran to Beirut via Baghdad and Damascus. The Iranian Oil Ministry will pull out old maps from its drawers to build the pipeline to pump Iranian oil and gas from Abadan (across Iraq) to Tartus [on the Mediterranean coast]. The Iranian Ministry of Roads and Transportation will dust off the national railways authority's blueprints for a new branch line from Tehran to Damascus, and possibly Beirut. Why not? … Tehran has been mulling over such projects for years without actually starting them.[49]

What chills about this commentary is its hidden projection of Saudi geopolitical ambitions masquerading as sectarian fear. At that time the Saudi government claimed, unconvincingly, to be 'unable' to prevent volunteers from joining the al-Qaeda affiliates in Syria and Iraq who were fighting what they saw as a legitimate jihad against infidel Shias backed by Iran. In actuality, young men, many of them from well-connected families, were motivated by the same ideology that brought the Al Saud to power in the 1920s: Muslims not subscribing to the Wahhabi version of Islam — and especially the Shia — were infidels deserving of death.

In March 2011 the Saudi government sent 1,200 troops across the causeway into Bahrain to assist the Sunni minority regime, led by King Hamad bin Isa al-Khalifa, to repress the movement of popular protest that erupted in the wake of the 'Arab Spring' uprisings in Tunisia and Egypt. This suppression of a burgeoning democratic movement based in the Shia majority does not seem to have disturbed

Khashoggi particularly, though he tried to take a balanced view of it. In 2015 he accepted the post of running a new al-Arab TV station based in Manama, the Bahraini capital. Financed by Prince Alwaleed bin Talal, the billionaire son of Prince Talal bin Abd al-Aziz – a 'free prince' who had been passed over for the kingship on account of his liberal views – the channel aimed to position itself midway between the relatively free approach of Al Jazeera, based in Qatar, and the more restrictive programming of Saudi-based television. 'We are going to be neutral; we are not going to take sides', said Khashoggi. 'We are going to bring in all sides in any conflict because right now we have a conflict in almost every Arab country.' The channel's inaugural broadcast came one day after Bahrain announced that it had revoked the citizenship of seventy-two Bahrainis on charges that ranged from supporting or engaging in terrorism to 'defaming brotherly countries' and 'inciting and advocating regime change through illegal means'. Al-Arab aired a segment on the decision and interviewed Khalil al-Marzouq, a former member of Bahrain's Parliament and a senior leader in al-Wefaq, the country's largest opposition party representing the Shia majority. 'When we talk about revoking citizenship, that is a human right for any human who lives in a given land', said Marzouq. 'So when we revoke that citizenship, you are making absent the legal personality of that person in his daily, official and other dealings.' The channel was taken off air, and had its licence revoked, leaving some 260 employees without jobs.[50]

While Khashoggi had long been seen as close to the Saudi elite, this was clearly a watershed. A crucial milestone was the break with Qatar, driven in part by the Gulf state's sponsorship of Al Jazeera, the television network that had pulled the veil off Arabic public discourse, exposing rulers to public criticisms in a way that had never happened before. Saudi officials regarded Al Jazeera as being 'far more dangerous' than the Western media because it hid behind the façade of Arab culture. Prince Nayef ibn Abd al-Aziz, who served as interior minister from 1975 till his death in 2012, regarded Al Jazeera as 'serving up poison on a silver platter'.[51]

The platform that Al Jazeera provided for Sheikh Yousuf al-Qaradawi, widely regarded as the most eloquent voice of the Muslim Brotherhood, infuriated the Saudi religious establishment. While staunchly anti-Shia, al-Qaradawi endorsed moderate expressions of Sufism or mystical practices such as are found in Egypt, as well as the celebration of the Prophet Muhammad's birthday (anathema to Wahhabis). Correctly he saw the Salafists as providing the theological underpinning of movements such as ISIS, Boko Haram, al-Qaeda, the Taliban, the Somali Shabbab and similar Sunni extremists. While his defence of suicide bombings in Palestine caused al-Qaradawi to be banned in several countries, including Britain and France, his sermons and popular TV show *Sharia and Life* reached tens of millions of Muslim households, upsetting rulers (excepting the ruling Qatari family, who remained 'off-limits') with harsh criticisms and annoying them and their American ally with his support for Hamas and the Muslim Brotherhood. The knowledge that al-Qaradawi had been awarded the 1994 King Faisal International Prize, recognizing exceptional service to humanity in religious scholarship or the secular sciences, must have been especially galling for the Saudis, for it demonstrated the extent to which they had abandoned the legacy of the sainted King Faisal when he had presented himself as the leader of the Islamic world, a quasi-caliph whose support for the Brotherhood undermined their current efforts to blacken that organization as 'terrorist'.

As a supporter of al-Qaradawi, Khashoggi had been dismissive of MBS's claims to be reverting to 'moderate Islam', asserting that MBS did not understand what moderate Islam meant. As he explained to Al Jazeera in 2017, it was the Muslim Brotherhood's more forward-looking scholars like al-Qaradawi and Sheikh Ali Tantawi (1909–99), another recipient of the King Faisal Award, who were the true moderates. MBS, he stated, was confused about the proper meaning of moderation. 'The Muslim Brotherhood are moderates, but he does not want to admit that.'[52]

In June 2017 Saudi Arabia took the step of severing diplomatic ties with Qatar, demanding that the Al Jazeera network be shut down for broadcasting propaganda contrary to the Saudi interest and launching a regional standoff lasting years. Two weeks afterwards came the palace coup that brought MBS to power.

Since the death in 1953 of the modern kingdom's founder, Abd al-Aziz Al Saud (generally known as Ibn Saud), succession has passed down the line of his sons, skipping those considered unsuitable, such as the liberal-minded prince Talal bin Abd al-Aziz, father of Waleed. The present king, Salman, reportedly Ibn Saud's twenty-fifth son, inherited the throne in 2015 on the death of his half-brother Abdullah. While the ageing Abdullah lacked energy and initiative, Salman, former governor of Riyadh and minister of defence, was initially seen as much more energetic, being named in the Saudi press as *malik al-hazm* – 'King of Decisiveness'.[53] At eighty-eight, however, Salman is now in fragile health: he has had two strokes and is believed to be suffering from Alzheimer's. On 21 June 2017 he promoted his favourite son, the thirty-one-year-old MBS, to crown prince, putting him in line to be the first of the third generation – Ibn Saud's grandsons – to occupy the throne.

According to the *New York Times*, MBS's elevation at the expense of his older cousin, Crown Prince Muhammad bin Nayef (known as MBN), was the result of a cleverly executed plot. MBN had been highly regarded by the US and its allies: as head of the interior ministry and chief of Saudi intelligence he presided over operations against al-Qaeda in the Arabian Peninsula; he had attended training sessions with the FBI and was a powerful advocate of continued close relations with the Americans. In February the CIA honoured him with the George Tenet medal, in recognition of his 'excellent intelligence performance in the domain of counterterrorism and his unbounded contribution to realize world security and peace'.[54]

On the night of 20 June, the eve of the 'Eid al-Fitr festival that ends the holy month of Ramadan, MBN was summoned along with other senior princes for an audience with the senile king. Courtiers answering to MBS – who was already chief of the royal court, a position that made him the gatekeeper to his father, as well as the world's youngest minister of defence – removed his phones and pressured him to relinquish his posts. MBN at first refused but eventually gave in and is now said to be under palace arrest. Afterwards, clips of MBN paying allegiance to his younger cousin were shown on Saudi media to demonstrate a smooth transition, and it was put about – this time by US as well as Saudi officials – that MBN had been suffering from the effects of the 'arsehole bomb' attack in 2009, when an al-Qaeda operative masquerading as a petitioner approached him and blew himself up with an IED hidden in his rectum. MBN survived the attack but was said to have become addicted to the medication he had been taking to mitigate the effects of the trauma. Members of the Allegiance Council, a body of senior princes established by King Abdullah in 2006 to resolve disputes by approving changes in the line of succession, were told that MBN had a drug problem and was unfit to be king. Despite private reservations, the council deferred to King Salman and rubber-stamped their approval, in a vote of thirty-one to three. One prince who voted against young Mohammed and refused to give him his *baya* (oath of allegiance) is Prince Ahmed ibn Abd al-Aziz, born in 1942 and the youngest surviving son of the kingdom's founder by his favourite wife Hussa bint Ahmed Al Sudairi. In the event of MBS's removal, Prince Ahmed's royal lineage could make him a credible candidate to succeed his full brother Salman.

While not dismissing the claims about MBN's health, at least one foreign diplomat and a well-placed Saudi source suggested that his opposition to the Saudi-led embargo of Qatar was the real reason for his fall. As in early modern Europe, palace politics in Arabia and the Gulf are not just driven by private ambitions but reflect wider geopolitical struggles. MBS is said to be close to his mentor Mohamed bin Zayed (sometimes known as MBZ), crown prince of Abu Dhabi and deputy commander of the armed forces of the UAE, the region's most effective – and most interventionist – military power. Emirati successes include taking the ports of Mukalla and Shihr in southern Yemen from the al-Qaeda affiliate al-Qaeda in the Arabian Peninsula as well as two strategic islands in the Bab al-Mandab strait between Arabia and Africa, through which tankers bearing some 4 million barrels of oil must pass each day. Emirati special forces have also been active in fighting the Houthi rebels in Yemen, Islamist groups in Somalia and northern Sinai, and are known to support General Khalifa Hafter in Libya, the US-trained leader of the Libyan National Army now contesting power with forces loyal to the official UN-backed government in Tripoli. MBZ has been influential in Washington, especially with the Trump administration. He is virulently hostile to the Muslim Brotherhood, which he sees as a dangerous threat to dynastic rule throughout the Gulf. He is thought to have been the driving force behind the 2017 blockade of Qatar which MBN was resisting. As one commentator tweeted cheekily, 'bin Zayed has become the real ruler of Egypt and Saudi Arabia, the two largest Arab countries. Congratulations to the people of these two countries.'

As defence minister, MBS was already in charge of launching the Emirati-backed intervention in Yemen, which has been responsible for the killing of thousands of civilians in air strikes and the displacement of more than 3 million people. It has 'weaponized' famine by deliberately bombing food imports, using starvation as an instrument of war. According to the UN, 80 per cent of Yemen's population is now in need of humanitarian aid that can't reach the country thanks to the Saudi blockade; the lack of food and clean water has led to widespread malnutrition and at least 500,000 cases of cholera. A Saudi–Iranian rapprochement engineered by China brought a pause in the fighting in March 2023, with Iran agreeing to halt arms supplies to the Houthi rebels who opposed official president Abdrabbuh Mansour Hadi. Saudi Arabia has consistently accused the Houthis, who belong to the Zaidi Shiite sect, of being Iranian proxies, a charge that was once untrue but came to have the force of prediction as the Islamic Republic stepped up its aid.

After the Israeli attack on Gaza in response to the atrocity of 7 October 2023 when Hamas operatives broke through the border fence between Israel and Gaza brutally killing more than 1,200 Israelis and capturing some 250 hostages, the Houthis helped Hamas in its war against Israel by preventing Israeli shipping or cargoes destined for Israel from passing through the Red Sea, a move that threatened to widen the conflict by involving shipping of other nations.

In a twist to this complex story of dynastic intrigue, tribal dynamics and geopolitical ambitions framed by sectarian rivalries, MBS – with UAE backing – persuaded Ali Abdullah Saleh, the former Yemeni strongman – to abandon his alliance he had forged with the Houthis after he was forced from office in 2014. MBS and MBZ hoped that a return to power by Saleh, or his son Ahmed, a powerful military chief who had served as ambassador to the Emirates, would help extricate the Saudis and their UAE allies from an unwinnable war. On 4 December 2017, the Houthis dealt with this betrayal by their former ally by killing Saleh in a battle around his home outside

Sanaa, the Yemeni capital, which they had taken over, blocking Saudi control.

As with Saudi engagement with Yemen, the diplomatic and economic campaign against Qatar can be seen as part of an expansionist drive in the Saudi–UAE effort to counter what they present as Iranian influence. This move also appears to have backfired, by driving Qatar closer to the Islamic Republic. As Richard Sokolsky and Aaron David Miller put it in *Politico*:

> The crown prince engineered this dispute not to punish Qatar for its financing of terrorism (a hypocritical comment coming from the Saudis, whose own citizens have provided funding to radical extremists over the years), but rather to end Qatar's independent foreign policy and especially its support for the Muslim Brotherhood and its ties with Iran. Simply put, the Saudis want to turn Qatar into a vassal state – as they have done with Bahrain – as part of their plan to establish Saudi hegemony over the entire Persian Gulf.[55]

But Qatar has its reasons to cooperate with Iran – not least the fact that the countries share ownership of the world's largest natural gas field – and, partly through the offices of Al Jazeera, the only measurably independent news organization in the region, it has shown itself more tolerant than any of its neighbours of the dissenting political movements whose fortunes improved with the Arab Spring. Like the Saudis, the Qataris follow Wahhabi teachings, although their version is known as 'the Wahhabism of the Sea' in contrast to 'Wahhabism of the Land'. Qatari Wahhabism embraces a higher degree of religious pluralism than the Saudi version, with Christians (who comprise some 13 per cent of the immigrant population) permitted to construct churches and Hindus (who comprise another 13 per cent) granted freedom of worship. In contrast to Saudi Arabia, where the religious establishment was part of the historic duopoly with the Al

Saud family, the Qatari rulers kept the Wahhabi clerics firmly under royal control. As Hakim al-Karoui, advisor to President Macron, pointed out in his report for the Institut Montaigne, the Muslim Brotherhood has been entrenched in the country's educational system since the 1970s. Along with the influence of al-Qaradawi, the most prominent of the Brotherhood voices, members of the fraternity are present in all levels of society, as well as in ministries such as education and religious affairs. For the Qataris, who resisted inclusion in the UAE after Britain's withdrawal from the Gulf in 1971, the Brotherhood represents an important element of 'soft power', an ideological resource against the 'hard power' of Saudi Arabia and the UAE, whose hegemonic aims in the peninsula they perceive as threatening.

For the Saudi princes, like their Emirati peers, the Muslim Brotherhood is an internal threat not to be countenanced, especially in the aftermath of the Arab Spring insurgencies that erupted throughout the region in 2011. In this sense, the military offensives against Yemen on the part of Saudi Arabia and the UAE as well as the diplomatic standoff with Qatar were not just part of a plan for regional domination but also a defensive operation designed by the regime to stoke up anti-Iranian and anti-Shia feeling at home – even when the Iranian influence is largely invented. 'We are a primary target for the Iranian regime', MBS said in May 2017, shortly before Trump's visit, accusing the Iranians of seeking to take over Islamic holy sites in Saudi Arabia. 'We won't wait for the battle to be in Saudi Arabia. Instead, we'll work so that the battle is for them in Iran.'[56]

Khashoggi was a particular threat to MBS because he was a 'soft' Islamist, a fellow traveller of the Muslim Brotherhood whose affiliates include not only 'hardened' jihadists but constitutionally minded politicians such as Rachid al-Ghannouchi, leader of the Ennahda party in Tunisia, who has reluctantly conceded that democracy 'trumps' Islam, when it comes to politics. He was also close to the Turkish president Erdogan, Saudi Arabia's principal competitor for Sunni leadership, who could also be described as a 'soft Islamist' friendly to the Muslim Brotherhood. When he visited Cairo at the start of the Morsi presidency, Erdogan was mobbed in the streets by the Brotherhood and its supporters. He may be highly authoritarian and is certainly no friend of intellectual freedom – there are more journalists serving time in Turkish prisons than in Chinese jails – but, although an authoritarian Sunni, Erdogan takes a much more nuanced view of the conflicts in the Middle East than the Saudis and their American friends, especially with regard to Iran. While the Saudis consider Iran their arch-enemy, the Turks have common interests with the Islamic Republic – including a shared frontier and similar problems in managing their Kurdish minorities; rather than following the Saudis and their Gulf allies in pursuing active confrontation with Iran they have 'chosen the path of active diplomacy and constructive dialogue'.[57]

As a high-profile moderate with access to power and authority, especially in the United States, Khashoggi was not just a 'soft Islamist': he was also a personal threat to the prince, being on familiar terms with rival royals, such as Prince Turki al-Faisal and Prince Ahmed, the surviving Al Sudairi sons who would have a strong claim to the throne on the death of King Salman. A well-known 'insider', he was better placed than anyone to expose the emerging dictatorship behind MBS's liberalizing rhetoric and to challenge the direction along which he had been leading the country. Vali Nasr, one of the most perceptive observers of Middle East politics, saw the Khashoggi affair as 'a watershed event' that 'brought into sharp relief the weakness at the core of Mr. Trump's strategy, even as it weakened the crown prince himself, along with support for his partnership with America'.[58]

In the wider game of geopolitics, however, it was far from clear that Trump's strategy of helping Israel by boosting support of the Gulf states, including Saudi Arabia, in confronting Iran was doomed to fail. In August 2020 the so-called Abraham Accords between Israel, the UAE and Bahrain (along with Sudan and Morocco), negotiated by Jared Kushner and the White House official Ari Berkowitz with Riyadh's blessing, produced a full-blown peace treaty between Israel and two Gulf Arab states, the first since its treaty with Jordan in 1994. The deal legitimized de facto connections between Israel and the Gulf states (including Qatar) that had been in place for many years, converting what one Israeli commentator saw as long-standing 'mistress relations' between the parties into 'open and legitimate relations'.[59]

While hailed as a triumph of diplomacy by Trump's supporters, who pointed out that the deal involved the abandonment of Israeli premier Benjamin Netanyahu's plans to formally annex the Arab territories Israel had been occupying since 1967, critics on both sides of politics had their concerns. On the left the accords could be seen as the final abandonment by financially powerful Arab states of any remaining concerns for the rights of Palestinians under occupation. In the Israeli centre there was concern that the construction of an anti-Iranian front could require Israel to take military action 'on behalf of its new allies even in situations where there is no existential threat to the Jewish state', a particular concern in the case of Bahrain where Iran has territorial claims.[60]

Biden's victory in the 2020 presidential race did not alter the strategic calculation. Though a more nuanced supporter of Israel than Trump, who, before the accords, had supported Netanyahu's policy of Israeli annexation, he nevertheless maintained his predecessor's policy of withdrawing America's commitments in the region, most notably in his controversial decision to remove all US troops from Afghanistan in 2021. Once in power the Biden administration found itself holding a delicate hand. On one side it wanted to restore the JCPOA (Joint Comprehensive Plan of Action) – the so-called 'nuclear deal' with Iran made by the Obama administration, backed by China, Russia, France, Germany and the United Kingdom, according to which Iran would abandon any plan to 'weaponize' its nuclear facilities in exchange for the lifting of the sanctions imposed on it when the Trump administration unilaterally abandoned the deal. At the same time the Biden administration quickly came to recognize that withdrawing its support for Saudi Arabia, the largest and potentially most powerful of the Gulf states facing Iran, would weaken its negotiating posture in the revived talks with Iran.

The predicament facing the new administration in Washington was illustrated by Biden's 'wobble' over Khashoggi. Within days of his coming to power in January 2021 Biden made it clear that he still saw MBS as a 'pariah', insisting he would only deal with the Saudi kingdom through its ruler, King Salman. Going even further, he appeared to rub salt into MBS's wounded reputation by authorizing the official release of the redacted CIA report on the Khashoggi murder (most of the details of which were already widely known, having been leaked to the *New York Times* and *Washington Post*).

However, no sooner had Biden authorized the CIA report's publication than members of his team, or indeed the president himself, leaked to the *New York Times* that the crown prince would not be punished because the 'diplomatic cost' would be 'too high'. His immunity was provided with legal authority after September 2022 when his father King Salman promoted him to the rank of prime minister. Customary law – though not formally enacted – holds that servicing heads of state and government as well as foreign ministers are immune from prosecution in jurisdictions outside of their countries.[61] As Karen House, an astute observer of the kingdom, who we shall meet in Chapter 4, observed: by 'waffling' over the prince,

The president has unleashed a potentially dangerous game. He will be under pressure from the Democrat left to punish Saudi further. MBS wants good relations with the US. But make no mistake, his top priority is his survival ... If the crown prince faces backlash from royals, religious or frustrated youth, he won't dither and depart as the Shah of Iran did four decades ago under US Human Rights pressure. MBS will crack down.[62]

As may be read in Chapter 10, the Saudi blogger who calls himself Mujtahid sees MBS as a 'Machiavellian and narcissistic psychopath' who enjoys psychologically, even physically, torturing other people. This is not to say that he is worse than Hitler, Stalin or Mao Zedong. It is rather a recognition of the unpleasant fact of life that power not only corrupts, but has a tendency to gravitate towards 'narcissistic psychopaths', a tendency unlikely to be reversed with President Trump's return to power in 2025.

2
The Wahhabi Mission

Around the year 1741 when Louis XV was king of France and people in Lille were being entertained by Voltaire's scurrilous drama *Le Fanatisme, ou Mahomet le prophète, tragédie* (a coded attack on the Catholic church masquerading as a satire on the founder of Islam), a lonely figure might have been spotted wandering away from the busy port of Basra on the Persian Gulf. Muhammad ibn Abd al-Wahhab, scion of an established family of clerics from the town of al-Uyayna, some 50 km north-west of Riyadh in the arid uplands of Nejd in northern Arabia, had been expelled by Basra's ruler at the behest of local clerics or *ulama* – 'the learned men' who acted as guardians of scriptural correctness. Sheikh Muhammad had scandalized these clerics, who prided themselves on scholastic knowledge of the Quran, its exegesis, the life of the Holy Prophet and his sayings and deeds as relayed through the corpus of hadiths (reports or 'traditions' relayed through chains of transmitters over time). They had been outraged by what they regarded as the cleric's ill-informed and fanatical attacks on local practices, such as veneration of saints through whom people sought intercession with God. By some accounts, the sheikh had already arrived in Basra, a regional centre of scholarly learning, with a track record of attacking 'idolatry' – the most heinous of theological sins in the Islamic book.

After studies with his father and in the holy city of Medina, where he is believed to have come under the influence of Sheikh Abdullah ibn Ibrahim al-Nejdi, an important scholar in the neo-Hanbalite tradition that followed the austere puritanical teachings of the medieval scholar Ibn Taymiyya (d. 1328), he travelled to Basra, and possibly to places further afield, including Damascus and Cairo, though this is not known for certain. Practices that Ibn Abd al-Wahhab attacked in his native Nejd included the cult of Dha'l Khilsa, a fetish or image against which infertile women rubbed their genitals in the hope of getting pregnant, praying to the souls of the dead and seeking supplication at their tombs, and celebrations at the festivals of holy people. Among other practices that were anathema to him was honouring the Prophet Muhammad's *mawlid* or birthday, a festival widely observed in other Muslim regions.

In Basra, however, there was a large Shia population – something unknown in Nejd. We can be sure that this provincial outsider from a rural backwater would have been horrified by Shiite ritual practices, such as the processions and flagellations that took place during the month of Muharram, when Shias commemorate the death of Husayn ibn Ali, grandson of the Prophet Muhammad, and the first of their imam martyrs. Inspired by the sheikh's teachings, Wahhabis have always been virulently anti-Shiite.

In Basra the sheikh is said to have had some kind of mystical experience: according to his grandson it was while he was studying with the city's scholars that God revealed to him hidden aspects of *tawhid*, the divine unicity – the theology that would inform the *Treatise on God's Unity* or 'monotheist manifesto' that he would compose on returning to Nejd. But even before this, his call to the people of Basra to affirm God's unity and to reject 'idolatry' had infuriated the local ulama, not just because its claim to direct inspiration from God challenged their religious authority, but because his radical doctrine threatened the social peace in a thriving port city which had large populations of Jews and Christians along with its Shiite majority. The first Wahhabi chronicler, Husayn ibn Ghanam, relates that the city's ruler expelled the would-be reformer or 'renewer' (*mujaddid*) of Islam at the height of summer (when temperatures regularly exceed 50 degrees Celsius). After his expulsion, according to a narrative of persecution and exile that echoes standard accounts of the life of the Prophet Muhammad, the preacher departed the city on foot and nearly perished from thirst until rescued by a kindly stranger who gave him water and let him ride his donkey until he reached the nearby town of Az Zubayr. From there he moved to Huraymila (around 90 km north of Riyadh, the present Saudi capital) where his father had been appointed judge, before moving to nearby al-Uyayna where he benefited, briefly, from the support of the local emir, Uthman ibn Mu'ammar. Here he 'resumed his mission of combating popular veneration of trees, stones, tombs, shrines' erected over the graves of the Prophet Muhammad's Companions and holy men, along with the 'places where folk slaughtered animals to seek good fortune'.[1] As in Basra, however, Sheikh Muhammad's preaching soon generated opposition from the local ulama, who contacted the ruler of al-Ahsa, the region's distant overlord, persuading him that Sheikh Muhammad's mission threatened his right to collect taxes. The ruler ordered the Emir Uthman to expel him from al-Uyayna, so once again the preacher found himself driven into exile, a lonely and persecuted figure.

Two highly contentious actions feature in this narrative. The first was the sheikh's part in the destruction of the dome covering the grave of the Prophet's Companion Zayd ibn al-Khattab, brother of Umar ibn al-Khattab, the second of the four 'rightly guided' caliphs or leaders who succeeded Muhammad and are revered by all Sunni Muslims. The second was his order to stone to death a woman accused of adultery, an act that was widely noted because of its extreme rarity: though we do not have records of stoning in Nejd at that time, in some five centuries of Ottoman legal documentation there is only one case of a stoning imposed by an Ottoman court, and 'the outrage it caused was such that it never occurred again under Ottoman rule'.[2]

The destruction of Zayd's tomb occasioned a lively polemic from Sulayman ibn Suhaym (c. 1718–67), a scholar based in Riyadh, who – at that time – was highly resistant to Sheikh Muhammad's claim to be reviving 'true Islam'. The tomb, said Ibn Suhaym, had not been erected for idolatrous reasons, but because the ground was too rocky for a grave: Zayd's Companions had erected the tomb above ground to prevent his body from being savaged by wild animals. The sheikh, moreover, did not stop his iconoclastic attacks at the tomb of Zayd. He had already destroyed a nearby mosque for no good reason and given the opportunity he would have destroyed the tomb of the Prophet himself in Medina along with other acts of desecration.

Broadening his attack on Muhammad ibn Abd al-Wahhab, Ibn Suhaym noted that Sheikh Muhammad claimed that all those who refused to share his denunciation of the cultic practices of which he disapproved, such as praying at the tomb of saints or making sacrifices to ward off evil, were unbelievers deserving of death. According to this standard, not only were Sufi masters, such as the poet Ibn al-Farid and the great mystic Ibn Arabi, anathematized as infidels, but so too were all those descendants of the Prophet known as *sayyids* who accepted vows of allegiance from Muslims of lower status.

In a charge later taken up by Sheikh Muhammad's own brother Sulayman, Ibn Suhaym suggested that the would-be reformer lacked the scholarly qualifications needed to justify his attacks on popular beliefs and practices. He mentioned a letter that Sheikh Muhammad had sent to some of his followers stating that he had not obtained his knowledge of divine unicity from his father or any other teacher: a claim that seems to have been endorsed later by his grandson's account of the mystical experience in Basra. If this was the case, asked Ibn Suhaym sarcastically, from where did Ibn Abd al-Wahhab obtain his so-called knowledge? Was it God who inspired him, in a dream? Or was it perhaps Satan who had been his teacher?

Sulayman's critique of his brother was even more pertinent than Ibn Suhaym's, raising the issue that would become pivotal in subsequent arguments between Wahhabis and their Muslim critics. He, too, accused his brother of undertaking independent legal reasoning (*ijtihad*) without the necessary scholarly qualifications. In particular, his handling of proof texts from the Quran and the sunnah was deficient. If he had discussed his views with other ulama, he would have avoided his erroneous conclusions. The most serious charge levelled by Sulayman was his brother's branding of other Muslims as infidels. On this matter, as Commins explains,

> Sulayman anticipated a perennial controversy between Wahhabis and their Muslim adversaries. The Wahhabis would always maintain that they never regarded Muslims as infidels while their opponents insisted that the fundamental problem with Wahhabism is its exclusion of Muslims from the community of believers. Sulayman asserted the general view, accepted by the vast majority of scholars, that to proclaim the creed ('There is no god but God and Muhammad is the messenger of God'), to perform the obligatory acts of worship and to believe in God, His angels, books and messengers qualify one as a Muslim. In contrast Sheikh Muhammad argued that if someone violated God's unity by invoking a dead or living holy man or by a similar practice, then that person was guilty of idolatry even if he sincerely proclaimed

the creed. According to Sulayman, the Muslim consensus viewed such violations of God's unity as 'lesser idolatry' which falls short of apostasy, for which one may be put to death.[3]

In invoking charges of apostasy against supposed idolators, a charge known by the term *takfir* – (declaring someone a *kafir*, or unbeliever) – Sheikh Muhammad had claimed the authority of – among others – Ibn Taymiyya (d. 1328), a scholar in the legal tradition of Ibn Hanbal to which both brothers belonged. Sulayman, however, states that Ibn Taymiyya endorsed the consensus view of 'lesser idolatry'. That Ibn Taymiyya is invoked in the polemics between the two brothers is significant, if not surprising, as his legacy is still controversial and contested between different Islamist groups today. An iconic figure for modern jihadis, often seen as the foremost medieval authority for Islamic radicalism among the Sunnis, the Syrian jurist, who died in a Damascus prison, was a polemicist who inveighed against Sufis, philosophers and Christians in his earlier writings.

He was especially hostile to mystical theology associated with Muhyi'l din ibn Arabi (d. 1240), who saw all creation as a 'mirror to the Creator', an outlook that could be seen to 'minimise the importance of the divine law and daily acts of worship' leading to polytheism, and to the popular practice in his time of praying at the tomb of saints, which he saw as imitating Christians and other unbelievers, implying that 'the dead share in God's divine power', a practice that could also lead to polytheism.[4]

Living at a time when the Mongols had invaded his native Syria, Ibn Taymiyya issued two famous fatwas comparing the Mongol invaders (who had adopted Islam formally, while maintaining elements of their pre-Islamic *yasa* code) to the early Kharijites, the militant group who had fought against the first caliph Abu Bakr

(r. 632–4) and murdered the fourth caliph Ali. They were considered legitimate targets by other Muslims, not least because they themselves declared that grave sinners could not be regarded as Muslims and hence were liable to attack. Towards the end of his career, however, Ibn Taymiyya modified his position on *takfir*, stating that he did not 'deem anyone from among the Muslims to be an unbeliever'. At several points Sulayman accused his brother of disrupting Muslim unity by abandoning the consensus view of 'lesser idolatry', a course that would take him and his followers down the same misguided path as the early Kharijites. The charges of 'takfirism' and Kharijism would become standard accusations levelled against Wahhabis and other militant groups in the course of the following centuries.

This fraternal dispute about idolatrous worship might have remained an abstruse argument between religious scholars, such as is found in every tradition, had it not been for the harnessing of theology to power. The event that sealed the theological–military axis of Saudi-Wahhabism, one that would have huge consequences for the future of the Islamic world and beyond, was the meeting in 1744 between Muhammad ibn Abd al-Wahhab and Muhammad ibn Saud, the emir who controlled the oasis of al-Diriyah, where Sheikh Muhammad had settled after his expulsion from al-Uyayna. Muhammad ibn Saud (d. 1765) was a relatively minor lord without connections to the larger tribal confederations of northern Arabia and Nejd. He was a landowner and broker able to finance the caravans of some long-distance merchants, exacting tribute from the settlement in exchange for defending its inhabitants, some of whom served in his militia alongside his slaves.[5] According to one of the chronicles it was a Bedouin wife of the emir who persuaded Ibn Saud to meet with the refugee preacher. Sheikh Muhammad's pitch seems to have been flawless. Invoking the canonical narrative of the *sirat* – the Prophet's biography, a subject he had studied in Basra – he told the emir that the people of Nejd were currently living in the same condition of ignorance or *jahiliyya* as the pagan Arabs of the Prophet Muhammad's time. To put matters right they must emulate the Prophet and take up the cause of *tawhid* against the idolaters – those who would wrongfully allow 'partners' to share in God's divinity.

Seeing his opportunity to enlarge his territory at the expense of his neighbours, the emir agreed to back the sheikh's campaign against unbelief and idolatry on two conditions: first the preacher's support for the emir must continue even after their campaign had triumphed; second the preacher must approve of the emir's right to tax al-Diriyah's harvests. After agreeing to the first condition, the sheikh cunningly suggested that with regard to the second, God might choose to compensate the emir with booty far greater than any he would obtain from the meagre harvests of the cereal and date cultivators on which he relied at present. The scene was set for a series of conquests, modelled on the Prophet Muhammad's original mission, that would effectively unite Arabia under a single regime that combined the military power of the tribe with the religious authority of the scholar. As the historian al-Rasheed explains,

> Wahhabism provided a novel impetus for political centralization. Expansion by conquest was the only mechanism that would permit the emirate to rise above the limited confines of a specific settlement. With the importance of *jihad* in Wahhabi teachings, conquest of new territories became possible. The spread of the Wahhabi *da'wa* (call), the purification of Arabia of unorthodox forms of religiosity and the enforcement of the shari'a among Arabian society were fundamental demands of the Wahhabi movement ... Wahhabism impregnated the Saudi leadership with a new force which proved crucial for the consolidation and expansion of Saudi rule. Wahhabism promised this

leadership clear benefits in the form of political and religious authority and material rewards, without which the conquest of Arabia would not have been possible.[6]

This process of political centralization, the beginning of state-building, worked by inverting the system of tribal alliances that had prevailed in Arabia in the past and would resume, short-term, after the collapse of the first two Saudi emirates in the nineteenth century. Under the old system, a leading clan would offer protection – *himaya* – to other clans, creating a layered confederation of tribes which extracted payment of *khuwwa* (tribute) from farmers and traders, turning them into vassals, without fundamentally altering their relations or interfering with their activities. As a tribute the *khuwwa* was a tax 'levied not on the collector's own community, but rather on a conquered group which remained more or less autonomous'.[7]

The Al Saud, however, were not tribal nomads, but primarily farmers and traders. Their territory at al-Diriyah was small. They had no tribal confederation to support expansion beyond the settlement and 'no surplus wealth that would have allowed Muhammad ibn Saud to assemble a fighting force with which to conquer other settlements. The key to expansion – as in the time of Muhammad – was 'submission' – a word normally used to translate the Arabic word *islam* into European languages.[8] In Muhammad's time the submission of the tribes to God and His Prophet enabled the Arabian tribes to channel their energies towards the phenomenal world-conquest that followed the death of the Prophet in 632 CE.

In eighteenth-century Arabia the idea of submission entailed the replication of Muhammad's original movement. In this case submission was not to the existing idea of 'Islam' – a diversified system of religious and power relations focused on formal allegiance to a sultan-caliph based in distant Istanbul – but to the revitalized tenets of the religion engineered by Muhammad ibn Abd al-Wahhab in alliance with Muhammad ibn Saud. While this may have represented a departure from Ottoman-style acceptance of plurality of religious practices and legal rulings allowing for a variety of customary procedures, it resonated powerfully with the original narrative of the Prophet Muhammad's life. In both cases, internecine strife between competing tribal systems, symbolized by a variety of devotional practices, was to be abandoned under the rubric of the one true singular God and His Prophet.

As al-Rasheed explains, submission to the tenets of Wahhabi Islam among the population, both sedentary and nomadic, led (as in the Prophet Muhammad's time) to the creation of a supra-tribal confederation with which to conquer further territories in the name of true Islam. Like other religious groups in Islamic history, Wahhabis eschewed the sectarian label, avoiding the term Wahhabi in preference for *muwahhidun* – 'unitarians' – as befitting the theology of *tawhid*. Additional to the expansionist rubric of jihad was the consolidating force of *zakat* – the alms tax or purifying dues that is one of the five obligatory pillars of the Islamic faith. As a religious duty *zakat* differs from *khuwwa*, for while the latter involves recognition of the superiority of one tribe over another, the former is a universal duty owed to God. The key to Saudi-Wahhabi strategy was fusion of religion and politics embodied in *zakat*: for while its payment was a token of political submission, it was also a *religious* obligation. Communities, both tribal and nomadic, who submitted to Wahhabism were expected to demonstrate their loyalty by 'agreeing to fight for its cause and pay *zakat* to its representatives' while those who resisted 'were subject to raids that threatened their livelihood'.[9] By means of *zakat* the Saudi-Wahhabi polity extracted wealth from the trade of the Qassim area, whose rival cities of Buraydah and

Unayza sat astride the important route between Medina and Basra and Kuwait, where the Unayza traders had a stake in its famous pearl fisheries.

In the short term, the Saudi-Wahhabi formula, the fusing of jihad and *zakat*, proved remarkably effective. Under the leadership of Muhammad ibn Saud's son Abd al-Aziz (1765–1803), the polity expanded into the domains of Riyadh, Kharj and Qassim. Towns in central Nejd received judges from a new corps of Wahhabi-trained ulama who ruled in strict accordance with the Hanbali *madhhab* (law school). The subjugating of Qatif opened the way to the Gulf Coast and Oman. Qatar acknowledged Saudi authority in 1797, followed by Bahrain. By 1800, most of the emirs of Nejd had submitted to the Saudi leadership: they were allowed to remain in place so long as they paid the *zakat* to the Saudi leader.

Beyond the steppelands of Nejd (a word that signifies 'elevated, stony table-land'), the situation was much less stable. In the Hejaz, the western region containing the holy cities of Mecca and Medina, a rich human patina of cosmopolitan and ethnic diversity attests to centuries of settlement by pilgrims from every part of the Muslim world. Here the Saudis faced resistance from the Ottoman-appointed sharif who submitted temporarily while remaining resentful of the destruction of the tombs of the Companions in Medina, including that of the Prophet himself, in accordance with Ibn Abd al-Wahhab's iconoclastic doctrines.

In 1802, the Wahhabis further scandalized the wider Muslim world, by sacking the Shiite shrine city of Karbala in Iraq, a centre of learning and pilgrimage focused on the tomb of the Prophet's grandson Husayn, first imam of the Shia. Some 4,000 of Karbala's people are reported to have been slaughtered, with the Arab invaders ripping the fetuses from pregnant women, leaving the fetuses to rot beside their corpses. According to one chronicle, 4,000 camels were deployed to bring back booty brought to Karbala over the centuries by Shiite pilgrims from Persia, central Asia and India.

The Saudi occupation of the Hejaz, though mild compared with the devastation of Karbala, directly threatened the Ottoman sultan's standing as Guardian of the Two Shrines of Mecca and Medina, finally causing the empire to act. In 1811, Mehmet Ali, the powerful and virtually autonomous Ottoman viceroy in Egypt, sent his son Ibrahim Pasha to eliminate the Saudi-Wahhabi menace. After initially repulsing the Egyptians, the Saudis eventually succumbed to their better organization and superior fire-power, withdrawing from Medina after a brief siege in November 1812 and from Mecca in January 1813. Many of the tribal confederations that had suffered under the Wahhabis switched their allegiance back to the Ottomans, allowing Ibrahim to consolidate his authority in the Hejaz. In 1815, the Ottoman-Egyptians made a major thrust into Nejd, marching into al-Qassim where inconclusive fighting produced a truce resulting in an Ottoman withdrawal to Hejaz.

Furious at the way some of the chiefs had switched their allegiance and even invited Ottoman troops into al-Qassim, the Saudi emir Abdullah, who had succeeded his father Saud in 1814, razed the walls of two towns and took their chiefs hostage, an act that provoked Mehmet Ali into resuming the war. In 1818, Ibrahim arrived at the gates of Diriyah with a force of 3,300 Egyptian and Moroccan cavalry, 4,300 Turkish and Albanian infantry, along with some 180 gunners, weapons technicians and engineers. Finally, after five bitter years of conflict and the complete destruction of the city and its fortifications, the Saudis surrendered. Diriyah never recovered: the ruins of its ancient mud walls, a favourite picnicking place for Riyadh families, is now being restored as a UNESCO World Heritage Site. After Ibrahim Pasha's troops had massacred several of the Wahhabi ulama, the Emir Abdullah was brought in a cage to Istanbul.

He was beheaded before the great mosque of Hagia Sophia, amid fireworks and public rejoicing.

While the Ottomans remained in the Hejaz, they did not have the resources to occupy Nejd, and 1824 saw the return of Turki bin Abdullah Al Saud, son of the beheaded emir, to Riyadh near Diriyah. After expelling the Egyptians he was able to extend his control over adjacent areas, and while his authority in Hail and Qassim was minimal, by 1830 he was able to enforce recognition of Saudi authority in al-Ahsa.

There followed another period of turbulence which lasted until the beginning of the twentieth century as individual members of the Al Saud family vied with each other for power against the background of external pressures from the Egyptians, the Ottomans and eventually the British. This picture of Mafia-style tribal politics, with rival 'godfathers' competing for power against other members of the 'family', is not very different from the pattern that would unfold in the early twenty-first century against the backdrop of Arab, Israeli and Iranian rivalries and the broader strategic interests of Russia and the United States. Although the Emir Turki was a loyal Wahhabi, he avoided provoking the Ottoman-Egyptian troops in the Hejaz by attacking the pilgrim caravans, but he was unable to deal with dissent within his family. In 1834 he was assassinated by a cousin when leaving a mosque after Friday prayers. With help from the pro-Ottoman governor of Hail, Turki's son Faisal succeeded his father as emir.

Faisal's rule as an autonomous leader, however, lasted barely three years. In 1837 the Egyptians sent a new expedition to Riyadh when he refused to pay them tribute. Faisal was taken as a hostage to Cairo while the Egyptians appointed a cousin, Khaled, to rule in southern Nejd. But following the Treaty of London (1840) the Egyptians withdrew from Arabia under pressure from Britain, Russia, Prussia and Austria. Abdullah ibn Thunayan, who belonged to a different branch of the family, took power in Riyadh, leaving Khaled to flee to Jeddah in the Hejaz which remained under Egyptian protection. In 1843 Faisal escaped from Cairo, returned to Riyadh and killed Ibn Thunayan, resuming his chieftainship and inaugurating the relatively calm period known as the second Saudi emirate.

Instead of continuity, however, Faisal's death in 1865 initiated a new period of dynastic disruption. His succession by his eldest son Abdullah was challenged by Abdullah's younger half-brother Saud, who conspired with the rulers of Asir (near what is now the international border with Yemen) and leaders of the Murra, Ajman and Dawasir tribal confederations with a view to supplanting Abdullah. The protracted military struggle sapped the strength of the Al Saud dynasty, opening the way to the fall of the second Saudi emirate in 1891 and the triumph of the pro-Ottoman Rashid family, who were part of the great Shammar confederation of north-Arabian tribes.

In 1870 Abdullah appealed to Muhammad ibn Rashid, the ruler of Hail, to support him in his struggle with Saud and his sons. Seizing the opportunity, Ibn Rashid marched on Riyadh and took charge, having expelled Saud and his men. After Saud's death in 1875 his brothers Abdullah and Abd al-Rahman resumed the struggle, with Abdullah ruling the city as a vassal of the al-Rashids. After failing to regain full power with the help of allies from al-Qassim, Abdul Rahman abandoned Riyadh, seeking refuge in the Rub al-Khali (the 'Empty Quarter') desert where the al-Murrah tribe protected him before he moved to Kuwait under the protection of the ruling Al Sabah family, with a pension from the Ottoman government. It was Abdul Rahman's son Abd al-Aziz ibn Saud who would restore the family's fortunes at the start of the twentieth century.

These dynastic struggles involving external forces posed real dilemmas for the Wahhabi establishment, dilemmas that would still resonate powerfully in the late twentieth and early twenty-first centuries in the frame of a modern state. Given the absence of celibacy as a requirement for religious leadership in the Islamic tradition, religious expertise is often passed down the generations in a patriarchal line that mirrors the dynastic patterns of the military tribal sphere. Descendants of Muhammad ibn Abd al-Wahhab — known as the Al ash-Sheikh (House of the Sheikh) — 'played the central role in perpetuating the Wahhabi mission and assumed an unrivalled position of prominence as a hereditary line of religious leaders for two centuries'.[10]

Abdullah was the most prominent of Sheikh Muhammad's four sons after his father's death, acting as chief counsellor to the Al Saud and overseeing the appointment of teachers and *qadis* (judges). As the supreme religious authority, he took part in the conquest of Mecca in 1803, making a special effort to place the Wahhabi mission, with its linkage to the Hanbali school of law, in the mainstream of the Sunni scholastic tradition, citing well-known authorities on Quranic exegesis and hadith to counter accusations of unorthodoxy. In one of his epistles he states unequivocally that Wahhabis follow the Hanbali *madhhab* but do not reject other schools, although Shias are beyond the pale.[11]

During his era, Wahhabi epistles were sent to religious scholars in Syria, Egypt and beyond to the Maghreb. Messages condemning many accepted forms of worship as idolatry invited ridicule, with ulama loyal to the Ottoman sultan regarding them as a 'rustic, misguided and fanatical — and hopefully temporary — intrusion' into their religious lives, except in the Islamic far west, where the Wahhabi discourse helped boost the sultan's religious authority vis-à-vis the local marabouts or holy men.[12] Moroccan pilgrims passing through Cairo on their way home from Mecca gave the historian Abd al-Rahman al-Jabarti a generally favourable account of the Hajj of 1809 when the Saudis were occupying the holy city, leading him to conclude that stories about their cruelty came from corrupt denizens of Mecca and Medina who profited from extorting gifts and fees from pilgrims.

In addition to arguments about what religious practices constituted idolatry, much of the debate between Wahhabi scholars and their mainstream Sunni opponents concerned the conduct of relations between the true 'unitarians' and others. In 1815 when Ottoman forces withdrew to the Hejaz and men from al-Qassim went to Cairo to ask Mehmet Ali to return to Nejd, despite the truce between the Saudi Emir Abdullah and Ibrahim Pasha, Sulayman ibn Abdullah, a member of the Al ash-Sheikh, wrote an important thesis elaborating two related questions: is it permitted to travel to the land of idolatry, and is it permitted to befriend idolaters? In answer to the first he stated it was permissible on two conditions: one must be permitted to practise one's religion but must refrain from befriending the idolaters. A verse from the Quran (al-Nisa' 140) that urges the believers not to remain in the company of those who reject or deride God's revelation is cited in support of this position. A hadith in the canonical collection of Abu Dawud underscores this message, and features prominently in Wahhabi writings: 'Whoever associates with the idolater and lives with him is like him.' In due course the doctrine known as *al-wala' wa'l-bara'* (loyalty and disassociation), encouraging believers to actively distance themselves from non-Muslims and their world, became a standard Wahhabi trope, one that informs the reluctance of many contemporary Salafists to engage with outsiders, reinforcing an 'us-versus-them' mentality.

The religious permissibility of allowing true believers to associate with those they regarded as idolaters or unbelievers came to a head during the period of infighting between Abdullah ibn Faisal, his half-brother Saud and their respective clans. In 1869 Abd al-Latif, chief of the Al ash-Sheikh and leader of the Wahhabi mission, faced the delicate task of negotiating the surrender of Riyadh to the forces of Saud after Abdullah ibn Faisal had abandoned the Saudi capital for al-Ahsa on the coast, where the Ottomans were entrenched. Citing necessity, Abd al-Latif recognized Saud as the legitimate ruler even though he had previously made a pronouncement of *takfir* against him.

As Commins comments, Abd al-Latif's commitment to Abdullah 'may have been diluted by the beleaguered ruler's bid to forge an alliance with the Ottoman governor of Baghdad. The Wahhabis condemned any such move that might bring the "infidel" Ottomans into Arabia and they made no allowance for Abdullah's desperation in the face of Saud's threat.'[13] The difficulty facing the Wahhabi leader in the face of internecine strife, with one of the contending parties being accused of acting in the interest of foreign 'infidels', is virtually identical to the predicament faced by Abd al-Aziz bin Abdallah ibn Baz (1910–99), grand mufti of Saudi Arabia and chief Wahhabi cleric in 1990–1, when King Fahd ibn Abd al-Aziz placed him under pressure to authorize the presence of 'infidel' American troops to defend the country after the Iraqi invasion of Kuwait. Ibn Baz's fatwa justifying the presence of the Americans on the grounds of necessity was openly condemned by other leading clerics, becoming a major source of contention within the Wahhabi-Salafist movement, not just in Saudi Arabia but in its global outreaches.

In Riyadh, the original Wahhabi response was uncompromising, with Abd al-Latif issuing epistles 'condemning allegiance to infidels as a violation of God's explicit word in the Quran. On the contrary, it is an obligation to sever ties with them, to wage war against them and to grow closer to God by hating them.'[14] This may have been the dominant view, but it was not the only one. Muhammad ibn Ajlan, a Wahhabi scholar who remained loyal to Abdullah ibn Faisal and travelled with him to Baghdad to solicit

Ottoman help against Saud, regarded Abdullah's invocation of Ottoman support acceptable. Initially, Abd al-Latif rejected Ibn Ajlan's position 'without qualification' but when Saud left Riyadh in 1871, a move that allowed Abdullah to return to defend his patrimony against Ottoman encroachments, Abd al-Latif rapidly changed his tune once again and recognized Abdullah as the legitimate ruler.[15] 'He explained his switch by declaring that he had nothing to do with Abdullah when he brought the Ottomans to Arabia, but that the Saudi contender had since proclaimed repentance and remorse.'[16] When Saud returned two years later to oust his half-brother again, Abd al-Latif and other ulama were forced to renew their allegiance to him. When Saud died soon afterwards, in 1875, Abd al-Latif and some other ulama chose to consecrate the youngest of Faisal's sons, Abd al-Rahman, as the new leader. This did not prevent Abdullah from marching on Riyadh the following year, at which point Abd al-Latif persuaded Abd al-Rahman to step down temporarily and to re-instate Abdullah in the interest of resisting Saud's sons. While this may have concluded a decade of internecine fighting among the Al Saud, the internal strife enabled the pro-Ottoman Rashids to annex al-Qassim, with its palm groves and trading cities, to their realm.

The decade of Rashid rule that followed, sealed by the Battle of Mulayda in 1891, when Ibn Rashid overcame resistance of Faisal's surviving son Abd al-Rahman and an alliance of al-Qassim emirs, did little to weaken the force of the Wahhabi *da'wa* (mission). Wahhabi clerics, such as Abdallah ibn Abd al-Latif who succeeded his father as head of the mission in 1876 after he died of an apparent heart attack when a Saudi pretender shot one of his rivals in Riyadh's central mosque, continued to rant against the Rashids calling them enemies of *tawhid* for inviting the infidel Ottomans into Nejd.

The issues of the permissibility of intercession and of travelling to the lands of infidelity continued to generate heated arguments.

Some pro-Ottoman, anti-Wahhabi ulama, such as Abdullah ibn Amr (c. 1870–1908), would accuse Wahhabis of fomenting ill-will in al-Qassim, 'because of their arrogance and habit of pronouncing takfir on ordinary folk with insufficient cause. But the Rashids failed to undertake the kind of purge that would rid Wahhabi extremism from their realm.'[17] Indeed, outside of the al-Qassim area, the Rashids kept Wahhabis in place as *qadis* throughout Nejd, including their capital Hail. As Commins concludes 'by the 1880s generations of Nejdi townsmen had lived in a Wahhabi milieu. The strict monotheistic doctrine had been naturalized as the native religious culture.'[18]

In following the trajectory of this complex interaction between theological issues, clan rivalries and hegemonic Ottoman power, a distinctive pattern emerges. While it would be simplistic to describe Wahhabism, with its puritanical extremes, as a type of proto-nationalism, it can certainly be seen, like other nineteenth-century nationalisms, as a force rooted in local identity and feeling that challenged the imperial hegemon, represented in this case by Ottoman paramountcy. A local movement anchored as 'a distinctive regional religious culture wherever Saudi power could ensure conformity', it had the capacity to project itself in a universalist Sunni milieu as an authentic return to origins.[19]

Modern Salafism, into which the Wahhabi movement would evolve, with its sartorial obsessions and strict rules of gender segregation, might be called a type of 'Islamic pristinism' – 'philosophy that believes in progression through regression' where the 'perfect life is realized only by reviving the Islam of its first three generations ... a redemptive philosophy based around an idealized version of Islam that enshrines both authenticity and purity'. In the words of American scholar Ahmad Dallal, it offers 'a grim and narrow theory of unbelief, which fails to link the creedal to the political or the social' or to generate a meaningful discourse that could justify its perpetuation as a comprehensive reading of Islam, but this is also the source of its strength.[20] By paring away centuries of cumulative religious tradition while avoiding social or political issues, it offered the perfect platform for projecting dynastic power.

Some scholars have suggested that Muhammad ibn Abd al-Wahhab's movement was part of a wider reformist trend that swept through the Muslim world in the eighteenth century, and he may certainly have come into contact with reformist trends including the revival of hadith reports during his period of study in Medina. According to Commins, however, 'his doctrine bears little similarity to the teachings of other eighteenth-century religious revivalists and the very notion of a common revivalist impulse during that era is not firmly established'. His idea of *tawhid* is certainly narrower and much more anti-mystical than that of two important contemporaries.[21]

A contrasting view of *tawhid* was offered by Shah Wali Allah of Delhi (1703–67) who was born in the same year as Muhammad ibn Abd al-Wahhab. But, unlike his Nejdi contemporary, Shah Wali Allah had serious social concerns. Being interested in unity as a social as well as a religious ideal, his understanding of *tawhid* included Sufi ideas based on the all-embracing mystical theology of Ibn al-Arabi who saw reality as a continuum linking God with His creations. Unlike Ibn Abd al-Wahhab, Shah Wali Allah took care not to antagonize the majority of Muslims by making pronouncements of *takfir* (infidelity). He did not regard 'actions as extreme as prostrations to trees, stones, idols and stars' as final evidence of unbelief because there were no explicit texts defining them as such.[22] Shah Wali Allah challenged the monopoly of the Arabic-speaking ulama by translating the Quran into Persian, the language of most educated Indian Muslims at that time. His more inclusive understanding of *tawhid* was much more appropriate than Wahhabism in India's pluralistic culture, where there are shrines to Hindu deities everywhere and *baraka* or holiness takes a myriad of different forms. Hindus often worship at the shrines of Muslim saints, such as Nizamuddin in Delhi or Muhiuddin Chisti in Ajmer.

Another example of 'indigenous' renewal comes from the Sahel region of Africa where a series of 'jihad' movements led to the creation of Muslim states during the eighteenth and nineteenth centuries. Most of these movements involved rebellions by nomadic tribesmen against nominally Muslim rulers who mixed African concepts of divine kingship, pagan or animist practices with Islamic symbols of power and authority that lent these rulers prestige. The leaders were members of the ulama – scholars, teachers and students – who had studied with Sufi masters or in major centres such as Mecca or Medina. The most famous was Usman Dan Fodio (1754–1817), a 'mallam' (*alim*) from a family of religious scholars in the Hausa kingdom of Gobir. After condemning the ruler for mixing Islamic with pagan practices, Dan Fodio emulated the Prophet by making a *hijra* outside the kingdom's borders before waging jihad against the king and other Hausa rulers in the name of a purified Islam. By 1808 his movement had overthrown most of the Hausa kingdoms, and in the next two decades it expanded to include what is now northern Nigeria and northern Cameroon. In 1817 he retired to a life of reading, writing and contemplation, leaving his son Muhamad Belo to run the Emirate of Sokoto, now a constituent part of Nigeria.

In emulating the Prophet, Dan Fodio conveyed a powerful message of social justice, combining his attacks on *shirk* (idolatry) with condemnations of illegal taxes, dishonest business practices, sexual laxity and violations of Islamic inheritance laws. He declared that rulers who failed to govern according to Islamic norms were guilty of infidelity, but (unlike Ibn Abd al-Wahhab) he made a distinction between the political disbelief (*kufr*) of the rulers and the laxity or unbelief of individuals. Muslims guilty of political *kufr* might be criminals, but they were not apostates outside the Islamic fold. His agenda was political as well as religious. In Ahmad Dallal's words 'both Dan Fodio's thought and his actual practice exhibit a model of political radicalism and social tolerance'.[23]

3
Ibn Saud: Founder of a Kingdom

If there is any nation-state in the world whose very existence is the result of the actions of a single individual it has to be modern Saudi Arabia. Its founder Abd al-Aziz Al Saud (Ibn Saud) is thought to have been born around 1875 (though the exact date remains uncertain, given the absence of a clear record). He appears to have inherited his larger than average physique — the 1.9 m he achieved on maturity — from his mother Sarah Al Sudairi of the Dawasir tribe south of Riyadh.

His father Abd al-Rahman was slighter of build. As we saw in the previous chapter, Abd al-Rahman, the youngest son of the Emir Faisal, left Riyadh in 1891 with his family at a time of internecine conflict when the Saudis had been forced to accept a pro-Ottoman Rashidi governor in their capital. After leaving Riyadh they spent some time as guests of the al-Murrah tribe in the sands of the eastern peninsula while seeking permission to reside in Bahrain or Qatar, beyond the reach of their Rashidi enemies. Their sojourn with the al-Murrah is said to have given the teenage Ibn Saud more than just a taste of Bedouin life: it provided him with a vital apprenticeship in the skills of desert existence, such as camping in black goat-hair tents, tracking, horsemanship and camel-riding, as well as the use of sword, rifle and dagger.

The young man's immersion in the al-Murrah tribe with its distinct dialect would cause many difficulties for his interpreters in future years. In 1945 the Egyptian monarch King Farouk found it impossible to follow Ibn Saud's 'breathy Bedu colloquialisms' while the British diplomat and Arabist Sir Laurence Grafftey-Smith admitted that the Saudi ruler's 'Arabic was not easy for me to understand, being a mixture of the classical (which I could follow) and tribal and Bedouin locutions (which I could not)'.[1]

After sojourns in Bahrain and Qatar, the Ottoman authorities granted the family permission to settle in Kuwait, with a small pension from the Ottoman government. Ruled by the Al Sabah family since the early eighteenth century, Kuwait was a thriving port city famed for its boat construction. It had maritime links with India and East Africa and was an important entrepot of trade across desert to Damascus and by river to Baghdad. The family circumstances were far from lavish. The best they could afford was a three-bedroom flat-roof house made from adobe (baked mud). They had so little cash that Ibn Saud's first wedding when he was about eighteen (somewhat older than his Bedu peers who were usually married soon after puberty) had to be paid for by a local Kuwaiti merchant. Exposure to foreign influences combined with an exiled aristocrat's sense of loss and entitlement fuelled the young man's ambition: he would have been conscious that his family, now fallen low, had once ruled over vast territories, and that the fratricidal power struggle between his uncles Abdullah and Saud had led to the collapse of the second Saudi emirate, allowing the Rashidis to take power under Ottoman suzerainty. He would also have understood the value of military technology and how fragile the alliances on which the Al Saud depended had been: the two main reasons for the failure of the first Saudi dynasty being the ability of the invading Egyptians to buy the support of Bedouin tribes and the modern field artillery they had at their disposal.[2]

Despite the family's impoverishment, Ibn Saud is thought to have received a better than average education for a man of his time. His father – a devout Wahhabi – and Qadi Abdullah al-Kharaji, a local Hanbali judge – took charge of his religious instruction, teaching him the Quran, hadiths and life of the Prophet Muhammad (*sirat*) while instilling in him the basic disciplines of his faith, such as rising two hours before dawn for prayer. Although Ibn Saud would recall how impatient he had been with his lessons, and how much he preferred shooting instruction, the strict routines he received from the age of seven had a lasting effect. *Qaris* – professional Quran reciters, many of them blind – would be employed in his palaces in later years to intone the verses of the holy text. Ibn Saud was fortunate, however, in having another tutor in addition to his devout father and the *qadi*: the formidable Sheikh Mubarak, ruler of Kuwait.

In 1896 Mubarak Al Sabah – known to Kuwaitis as Mubarak the Great – became the ruler of the maritime city-state after killing his half-brother Sheikh Muhammad. A shrewd if ruthless operator, Mubarak saw that he could increase his freedom of manoeuvre by positioning himself between the Ottomans and the British, an increasing presence in the Gulf since the 1790s when the region was known as the 'Pirate Coast' from the frequent raids on British-Indian shipping by Arab buccaneers. British strategic concerns had also been raised by Napoleon Bonaparte's 1798 invasion of Egypt and France's military alliance with Persia (1807–9), both of which revived the spectre of France's designs on India following the defeat of the French and their Indian allies at the Battle of Plassey in 1757. In 1820 Britain signed the first of a series of treaties for the suppression of piracy that would transform the 'Pirate Coast' into the

'Trucial Coast'. The most important of these were the Maritime Truces beginning with the 1835 truce signed by the rulers of Abu Dhabi, Dubai, Ajman and the Qawasim families of Sharjah and Ras al-Khaimah. These were at first renewed annually, followed by a ten-year truce in 1843 and clinched with a perpetual maritime truce in 1853. The original signatories of what became known as the Trucial States are now the UAE.

In time, forty-seven other rulers were invited to join the system, including those of Kuwait (1841) and Bahrain (1861). Under the terms of these various truces, rulers gave up the right to wage war at sea in return for British protection against piracy and other forms of maritime aggression. A number of these rulers also signed exclusive agreements with Britain, including Bahrain (1880 and 1892) and the Trucial States (1888 and 1892). This version of Pax Britannica cast Britain in the role of protector, mediator and arbiter between competing sheikhdoms, as well as guarantor of the settlements between them. In arrangements similar to those between the British Raj and the rulers of Indian princedoms, the sheikhs and emirs of the Gulf bound themselves to exclusive political relations with Britain and ceded control over their external affairs to the British government of India.

From the time of his accession, which the Ottomans recognized with reluctance, Sheikh Mubarak would welcome the young Saudi prince into his *majlis* (assembly), where he would receive not only petitioners from among his own subjects, like any Arab ruler, but also representatives of foreign powers, including those of France, Russia, Germany and Britain, all of whom – in addition to Ottoman Turkey, the official suzerain – had an interest in the region. In addition to observing these proceedings – in itself a top-level introduction to international affairs and the realm of geopolitics – it is believed that Mubarak arranged for his young protégé to receive lessons in history, geography, mathematics and English.

The attention Mubarak lavished on the young prince was not entirely to the liking of his father Abd al-Rahman, who disapproved of what he regarded as Mubarak's loose morals – the sheikh's fondness for dancing girls, tobacco and other sensual delights disapproved of by Wahhabis. And Mubarak's concern – we may surmise – was neither mere companionship nor the disinterested improvement of a young man's mind. He saw in young Ibn Saud (rather than his father) a useful foil against the Rashidis, his rivals for power and influence in northern Arabia.

By the turn of the twentieth century, Ibn Saud, now in his early twenties, had acquired a significant knowledge of international affairs and a shrewd understanding of politics in the violent milieu of tribal Arabia. From Mubarak he learned that the essential survival skill was to surf the tide of British influence without antagonizing the formal suzerain, Ottoman Turkey – a difficult balancing act. In 1899 Mubarak joined the other Gulf rulers by signing a secret treaty of protection with Britain, whereby in exchange for Britain defending it against Turkey, or any other power, Kuwait agreed to 1) have no dealings with any foreign power without prior agreement from Britain and 2) not cede any of its territory without Britain's agreement.

Emboldened by the presence of British ships at the head of the Gulf, Mubarak decided to move against the Rashids, launching a large-scale raid on their capital Hail, while Ibn Saud took a raiding party to the ancestral Saudi headquarters of Riyadh. Although he defeated the garrison and succeeded in holding Riyadh for up to three months, the expedition failed overall, with the forces of Mubarak and his Saudi allies decisively beaten on the salt-pans of Tarajiya in March 1901, where the casualty rate was so high that 'the rain mingling with the blood of the fallen flowed in a broad red stream into the snow-white basin of salt'.[3]

Undeterred, Ibn Saud made a second attempt the following year (1902) having obtained permission from his father and Sheikh Mubarak. He took advantage of the knowledge he had gained in the earlier raid: the fortifications were inadequate and the garrison relatively small as the main Rashidi force was concentrated in their capital of Hail. The night of 15–16 January was moonless. Ibn Saud crept with his party through the palm groves and found a place where they could climb over the walls using palm trunks. By the following morning the Rashidi governor was dead; by noon Ibn Saud was leading the people of Riyadh in prayer before receiving their *bayas* (pledges of allegiance).

Ibn Saud had little difficulty in gaining the allegiance of surrounding tribes who had been harshly treated and taxed by the Rashids. The arrival of his father, Abd al-Rahman, the official imam or spiritual leader of the Wahhabis, gave further legitimacy to his rule: after consultations with the Wahhabi ulama, it was agreed that the father would retain the imamship, with his son the effective ruler. Ibn Saud would remain deferential to his father, in public and in private, until the latter's death in 1928, when Ibn Saud himself became imam. Daniel van der Meulen, the Arabist and scholar who was Dutch consul in the city of Jeddah at the time of its surrender to the forces of Ibn Saud in 1926, was astonished as the conqueror of the Hejaz knelt in the dust beside his father's horse while the old man eased himself onto his son's broad shoulders before stepping onto the ground. Muhammad Asad, the former Leopold Weiss, a journalist and scholar who converted from Judaism to Islam when covering Ibn Saud's campaigns for the *Frankfurter Allgemeine* in the 1920s, learned from Ibn Saud that he would never enter a room in the palace if he knew his father was on the floor below: 'for how can I allow myself to walk over my father's head?'[4]

Ibn Saud's military consolidation proceeded apace, with the Rashidis overcome in a number of engagements. While to outsiders these may have appeared to have been ordinary tribal skirmishes, with raids and counter-raids motivated by the demand for booty in the shape of camels, sheep and goats, two features account for Ibn Saud's growing superiority. A 'highly gifted amateur' without formal military training, he nevertheless understood 'the overwhelming value in war of economy of effort and the concentration of force' recognizing especially the importance of concentrated rifle-fire.[5] A striking example is a palm grove battle fought in the area of Dilam in southern Nejd in November 1902. Ibn Saud had obtained comparatively large quantities of ammunition from Kuwait as well as hiring the services of Kuwaiti marksmen. In the course of the battle, however, the ammunition was almost exhausted. In the words of Leslie McLoughlin:

> As the Rashidis advanced towards the palm groves, the Saudis and Kuwaitis lay concealed, waiting behind their camel saddles. They did not open fire until the Rashidis were almost upon them, achieving total surprise and killing and wounding numbers far in excess of the usual numbers of casualties in tribal raids. The Saudis then launched their cavalry against the Rashidis and a fierce battle raged from midday until the sun went down. By the end of the day the Rashidis had retreated and escaped from the pursuing Saudi cavalry ... Had the Rashidis known how close Ibn Saud had been to exhaustion of his stocks of ammunition they might have persevered in their attacks and there might have been a totally different outcome to this and the succeeding battles. Ibn Saud was never to forget this lesson in battle management and because of this in later years he was to be seen personally counting out rounds of ammunition.[6]

By the summer of 1903 Ibn Saud had established his writ in the major settlements north and south of Riyadh and was poised to advance into the Qassim region with its major cities of Buraydah and Unaizah. In later years he recalled to Ameen Rihani the relish he experienced in killing Ubayd al-Rashid in the battle that resulted in the capture of Unaizah in the spring of 1904. 'I struck him first on the leg and disabled him; quickly after that I struck at the neck; the head fell to one side, the blood spurted up like a fountain, the third blow at the heart I saw the heart which was cut in two palpitate ... It was a joyous moment. I kissed the sword.'[7]

The bloodthirsty recollection, aimed, one suspects, at impressing Rihani, a well-known Christian Lebanese–American novelist and poet who became friends with Ibn Saud in the 1920s, should not prevent us from recognizing the degree to which Ibn Saud subordinated the violence of war to his wider state-building project. The key to his strategy was to fight the Rashidis and their Ottoman allies while taking account of great power sensitivities, especially those of the British. Ottoman support for the Rashidis was based on the sultan's claim to sovereignty over Nejd. The British, while concerned with preserving maritime peace in the Gulf, were reluctant to become involved in the interior for fear of upsetting the Sublime Porte in Istanbul.

Concerned with maintaining the balance of power in Europe, they believed that overt support for Ibn Saud against the Rashids would drive Ottoman Turkey further into the arms of Germany, which was already extending its power in the region. The Germans were training the Ottoman army and building two railways, the Berlin–Baghdad railway that would give it access to the Gulf, and the Hejaz railway from Damascus to Medina that could be used to transport troops as well as pilgrims into the Muslim holy land. A request by Ibn Saud's father Abd al-Rahman for British protection in May 1902 was studiously ignored by London. Lack of response, however, did not diminish Ibn Saud's desire to gain British support against the Ottomans.

In March 1903 an opportunity presented itself when a Russian warship steamed up the Gulf, calling at a number of ports including Muscat and Kuwait. Invited on board, along with his brothers Muhammad and Saad and Sheikh Mubarak, Ibn Saud impressed the Russians with his account of taking Riyadh and told them of his fears of direct Turkish intervention. Despite his friendly reception by the Russians, he avoided accepting any offer of aid that would have drawn him into alliance with the tsar, believing that the 'key to his success was a good understanding with Britain in order to guarantee his own state's protection and independence'.[8]

His caution would soon be vindicated. In May 1903 the British government made it clear they would regard 'the establishment of a naval base or a fortified port in the Persian Gulf by any other power a very grave menace to British interest' that would be resisted by all means at their disposal. A few months later the viceroy of India, Lord Curzon, made the first ever visit to the sheikhdoms by the imperial ruler of India, telling his audience in Kuwait 'The peace of these waters must still be maintained; your independence will continue to be upheld; and the British government must remain supreme.'[9]

In summer of 1905 when Ibn Saud appeared on the borders of Qatar with an armed bodyguard – reviving fears of nineteenth-century Wahhabi attacks – Sir Percy Cox, the British political agent appointed by Curzon, politely but firmly warned him against proceeding further, eliciting from Ibn Saud an emollient reply stating that he had no harmful intentions. By the end of 1905 Sir Nicholas O'Conor, Britain's ambassador in Istanbul, was coming to recognize the growing power of Ibn Saud. In December he telegraphed London: 'Reports as to the actual state of Arabia have been somewhat complicating but according to the latest information the Saud party are apparently in the ascendant.'[10]

As Ibn Saud consolidated his power in northern and central Arabia, a new phenomenon began to appear – cantonments known as *hijras* or *hujar* (to use the Arabic plural) populated by settled Bedouin of the Mutair, Utaibi and other Arabian tribes. For a vital period, between 1912 and 1929, Ibn Saud gave his backing to this movement which was also supported by some Wahhabi clerics. It is not known for certain where the idea came from. One possibility is that Ibn Saud was influenced by the duplicitous behaviour of tribal leaders such as Faisal al-Duwaish of the Mutair, who tended to switch sides according to the fortunes of war when towns such as Unaizah and Buraydah were lost and retaken. Settling and converting them to agriculture would make them less volatile in their behaviour. One writer suggests that Ibn Saud's inspiration came from his favourite wife Jawhara bint Musaid (mother of the future King Khalid) who would die, to his great distress, in the great influenza epidemic of 1919. Whatever the origins of the movement, the *hijras* would become game changers in the fractious milieu of tribal competition.

The notion of *hijra* – emigration – based on the Prophet's migration from sinful, polytheistic Mecca to the oasis settlement of Medina where he founded the first 'Islamic state', is foundational in Islamic salvation history and teems with religious resonance. Emigration – from the lands of idolatry to those of true Islam – had been central to Wahhabi polemic in the nineteenth century when the ulama had inveighed against travel to and residing in 'idolatrous lands' – by which they usually meant territories under the 'infidel' Ottomans whose formal adhesion to Islam they refused to acknowledge. For these ulama 'emigration was a duty, just as it had been for seventh-century Muslims to quit Mecca and move to Medina'.[11] Early-twentieth-century Wahhabism, however, gave the idea a new perspective: it was no longer Ottoman authority from which the faithful should migrate but the rapacious nomadic lifestyle.

The Quran (9:97–9) provides explicit condemnation of the ways of some desert nomads while commending the pious attitudes of others:

> The Arabs [i.e. Bedu] of the desert are the worst in unbelief and hypocrisy and most fitted to be in ignorance of the command which Allah hath sent down to His Apostle ... Some of the desert Arabs look upon their payments as a fine and watch for disasters for you ... But some of the desert Arabs believe in Allah and the last day and look upon their payments as pious gifts bringing them nearer to Allah.[12]

The text provided a clear rubric for evangelizing recalcitrant nomads and changing their ways from a life based on animal husbandry to a more settled agricultural existence. In desert conditions pastoralists are dependent on seasonal fluctuations in rainfall. In good years their animals multiply and so do their children. In lean years the animals die, their children may starve, and tribes may seek survival by raiding other tribes or the farmers of settled regions. The awesome reputation of desert predators was a brutal consequence of the harsh environment in which they lived. Settling the nomads aided religious indoctrination. As a tribal section moved to a *hijra* its leader was sent to Riyadh for instruction in Wahhabism, which meant that in many cases the extremist ideology of *tawhid* and anti-idolatry constituted the Bedouins' first – and only – exposure to formal Islamic belief and practice. The *hijras* included religious officials known as *al-mutawi'a* (or *mutaween*) to enforce public morality and punctual observance of prayer – fore-runners of the Saudi kingdom's notorious 'religious police'.

The movement's success was consistent with the paradigm outlined by famous North African savant Ibn Khaldun (1332–1406), often seen as a precursor of such Western social theorists as Machiavelli,

Hobbes, Montesquieu, Comte, Marx, Weber and Durkheim. The most celebrated of Ibn Khaldun's ideas was based on the practical knowledge of North African politics that he acquired when working for a variety of different rulers. 'Leadership', he wrote, 'exists through superiority, and superiority only through *asabiyya*' – an Arabic word meaning 'group-feeling', 'social solidarity' or 'clannism' that appears more than 500 times in the text of his most famous book, the *Muqadimma* (Introduction) to world history.

According to Ibn Khaldun the origins of *asabiyya* lie in desert conditions, where the solidarity of the tribe is vital to human survival. When nomadic tribes unite, their superior cohesion and military prowess put farmers and urban dwellers at their mercy. Inspired as often as not by religion, they conquer the towns and create new dynastic states. But within a few generations the victorious tribesmen usually lose their *asabiyya* and become corrupted by luxury, extravagance and leisure. The ruler, who is no longer able to rely on tribal warriors for his defence, will have to raise extortionate taxes to pay for other sorts of soldiers, and this in turn may lead to further problems resulting in the eventual downfall of his dynasty or state. The geographer Yves Lacoste, in his discourse on Ibn Khaldun, distinguishes between egalitarian tribes in which the chieftain only has moral authority and tribes with good *asabiyya* in which the chief has succeeded in asserting his dominance.[13] The role of religion in the Khaldunian paradigm is complex: for while conquering tribes may have emulated the original Arab conquerors who swept through western Asia and North Africa after the death of Muhammad in 632 CE in maintaining their *asabiyya* before the empire fell apart, the Prophet himself is said to have opposed the very concept. According to a widely circulated hadith, someone once asked him: 'Does *asabiya* mean loving one's people?' 'No', he is reported to have replied, '*asabiya* means helping one's people in unjust actions.'[14]

The Khaldunian paradigm can therefore be said to reflect a dialectical tension between the force of *asabiyya* in terms of clannism or tribal solidarity – a force that is rooted in a particular tribe's identity and communal will to power – and a religious discourse that claims a mandate from God with spiritual benefits and universal justice for all. (The tension, one can argue, is present in the Quran itself, which proclaims a message aimed at the whole of humankind while acknowledging the difference between nations and tribes – see Quran 49:13.) The fusion of tribal *asabiyya* and religious enthusiasm was, for a period, unbeatable.

The newly settled nomads called themselves Ikhwan – brethren – in a gesture towards universal Muslim ideals of fraternity. They forsook the black *aghal* (headrope) – originally a double loop of rope used for hobbling camels, which the Bedouin placed on their heads when not in use – in order to symbolize their abandonment of nomadic ways. They cut their beards in imitation of what they were told was the Prophet's way of managing his facial hair and trimmed their gowns above the ankle in obedience to a hadith according to which he is said to have disapproved of men who displayed their wealth and status by trailing flowing robes along the ground. 'Yet while they abandoned their formal pastoral occupation, they did not give up the martial bent of nomadic tribes.'[15] A bent, one might add, rooted in the group solidarity of *asabiyya*. As the historian Robert Lacey observes, the settlements were more like military cantonments than pastoral villages: 'there were stables and fodder bins in the main square where the soldiers could be marshaled from the mosque roof, and central magazines where ammunition was distributed'.[16] Yet for all the appearance of a common profile and outlook, the settlements were not, as is sometimes argued, agents of 'de-tribalization'. On the contrary, Commins states that initially, at least,

The settlements were not melting pots for the blending of Arabians from different tribes and their transformation into homogenized Saudi subjects. Instead, each one was populated predominantly by members of a single tribal section. On the face of it, this was to be expected: When a tribal section agreed to settle at a *hijra*, it would prefer to remain in its home region. As a consequence, the renowned solidarity of tribal nomads would not have been diluted at all by this particular form of sedentarization by tribal sections.[17]

From the original settlement at al-Artawiya, midway between Riyadh and Kuwait, the movement spread exponentially. By 1917 there were already more than 200 *hijra* settlements located at strategic points throughout Nedj, none of them more than a day's march from another. A 'rapid deployment force' *avant la lettre*, they could be mobilized quickly. Moreover, as McLoughlin explains:

> Ibn Saud was spared the expense of maintaining a standing army. He had to bear the expense of paying modest subsidies and giving presents to the tribal leaders, of providing land and seeds, of paying for the preachers and to some extent of providing arms and ammunition, but he was spared the enormous overheads of accommodation, supply, administration, training and personnel problems.[18]

At the height of the movement there would have been in the region of 60,000 men of military age available to Ibn Saud. One consequence, as Lacey infers, is that within a matter of years, something like a quarter of a million men, women and children had shifted from living in black hair tents to permanent mud-brick settlements, making this 'a momentous transformation of the Nejdi way of life'.[19]

Although not de-tribalized, the nomads of the Ikhwan were now subject to the rigours of a sedentary economy and no longer dependent for their livelihoods on the seasonal fluctuations of their herds.

But, as Commins suggests, 'they did not take to agricultural work with enthusiasm, nor, it seems, did many pursue productive work in crafts and trade'. Indeed, if in sponsoring the movement Ibn Saud had hoped to gain financially through taxation, he was disappointed, as in effect the '*hijras* became consumers of dynastic largesse'.[20]

This, however, did not prevent the tribes from being subject to forms of taxation through the institution of *zakat*. Whereas under the old system nomadic tribes had offered protection (*himaya*) in return for taxation, Wahhabism made them subject to the centre. For the tribes 'to be considered anything other than idolaters they had to be incorporated into the political system whose core was (and still is) the Saudi clan. This entailed these tribes becoming tributaries to the centre of power in southern Nejd, and this in turn entailed not only their subjection to taxation (in kind such as camels) but also their exclusion from the political sphere.'[21]

In the long term, state Wahhabism had the effect of converting clans that had ceased to be nomadic into tributaries of Saudi power by tying them to a system of wealth distribution with clans stratified according to a particular pecking order under the Saudi dynasty. Instead of the former tradition of plunder, tribes may now enjoy subsidies and 'the privileges of citizenship, such as the legal sponsorship of foreign businesses (*kafala*) akin in many ways to the extraction of money (*khuwwa*)'.[22] Thus a form of tribalism prevails, 'not merely [as] a modus vivendi or traditional structure of society' but as a central part of the country's institutional structure.[23]

More immediately, however, Ibn Saud was able to benefit from the manner in which sedentarization enabled the aggressive militancy of tribes to be redirected in the interest of Saudi hegemony. Moreover, as Commins points out, the tribal propensity for warfare was now directed to religious ends, with devastating consequences for those who stood in their path:

What had formerly been mundane raids for lucre now had religious sanction. But in contrast to the conventions of nomadic combat, where warriors did their utmost to minimize killing and severe injury and refrained from attacking non-combatants, the Ikhwan became noted for ferocity in battle. Indeed, they earned notoriety for routinely killing male captives, and they sometimes put children and women to death in spite of reprimands from their ruler. The pretext for such slaughter was the Ikhwan's notion that the nomads they fought, particularly from 1912 to 1919, had to convert or be put to death. That they deemed themselves qualified and authorized to judge for themselves which nomads required conversion is evident from their letters to leaders of tribal sections that did not quit nomadic pastoralism.[24]

As Hafiz Wahba, Ibn Saud's Egyptian advisor and his first minister of education, would write:

> I have seen them hurl themselves on their enemies utterly fearless of death, not caring how man fall, advancing rank after rank with only one desire – the defeat and annihilation of the enemy. They normally give no quarter, sparing neither boys nor old men, veritable messengers of death from whose grasp no one escapes.[25]

The fusion of political and religious militancy, however, was far from stable. The period from the original formation of the Ikhwan in the second decade of the twentieth century to 1929 saw a constant struggle between tribal militancy linked to religious zealotry – a phenomenon that Ibn Khaldun would have recognized and understood – and the post-Westphalian international order predicated on discrete territorial units with recognized boundaries fixed in law. The conquest in 1913 of the coastal region of al-Ahsa (now the country's oil-bearing region known as the Eastern Province), Ibn Saud's first major push outside of Nejd, posed no great problem internationally, despite the presence of a substantial Shiite community in and around Qatif. In 1915, Britain, now at war with Ottoman Turkey, recognized Nejd and al-Ahsa as 'the countries of Bin Saud and his fathers before him' along with his descendants so long as they were not antagonistic to Britain.

In a treaty similar to those that Britain had made with Kuwait and other Gulf states Ibn Saud agreed not to commit aggression against any of the Gulf emirates and sheikhdoms with which Britain had agreements. In return for signing the agreement Ibn Saud received a loan of £20,000 (around £1.2 million or €1.4 million in today's values), 1,000 weapons and 200,000 rounds of ammunition, plus a monthly subsidy of £5,000 (around £300,000 today). In addition, the capture of al-Ahsa, a relatively wealthy area of farms and fisheries, doubled his annual income from taxes from around £50,000 a year (around £3 million in today's values) to £100,000.

The Hejaz and Iraq, however, were different matters entirely. Regarding the Hejaz, Britain had entered into secret correspondence with the Ottoman appointee, Sharif Hussein of Mecca, which led to the Arab revolt against Turkey led by the sharif's son Faisal with help from the British agent T. E. Lawrence ('Lawrence of Arabia') between 1915 and 1917. British backing for the sharif, who declared himself king of the Arabs – including the Hejaz – in 1916, and whose sons Faisal and Abdullah would be made the kings of Iraq and Transjordan under British auspices, remained the primary obstacle to his ambition in the Hejaz. Ibn Saud, who had fought the sharif's forces in 1910, knew he had the capacity to conquer the Muslim holy land. But he was restrained by his agreement with the British, along with the subsidy he received from them.

'If only you English would allow me to carve out my fortune by the sword', he told Harold Dickson, the British agent in Bahrain, in 1920, 'I would have Hejaz inside a week.' Gertrude Bell, the English political officer, traveller and archaeologist, thought his boast was justified. In comparing Ibn Saud with Sharif Hussein, she thought the Nejdi 'much the stronger of the two. It is only the fact that he has acted in accordance with our wishes which has prevented him gobbling up the Hejaz.'[26] Ibn Saud had impressed Bell, the first unveiled woman he would have met outside of his family at Basra, now in Iraq, in 1916. As Sir Percy Cox, the British agent, commented at the time 'Ibn Saud met Miss Bell with complete frankness and sang-froid as if he had been associated with European ladies all his life'.[27] For her part, Bell noted his intelligent approach to new technology: 'We took him in trains and motors, showed him aeroplanes, high-explosives, anti-aircraft guns, hospitals, base depots, everything. He was full of wonder but never agape. He asked innumerable questions and made intelligent comments. He is a big man.'[28] In due course, as we shall see, Ibn Saud would incur the hostility of religious conservatives for his enthusiasm for modern technology, including the wireless, telegraph and motor vehicles.

While recognizing the importance of keeping the British 'on side', however, he was far from prepared to act as their agent. In 1923, following the Ottoman defeat and in the face of post-war austerity, Britain decided to end its Middle East subsidies. With this constraint removed he prepared to invade the Hejaz.

Events in Turkey contributed to the fate of the Muslim holy land. Early in 1924 Mustafa Kemal, the new leader of the Turkish republic who had defeated the French and British at Gallipoli and driven the Greeks from the Anatolian mainland, abolished the caliphate – a great Sunni institution that had been used by the Ottoman sultans to bolster their spiritual authority over Muslim subjects worldwide, especially in Tsarist Russia and British-ruled India. In March the ruler of the Hejaz, Sharif (now King) Hussein, visiting his son the Emir Abdullah of Transjordan, responded by proclaiming himself caliph. His unilateral pronouncement annoyed Muslim leaders just about everywhere. It was done without consultation, and there were other candidates for the august title, including King Fuad of Egypt and the sultan of Morocco (who like the sharif claimed descent from the Prophet Muhammad). Indian Muslims, a large and important constituency, were especially unimpressed, not least because of the sharif's rebellion against the Ottoman sultan-caliph who had appointed him. The Wahhabi tribesmen were outraged. They had already been infuriated by Hussein's refusal to allow them to perform the Hajj, for fear that armed militants would terrify foreign pilgrims.

In June 1924 at a conference in Riyadh, the main tribal chiefs and ulama joined Ibn Saud's father Abd al-Rahman in deciding to invade the Hejaz. In August, Ikhwan of the Utaiba tribe joined with the emir of Turaba on the borderland between Hejaz and Nejd, and attacked the highland city of Taif, after troops commanded by Ali bin Hussein, the eldest but least warlike of the sharif's sons, had abandoned the city under cover of darkness. Contemporary accounts describe the horrors inflicted on the city, when the Ikhwan murdered hundreds of civilians, including men, women and children, in an outrage similar to the violence committed by ISIS and al-Qaeda in our time. Even the *qadi* and senior ulama who were sheltering in the mosque were dragged out and murdered.

The way to Mecca was now open, and with panic facing its citizens, King Hussein of the Hejaz appealed to Britain for help. He received no response, however. Convinced that their former ally was a broken reed, the British (influenced by a positive account of Ibn Saud from the likes of Bell and Cox) decided to let matters take their course. A cable to Ibn Saud warning him not to jeopardize the safety of British pilgrims (that is, Muslims from India who were British subjects) was their only official gesture. Hussein's decision to abdicate in favour of his son Ali at the request of Jeddah merchants proved to be just as futile as the request for British help, and King Ali of the Hejaz soon found himself joining his father in exile.

After conquering the Hejaz, Ibn Saud adopted a careful course, aiming to absorb the region containing the two holy cities of Mecca and Medina into his realm without disrupting the pilgrimage or disturbing the large number of non-Arabian residents from every part of the Muslim world who had settled there over the centuries. To reassure pilgrims he introduced tighter regulations on pilgrimage guides aimed at reducing their extortionate fees, introduced quarantine restrictions to reduce the danger of disease (the pilgrimage having been a notorious hub for the spread of cholera) and, ignoring the objections of Wahhabi ulama, he allowed Shiites to perform the Hajj. He also pioneered the use of motor vehicles to transport pilgrims from the port of Jeddah to Mecca.

At the same time, he needed to control his Ikhwan supporters by deploying the moral force of the Wahhabi clerics under his patronage. From 1914 he had joined with Wahhabi ulama in demanding that Ikhwan refrain from attacking believing nomads on the pretext that they had committed acts of unbelief, for viewing inhabitants of *hijras* as superior to villagers and townsmen or for discriminating against Nejdis who wore the *aghal* instead of the white headdress. When his warnings were ignored as sometimes happened, he ordered the dismissal of religious instructors for sowing extremist ideas.

His authority to do this was underpinned by a statement of royal supremacy produced by the leading Wahhabi ulama in 1919: 'He [the Muslim] should not be hostile or friendly except to those that the legal ruler orders. He who contravenes this goes against the way of the Muslims.' As Commins comments, the statement, issued in the 'conventional fashion of scholastic discourse', is unambiguous in its implication: 'Neither the Ikhwan nor even the Wahhabi ulama had the right to determine who is a friend or foe, who is believer or infidel; that distinction was reserved for Ibn Saud.'[29] The ruler followed up this statement by paying for the publication of a treatise by Ibn Sihman, a prominent Wahhabi scholar, who took Ikhwan to task for actions such as ostracizing people for minor slips or using physical coercion to enforce conformity. Other prominent scholars were sent to the important *hijras* of al-Artawiya and al-Ghat to dissuade the Ikhwan from belligerence.

Ibn Saud's position – as Commins points out – marked a signal departure from nineteenth-century Wahhabi discourse whereby infidels were identified on the basis of religious practice and belief rather than the ruler's discretion. It is not surprising, therefore, that radical elements would join with tribal forces in rejecting Ibn Saud's assertion of dynastic realpolitik.

A critical issue in relations between Ibn Saud and the Ikhwan before the Second World War was the post-Westphalian question of frontiers. Subjects of the British-backed regimes installed in Transjordan and Iraq looked to British protection to defend new boundaries that cut across grazing used by nomads and semi-nomadic pastoralists at different times depending on the sparse uncertainties of rainfall. Indeed, in 1925 before Ibn Saud even took power in the Hejaz he accepted – with reluctance – the Hadda agreement he negotiated with the British emissary Sir Gilbert Clayton in exchange for Britain's 'neutrality' over the Hejaz. Under this agreement the port of Aqaba that had been part of the Hejaz went to King Abdullah of Transjordan in exchange for the northern reaches of the Wadi Sirhan, traditional grazing grounds of the populous Shammar tribe whose territory reaches north into the steppelands of Syria. This is why part of the Saudi frontier now pushes northwards, east of the present Jordanian frontier. In Iraq, where sheep- and goat-herders were at the mercy of Ikhwan camel-raiders, the British constructed a series of forts aimed at containing the threat. The

Ikhwan tribesmen and their leaders were furious after Ibn Saud had made it clear that neither of their leaders, Ibn Bijad of the Utaiba, who hoped to become governor of Mecca, or Faisal al-Duwaish, leader of the Mutair tribe who had similar ambitions in Medina, would be rewarded with offices they regarded as their entitlement as conquerors of the Hejaz.

At a meeting at al-Artawiya in 1926 the Ikhwan leaders vented their frustrations. They accused Ibn Saud of sending his sons to idolatrous lands (Faisal to England and France for the 1919 peace conference, Saud to Egypt) and allowing nomads from idolatrous lands in Iraq and Transjordan to pasture their animals in the true Muslim territories of Nejd. In a letter of 1929 Duwaish revealed that, for him and his tribe at least, the idea of making a living by crafts and agriculture rather than raiding settlements had failed utterly. He complained about the impoverishment of his people since Ibn Saud had prohibited raids on other nomads and infidels. At a meeting with Harold Dickson, the British agent, Duwaish expressed his puzzlement at the prohibition on raids due to the new treaties on boundaries: 'How could we help it when our grazing grounds and wells had been taken from us and seeing that we were persistently encouraged to do so [before]?'[30]

The issue of the forts came up at a major conference Ibn Saud convened in Riyadh in November 1929, attended by thousands of tribesmen, Ikhwan and ulama. The dissident tribal leaders – Faisal al-Duwaish of the Mutair, Sultan ibn Bijad of the Utaiba and Dhaidhan ibn Hithlain of the Ajman – were notable for refusing to attend. In a growing atmosphere of crisis, the king kept the other tribesmen outside the city walls, reinforcing its defences with men from other cities. In a dramatic gesture he offered to abdicate if the people would not accept his rule. As expected, 'the uproar was immediate and unanimous. '"We'll have none but you to rule us", cried the delegates, and Abdul Aziz [ibn Saud] had the whole assembly behind him from that point onwards.'[31]

As Lacey astutely remarks, his offer was not an empty gesture made in the full knowledge that it would be rejected. It was

> also a reminder to his audience – and to the world – of the ultimate legitimacy on which Saudi rule rested ... The bedrock of [his] authority was the consent of the peoples that he governed; they offered him their baya voluntarily, and in now offering to release them from their oath [he] showed he had not forgotten what underpinned the structure of his newly adopted royal panoply.[32]

The scene was set for the final showdown with the dissenting Ikhwan. What appears to have been the last straw occurred in December 1928, when one of the chieftains attacked a caravan of merchants from al-Qassim, many of them from the staunchly Wahhabi city of Buraydah. To kill supposedly infidel herders in Iraq or Transjordan might complicate his relations with the British but massacring his subjects in the Nedji heartland was a brazen challenge to his authority. Efforts to mediate by the ulama failed, and in March 1929 he took on the rebels at the Battle of Sibila. Ibn Saud drove through the region in a motorcade bristling with weapons, buying the loyalty of tribal chiefs: each tribal leader received six gold pounds, while a common tribesman or townsman received three pounds for turning up, with the promise of more with the service completed.

By the time Ibn Saud's force, led by a 'motorized armada', along with tribesmen, camels and horses reached the plain of Sibila before al-Artawiya, it was three times as large as that of the rebels. Misinterpreting a movement among the Saudi advance guard as a retreat, the advancing Ikhwan were caught in the fire of a dozen machine-guns whose existence had been carefully hidden from them. 'Several hundred men went down immediately, the surviving Ikhwan turned in flight, and [Ibn Saud] launched his cavalry upon them.' The battle was over in less than an hour.[33]

The war against the rebels was followed by several attacks against the Ikhwan cantonments; while raids in Iraq, Kuwait and Transjordan were repelled from above by the British Royal Air Force — a tactic used in the suppression of tribal rebellions in numerous other regions, from Somalia to Algeria, in the early twentieth century. As al-Rasheed makes plain, 'the last thing Britain wanted to see was Ikhwan sympathisers among the Kuwaiti tribes, some of whom shared common descent with their Saudi counterparts'.[34]

The conquest of the Hejaz and suppression on the Ikhwan rebellion opened the way for Ibn Saud's final territorial accomplishment, the conquest of Asir on the border with Yemen, still one of the poorest and least developed parts of the Saudi kingdom. For centuries the terrain, which is divided between rugged highlands with peaks rising to nearly 3,000 metres and the coastal plain or Tihama, was riven by tribal conflicts. As in the area of Nejd, the clans tended to quarrel among themselves when not coalescing in the face of outsiders. In 1906 a charismatic scholar-king, Sayyed Muhammad al-Idrisi, connected to the Sufi or mystically oriented Sanusiyya order in North Africa, was invited to settle disputes between these warring tribes. Al-Idrisi's domain grew rapidly as tribes, attracted by his reputation for piety and justice, rallied to his cause against the Ottomans.

After backing the Allies in the First World War he hoped that the victors would reward him by preserving Asir's independence. All such hopes were dashed, however, following his death in 1922, when the region came under the growing sway of Ibn Saud's kingdom. In October 1926 Ibn Saud signed the Treaty of Mecca with al-Idrisi's successor Hassan ibn Ali. The Asiri leader acknowledged his status under the 'suzerainty of His Majesty the King of the Hejaz, Sultan of Nejd and its dependencies' and agreed not to 'enter into political negotiations with any government or grant any economic concession to any person except with the sanction of His Majesty'. Ibn Saud for his part agreed that the 'internal administration of Asir and the supervision of its tribal affairs' would be dealt with by the Idrisis.

For a period at least, Asir was allowed to coexist with Ibn Saud's dominions, but the status came to an end in 1930 when, in his drive for territorial expansion, Ibn Saud swallowed up most of the region, leaving the southern part to Idrisi's inveterate enemy, the imam of Yemen (who belonged to the Zaidi sect of Shiism). In the spring of 1934, two large armies of Ikhwan veterans and town levies commanded by Ibn Saud's sons Faisal and Saud advanced southwards in a pincer movement aimed at conquering Yemen from the former Emirate of Asir down to the border of the British protectorate of Aden.

While Prince Faisal's army, used to desert conditions, had little difficulty in advancing down the flat Tihama plain by the Red Sea Coast, Prince Saud's army got hopelessly stuck in the mountains short of Sanaa, the Yemeni capital (a fate very similar to that which would befall the Egyptian army sent by President Nasser in the 1960s). The peace agreement that was signed between the imam of Yemen and Ibn Saud in May 1934 marked the limit of his expansion in the south-west of the peninsula. Ibn Saud formally acquired Asir but failed to reach agreement on settling the Saudi–Yemeni border. Some 400,000 people are said to have been killed in the course of this conflict.

The Saudi annexation of Asir was followed by an invasion of religious clerics who imposed their Wahhabi-Salafist practices on Asiri society. In the comparatively well-watered region of farms and terraces that catch the monsoon rains, Asiri males were known as the 'flower men' from the flowers they wore in their hair (an indication of their status as cultivators rather than nomads). Even their turbans were adorned with flowers, grasses and stones. Asiri women were clothed in spectacular explosions of colour, their headdresses glittering with coins and jewellery.

The Saudi clerics forced young males to remove their 'un-Islamic' locks and headgear as well as the traditional daggers that symbolized their masculinity. The women were obliged to adopt the niqab (full facial veil) in place of the traditional headscarf. According to the anthropologist Akbar Ahmed, while Western countries were appeasing the Saudis to secure their oil supplies, the Saudis were systematically destroying the Yemeni-Asiri culture. During the 1960s this process was exacerbated by the civil war that brought 70,000 Egyptian troops into Yemen. Represented in the Western media as a Spanish-style conflict between 'progressive' republicans backed by Egypt and 'reactionary' royalists supported by Saudi Arabia, the war was really a conflict between tribal systems that had been drawn into supporting different sides.

The strategic demands of that war prompted the Saudi ruler, King Faisal, to build the famous Highway 15 linking Mecca with the Hadhramaut valley in southern Yemen. The construction magnate who undertook this formidable feat of engineering was Mohammed bin Laden, father of Osama. Twelve of the hijackers who attacked the World Trade Center and Pentagon on 11 September 2001 came from towns that lie along this highway, a key strategic asset in the programme of Saudi repression that accompanied the destruction of Asiri culture.[35]

While the British had supported Ibn Saud in suppressing the Ikhwan rebellion by using the RAF against the rebel nomads who were threatening the client regimes they had installed in Transjordan and Iraq, they saw no comparable interests at stake regarding the war in Yemen, despite growing interest in the region on the part of fascist Italy. London viewed the Saudi–Yemeni war merely as a local conflict over the buffer territory of Asir.

As al-Rasheed plausibly suggests, 'It is not unlikely that Ibn Saud interpreted Britain's reserved attitude towards this war as a failure to help him.' This was doubtless one reason why he chose to sign oil concessions with an American company rather than a British one, a company from a country whose government was 'considered to be neutral and without obvious imperial ambitions in Arabia'.[36] The momentous consequences of this decision will be considered in the next chapter.

4
Petroleum and Patriarchy

In 1930 a group of American geologists working for a subsidiary of Socal, one of the smaller American oil companies based in San Francisco, were prospecting in the British protectorate of Bahrain, the group of islands located off the east coast of the Arabian Peninsula. After finding oil under a rocky outcrop they observed similar outcrops on the mainland 25 km across the sea. The geological features were later found to be part of a single structure known as the Dammam Dome.

Three years later Ibn Saud was persuaded by his British friend, the maverick explorer and Arabist Harry St John Philby, that he could find the money he desperately needed by exploiting his country's mineral resources. Prompted by Philby, the king engaged an American geologist Karl Twitchell to interest the American oil companies in Arabian prospecting. Two larger companies – Exxon and Gulf – expressed no interest. They were bound in any case by the so-called Red Line Agreement not to prospect in territories claimed by the former Ottoman Empire (an arrangement designed to maintain the monopoly that the British-owned Iraqi Petroleum Company claimed as corporate successor to the Turkish Petroleum Company).

The Iraqi Petroleum Company, which was not much interested in Arabian exploration at a time of world glut, offered the king a paltry £10,000 to be paid in currency rather than gold. Its interest was to 'keep out the Americans' rather than to engage with Arabian exploration.[1] Philby, a brilliant explorer, traveller and former colonial official who had resigned over his government's failure to back Ibn Saud over the Hashemites, saw his opportunity. Advised by Philby, Socal made Ibn Saud a much more handsome offer: an immediate loan of £30,000 (£1.5 million in today's values), to be followed by £20,000 in eighteen months and an annual rent of £5,000 — all of it paid in gold. In return Ibn Saud granted the company a concession area around twice the size of Texas.

The agreement — signed in August 1933, netted Philby a salary of £1,000 per year (around £50,000 in today's values) and gave him the satisfaction of keeping out a British-controlled company in favour of the supposedly less imperially minded Americans. With the Bahrain oil already flowing, and the Arabian concessions promising, Socal realized it needed more capital and marketing outlets. It sold a half share in its Bahrain and Saudi concessions to Texaco, the only major company not to have been bound by the Red Line Agreement.

The story of 'Dammam no. 7' — the iconic well in the city of Dhahran that is now a local tourist attraction — reads like a modern fairy tale. Like the story of some magical chest, the suitors all fail at a succession of tasks before one hits the talismanic Well Number 7.

The 'wild cat' prospectors were not well equipped. Lacking dynamite, they prepared the ground for the derricks by breaking up the rock by hand and heating it with wooden fires, dousing them with cold water to force the rock to split. More than two years of drilling between 1935 and 1937 produced nothing in commercial quantities. Rig number 1 was abandoned; number 2, after an initial spurt, diminished to a trickle. Number 3 never produced more than a measly 100 barrels per day (b/d). Number 4 was a 'dry hole' producing nothing at all. Numbers 5 and 6 were just as disappointing. After drilling number 7 to a depth of more than 1,000 metres with only negligible results the San Francisco executives were minded to look elsewhere. 'Shouldn't the company pull out of Saudi Arabia altogether?' they asked. They had already 'poured millions of dollars down the holes in the desert'. Then on 8 March 1938 the drillers struck black gold. 'On that day, No. 7 flowed at the rate of 1,585 b/d. Three days later rate of flow had risen to 3,690 b/d.'[2]

The drillers had penetrated the principal oil reservoir of the Upper Jurassic sequence, now believed to hold around half the entire planet's store of oil and gas. One level of this formation, known as Arab D, connects with the gargantuan Ghawar Field, south-west of Dammam. Still a top producer, it is the world's largest known oil field.[3]

In May 1939 the king made his journey across desert to the new oil town of Dhahran just south of Dammam. There were banquets and inspection, and Ibn Saud was entertained on the deck of a tanker, the *D. G. Schofield*, named after the founder of Socal. The king turned the valve on the pipeline and oil began to flow. He was so delighted with the Socal–Texaco consortium (known as CASOC – the California-Arabian Standard Oil Company) that he increased the size of its concession to 444,000 square miles (just under 1.15 million sq. km) – an area more than twice the size of metropolitan France). The company would have exclusive rights in this area in exchange for a royalty that worked out at 22 cents a barrel.[4]

Although production was held back for supply and logistical reasons, the outbreak of the Second World War could only emphasize the strategic importance of oil. While Ibn Saud was pressing them for money to make up the loss of revenue from the Hajj, which saw the flow of pilgrims dry to a halt, Socal and Texaco became increasingly worried about the future of their concession. A particular concern was that the British, who were still subsidizing Ibn Saud's regime, might use their leverage to undermine the American consortium. When the companies approached the US government for lend-lease funding for Saudi Arabia they found a ready response. With war raging in both the Atlantic and Pacific theatres, the US recognized the importance of its Middle Eastern supply line. A memorandum to President Roosevelt from William Bullitt, under-secretary of the navy, explained that 'to acquire petroleum reserves outside our boundaries has become ... a vital interest of the United States'.[5] A proposal for a direct US government stake in the Saudi consortium and the US government funding the construction of a pipeline to bring oil from the Gulf to the Mediterranean foundered on the resistance of the oil companies who did not want to be dependent on the government. Instead, they decided to build the pipeline using private capital. A 30-inch-wide (762 mm) 'steel snake' was laid through the desert at a cost of some $200 million (around $1 billion in today's money). For a period, the Tapline would save Aramco the costs of tankers and Suez Canal tolls. It was, however, vulnerable to the stoppages resulting from the Arab–Israel dispute. Indeed construction was interrupted by the first Arab–Israeli war (1948), and it was not until 1949 that Syria and Lebanon allowed the pipeline to cross their territories.

The Arab–Israeli dispute, already a major problem for Britain as the mandatory power in Palestine before the outbreak of war in 1939, became even more critical when the war ended and the full horrors of the Nazi Holocaust were revealed. As pressure for Jewish immigration into Palestine increased, so Ibn Saud, as a leading Arab ruler, was drawn into a complex web of diplomatic engagements, disengagements and armed conflicts in one of the world's most volatile regions.

Before the United States entered the war against Germany and Japan in December 1941, Philby, concerned about falling Hajj revenues, had approached two leading Zionists Chaim Weizmann (later to be Israel's first president) and Moshe Shertock (its first foreign minister) with the suggestion that in return for a subsidy of £20 million paid to Ibn Saud, Jews should take over the western part of Palestine, apart from a Vatican-style enclave in the old city of Jerusalem. In exchange, according to Philby's plan, the Jews would accept the idea of 'Arab unity' under the leadership of Ibn Saud. Philby put his plan to Ibn Saud who did not turn it down immediately, saying 'he would give [him] a definite answer at the appropriate time'.[6] However, when President Roosevelt, who had been briefed by Weizmann, sent as his Arabic-speaking emissary Colonel Harold Hoskins to find out if Ibn Saud might enter into discussion with Weizmann, the king is said to have 'exploded', because Weizmann had 'impugned his character by offering a bribe of £20 million if he would accept Arab settlers from Palestine'.[7]

By the end of the war it was clear that the dominant influence in Saudi Arabia was the United States. In October 1943, concerned about US oil supplies, the secretary of the interior Harold Ickes sent an expedition to the Gulf headed by Everette Golyer, an eminent geologist. On returning to the US, Golyer stated in his report: 'The centre of gravity of the world of oil production is shifting from the [Mexico] Gulf-Caribbean areas to the Middle East, to the Persian Gulf area, and is likely to continue to shift until it is firmly established in that area.'[8]

In February 1945, on returning from his meeting with Stalin and Churchill at Yalta, Roosevelt entertained Ibn Saud aboard the US naval cruiser *Quincy*, which was moored in the Great Bitter Lake by the Suez Canal. The king arrived aboard the destroyer USS *Murphy* along with two of his sons Mansour and Muhammad, an entourage of fifty, including two senior advisors, and an official charged with the task of ensuring that the US navigation officer's indication of the *qibla* (direction of Mecca) for prayer was correct. The party included seven live sheep who were duly slaughtered in accordance with the requirements of *halal*.[9] The king, who by now had been crippled with arthritis, had to be hoisted aboard the *Quincy*. His meetings with Roosevelt lasted for five hours. The king brought gifts of swords and daggers; the president promised Ibn Saud an airplane – the DC-3 that would become the basis of the Saudi Arabian air force. While oil was discussed, the main topic was inevitably Palestine. When the president tried to persuade Ibn Saud to be more conciliatory towards Jewish immigration in view of the appalling suffering sustained by European Jewry under the Nazi regime, the king's reply was adamant: 'Give the Jews and their descendants the choicest lands and homes of the Germans who have oppressed them.' When the president countered by saying that Jewish refugees would prefer to go to Palestine the king replied by 'saying it was the criminal who should make amends, not the innocent bystander'.[10] In a subsequent letter to the king, the US president reaffirmed his position that the United States would not change its policy towards Palestine without consulting the Arabs. But two months later, Roosevelt was dead. His successor President Harry Truman would soon give full US support to the establishment of the new state of Israel.

After his meeting with Roosevelt Ibn Saud went on to meet Winston Churchill in Egypt. The meeting at a hotel in the Fayyum Oasis was far less successful than the encounter on the USS *Quincy*. Whereas the president – a chain smoker – had avoided offending the king by not smoking in his presence, the prime minister had sipped whiskey and continued to puff on his cigar. Britain's promised gift, a brand-new Rolls Royce straight off the production line in Derby, though politely accepted, was not in the same league as the American

DC-3. The British, moreover, had not done their homework on protocol. As it was a right-hand-drive vehicle, the king would have had to sit to the left of his chauffeur. Ibn Saud gave 'the best car in the world' to his brother Abdullah.[11]

It was clear that by now the centre of political gravity had shifted. As Sampson states, 'Churchill's reference to the King's "unfailing loyalty" could not conceal that he now looked across the Atlantic both for his defense and his income from oil.'[12] With the resumption of both oil exports and pilgrimage revenues his income was growing apace. In the first full year after oil exports were resumed, he received more than $10 million (around $130 million in today's values). The royalties were paid into a New York account operated by his trusted treasurer Abdullah Sulaiman, a clerk from Unayza in Nejd who had been with the king since the early days. With no distinction between Ibn Saud's personal wealth and that of the Saudi state (which barely existed as a political entity distinct from the ruler's person) accounting was chaotic. The challenge of managing this wealth would have been considerable for the ablest of financial advisors, given the demands of Ibn Saud's ever-growing family numbering hundreds of sons, daughters and grandchildren all of whom were entitled to share in his wealth. But Sulaiman was said to have had an alcohol habit. He was described by Laurence Grafftey-Smith, the British minister in Jeddah, as 'the only Finance Minister I ever met who drank methylated spirit'.[13] But accounts of his incompetence may have been exaggerated.

Despite his finance minister's problems, Ibn Saud managed to ratchet up the royalties he received from Aramco, forcing it to increase its royalty payments from 22 to 33 cents a barrel. Moreover, a revised agreement signed in 1948 required the company to give up blocks of its unexplored territory every three years, forcing the company to speed up its prospecting in a competitive oil race in which rival companies holding neighbouring concessions were provoked into similar spurts of activity.[14] By increasing pressure on Aramco in competition with its mainly British-backed rivals, Ibn Saud not only increased his revenues, but enlisted America's strategic support, as Aramco's profits were taxed by the US government. That support became crucial in the dispute over Buraimi, an oasis lying between the Trucial emirates and the Sultanate of Muscat, part of which a Saudi-backed force occupied in 1952 using Aramco trucks and supplies. The dispute centred over nine villages or settlements, three of them claimed by Oman and six by Abu Dhabi, both British protectorates. A British contingent based in Oman, which included two Lancaster bombers, prevented Saudi reinforcements and the standoff continued pending UN arbitration. (The arbitration descended into farce when the tribunal's international delegates led by the British minister resigned over crude Saudi efforts to influence the proceedings by bribing and interfering with witnesses.)

In 1949 Sulaiman discovered that, thanks to complex changes in the relationship between the company and its shareholders, Aramco was paying more tax to the US Treasury than it paid in revenues to the Saudi government. A solution was found in a 'fifty-fifty law' enacted by the government of Venezuela, whereby all oil company profits were subjected to a 50 per cent levy: if such a 'fifty-fifty law' had been applied to Aramco in 1949, the king could have received another $33 million from the company. A tax expert hired by the Saudis explained that the additional levy could be offset against the company's US tax liabilities. For the US government, the 'fifty-fifty' deal had an unintended result: as Barr explains, by approving the deal the Aramco board 'was effectively volunteering American taxpayers to subsidize the lifestyle of the Saudi royal family'.[15]

Ibn Saud's discussions with the Americans had included the idea of constructing a pipeline between the oil fields of al-Ahsa and the

Mediterranean. The king agreed with the oil companies that such a venture should be undertaken by the companies using private capital, and not the US government. In this, his instincts as well as interest coincided with those of the Americans. His feeling on Palestine allowed for no distinction between the Zionist project of colonizing Palestine as a refuge for the Jewish people – a matter of primary concern to Philby – and hostility to Jews in general. As he told the Anglo-American commission on Palestine in 1946, 'The Jews are our enemy everywhere. To every spot on earth to which they come they spread corruption and work against our interests.'[16] The same year he sent his ablest son and second successor, the Emir Faisal (king from 1964–75), to Washington to make clear to Truman his concerns about Palestine. In New York Faisal had to endure not only the failure of the Arab countries to prevent the United Nations vote for the partition of Palestine, but the boos and insults of Jewish demonstrators. Though satisfactory regarding oil, the meeting with Truman got nowhere when it came to Palestine. As US secretary of state Dean Acheson put it in his memoirs, 'their minds crossed but did not meet. The Amir was concerned about conditions in the Near East, the President with the conditions of the displaced Jews in Europe.'[17]

A contradiction that would be fundamental to US–Saudi relations was not so much masked as managed, leading to the emergence of an extraordinary two-track policy. On the one hand the US would be unequivocal in its support for Israel. Senators and representatives who opposed Israeli policies would soon find themselves unseated by the all-powerful pro-Israel lobby. But oil matters were treated differently: the extraction of oil, its marketing and distribution were 'business', not politics. As Sampson explains:

Two opposite American foreign policies were thus both firmly recognized; support for the State of Israel, which was critical for honor and votes, and support for Saudi Arabia, which was critical for oil. The State Department's solution ... was to delegate their diplomacy to the oil companies, and to regard them as an autonomous kind of government; and through this means the two policies were kept remarkably separate for the next twenty-five years.[18]

Ibn Saud breathed his last on 9 November 1953. His final years were marked by personal unhappiness as well as arthritis, blindness and other ailments that might be attributed to his excessive consumption of aphrodisiacs. His favourite son Mansour, who had been charged with defence, died of alcohol poisoning following a party hosted by his half-brother Nasser, governor of Riyadh, in which several foreigners also died.[19] Another son, nineteen-year-old Mishari, caused him even more serious loss of face – by shooting dead the British vice consul in a drunken fit. (The diplomat's widow accepted compensation for her husband's murder and Mishari was released from prison by his half-brother King Saud after serving just a few years.)

Ibn Saud was increasingly preoccupied by the rivalry between his two senior sons Saud and Faisal (b. 1906), both of whom were in constant attendance as his health declined. In 1951 Ibn Saud performed his last Hajj in brutal summer heat. By 1953 a journey to Mecca in the height of summer was out of the question. He was flown in the DC-3 to the coolness of Taif, the summer capital, after performing his last act as king – the signing of a decree establishing a cabinet or council of ministers, which the US embassy believed might help to bring 'order to the present chaotic state of the administration'. It was symbolic, perhaps, that the king died in the arms of his second son Faisal when Saud had left temporarily for Jeddah.[20]

Saud succeeded, having been appointed crown prince by his father in 1933. His mother, Wadhah bint Muhammad bin 'Aqab, came from the Bani Khalid tribe which had dominated in the al-Ahsa region and Qatif. Ibn Saud always made a point of keeping the tribes loyal by marrying their women. As McLoughlin comments 'he used with great skill the traditional ways of maintaining contact' with the tribes 'through marriage and hunting expeditions'.[21] US officials called this 'an active policy of serial polygamy' tied to state-building by conquest.[22] In this patriarchal, tribal culture, women, like booty, were the rewards of victory. The binding of subordinate tribes to the rule of the Al Saud was ensured by marriage bonds and emergence of children who would share in the same tribal-genetic pedigree. Through most of his adult life 'Saud enjoyed close relations with the tribes, was popular with them and loved to travel amongst them'.[23] After being named crown prince, he received the *baya* (fealty) from his younger brothers annually as well as from tribal leaders.

Ibn Saud sired forty-three sons and an unnamed number of daughters. His son Saud (r. 1953–64) had an equally formidable number of progeny. Both leaders demonstrated a striking correspondence between virility and power. Such a correspondence may have been accentuated in the primitive conditions of tribal Arabia, but it is far from being unique to tribalism. The Chinese emperor typically disposed of a vast harem of concubines, indicative of primordial links between virility and power. Medieval notions of chivalry, based on radical gender distinctions, with virility seen as integral to heroic military virtues, were as typical of medieval Europe as of the twentieth-century Middle East. For example, in the case of Henry IV of Castile (1425–74), known as 'the impotent' from his failure to consummate his marriage to Blanca da Navarra (who was declared a virgin when the marriage was annulled after a union of thirteen years), the monarch's presumed homosexuality and other sexual inadequacies were seen as the cause of political disarray. As Thomas Devaney explains 'the king's impotency ... pertained to more than the royal bedchamber' with the king's weakness in this arena directly linked to 'a general inability to prevent abuses of power that were ruining the kingdom at that time'.[24]

In their 1981 book *The House of Saud*, written by the British journalist David Holden (who is thought to have been a CIA agent) and completed by Richard Johns of the *Financial Times* after Holden was murdered in 1977, the authors recount a story that might seem malicious were it not for the insight it sheds on the correspondence between virility and power that is comparable in some respects with the culture of fifteenth-century Iberia.

The year 1961 was a time of extreme tension between Ibn Saud's successor Saud ibn Abd al-Aziz and his brother Crown Prince Faisal who would replace him after Saud was eventually forced to abdicate in 1964. Much of the tension, as Philby would relate, was due to Saud's extravagant habit of building palaces with hundreds of slaves and concubines rather than addressing the sober business of government. The enmity between the brothers, which would eventually be resolved in Faisal's favour, was a serious cause for concern among the princely elite, not least because the regime was vulnerable to anti-monarchist propaganda from Nasser's Egypt.

At sixty-one King Saud's declining health involved a multiplicity of ailments, including stomach troubles, high blood pressure and sagging legs unable to bear the weight of his 200-pound (90 kg) frame. In addition, rumours abounded in court circles – and doubtless in the *suqs* of Riyadh and Jeddah – that the king had a penchant for what were politely called 'irritating liquids' (notably Cointreau), a habit that clearly distinguished him from the more austere and sharia-minded brother Faisal. The tension between the two half-brothers reached a climax at a cabinet meeting on 15 November when the king was apparently furious about a commission that Faisal's brother-in-law, Kamal Adham, had received from a Japanese oil concession – a portion of which was claimed by Faisal and his wife Iffat. Later that night Saud is reported to have collapsed with acute stomach pains. Before departing for treatment at Aramco's hospital in Dhahran, however, he made what Holden and Johns call 'an extraordinary attempt to reassure his subjects of his physical fitness to govern. He insisted on his favourite wife, the fat Umm Mansour, being brought to him. With the physical support of four slave girls he successfully had intercourse with her.'[25]

Soon the 'glad tidings' about the king's virility were spreading around the capital, confounding the doubters. In the hospital he was examined by specialists, who found he was suffering from severe internal bleeding caused by alcohol. With the agreement of his brother, he flew to Boston for surgery, where his entourage ran up bills amounting to $3.5 million. Aramco picked up the tab on the understanding that it would be reimbursed a year later. Though clearly overdue already, the abdication did not actually happen for another three years.

It would be wrong to suppose that this story represents a manifestation of 'royal decadence' although in the changing values that accompany modernization it is hard to avoid seeing it as such. During his declining years Ibn Saud, half blind from a cataract and barely able to walk, made similar efforts to quash rumours about his virility, by having injections against impotence and selecting a bride from one of the tribes and (no doubt audibly) 'consummating the marriage behind the woollen walls of the royal tent'.[26] In the warrior society to which both Saud and his father belonged, virility was a vital dimension of leadership. The tribal leader is a 'father to his people' in more than a metaphorical sense, with the act of fathering closely connected to the exercise of power.

In his prime Ibn Saud had been romantically attached to Jawhara bint Musaid, who died of influenza in 1919, as did his eldest son Turki. Jawhara remained a vivid memory. Indeed, in the 1930s while talking of her with Muhammad Asad he would almost break down.

> Whenever the world was dark around me and I could not see my way out of dangers and difficulties that beset me I would sit down and compose an ode to Jawhara, and when it was finished the world was suddenly lighted, and I knew what I had to do.[27]

Yet there is no sense that this romantic attachment inhibited sexual relations with numerous other women. Indeed the sexual act seems to have been integral to battle itself – an expression of masculine prowess as totemic as swords and guns. Among other writers, Ibn Saud's Arab biographer, Khair al-Din Zirkili, relates that after a battle with the Ajman tribe in 1915 when his brother Saad was killed, Ibn Saud, though wounded himself, demanded a 'bride' and succeeded in reinvigorating his dejected forces by a 'demonstration of conjugal strength ... when cries from the tent indicated that [he] had lost none of his vigour'.[28] Zirkili's story is consistent with Holden and Johns's account of King Saud's need to reassure the *suq* of his masculine prowess nearly half a century later. Ameen Rihani, who spent six weeks with Ibn Saud's entourage in the early 1920s, was told by his Bedouin troops, 'We desire women all the time ... and he whose desire is strongest is the Imam.'[29] Later Ibn Saud disclosed to Philby that by 1930 he had enjoyed sexual relations with 135 virgins and about 100 other women, but that he planned from now on to take only two new wives annually. This would still enable him to maintain a lifestyle of four legitimate wives, 'four concubines, wives in all but name ... and four slave-girls, to say nothing of his right to select from the damsels at his disposal'.[30]

At the same time, according to Philby, the king 'held himself free to absent himself from all domestic festivities occasioned by normal events like marriage and births' when he would generally take himself off to camp. He would see 'new-born babes only some days after their arrival and as for relations with their mothers these would resume after an interval of 40 days'.[31] Philby also states that Ibn Saud never allowed a woman to eat in his presence and believed that while it was permissible for women to listen to recitations of the Quran and other scriptures, the ability of a woman to read and write was 'an accomplishment unsuitable in a woman though not forbidden'.[32] The fact that such attitudes were prevalent in the mid-twentieth century gives some indication of the challenge facing Saudi women in the twenty-first, when gender parity in education – if not politics – became a norm to which the vast majority of countries, including Saudi Arabia, now aspire.

The impact of the oil boom, traumatic for many yet empowering for some, is captured in the five-part novel *Cities of Salt* (1984–9) by the Saudi–Iraqi novelist Abdul Rahman Munif (1933–2004). A trained economist who had worked in the oil industry, Munif charts the fortunes of characters who originally lived in the fictional oasis of Wadi al-Uyun before moving to the city of Harran on the Gulf, where two townships grow up side by side, one for the Americans and the local elites they benefit, including the emir, and the other for the displaced Arab labourers. The 'iron columns' of the oil rigs appear everywhere in this desolate landscape. 'How is it possible', asks one of the characters, 'for people and places to change so entirely that they lose any connection with what they used to be? Can a man adapt to new things and new places without losing a part of himself?'[33] Munif describes the disruptive impact of the American invasion through the consciousness of his local characters.

The familiar houses of old Harran are demolished by 'hellish yellow machines' that arrive like sea-monsters and charge about destructively like untamed camels.[34] A steel crate gallops like a gazelle yet never tires; a magic box talks, sings and even emits the sounds of prayer. The emir views his domain through a spyglass that can show you a single hair from a distance. He insists that his new home must be as fine as the ones the Americans have, slapping the wall to ensure its solidity. Further down the social scale the baker falls in love with an American woman he spies from afar and plasters the walls of his shop with pictures of women cut from Western magazines. The arrival of the 'satanic ship' bringing the Americans resonates with what Charles Dickens tellingly called the 'attraction of repulsion' – inviting both lust and horror from people unused to the sight of female bodies.

> Women were perfumed, shining and laughing, like horses after a long race. Their faces, hands, breasts, bellies – everything, yes, everything glistened, danced, flew. Men and women embraced on the deck of the large ship and in the small boats but no one could believe what was happening on the shore ... The people had become one solid mass, like the body of a giant camel, all hugging and pressing against one another ... The astonished people of Harran approach imperceptibly, step by step, like sleepwalkers. They could not believe their eyes and ears. Had there ever been anything like this ship, this huge and magnificent? Where else in the world were there women like these, who resembled both milk and figs in their tanned whiteness? Was it possible that men could shamelessly walk around with women, with no fear of others?[35]

The Americans also bring musical instruments. Both silence and social conformity are shattered by blaring music, dancing and scenes of sexual mayhem with men stroking women before suddenly seeming to attack them with hugs and kisses. Unsurprisingly, Munif's novel was banned in Saudi Arabia and other Arab countries, and he was stripped of his Saudi nationality. After working in the oil industry in Syria he spent the remainder of his life as a writer and editor in Iraq, Lebanon, France and Syria.

Cities of Salt is clearly impressionistic in its account of the impact of oil on the lives of ordinary people. But it is not inconsistent with more factual and positive accounts. In describing the new employment opportunities, Munif states that the first Arab workers had some power in dealing with the oil company, with jobs distributed on the basis of seniority and clan membership before the Americans gradually changed the criteria, bringing in books and asking questions about education. 'They said they had come to help the people and search for water, that there was gold underneath the sands and that they would extract it and distribute it among the people, but what did any of that have to do with their books or the questions they asked?'[36] In his memoir, Frank Jungers, the former president, chairman and CEO of Aramco (the great oil giant that Socal became after 1944), shows how the new meritocratic system offered incentives to enable Saudis regardless of older criteria of status and clan.

> Naturally problems arose – social frictions and rivalries – when the various levels of employees were brought together. At first the lowest grades were Saudis – they were starting off with absolutely no experience in industrial activities that their country had never seen before. The employees at the next level, who had more education and skills – especially clerical and white-collar workers – were nearly all foreigners, and were housed in an intermediate camp, which had better facilities than existed in the general camp where the lower-level and blue-collar and general Saudi labor lived. On the positive side, the promotion ladder for the first time offered promise to the lower-level workers, and

the Saudi laborers at Ras Tanura knew that the more education and training they received and the more experience they accumulated the more employee benefits they would enjoy.[37]

What emerges from this narrative – though Jungers does not state this explicitly – is less a comprehensive social transformation than the burgeoning of a parallel technocratic and privileged society, composed of foreigners as well as some Saudis, that grew up in the company's residential and industrial compounds. The compound was not wholly insulated from the rest of the country because generally lower-level Saudis lived in bachelor dorms and were taken home by bus on their days off. The craftsmen and white-collar workers – mostly South Asians, Sudanese and other foreigners – were housed in intermediate bachelor quarters that were superior in quality and more private. The system involved de facto discrimination till Saudis climbed up the ranks acquiring more skills and thus earning better quarters.

The Saudi employees, writes Jungers, were keen to acquire training in 'craft and operating jobs' in addition to their basic schooling. The ablest and perhaps the luckiest were even sent for training in the United States. Local instruction was provided by American craftsmen – mainly from the oilfields of Texas and California – 'tough workers who understood long hours and hard work' but had not been instructed as trainers. Later these American expats would be joined by employees from sparsely populated states such as Wyoming, North Dakota and Oklahoma – graduates with technical degrees who needed work and money. The earliest Arab employees, Jungers writes, included many Bedouins from Nejd and the north-eastern deserts, with few from commercial areas around Jeddah or the holy cities of the Hejaz (just as few Americans came from the Eastern Seaboard). 'As the workforce grew other Saudis from the Eastern

Province – from towns like Qatif and Safwa and from the great oasis of al-Ahsa – were hired as camp workers, to be trained as masons, carpenters, plumbers, electricians, cooks and domestic help.'[38]

A high proportion of the latter belonged to the Shia minority. While American employment policies discriminated on national lines (with Americans, like other workers of European extraction, earning considerably more than local Saudis or immigrants from Asia) 'they did not distinguish between sects and were "colour-blind" in their employment of Shia who did jobs the Bedouins refused to do'.[39] Jungers explains the issue somewhat differently: 'the company was very careful, as a matter of policy, not to allow this religious difference to become a factor in the training or evaluation of an employee.'[40] At the same time, according to Matthiesen:

> The Arabian Affairs Division, the research and intelligence gathering unit of the company, carried out several in-depth studies of Shia communities and was aware of religious discrimination and animosities between members of the two sects. Workers had to state whether they were Sunni or Shia on forms of the company's medical center. Especially Shia employees were vehemently opposed to this practice since they felt it would make government discrimination against them easier.[41]

Nevertheless, from the 1960s the Shia, whose sedentary background and proximity to the oil installations made them a new 'petite bourgeoisie', constituted at least a quarter of the company's workforce, rising to more than half of its 22,000 employees by 1979.[42] This would create problems as workers became increasingly susceptible to demands for better conditions. In October 1953, shortly before the death of Ibn Saud, around 17,000 of Aramco's 19,000 workforce went on strike for better pay and working conditions. The strike had been triggered by a petition presented in May by Saudi and other non-American employees for better housing.

As many writers have observed, the company's residential compound, known as 'Little America' or 'Mainstreet USA', was in marked contrast to the streets of hot mud-brick houses where most Aramco employees lived. Here, wide streets, manicured lawns and low bungalows resembled a California suburb. Robert Lacey, who visited it in the late 1970s for his blockbuster book *The Kingdom*, provided a vivid description of it.

> Neat white weatherboard houses, gauzed porches and pitched red roofs, [where] sprinklers play on the lawns, mowers chatter across the verges, and the yellow school buses never fail to halt at the crossing signs. There are oleander hedges, barbecue pits, soda fountains and baseball bleachers ... All the picture lacks is a church spire poking above the trees and some sort of bar or tavern ... You can easily live inside Aramco's Dhahran township and never realize you are in the Kingdom. There is a cinema beside the hamburger bar, and women are allowed to drive inside the compound.[43]

The American journalist Karen House even notes that until the 1980s when 'religiosity gripped the kingdom', pork and alcohol were permitted in the compound, and 'Christmas was celebrated complete with wise men riding camels to see baby Jesus'. While indulgence in Christmas and alcohol disappeared after 1979, when the Iranian revolution, Shia unrest and the siege of Mecca induced a religious crackdown (see Chapter 5), men and women continued to mix freely inside the compound, and women continued to be allowed to drive inside the perimeter.[44]

For a period, the Dhahran compound may have insulated most of the Saudi population from what tribal leaders, the Wahhabi ulama and their conservative supporters would have seen as the corrupting effects of Western influence, but its very isolation as a Western ghetto in the desert enabled it to act as a formidable incubator of change. While the broader implications of keeping this enclave of suburban modernity (a cancerous tumour for conservative critics) next to the pulsating heart of the oil industry will be discussed in a later chapter, we may note at this point the challenge it must present to long-held assumptions about gender.

According to House, the company – called Saudi Aramco since its formal nationalization in 1988 – now allows young women to compete for its coveted College Preparatory Program which accounts for 75 per cent of all new hires. In the standardized tests given to all applicants the young women tend to outperform the men. As House describes it, 'In a country where young women are kept under constant family surveillance until marriage' when the custodianship passes from father to husband, the very fact that these bright young women, however much they are supervised in their separate dormitory, are living away from home represents a 'big break from tradition'.

> Here they attend classes to prepare for entry into foreign universities to earn degrees mostly in engineering, management or finance and eventual employment at Saudi ARAMCO in jobs typically held by males. They are taught, among other things, how to manage contemporary social issues such as handling confrontations for foreigners or explaining the hijab if they choose to wear a head scarf when abroad.[45]

The education of women, pushing them to the forefront of Saudi Arabia's technological elite, may be a high-risk strategy for the regime, as House implies. For as she suggests it does not mean just the empowering of women, but a fundamental re-ordering of gender relations that must challenge the fundamentals of Wahhabism, not to say Islamic ideology as understood in much of the wider Muslim society. Her conversations with young millennials of both sexes convinced House that the current generation of young people, many of them much better educated than their parents, would be likely to bring about 'the kind of societal change in attitudes that baby boomers forced on America starting in the 1960s. America proved resilient enough to weather that generational storm. With all the entrenched rigidities of religion and regime, Saudi Arabia is unlikely to prove anywhere near as resilient.'[46]

That challenge, as reckoned by House, is now being addressed by the new crown prince, with consequences that are yet to be seen. As will be shown in Chapter 10, change appears far-reaching, without discernible resistance at this time. Andrew Hammond has suggested Wahhabism may have been 'defanged' but has yet to be 'dethroned'.[47] A rising generation may benefit from the loosening of social restrictions and the arrival of new opportunities in employment and activity. Deeper sources of tension, however, due to growing social inequalities in a sectarian system claiming a universalist religious hegemony and the replacement of a tribal consensus by a royal dictatorship, have yet to surface politically, though they may not be long in coming.

5
Managing the Ulama and Mismanaging the Hajj

On 12 November 2008, seven years after 9/11 and a week after Barack Obama had won the election to be the first US president of partly African origin, King Abdullah of Saudi Arabia visited the United Nations in New York. At a special conference devoted to interfaith dialogue the king urged the assembled dignitaries to learn the lessons of the past and to

> state with a unified voice that religions through which Almighty God sought to bring happiness to mankind should not be turned into instruments to cause misery. Human beings were created as equals and partners on this planet; either they live together in peace and harmony, or they will inevitably be consumed by the flames of misunderstanding, malice and hatred ... Terrorism and criminality are the enemies of every religion and every civilization. They would not have appeared except for the absence of the principle of tolerance. The alienation and the sense of being lost which affects the lives of many of our young, leading them to drugs and crime, became widespread due to the dissolution of family bonds that Almighty God intended to be firm and strong.[1]

In visiting the United Nations – the first Saudi king ever to do so – Abdullah was building on the quasi-caliphal role he adopted as Custodian of the Two Holy Shrines – the Ottoman title previously used by King Faisal (r. 1964–75), but given prominence by King Fahd (r. 1982–2005) who had sought to play down his reputation as a playboy capable of losing $1 million in a single scotch-fuelled gambling spree in Monte Carlo.[2]

In promoting interfaith dialogue, King Abdullah had visited the pope in Rome, where he grandiloquently offered the pontiff 'peace and friendship' on behalf of the Muslim world. Spiritually empowered, no doubt, by his reception by Pope Benedict (who had been trying to live down a speech widely perceived as condemning Muslims for terrorism delivered at Regensburg the previous year), Abdullah hosted a gathering in Madrid attended by representatives from the Vatican, the Anglican Church, Judaism, Hinduism and other faiths. The Saudi king's message of toleration might be viewed with scepticism by people familiar with the actual state of religious pluralism in Saudi Arabia, where some 1.5 million workers from Catholic countries such as the Philippines are prevented from worshipping publicly and Shiites remain subject to a variety of disabilities. In June 2008, while the king was chairing an international conference in Mecca for the promotion of interfaith dialogue, with many Iranian scholars present, twenty-two Wahhabi scholars signed an open letter condemning the Shia.[3]

Despite contradictions at home, there was no ambiguity about the role of 'leader of the Muslim Umma' that the ageing monarch wanted the world to recognize. UN officials who worked with the Saudis on the visit saw that his 'primary goal was to present himself as "pope" of all Islam, thereby diminishing Iran's Shiite sect and pleasing the conservative clerics in Riyadh for whom Shiites are heretics'.[4] For this reason, according to House, the king's staff insisted that protocol for King Abdullah's visit should match that of Pope John Paul's landmark visits to the UN in 1979 and 1995. 'The chief of protocol, the Saudis insisted, must meet the king at the airport, and the UN secretary general must greet him at the base of the escalator bearing him up to the General Assembly auditorium, an honor given to no other head of state.'[5] In order to meet the Saudi requirement, House relates, the 'hapless' UN secretary general Ban Ki-moon had to cancel a previously scheduled trip to Hollywood with California's governor and several movie stars, including Angelina Jolie.

When the UN conference concluded, the Saudi foreign minister Prince Saud al-Faisal stood beside the secretary general, who read a statement said to represent a 'sense of the United Nations' in support of greater religious tolerance. This statement, however, was not a resolution. The Saudis had made it clear that they did not want a resolution that would have to be negotiated among more than 190 UN members. The statement, moreover, was not reported in the official Saudi press. As House comments, the affair represented 'Saudi foreign policy at its most elaborately artificial'.[6]

To say that the Saudi leadership has a difficult role in dealing with Wahhabism would be a serious understatement. Since Ibn Saud defeated the Ikhwan rebels in 1929 the Saudi dynasty has had to manage challenges both to its legitimacy and to its modernizing agenda posed by the conflicting forces of Islamic thought and activism. While the regime is sometimes presented as 'totalitarian' in the manner of some European states in the mid-twentieth century, the reality is a good deal more complex, not least because Islam, even in the Hanbali–Wahhabi version that now predominates in the kingdom, is far from being a theological monolith. While Wahhabism still contains elements of militancy (as will be explored in Chapter 6), it is far from being the only source or style of Saudi religiosity. Like Judaism and Christianity, the Islamic tradition contains powerful millenarian or 'eschatological' impulses that may lie dormant but can be activated at times of social conflict.

In November 1979 a group of militants seized the Grand Mosque of Mecca – Islam's holiest site – in a three-week siege that was only suppressed with the help of French special forces. The group's leader, Juhayman al-Utaybi, had been a part-time theology student who had spent some eighteen years as a member of the Saudi National Guard, the militia commanded by Prince (later King) Abdullah, which contained many tribal elements of the disbanded Ikhwan. At the Islamic University of Medina he had come into contact with members of the Muslim Brotherhood who had found refuge there after the crackdown of the Brotherhood in Nasser's Egypt. But while he may have absorbed some Brotherhood ideas, his was primarily an indigenous Saudi movement.

Born in the 1930s to a Bedouin family in the Ikhwan *hijra* of Sajir in western Nejd, his family belonged to the Suqur branch of the large Utaiba tribe to which many of the Ikhwan belonged. His father, Muhammad bin Sayf, had fought with the Ikhwan rebels at the Battle of Sibila in 1929 and lived until 1972. Juhayman was proud of his father's exploits and was keen to evoke the memory of the old Ikhwan to his comrades in Jamaʻa al-Salafiyya al-Muhtasiba (JSM, the 'Salafist Group for Commanding the Right and Forbidding the Wrong'). The group's spiritual guide was the charismatic Sheikh Abd al-Aziz bin Abdallah ibn Baz, vice president of the university.

As well as guiding his students towards the paths of righteousness, Ibn Baz wrote a famous essay based on his Quranic reading asserting that the sun revolves round the earth and condemning secular Riyadh University for teaching students the Copernican view. His fatwa stating that any Muslim who rejected the geocentric model was an apostate deserving of death doubtless irritated the ruling family. In June 1985 Prince Sultan bin Salman bin Abd al-Aziz (a son of the present king) was orbiting the globe as a payload specialist aboard the US space shuttle *Discovery*. However, Ibn Baz's religious authority was such that it did not prevent him from rising to become the kingdom's chief mufti or religious authority from 1992 until his death in 1999 and receiving the King Faisal Award for services to Islam.

The Salafist group that Ibn Baz patronized had come to prominence in the 1960s when members were arrested for smashing pictures and photographs they regarded as *haram* or forbidden and attacking shop windows displaying female mannequins. They even made a habit of defacing banknotes containing pictures of the monarch. Initially, Ibn Baz had intervened with the authorities on their behalf, pointing out they were just pious Muslims who were justified in rejecting imported cultural practices. Like the Muslim Brotherhood in Egypt in the 1930s and 1940s the group appealed to Saudis disturbed by the pace of urbanization and consumerism brought about, in this case, by the sudden wealth flowing from the quadrupling of oil prices after the 1973 Arab–Israeli War. (In that first decade of a great oil boom, the kingdom's revenue grew from $1.2 billion in 1970 to $22 billion by 1974 and reaching $100 billion a year by 1980.)

By 1976, the JSM already had followers based in several Saudi cities, including Mecca, Riyadh, Jeddah, Taif, Hail, Abha, Dammam and Buraydah.[7] Many of the followers appear to have been young men from Bedouin backgrounds who had lost out in the course of modernization. Others were foreigners, with or without Saudi nationality.

The group that seized the Grand Mosque was a radical faction of the JSM that split from its main body, not because of arguments about violence, but because of disagreements over ritual. Among other details Juhayman's group thought the fast of Ramadan could be broken by shutting out light in a darkened room rather than having to wait for sundown. Their split with the majority doubtless radicalized

Juhayman, who came to regard his former mentor Ibn Baz and the rest of the Wahhabi establishment as government stooges. It also concerned the authorities, who issued orders for Juhayman's arrest. Though other members of the group were arrested and detained, he escaped after a tip-off from a fellow Utaibi tribesman working for the police.

After leaving Medina, Juhayman spent two years in desert regions remote from police surveillance. He maintained contact with family and supporters, however, and gave expression to his ideas via audio cassette and essays or 'epistles' which were smuggled to Kuwait and published later by one of its newspapers. In the most political of these missives, he accused the Saudi regime of 'making religion a means to guarantee their worldly interests, putting an end to jihad, paying allegiance to the Christians (America) and bringing over Muslims' evil and corruption'.

As the Al Saud were not members of the Quraish, the Prophet's tribe, they were not entitled to Islamic leadership, making the *baya* (oath of allegiance) to them invalid. Interestingly, however, he did not go so far as to declare them infidels as more radical Islamists tend to do under the principle of *takfir*. While the state was illegitimate, pronouncing *takfir* on its rulers was prohibited so long as they called themselves Muslims. As two recent scholars have noted, these views do not diverge significantly from those of traditional Wahhabism rooted in the doctrine of *al-wala wa'l bara* (loyalty and dissociation).

The most radical of Juhayman's ideas, which appears to have come to him in the desert, was the appearance of the Mahdi – the Islamic Messiah – a subject to which he devoted the first of his seven epistles. This text, according to Hegghammer and Lacroix, 'presents all the authentic hadiths (prophetic traditions) about the Mahdi, correlating them with recent events in the modern history of the Arabian Peninsula to demonstrate the imminence of the Mahdi's coming'.[8]

In late 1978 Juhayman claimed he had a dream that his Companion Muhammad al-Qahtani was the expected Mahdi.

A young man with unusually fair skin, straight hair and honey-coloured eyes, al-Qahtani possessed several of the Mahdi's attributes as described in the hadiths: like the Prophet, his name was Muhammad bin Abdullah; he belonged – so he claimed – to the *ashraf*, or Prophet's lineage; his facial appearance 'a wide forehead and hooked nose' was in conformity with the descriptions of the Mahdi in religious tradition. The timing of the attack was also significant, coinciding with a Sunni tradition whereby a great scholar known as the 'renewer of the century' (*mujaddid al-qarn*) is supposed to appear at the beginning of each *hijri* (Islamic) century.

After purchasing an arsenal of automatic rifles and other weapons with funds from wealthier members of the group and bribing the guards to look the other way, Juhayman and his followers smuggled them into the *haram* area, where the Binladen Group – the kingdom's largest contractors – was doing construction work. Then at dawn on the First of Muharram (21 November 1979), the first day of the Islamic (*hijri*) year 1400, the rebels took over the mosque, making sure that all the gates were locked with snipers posted above the gates. After grabbing the imam's microphone Juhayman passed it to Muhammad al-Qahtani's brother Sayyid who delivered a sermon in the finest classical Arabic denouncing the House of Saud for corruption and debauchery. The *Wall Street Journal* correspondent Yaroslav Trofimov summarized his speech:

> The kingdom's rulers, pawns of the infidels, were unworthy of true believers' respect. The oath of baya [allegiance] that Saudi subjects had given their king was no longer valid because the royal family had demonstrably failed to govern in accordance with the laws of Islam. But relief was at hand. According to well-attested hadiths, the Mahdi

had arrived. 'The good man is here with us, and he will bring justice to Earth after it had been filled with injustice. If anyone doubts, come here to check. We are all your brothers.'[9]

While the millenarian vision of an Islamic utopia associated with the Mahdi is alien to Wahhabism, end-time scenarios involving the return of a messianic figure who will bring peace and justice to a world torn by strife are as common to Islamic traditions as they are to those of Judaism and Christianity. Though institutionalized in Shiism in which the ulama claim to be deputies of a Hidden Imam, they are more diffused but nonetheless present in the majority of Sunni traditions and have inspired radical movements throughout Islamic history. In 1881 the Sudanese Muslim cleric Muhammad Ahmad declared himself Mahdi, conquered Khartoum, and created a state that lasted until it was overthrown by the British in 1898.

The scenario maintains a certain plausibility – not to say attraction – even in the twenty-first century: a hadith in the collection of Ibn Kathir, an influential scholar who lived in Syria and died in 1373, describes 'signs of the Last Days' that instantly call to mind both the contemporary Sunni–Shia divide and the burgeoning towers that now dominate the skylines of many Gulf and Arabian cities.

> The Hour will not come till the following events have come to pass: people will compete with one another in constructing high buildings; two big groups will fight one another, there will be many casualties – they will both be following the same religious teaching; earthquakes will increase; time will pass quickly; afflictions and killing will increase.[10]

A central figure in the Muslim end-time scenarios is Dajjal – the one-eyed false messiah who corresponds to the Antichrist of the Book of Revelation. The details vary but most versions of this story agree that the final battle – the Islamic Armageddon – will take place in Syria east of Damascus when Jesus will return as messiah, kill pigs and other unclean animals, destroy Dajjal, and break the Cross in his symbolic embrace of Islam. In recent years this end-time scenario has been popularized by Daesh or ISIS – the extremist Islamic State group that took over large swathes of territory in Iraq and Syria after the 2003 US invasion of Iraq and the civil war in Syria that started in 2011.

While there may not be a direct textual connection linking the millenarian movement of Juhayman with that of Abu Bakr al-Baghdadi, the self-styled caliph of ISIS, they clearly draw on common sources and impulses. The parallels with the beliefs adopted by Christian fundamentalists known as 'premillennial dispensationalists', who want all the world's Jews to settle in Israel as a precondition for the Second Coming of Christ, are compelling.

Unwilling to test the loyalty of the National Guard, many of whose members belonged to Juhayman's Utaiba tribe and, as pious Muslims, were reluctant to fight in the Sacred Mosque, the Al Saud enlisted the GIGN (the Groupe d'Intervention de la Gendarmerie Nationale) – the elite French force widely regarded as being the most effective in special operations. Without actually taking part in combat, the GIGN squad led by Captain Paul Barril arranged for Saudi workmen and soldiers to drill apertures in the mosque's vast courtyard so the rebels holed up in the labyrinthine basements could be flushed out with CS gas, a chemical that blocks respiration, inhibits aggressiveness and can be lethal in a confined space. After some Saudi troops had suffered casualties from rebels who surprised them by firing through the apertures, the operation was successful. Rebels eventually captured, killed or executed included thirty-nine Saudis, ten Egyptians, six Yemenis and a number of Kuwaitis, Iraqis and Sudanese, as well as two African American converts whose status would pose a headache for the US ambassador John Carl West.

While one of the latter appeared to have been killed or executed, the second was 'spared the executioner's sword' and eventually allowed to return to the United States where Trofimov suggests he may now 'be alive and well today, resident in Anytown, U.S.A.'.[11] Independent observers, including the US ambassador, believed that the casualties of the three-week siege greatly exceeded the official figure of 270 deaths announced by the government, with deaths numbering at least 1,000.

The Mecca siege was not the only crisis to afflict the Saudi state at this time. Inspired by the Islamic revolution in Iran, where Ayatollah Khomeini, a senior Shiite cleric, had taken power in February 1979 after returning from exile in France, radicals of an underground Shia organization called the Movement of Vanguards' Missionaries (MVM) mounted a massive demonstration in Qatif in the Eastern Province. The decision to hold the rituals of Muharram, when Shias mourn the death of the Imam Husayn, the Prophet's grandson, in 680, in the streets of Qatif was seen as 'an open act of defiance of the government'.[12] In previous years the rituals had been held in the relative privacy of halls known as *husseiniyas* or in small towns or villages remote from the gaze of Wahhabi clerics.

In Iran, the mourning rituals of Muharram had been a critical element in the street protests in Tehran and other cities that led to the fall of the shah. Although as Wahhabi-inspired fundamentalists the Utaibi group who seized the Grand Mosque were very far from being Shiite sympathizers, the Al Saud and their American sponsors were inclined to see them as different sides of the same anti-American, anti-regime coin. Their apprehension was fuelled by the fact that Shiite demonstrators – inspired by Khomeini's deliberate avoidance of sectarian labels – couched their protests in the language of religious solidarity, chanting slogans popularized during the Iranian revolution such as '*la sunniyya, la shi'iyya ...*

thawra thawra islamiyya!' ('Not Sunni, not Shia ... Islamic revolution, revolution!') Echoing the Iranian protesters' slogan 'Death to America!' some even chanted 'Death to the Al Saud!' A letter sent to American employees of Aramco warning that they would be targeted if the US attacked Iran from Saudi soil alarmed the US government, which asked the embassy to draw up contingency plans for an evacuation of American nationals. Ambassador West replied that if the Americans were evacuated from the kingdom 'it would wreck the armed forces, oil production, transportation etc. and ... would lead to the overthrow of the Saud regime'. In any case, he told the State Department, the interior minister Prince Bandar ibn Abd al-Aziz[13] had assured him that the Saudis were confident of crushing the Shiite uprising 'as long as [Washington] didn't complain too much about human rights violations'. As Trofimov sardonically comments, 'The Iranian lesson had been learned, and no such complaints were forthcoming.'[14]

The crackdown did not just affect Shias politically and socially. It diminished their economic prospects as well. With the security of the oil and gas industry under threat, a special manpower committee was established in the Ministry of Interior with responsibility for deciding who should get important or sensitive jobs. Anti-Shia discrimination became more evident as the 'Saudi-ization' of Aramco took effect. By 1980 the Saudi government had nationalized the company buying out its foreign shareholders. Ali al-Na'imi became the first Saudi chief executive officer, with the company formally renamed Saudi Aramco in 1988. Whereas the Americans had adopted a non-sectarian policy of recruitment based on merit, the manpower committee adopted an unwritten rule:

> that Shia should not be hired in security or any other key sector of the oil industry. If Shia were hired at all, they were employed as drivers,

clerks, gardeners or in storehouses, food and community services. The recruiters would look at first or last names, locations of issuance of their national identification cards, or locations of high schools to find out who was a Shia.[15]

As Matthiesen concludes, instead of starting a revolution the Qatif uprising led to a 'spurring infighting between the radical elements who had taken part in the uprising and the families of Shia notables who had previously succeeded in keeping order'. With the power of the notables fading in the face of increasingly overt discrimination, many of the more radically minded Shia went into exile.

Since the 1980s, it has been difficult for anyone in the Shia opposition to find solidarity across sectarian boundaries. Radical opposition activists such as Sheikh Abdullah ibn Jibrin, who with others founded the London-based Committee for the Defence of Legitimate Rights, issued fatwas denouncing Shia as infidels deserving death; in the 1990s, Safar al-Hawali, former dean of Islamic studies at the Umm al-Qura University in Mecca and a leading critic of the Al Saud, circulated audio cassettes denouncing Shias as deviants. Loyalist Wahhabi scholars operating under the regime's protective umbrella ensured that boundaries were maintained, issuing fatwas forbidding intermarriage between Sunnis and Shias, and forbidding Sunnis from eating meat slaughtered by Shia butchers.

All this appears to have been part of a deliberate government strategy to persuade the Shia, as Matthiesen puts it, that 'they would fare even worse under Islamists than they would under the royal family'.[16] Al-Rasheed writes that 'the regime sees the perverse benefit of attacks on Shia worshippers by radical Sunni groups', as such attacks allow it to present itself 'as the best protector of the Shia', since the only alternative 'would be radical jihadists'.[17]

Despite the boost in revenues, the spectre of political and social unrest remains a constant concern of the regime. As already suggested, the Saudi regime, however repressive in practice, does not conform to the models of totalitarian rule that took hold in Europe in the twentieth century. The Wahhabi establishment supports the regime providing it with legitimacy under the rubric that the faithful are required to obey the existing authority unless it deviates from the true path of Islam, a proviso that allows for a good deal of interpretative space. As Muhammad ibn Abd al-Wahhab stated in the *Book of God's Unity*, 'to obey the rulers in permitting something forbidden by Islamic law is tantamount to idolatry'.[18]

According to Ibn Taymiyya, Abd al-Wahhab's medieval predecessor and guide, the only ground for disobedience to a ruler 'is if he commands a believer to violate something prohibited by the shari'a'.[19] The practical implications of this doctrine are problematic, not least because Islamic law in its classical formulations does not cover many areas of modern life. As Commins explains, while Ibn Taymiyya's formulation

> appears to give unlimited powers to the ruler, the proviso for respecting shari'a limits is significant, since it includes, in Wahhabi doctrine, respect for the independence of *qadis* [Islamic judges] in matters within their jurisdiction. Hence the ruler may not interfere in their deliberations. Building on this limitation on a ruler's power, the ulama have preserved their autonomy in the legal sphere by refusing to participate in the codification of law and the formation of a uniform system of law courts.[20]

One consequence has been the unpredictability of the Saudi legal system and the reluctance of *qadis* to adjudicate issues that appear to lie outside the purview of sharia, permitting the dynasty to issue decrees or statutory regulations (now numbered in thousands) covering matters without any obvious bearing in Islamic law. In the 1930s Ibn Saud issued regulations on matters such as 'firearms, nationality, government collections and motor vehicles' under the principle allowing the ruler to issue decrees that do not contradict sharia. Since the ulama refused to involve themselves in adjudicating these non-sharia regulations, Ibn Saud established a system of special tribunals or statutory courts. The outcome has been the emergence of a two-track legal system, 'one responsible for religious law and another for statutory regulations'.[21]

One consequence of the two-track system has been to enlarge the remit of the Wahhabi establishment while incorporating the ulama within a state-dominated system through a process of bureaucratization. To describe a very complex process somewhat simplistically, the regime made a 'deal' with the ulama whereby in exchange for maintaining a degree of cultural influence and a level of autonomy far greater than they enjoyed in former Ottoman territories such as Egypt and Greater Syria, they ceded control over large areas concerned with industrialization and modernization.

Commins notes the 'persistence of *qadi* independence' after a unified legal system was introduced in the 1950s. Although the regime instituted a Board of Review to hear appeals, of some 8,000 cases that went for review in 1979–80, only 1 per cent were reversed on appeal. The individual *qadi*'s independence remained a source of unpredictability in the Saudi legal system about which foreigners often complained.[22] Although the system of statutory regulation dealt with many matters outside the purview of the traditional sharia, the 'deal' enabled the ulama to extend their remit beyond the traditional bounds of Islamic jurisprudence. For example, in 1981 the Board of Senior Ulama issued a fatwa extending the Quranic definition of brigandage to include assaults on sexual honour, bringing them within the scope of *huddud* crimes subject to amputation and execution.

In 1988 terrorism and sabotage were brought into the category of *ta'zir* crimes, the punishment of which, not being specified by the Quran, can be left to the *qadi*'s discretion. The regime thereby legitimized the escalation of harsh penalties for acts such as 'blowing up houses, mosques, schools, hospitals, factories, bridges, storehouses of arms or water, sources of public revenue such as oil wells, or by blowing up or hijacking airplanes' under the rubric of *siyasa* (political) measures that permit Islamic rulers to issue decrees so long as they do not contradict sharia. Such crimes could now be included under the Quranic category of 'spreading corruption upon the earth' for which culprits may be 'slain, or crucified, or have their hands or feet cut off' (cf. Quran, 5:33–4). Commins remarks that by delegating such crimes and misdemeanours to the religious courts,

> the Saudi rulers essentially gave away their prerogative under the category of *siyasatan* punishment. Perhaps they hoped that such an approach would legitimize a harsh crackdown on crime and political violence. It probably does. But at the same time it may have the paradoxical effect of weakening legitimacy of official religious institutions by implicating them in measures that sustain the very political structure that has tenuous support from the population.[23]

In commenting on the public executions that characterize Saudi justice, the Syrian scholar Aziz al-Azmeh suggests that the Saudi–Wahhabi alliance is reminiscent of one of the principles of Roman statecraft, *panis et circenses* (bread and circuses). John Bradley, a British journalist who worked for the English-language *Arab News*, provides a vivid account of the execution of two men that he witnessed in Jeddah in his 2005 book *Saudi Arabia Exposed*.

> In the square, which doubled as a parking lot, armed cops were stationed every 10 yards, their backs turned to the block and their eyes

fixed sternly on the crowd. They were there in case the relatives of the men to be slain tried to sabotage the executions at the last minute.

The executioner himself, Muhammad Saad Al-Beshi ... a huge black man with piercing eyes and massive hands ... was dressed in an immaculate white robe and a red checkered headscarf. He gripped his beloved sword firmly in his hand, clearly wallowing in the extraordinary solemnity of the occasion.

The sound of police sirens could at last be heard, and soon afterward two police cars, lights flashing, sped into the square. Behind them came two police vans, followed by three more police cars. From the back of each of the vans emerged a man, blindfolded and with his hands tied behind his back. Each was escorted to the block by a policeman. They were obviously drugged. So sluggish were they that they needed the support of the policeman to walk the short distance. They were made to kneel on the block and were fixed in place with their heads slightly bowed. Their nationalities (Pakistani), ages (both in their thirties) and crimes (smuggling heroin into the kingdom) were broadcast over loudspeakers.

A verse from the Quran was recited.

The executioner leaned over to the Pakistani nearest to him and whispered into his ear that he should say the shahada, the Muslim declaration of faith. There was no indication that the man could even comprehend what was being said, let alone the nightmare his short life had culminated in. The executioner stepped back, raised the sword, and with a precise but powerless swing managed to sever half of the man's head from his body. His suddenly lifeless torso fell, as if in slow motion, toward his compatriot awaiting the same fate. Then it tumbled completely off the block. The executioner took the man's head by its hair and hacked two or three times at the skin and muscle still attached – all with the cool, matter-of-fact diligence of an expert butcher.

After wiping the blood from the sword with a white cloth, he dealt the same fate to the second Pakistani. For all his talk in the Arab News interview about the years of practice it takes to get to his position as chief executioner, he botched the job again, failing to sever the head completely from the body, necessitating once again a bout of follow-up, close-quarter hacking.

An ambulance pulled up. Both heads and bodies were put on separate stretchers. As the blood was hosed down with a powerful jet of water by the local fire brigade, the loudspeakers were already urging the crowd to disperse, to the inevitable chants of 'Allahu Akbar' (God is greatest!)[24]

It is especially chilling to read in Bradley's description a medieval-style execution abetted by ambulances and fire-engines, vehicles the modern world normally entrusts with saving human lives.

As will be seen in the next chapter ('Conflicting Currents') not all the Wahhabi ulama, however privileged, are satisfied with the control they exercise over legal processes or their privileged treatment by the regime. A signal obstacle was the fatwa Ibn Baz issued after the Iraqi invasion of Kuwait, allowing the presence of 'infidel' US and international troops to defend the kingdom against a possible Muslim invader in the shape of Saddam Hussein. Religious opposition to the regime comes from two sources: from within the Wahhabi discourse the Sahwa (awakening) movement attacks the regime's corruption and departure from Islamic ideas of justice; from outside the Wahhabi discourse, Islamist radicalism, inspired by the Iranian revolution, is still a threat to the regime's hegemony.

Both present dangers that may be exacerbated by any turmoil within the ruling family in the wake of the Khashoggi murder and the humanitarian disaster in Yemen. At this writing, however, the regime maintains its control over its two main pillars of power and legitimacy: the oil wells of the Eastern Province now managed by Saudi Aramco, and the holy city of Mecca, focus of the pilgrimage to which all observant Muslims aspire.

While Saudi hegemony over the Hejaz and the two holy cities of Mecca and Medina may appear strong, the challenges are many, not least in ensuring the safety of the 3 million pilgrims who descend on Mecca every year for the annual Hajj. Here Saudi stewardship has been marred by disasters. In addition to the Siege of the Haram area in 1979, the Hajj has seen a scandalous number of fatalities. Some of these have been political or sectarian, such as an unauthorized protest by Shiite pilgrims suppressed by Saudi troops in 1987, in which some 400 people, including 275 Iranians, were killed, and an attack on the outside of the Haram in 1989 in which one person was killed, for which sixteen Kuwaiti Shias were found guilty and executed.

But most of the fatalities can be attributed to poor management of an admittedly difficult area, with its complex of physically demanding rituals. In 1990 a stampede in a tunnel near Mina after the failure of its ventilation system killed 1,426 mainly Asian pilgrims; in 1994, 270 were killed in a stampede at walkways adjacent to the ritual stoning at the Jamaraat Bridge; 1997 saw 343 pilgrims burned at the tent city of Arafat in a blaze fanned by strong winds; the pilgrimage seasons of 1998, 2001, 2005 and 2006 saw further fatalities at the Jamaraat stoning, with more than 360 pilgrims killed in 2006 and 310 killed at a stampede in 2015. The same year saw the collapse of a construction crane in the Haram area, killing 118 pilgrims and injuring almost 400. A spokesman for the Binladen Group refused to take responsibility, telling the press that 'What happened was beyond the power of humans. It was an act of God.' A similar response had come from King Fahd after the 1990 stampede: 'It was God's will, which is above everything. It was fate.'

Mustafa Akyol, one of the most astute commentators on modern Islam, argues that Fahd's statement and that of the Binladen Group spokesman were not just excuses aimed at avoiding responsibility. They are rooted in the Asharite and Hanbali theologies governing much of the Sunni world in contrast to the Mu'tazilism or rationalism prevailing among the Shia. He pointed out that after a terrible fire that killed 301 Turkish miners in 2014, Mehmet Gormez, Turkey's leading cleric, had warned his countrymen against producing excuses attributing the consequences to 'divine power' that should be levelled at human agency. 'The laws of nature', he said, 'are the laws of God. God's will is for humans to take the necessary precautions against the physical causes of disasters.'

Akyol argues that the Turkish cleric's statement was:

> Unmistakably grounded in certain medieval Islamic schools of thought, such as the Maturidis and the Mutazilites, who believed human beings possessed free will and could be 'the creator of their own deeds'. They also believed that humans could use reason to interpret scripture and establish moral truths. But such rationalist Muslim schools had powerful rivals, such as the Asharites and the even more rigid Hanbalis, the precursors of today's Salafis. These dogmatists played down human free will by emphasizing God's predestination and discredited human reason. They also denied the existence of natural laws, assuming that causality is an infringement on God's omnipotence.[25]

Akyol concludes that while 'today most Muslims have little knowledge of these ancient debates', they continue to 'live within cultural codes largely defined by the dogmatists, who gained the upper hand in the war of ideas in early Islam. In these codes, human free will is easily sacrificed to fatalism, science and reason are trivialized, and philosophy is frowned upon.'[26]

Since their accession to power in 2015, King Salman and his son have resisted giving any ground to dogmatic fatalism. At the height of the Covid-19 pandemic in 2020 the government closed the holy sites of Mecca and Medina to prevent the spread of the virus and had the precincts sterilized before reopening them only for pilgrims resident in the kingdom. The approach was consistent with the king's refusal to accept the Binladen Group's argument that the crane's collapse was an 'act of God' – the company was suspended from work, pending an investigation. Intervention, however – whether divine or royal – would have no bearing on why the crane was there in the first place. Under the Al Saud, Mecca, sacred hub of Islam, has long been a massive construction site. Discerning visitors say the holy city now resembles Las Vegas, with hotels such as the Raffles Makkah Palace and the Makkah Hilton towering over the Kaaba, the cube-shaped temple to which Muslims everywhere bow in the direction of prayer. Overlooking the Sacred Mosque stands the Mekkah Clock Royal Tower, a kitsch rendition of London's Big Ben around five times as high – and now one of the world's tallest buildings.

Wealthy Gulf pilgrims are expected to pay premium prices for rooms and apartments in these skyscrapers, as part of the effort to balance declining oil revenues. Even the historical legacy of the Prophet Muhammad is not immune from the corrosive effects of an unholy alliance between real estate vandalism and Wahhabi iconoclasm, which regards any veneration of the Prophet (as distinct from the worship of God) as forbidden idolatry. The site believed to have been occupied by the home of Khadija, Muhammad's first wife, where he received his first revelations and where five of his children were born, is now occupied by a row of public toilets.

Before his assassination by a nephew in 1975 (see Chapter 6) King Faisal authorized a Hajj Research Centre in Jeddah. This institution, established by the Saudi architect Sami Angawi in 1974, was intended to rescue Islam's holiest city from an onslaught of developers while accommodating the increase in pilgrims from around 200,000 in the late 1950s to more than 800,000 in the mid-1970s. Despite receiving formal legal recognition, Angawi's project for a carefully calibrated development in the vicinity of the Sacred Mosque, with the holy

Kaaba at its centre, met with resistance from the real estate developers, including members of the vast and parasitic ruling family. So the project never got off the ground. As Ziauddin Sardar, the British writer who worked at the centre in the 1970s, explained:

> Astronomical sums of money were being poured into making Mecca look like Houston, where many of the government ministers had spent time pursuing higher studies. There was a 'master plan for the Holy City of Mecca' but it was never adhered to as a guide for developers, and Western consultants were producing ever more grandiose plans of a damaging nature. If implemented these plans would level the mountains, introduce skyscrapers and rip apart the very fabric of the Sacred City. The challenge facing Mecca, Angawi declared, was to synthesise tradition and modernity, and thus to 'fit the variables into the constants'.[27]

Angawi lost his battle. As Sardar describes it, 'the skyline above the Sacred Mosque is no longer dominated by the rugged outline of the encircling mountains.' It is surrounded instead by the brutalism of rectangular steel and concrete buildings resembling the 'downtown office blocks in any mid-American city'.

Though Saudi officials have argued that the building is necessary to accommodate the increasing numbers of pilgrims, now approaching 3 million each year, the motives are largely financial. As Angawi told the *New York Times* in 2010, 'it is the commercialization of the house of God ... the closer to the mosque, the more expensive the apartments. In the most expensive towers, you can pay millions for a 25-year leasing agreement. If you can see the mosque, you pay triple.'[28]

Critics see the holy city, where the shared experience of pilgrimage induces a feeling of common humanity, as being fractured by divisions of wealth and class, with the rich sealed inside exclusive air-conditioned high-rises encircling the Grand Mosque and the poor pushed increasingly to the periphery. With a few honourable exceptions, such as Angawi himself, the Meccans, according to Sardar, have only one true love which is wealth.

Ironically Sardar's critique of Meccan commercialism and real-estate corruption echoes the criticism Ibn Saud made of Hejazi greed and corruption during the era of Hashemite rule. In the holy city the vision of brotherhood and equality exemplified in the Hajj ceremonies is conspicuous by its absence. As Sardar now sees it, Mecca is not so much a city as an un-integrated collection of villages that are 'riddled with racism, bigotry and xenophobia'. In short, he concludes, the sacred city is a microcosm of today's Muslim world. 'What happens in Mecca not only reverberates throughout Muslim societies, but it also actually defines the state of Muslim civilization.'[29]

On 19 October 2018, less than three weeks after the Khashoggi murder, Sheikh Abdulrahman al-Sudais, the officially appointed imam of the Grand Mosque in Mecca, delivered his Friday sermon from a written script. According to Khaled Abou el-Fadl, professor of law at the University of California, Los Angeles (UCLA), and a world-class authority on Islamic affairs, such sermons 'carry a great deal of moral and religious authority' being broadcast live on cable networks and social media sites and 'watched with great reverence by Muslims everywhere'. In his sermon the imam referenced the same hadith that Juhayman had used, according to which Muhammad is reported as saying: 'Once every century, God sends a *mujaddid*, a great reformer or renovator to reclaim or reinvigorate the faith.'

It would not, however, be Juhayman or his deceased friend the 'Mahdi' Muhammad al-Qahtani who was to be this century's great renovator capable of addressing 'the unique challenges of this era' but King Salman's beloved son, Crown Prince Mohammed bin Salman.

As the imam declared, from the pulpit where Prophet Muhammad is supposed to have delivered his last sermon:

> The path of reform and modernization in this blessed land ... through the care and attention from its young, ambitious, divinely inspired reformer crown prince, continues to blaze forward guided by his vision of innovation and insightful modernism, despite all the failed pressures and threats.[30]

Invoking the arguments that followed the Khashoggi murder in the office of the Saudi consul in Istanbul, Turkey – a crime which the normally reticent CIA attributed directly to Crown Prince Mohammed bin Salman, Imam Sudais warned Muslims against believing ill-intended media rumours and innuendos that sought to cast doubt on this new great Muslim leader. Such rumours, he implied, were part of the web of conspiracies against the prince, plots aimed at destroying the whole of Islam and all Muslims. 'All threats against his modernizing reforms are bound not only to fail, but will threaten international security, peace and stability', warned the imam.[31]

El-Fadl notes that since coming to power the crown prince has imprisoned hundreds of prominent Saudi imams who have shown even a modicum of resistance – including very prominent and influential jurists such as Sheikh Saleh al-Talib and Sheikh Bandar bin Aziz Bilila, former imams of the Grand Mosque itself. Saudi prosecutors have even sought the death penalty for Salman al-Awdah, the prominent member of the al-Sahwa group who was arrested in September 2018 (see Chapter 6). At this writing (October 2024) Saudi Arabia has been executing people at a record rate. In July and August alone there were 80 executions, making 2024, with 215 executions, the bloodiest in the Kingdom's modern history. A 2023 report by Reprieve and the European Saudi Organisation for Human Rights showed that since January 2015, when Crown Prince Mohammed bin Salman achieved de facto power, the annual rate of executions has doubled, with the execution of 1,459 people thus far. In 2024, despite its active lobbying efforts, the Kingdom failed to regain the seat on the United Nations Human Rights Council it lost in 2020. In his conclusion, el-Fadl says that 'by using the Grand Mosque to whitewash acts of despotism and oppression' such as the Khashoggi murder, Prince Mohammed has placed in question the 'very legitimacy of the Saudi control and guardianship of the holy places of Mecca and Medina'.[32]

While the imam's sermon certainly invited some outrage and ridicule on social media, it does not seem to have seriously dented the crown prince's appeal among Saudi youth. Who cares about a Saudi royal appropriating the Prophet's hadith about renovators, when the holy city of Mecca – Islam's answer to Rome – is a magnificent glittering imitation of Las Vegas?

6
Conflicting Currents

Saudi Arabia's path to modernity was never going to be smooth. When television was introduced in 1965, it was opposed by most of the Wahhabi ulama, who regarded any representation of the human form as *haram* (forbidden), even though there was strict censorship against showing people drinking alcohol or men and women in situations that might violate rules of gender segregation. The first transmission triggered violent protests, including an attack on a TV station in Riyadh in which no less a person than Prince Khalid ibn Musa'id, a grandson of Abd al-Aziz, was shot by a policeman. Ten years later Khalid's younger brother Faisal, who had been a student in Berkeley, California, and may have been into drugs, avenged his brother's death by murdering their uncle King Faisal, the most able of the sons of Ibn Saud. Despite ulama protests, TV stations were introduced in Medina, Mecca, Taif, Buraydah and Dammam.[1]

The regime sought to contain the ambiguities and disruptions of the two-track legal system described in the previous chapter by establishing a Higher Judicial Council to supervise procedures and judicial appointments, with a special office (Dar al-Ifta) that issued fatwas (legal opinions) under the authority of the chief mufti. Prior to his death in 1969, the then chief mufti Muhammad ibn Ibrahim ibn

Abd al-Latif gave his backing to using the media in order to counter nationalist propaganda from Nasser's Egypt which threatened both the Saudi dynasty and the Wahhabi establishment.

The ideological counter-attack to Nasser's mix of nationalism, republicanism and socialism entailed Saudi funding for pan-Islamic organizations, such as the World Muslim League founded in 1962 and the World Assembly of Muslim Youth founded in 1972 which promoted versions of Sunnism close to the Wahhabi outlook. It included groups such as Deobandis, Ahl-e-Hadith and Jamaati Islami in South Asia. All these movements aimed to combat Sufism, liberal and esoteric versions of Islam such as Ismailism or groups considered heretical such as the Ahmadiyya sect, along with attacks on religious syncretism and popular religious practices.

The World Muslim League sent missionaries to West Africa, where it funded schools, distributed religious literature and provided scholarships for Saudi universities, such as the Islamic University of Medina. The Saudi outreach abroad entailed some loosening of Wahhabi doctrines with input from other currents that can loosely be described as conservative and reactionary. While petrodollars provided much of the fuel for this momentum, it would be a mistake to see it as uniformly Wahhabist in inspiration or delivery. The Salafist tendency outlined in Chapter 2 was certainly the beneficiary of Saudi largesse, at the expense of Shia or Sufi tendencies and orientations. As Roel Meijer suggests,[2] Wahhabism's contribution to Salafism involved increasing its xenophobic tendencies, by framing the struggle for piety in terms of distance, not to say enmity, towards outsiders. Ibn Baz, for example, said that Muslims should withhold greetings such as *salam aleikum* ('peace be upon you') from non-believers, an attitude rooted in the imperative of *wala wa'l-bara* ('loyalty and disavowal').[3] As a social attitude, rather than an articulated political doctrine, the Salafist approach may resonate in a variety of different contexts. In Indonesia, pious-minded worshippers known as *santris* differentiate themselves from the more syncretic *abangan*, whose ritual observance has absorbed some Hindu influences. In the European *banlieues*, Muslim migrants who find themselves having to mix with infidels adopt a Salafi lifestyle that allows them to feel 'good about themselves' or even superior when shopping or riding on public transport.[4]

Many Salafist tendencies are explicitly non-political, based on the believer's duty to obey governments that rule in accordance with sharia, and such a quietist approach can include Salafists living as minorities, where pietistic displays such as veiling and beards can be adopted – and seen – as 'lifestyle choices'. However, as the siege of Mecca demonstrated, the original quietism of a group that follows the injunction to accept the political status quo can easily morph into armed rebellion. As Meijer suggests, the more a group concentrates on religious knowledge and purity of belief, the greater tension with reality it encounters, a trajectory that may lead it to criticize the political establishment as deviant, corrupt and un-Islamic. 'Political *takfir* [anathematization] is a monster that mainstream Salafism desperately tries to keep in its cage while other currents within the movement have done their best to let it escape.'[5]

Examples that come to mind include two major movements – the Muslim Brotherhood and Tablighi Jamat – that are not usually described as 'Salafist' in the formal sense, but which share important 'family resemblances' with the Salafist outlook. Both have been major recipients of Saudi patronage.

The Muslim Brotherhood, founded in Egypt in 1928 by the schoolteacher Hasan al-Banna (1906–49), was a movement influenced by some reformist ideas of Muhammed Abduh and his more conservative disciple Rashid Rida (1865–1935). After the 1924 massacre of Taif (see p. 85 above), Rida found himself unable to condemn Ibn

Saud's Wahhabi fanatics, arguing that such actions 'happened in all wars and were generally the result of mistakes or personal grudges'.[6] Ibn Saud's victories drew scholars to the Saudi kingdom even before the money it obtained from oil enabled it to develop its formidable network of transnational proselytism through organizations such as the World Muslim League and World Assembly of Muslim Youth. From the 1970s the purist version of Salafism exported from Saudi Arabia spread throughout the world, overshadowing earlier versions regarded as more 'rationalist' or 'renewalist' in orientation.

Saudi patronage of pan-Islamic movements entailed some compromise with strict Wahhabi doctrine. The Muslim Brotherhood's founder, Hasan al-Banna, was connected to the Hasafiyya Sufi brotherhood, a mainstream or 'orthodox' mystical order. They believed in dreams and the power of prayer while rejecting the ecstatic displays of other Sufi orders. Al-Banna, however, shared some Wahhabi views. He was intolerant of what he saw as 'deviations from the "straight path"' of Islamic practice and expressed disgust at lifestyles and types of behaviour he saw as having been introduced by Europeans.

The Brotherhood, which he launched in 1928, was a blend of the traditional and the modern. While its organization drew on the traditional structure of the Sufi order dominated by a leader or spiritual guide, with followers graded according to their understanding of spiritual practices and esoteric knowledge, the content entailed a thoroughly this-world agenda, addressing the issues of the day:

> Islam is worship and leadership, religion and state, spirituality and action, prayer and jihad, obedience and government, the books and the sword. None of these can be separated. God will subdue with might what cannot be subdued through the Quran ... We are at war with every party leader, party chief or organization that does not work to support Islam and does not move to restore the rule and glory of Islam.[7]

The Egyptian leader Abd al-Nasser's suppression of the Brotherhood, after a very brief honeymoon that followed the coup that brought the Free Officers to power in 1952, was prompted by an unsuccessful attempt on his life at a public meeting in Alexandria. During a long period of exile in Saudi Arabia and the Gulf, Brotherhood survivors benefited from the political patronage provided by conservative monarchies threatened by Nasser's republican nationalism, and especially from the patronage they received from the Saudi crown prince, and later king, Faisal, who saw the Brotherhood as a bulwark against the spread of Nasserism, communism and socialism in the Middle East. As Stéphane Lacroix explains:

> Faisal understood the necessity of not surrendering the ideological arena to a master of propaganda like Nasser. To confront Nasser's pan-Arab socialism, he had to make Islam, the kingdom's chief symbolic resource, into a counter-ideology, but the very traditional Wahhabi ulema were quite incapable of engaging in a political debate of this magnitude. Thus the members of the Muslim Brotherhood in Saudi Arabia were increasingly brought into the anti-Nasser propaganda apparatus and became its core by 1962. No one but these experienced Islamists, sometimes themselves Nasser's victims, was in a better position to denounce the 'ungodliness' of his secular government and to use Islam as a weapon against it.[8]

Brotherhood scholars who benefited from Saudi patronage included Selim Azzam, long-time chair of the Islamic Council of Europe prior to his death in 2008, and Muhammad Qutb, young brother of Sayyid Qutb, the Brotherhood's leading intellectual who was executed by Nasser in 1966. Muhammad taught at the Umm al-Qura University in Mecca after his release from prison in Egypt and at the King Abd al-Aziz University in Jeddah, where Osama bin Laden attended his lectures.[9] The Palestinian brother Abdullah al-Azzam, the leading Arab proponent for the jihad in Afghanistan after the Soviet invasion in 1979, also found refuge in the kingdom. Azzam, who judged the jihad against communism as a *fard ayn* (an obligation like prayer and fasting incumbent on individuals), became bin Laden's mentor in Peshawar, Pakistan, where he used bin Laden's money to create the Maktab al-Khidamat (Office of Services) that would evolve into the al-Qaeda organization.[10]

In addition to making available his brother's work, Muhammad Qutb worked to advance his ideas by smoothing away differences between Sayyid's radical supporters and more conservative Muslims. Muhammad took a less radical view of *jahiliyya*, the condition of ignorance classically applied to pre-Islamic Arabs that Sayyid Qutb – adapting the discourse of the South Asian writer Abu Ala al-Maududi – had applied to contemporary Muslim governments. Denying – not unreasonably – that the kingdom that had given him refuge could be regarded as part of the *jahiliyya*, Muhammad Qutb came out against *takfir*, working actively to reconcile the doctrine of the Muslim Brotherhood with the more traditional Salafism that prevailed in his host country.

Perhaps the most significant contribution made by Brotherhood exiles and by the Saudis who engaged with them was in education. Lacroix remarks that:

> since the late 1960s hundreds of the movement's grassroots militants had permeated the various levels of the Saudi educational system, where they taught all subjects, religious and secular [and] ... made up the bulk of the personnel in the religious secondary schools, called Scientific Institutes (*ma'ahid ilmiyya*) of which there were 27 in the kingdom in 1970.[11]

Brothers who taught at the Institutes included Sa'id Hawwa, ideologue of the Syrian Muslim Brotherhood whose book *Soldiers of*

God: Culture and Morals (1979) would become essential reading for Islamists throughout the region. Members of groups who taught at the Institutes without being directly connected to the Brotherhood included the blind Sheikh Umar Abd al-Rahman who authorized the assassination of Egyptian president Anwar Sadat in 1981. Sheikh Umar died in a US prison in February 2017 after serving a life sentence in the US for the bomb attack on the World Trade Center in New York in 1993.

The overlap between Wahhabism and the more reformist-oriented Brotherhood is also evident in the adoption by both of *hisba*, the duty of 'commanding good and forbidding wrong' which can merge with vigilantism if suitably encouraged. Al-Banna had exhibited an air of rectitude during his youth in the Nile Delta, informing the police against boat-builders who carved prows with female forms and denouncing villagers who failed to observe the Ramadan fast. His holier-than-thou approach may have been softened to some degree by his membership of one of the mystical Sufi brotherhoods. But he was intolerant of rulers who had 'brought their half-naked women into these regions, their liquors, their theatres, their dance halls, their entertainments, their stories, their newspapers, their romances, their phantasies, their frivolous pastimes and their insolent jokes'.[12] Although they diverged from the Brotherhood in terms of leadership and organization, the *jama'a al-Islamiyya* (Islamic associations) that came to the fore in Egyptian Universities and professional associations in the 1970s shared al-Banna's view that piety entailed a struggle against 'moral corruption'. In Egypt, members of associations disrupted musical performances and Western film shows and attacked other forms of 'corruption', such as Christian liquor stores, video shops and male and female mixing.

Inside Saudi Arabia, and especially in Riyadh, the duty of *hisba* ('commanding the good and forbidding the evil') had been entrusted to the Committee for the Promotion of Virtue and Prohibition of Vice since the 1920s. Dubbed the 'religious police' by Westerners or *al-mutawi'a* or *al-hay'a* (the 'Committee') by Saudis and Arab residents, its duties included enforcing strict gender segregation and female dress codes, ensuring that shops and businesses were shut during prayer times, and preventing public displays of behaviours they considered un-Islamic, such as playing music.

In the 1970s and 1980s Saudi patronage of the Muslim Brotherhood and like-minded movements, such as the Jama'at al-Sunna al-muhammadiyya in Egypt and Deobandi movement in Pakistan that underpinned the 'Islamization' measures of General Zia-ul-Haq (1924–88), became closely allied to the country's foreign policy – a momentum that reversed dramatically after the Iraqi invasion of Kuwait in 1990 which the Brotherhood supported as did the Palestinian leader Yasser Arafat.

The Brotherhood's pan-Islamic militancy had originally been forged in the conflict over Jewish settlement in Palestine. In the mid-1930s, long before it became a major player in Egyptian politics, it had taken a 'leading role in mobilizing public support for the Palestinian Arabs by issuing publications and organizing special events'.[13] After 1945 the conflict grew sharper, with survivors of Hitler's genocide landing in Palestine and joining the Jewish militias. During the first Israeli–Arab war of 1948, Brotherhood volunteers fought alongside Egyptian troops in the southern Negev, earning the respect of many Egyptian officers, including Nasser.

Much of the opposition to Jewish settlement had sound territorial reasons, given the experience of ethnic cleansing suffered by Palestinians during and after the war, which Israelis call their War of Independence and Arabs call the *nakba* – the 'catastrophe'. There were, however, deep-rooted 'Judaeophobic' tropes in Islamic history that could be drawn upon, despite episodes of Jewish achievement and success in Muslim lands, such as the time when the exilarch – leader of the large and prosperous Jewish community in Baghdad – occupied an honoured seat next to the caliph in a resplendent vision described by the Spanish–Jewish traveller Benjamin of Tudela (1130–73).

The Quran informs the faithful that, like the Christians, the Children of Israel distorted the true teachings revealed by their prophets – teachings that Muhammad had been sent by God to restore and correct. According to a document known as the Constitution of Medina preserved in the earliest account of the Prophet's life, Muslim emigrants from Mecca and their helpers in Medina formed an alliance with three Jewish tribes against the Meccan Quraish who had rejected Muhammad's message. After the Battle of the Ditch, however, when the Muslims repelled the Quraishite attack, Muhammad accused one of the Jewish tribes, the Banu Qurayzah, of treachery, endorsing the massacre of their men and the enslavement of their women (a standard practice at that time).

Martin Kramer (an Israeli scholar who can hardly be regarded as biased towards Arabs or Muslims) rejects the idea that the supposed betrayal (communicated to the Prophet supernaturally) became the source of a type of generic hostility towards Jews that we have come to call antisemitism. According to Kramer:

> Islamic tradition did not hold up those Jews who practiced treachery against Muhammad as archetypes – as the embodiment of Jews in all times and places. This makes for a striking contrast with a certain Christian concept of the eternal Jew, who forever bears the mark of the betrayer of Jesus. The Qur'an also includes certain verses which attest to the Prophet's amicable relations with some Jews, and while religious supremacism always coloured the traditional Islamic view of the Jews, it also coloured the Islamic view of Christians and all

other non-Muslims. In the Islamic tradition, the Jews are regarded as members of a legitimate community of believers in God, 'people of the Book,' legally entitled to sufferance. The overall record of Islamic civilization's tolerance of Jews is not a bad one, especially when compared with the record of Christendom in most periods.[14]

If there is a theological basis to strands of contemporary Muslim antisemitism that seems to be current in places ranging from western Europe to central Asia and even the Americas, it is suggested by Kramer's concept of 'religious supremacism', based on the doctrine that Islam corrects or supersedes the previous revelations of Judaism and Christianity. This idea may be complemented by what I have called the 'argument from manifest success', according to which the early conquests of Islam from central France to the borders of China were proofs of divine favour and a vindication of Islam's 'supercessionist' doctrine. The argument from manifest success worked well during periods of historical triumph, but became highly problematic when the vast majority of the world's Muslims became the subjects of 'Christian' nations whose religion was supposed to have been 'superseded' by the revelation of Islam. In this context the scandal of a Jewish state occupying Arab lands extends beyond objections to the 'colonial' appropriation of a territory assumed to belong to others and their expulsion or dispossession (issues that concern Israel's non-Muslim critics as well as its Muslim opponents). The idea that the presence of Israel is a violation of the cosmic order, rather than just a dispute about land, renders Islamists highly susceptible to antisemitic ideas imported from Europe, and it is clear that Saudis, Wahhabis and Muslim Brothers found common ground in promoting and exporting them.

Sayyid Qutb, the Brotherhood's leading intellectual, was a rabid antisemite. His tract *Our Struggle with the Jews* (thought to have been written in the 1950s, although there is no date of publication) was reprinted and disseminated in the 1970s by the Saudi government as part of a collection of his essays.

Like other Islamist writings, Qutb's diatribe against the Jews claims to be based exclusively on original Islamic sources, including the Quran and the hadith reports that form the base of the literary-canonical tradition of Islam. There is no explicit reference in his tract to antisemitic literature imported from Europe, although it is well known that this literature — notably the *Protocols of the Learned Elders of Zion* — has been reproduced uncritically in the Arab world since the 1930s. (I myself was presented with a copy by a Jordanian army officer in 1972, who clearly saw the tract as 'proof' of Jewish perfidy.) Ronald Nettler, a British scholar who has translated and analysed Qutb's pamphlet, is in no doubt that Qutb was conversant with the *Protocols*.[15] The Saudi editor of the 1970 edition, Zayn al-Din al-Rakkabi, makes numerous quotations from the notorious tsarist forgery in order to demonstrate the correctness of Qutb's views.

For an insight into the style of thinking that leads to attacks on Jewish schoolchildren or the desecration of Jewish cemeteries, when these have been perpetrated by angry young Muslims rather than neo-Nazis, one need look no further than Qutb's pernicious tract. His ideas — like those contained in Hitler's *Mein Kampf* or the *Protocols of the Learned Elders of Zion* — have been diffused far beyond the circles of those who have actually read the text. As the official US report into the events of 11 September 2001 recognized, they are present in the attacks on 'Jews and Crusaders' by Osama bin Laden and his colleagues, as broadcast by Al Jazeera, as well as in the bloody attack on Jews from pulpits in Gaza, whose Hamas government references the *Protocols* in its charter.

There can be little doubt that Qutb's abandonment of liberalism and rejection of the Western culture, to which he had initially been attracted, was motivated in part by his sympathy for the Palestinians and the trauma of the defeat of the Arab armies by the Haganah – the Jewish army in Palestine – in 1948. There is very little in his pamphlet, however, to indicate that his attitude towards 'the Jews' (not some Jews, or even particular currents such as Zionism within the variety of Jewish traditions) is conditioned by recent political events. As a 'born-again' Muslim he relies entirely on religious rhetoric derived from the Quran, a feature that would make his discourse acceptable to Saudi editors who, interestingly, are the ones to demonstrate his consistency with mainstream 'European antisemitism'. Nor is there any discernible attempt to analyse the causes of Arab defeat, or to explain to his readers where 'the Jews' might be coming from. The only allusion to the Nazi genocide is a laconic reference to one of many divine punishments meted out for Jewish obduracy: 'Then Allah brought Hitler to rule over them': the Nazi dictator, far from being the personification of evil, is the instrument of Allah's will.[16]

In Qutb's analysis, Jews are inherently decadent and anti-religious. They are actually worse than the idolaters fought by Muhammad, since they are cunningly able to undermine and destroy Islam, the only true religion, from within. During Muhammad's struggles in Medina, they joined the 'hypocrites' in resisting his divine authority and made treacherous alliances with the polytheists.

According to Qutb, the current leaders who have been foisted on the Muslim community in the guise of 'heroes' (one assumes that he may be referring here to some of the Arab leaders, possibly even Nasser himself) have been manufactured by Zionism for its own purposes. Here the Saudi editor helpfully appends a footnote quoting directly from the Arabic translation of the *Tenth Protocol of the Elders of Zion*: 'In the near future we shall make the president someone who is accountable (to us). At that time we will never again be hesitant in boldly affecting our plans, which this person as our "effigy" will be responsible for.'[17]

Apart from the explicit references to the *Protocols* by the Saudi editor, it is interesting to see if there are discernible Nazi influences in the text. At face value there is an important difference between the concept of Jewishness decried by Qutb and Nazi ideas of Jewish racial inferiority. Qutb's essentialist Jew is a malevolent moral agent responsible for Islamic decline as distinct from the 'parasite among nations' described by Hitler in *Mein Kampf*. The difference, however, is only superficial. In basic character, Hitler's and Qutb's Jews are both deceivers. For Hitler the Jew 'is obliged to conceal his own particular character and mode of life that he may be allowed to continue his existence as a parasite among the nations. The greater the intelligence of the individual Jew, the better will he succeed in deceiving others.'[18]

For Qutb: 'One Jew confides only in another ... Then they make a great display – some of them at least – of the very opposite of what they really want and what they are plotting.'[19] For Hitler, the Jew aims to bring about the destruction of the state by economic sabotage. For Qutb it is Islam itself that the Jew aims to destroy. Both ideologues attribute the predicament of their respective societies to the evil machinations of the Jew. For Hitler the 'Jew uses every possible means to undermine the racial foundations of a subjugated people' by seducing German girls and 'bringing Negroes into the Rhineland'.[20] For Qutb it was a Jewish convert who instigated the assassination of Uthman, the third caliph, in 656 CE, which brought about the schisms from which Islam has never recovered. For Hitler and his followers, Marxism is a 'weapon in the hand of the Jew', which fills the German people with fear.[21]

Qutb expands this malevolent intellectual legacy to embrace Sigmund Freud and Emile Durkheim: 'Behind the doctrine of atheistic materialism was a "Jew"; behind the doctrine of animalistic sexuality was a Jew; and behind the destruction of the family and the shattering of sacred relationships in society ... was a Jew' – to which the Saudi editor adds the inaccurate note: 'These three are, in order, Marx, Freud and Durkheim. Additionally, behind the literature of decadence and ruin was a Jew – Jean Paul Sartre' (who, of course, was not Jewish but a Frenchman born in the contested Franco-German province of Alsace).

One could extend the analogies further, on many points of detail. Both writers regard the Jews as fundamentally cowardly and responsible for all the symptoms of cultural, moral and political decline afflicting their societies. The principle difference between them is that Hitler describes this decline in political and secular terms, and above all in terms of 'race', while Qutb sees secularism itself – and the whole legacy of Enlightenment thought he regarded as 'corrupting' his society – as the result of Jewish machinations.

Judging from Saudi sponsorship of the *Protocols*, there seems little doubt that Muslim antisemitism owes much to Saudi dissemination. Olivier Roy has noted the evolution of the image of the Jew in Afghanistan where *mujahidin* rebels who fought the Soviet occupation after 1979 became recipients of generous Saudi as well as covert US aid. 'Before the war in Afghanistan', wrote Roy in 1995, 'the Pakhtun tribes boasted of being descended from a lost tribe of Israel; during the war, many traditionalist mullahs could be heard extolling the virtues of the Torah (in opposition, of course, to the atheist communists), but today many Afghan neo-fundamentalists harp on the Zionist plot.'[22] As Martin Kramer observed:

> If, in the highlands of Afghanistan, the Pakhtuns are having second thoughts about their descent, I think this speaks volumes about the extent of antisemitism in Muslim lands, and particularly its dissemination by

Islamists. The existence of a Jewish conspiracy against Islam is integral to the Islamist ideology, not tangential. Everywhere that ideology is preached, everywhere it is embraced, the conspiracy of the Jews is included in the package, which is to say that we should hardly be surprised when it surfaces even in the most unlikely places in Asia and Africa.[23]

The dissemination of antisemitic ideas imported from Europe is far from being confined to places close to the Palestine conflict or to regions such as Afghanistan where Muslims find themselves in conflicts with forces, whether Russian or Western, that can be imagined as belonging to the Judaeo-Christian enemy. The King Fahd Academy in London, a Saudi-funded private school patronized by Muslims residing in Britain including many Arab diplomats, had the following reference to the *Protocols* in a first-grade high-school textbook:

> *Protocols of the Elders of Zion*: It is a secret document which is thought to come out of 'the conference of Bal.' [sic] It was revealed in the nineteenth century. The Jews tried to deny its existence, but there is a great deal of evidence which proves its existence and the fact that its source was indeed the Elders of Zion. We can summarise the content of the protocols with these points:
>
> 1 To shake the foundation of the current world society and its system of governing, in order to allow Zionism to exclusively rule the world.
> 2 The destruction of Nationalism and religions, especially the Christian nations.
> 3 To work towards increasing the corruption of the current governing European regimes, for Zionism believes in their corruption and elimination.
> 4 Controlling of media, propaganda, and newspaper venues. Using gold to instigate instabilities. Tempting the masses with physical pleasures and spreading pornography.

> The indisputable evidence of the truth of the existence of these Protocols and their contents of the hell-raising Jewish plans is: the fact that a lot of the schemes, conspiracies, and instigations found in it have been implemented. Although it was written in the nineteenth century, it will become clear to anyone who reads it the extent of how many of its articles have been implemented.[24]

Nazi-style antisemitism is far from being the only product of Saudi outreach. To look at a different area, 'creationism' – a pseudo-scientific doctrine patronized by American Christian fundamentalists – also has its place. Evolutionary biology can be seen as something of a litmus test in the struggle for modernization. The Saudi regime has ambitious plans for healthcare, with modern hospitals serving the whole population with state-of-the-art facilities. The programme also includes an important research element, comprising a molecular diagnostics and personalized therapeutics unit (MDPTU) based at the University of Hail. Established in 2013, the unit is intended to serve as an example of the progressive research that is being conducted in the kingdom. According to Oxford Business Group, the MDPTU infrastructure includes:

> high-throughput DNA sequencing platforms that can perform genomic analysis, namely sequencing, genotype processing and bioinformatics. The unit should help gather the critical mass and expertise necessary to strengthen the competitiveness of the Kingdom's health care sector and attract large international projects. This research is being done in Hail in collaboration with Cambridge and Nottingham universities. In addition, the MDPTU was selected as one of the centres for the Saudi Genome Project to help in identification of hereditary diseases in the northern region of Saudi Arabia.[25]

On reading this and similar promotional texts one wonders if molecular research into the Saudi genome can be undertaken by Saudis who have been through an educational system that explicitly bans the teaching of evolution. As Theodosius Dobzhansky, the Ukrainian-born biologist and a practising Orthodox Christian, stated in a famous 1973 essay in which he explicitly attacked Ibn Baz's pre-Copernican views, 'Nothing in Biology Makes Sense Except in the Light of Evolution.'

> It is a blunder to mistake the Holy Scriptures for elementary textbooks of astronomy, geology, biology, and anthropology. Only if symbols are construed to mean what they are not intended to mean can there arise imaginary, insoluble conflicts ... the blunder leads to blasphemy: the Creator is accused of systematic deceitfulness.[26]

In an overview of the teaching of evolution in different parts of the world, including India, China and Japan, Rasmus Nielsen of the University of California at Berkeley notes that the teaching of evolution in those countries has been largely uncontroversial, with the possible exception of certain Darwinian ideas during the Cultural Revolution in China. The same by and large applies to Europe and to Latin America, especially after the 1996 declaration of Pope John Paul II that 'new knowledge has led to the recognition of the theory of evolution as more than a hypothesis'. Pockets of resistance remain in the United States, where school boards dominated by protestant fundamentalists have obliged teachers to explain the controversies surrounding 'ideas of evolution' rather than evolution as such.

However, the main exception to this picture, according to Nielsen, is the Middle East and North Africa, including relatively secular countries such as Turkey. In these places, culture wars over evolution, reminiscent of those that occurred in the US during the 1970s and 1980s, are currently raging, thanks to a contradictory blend of influences comprising Salafi literalism and 'creation science' exported from the US. According to Nielsen, the most egregious example of anti-evolution teaching is to be found in Saudi Arabia, where evolution is not mentioned in education texts, except in the more advanced biology course in twelfth grade or senior year (usually age seventeen or eighteen). Here it is introduced as 'a fallacious and blasphemous theory', with the following preamble:

> Nevertheless in the West appeared what is called 'the theory of evolution' which was derived by the Englishman Charles Darwin, who denied Allah's creation of humanity, saying that all living things and humans are from a single origin. We do not need to pursue such a theory because we have in the Book of Allah the final say regarding the origin of life, that all living things are Allah's creation.[27]

'One might wonder', Nielsen asks, 'how it is possible to provide more advanced biology education while altogether avoiding the topic of evolution.'

Nielsen also makes the important observation that Iran, the kingdom's regional rival which is opposed by many Western governments in contrast to the support they give to their 'ally' Saudi Arabia, stands at the opposite end of the spectrum when it comes to the teaching of evolution. He cites an analysis by the researcher Elise K. Burton of a standard biology textbook used in Iranian high schools:

> The evolution chapter, divided into three sections, provides a comprehensive introduction to the development of evolutionary theory, with the first section devoted primarily to Darwin and his influences and culminating in the formulation of the new synthesis; the second section to evidence of evolution, including palaeontology, molecular and structural homology, and embryology, with discussion of evolutionary rates and punctuated equilibrium; and the third section to examples of

natural selection, such as peppered moths and the work of Peter and Rosemary Grant on Darwin's finches.[28]

The high-school teaching of evolution in Iran, Nielsen concludes, appears to be on a par with the education in most countries in Europe, the Americas and East Asia. This will come as no surprise to anyone even modestly conversant with Shiite theology. Whereas the counter-rationalist Hanbalis and Asharites (see p. 134 above) regard natural laws as subject to the will of an omnipotent deity who maintains the capacity to transcend them supernaturally, the Shia have been strongly influenced by the rationalism of the Mu'tazila – the early intellectual tradition Wahhabis regard as heretical. Unlike the clerics who still hold some sway in the Saudi kingdom, the ayatollahs of Iran have no problem incorporating evolution into their vision of a divinely appointed natural order.

7
A Sectarian Outreach

As already suggested, it would be wrong to argue that Wahhabi outreach with its vast funding capacities is narrowly sectarian: it would be better to describe it as 'broadly traditional' or perhaps 'broadly sectarian' in the sense that it supports Islamic movements that like itself are hostile to Shiism and to more mystically oriented traditions within the Sunni fold such as the more majoritarian Barelwi movement in Indo-Pakistan. A leading beneficiary of Saudi largesse has been the 'Society for Propagation', Tablighi Jamaat (TJ) – one of the world's largest pan-Islamic organizations.

Beginning in pre-partition India in 1926, its founder Maulana Muhammad Ilyas started his mission among Meo cultivators in the Mewat region south of Delhi. Although regarded as Muslims, the Meos followed a number of Hindu practices such as walking around fires at weddings and celebrating Hindu festivals in the same way they celebrated Muslim festivals. Influenced by the reformist Deobandi movement, which was equally opposed to syncretism, the Tablighi movement grew ever stronger after the partition of India and now has a following estimated at between 12 and 80 million, ranged across 150 countries. Like other Muslim *da'wa* (evangelical) organizations, TJ has been a recipient of Saudi largesse. Its headquarters in the United Kingdom, the Markazi Masjid at Dewsbury in West Yorkshire, one of the largest mosques in Europe with a capacity of 4,000 worshippers, was built with Saudi money. The Masjid also houses an Islamic Institute of Education and independently funded boarding school for boys aged thirteen to nineteen.

While critics will claim TJ preaches Wahhabism, this is not strictly accurate. The grand mufti Abd al-Aziz ibn Baz took a somewhat nuanced view in his 1998 fatwa, when he stated that because of some 'innovations' and 'deviations' in its teaching, TJ preachers should always be accompanied by Wahhabi brothers to 'guide and advise them'.[1] While two distinguished scholars of Islam, Olivier Roy and the South Asian specialist Barbara Metcalf, regard TJ as completely 'apolitical and law-abiding', security experts in France, the UK and the US have seen it as an 'antechamber of fundamentalism' where Tablighis preach 'a creed that is hardly distinguishable from the radical Wahhabi-Salafi-jihadist ideology that so many terrorists share'.[2] As Alex Alexiev puts it, 'While Wahhabis are dismissive of other Islamic schools, they single out Tablighi Jamaat for praise, even if they disagree with some of its practices, such as willingness to pray in mosques housing graves.' Like the South Asian Deobandi movement from which it derives, TJ has been the recipient not just of Saudi largesse, but of the full panoply of Saudi-Wahhabi teachings about Islam and other religions.

In 2007 a British scholar Denis MacEoin published a controversial report on the state of Islam in Britain for Policy Exchange, a conservative think-tank. Given the fact that the majority of Muslims in Britain have roots in South Asia, MacEoin addressed the ongoing rift between two major South Asian Islamic traditions, the mystically inclined Barelwis who, while orthodox in discourse, include some Sufi-style rituals in their religious practices, and the Deobandis, whose style has much closer affinities with Wahhabism.

In Pakistan, he asserts, the non-Pashtun population is predominantly Barelwi, with Punjab, the largest province by population, being a key stronghold.

> In total, according to one estimate, 50% of Pakistan's population can be categorised as Barelwi, as compared to 20% Deobandi. Yet significantly, these statistics are virtually inverted when the question of control of religious schools (*madrassas*) is considered: some 64% of the total seminaries are run by Deobandis, as against 25% by the Barelwis (with 6% under the control of the Ahl-e-Hadith movement and 3% operated by various Shia organisations).
>
> Thanks to the windfall of cash Saudi Arabia received following the oil crisis of the early 1970s, Wahhabi money has bankrolled the proliferation of Deobandi *madrassas* throughout southern Asia, which now – according to some estimates – number upwards of 15,000. Some of these seminaries have served as the ideological incubators of the Afghan Taliban movement; of much of the anti-Shia and other forms of sectarianism through-out the region; and of a number of terrorist groups active in the ongoing conflict in Kashmir.[3]

Ebrahim Moosa, a Muslim scholar trained in the US who had studied at several Indian madrasas in the 1970s and 1980s and revisited them in the 2000s, sees them as repositories of genuine Islamic learning. Accounts in the Western media that regard them as seed beds of terrorism are 'gross distortions generated by the fogs of military and cultural wars'.[4] Citing Mawlana Abu Saud, a prominent scholar in a madrasa in Baruch, India, he sees madrasas as the 'true representative of Islamic learning', which the mawlana thinks the Americans want to eliminate. In Abu Saud's view the West's anti-madrasa propaganda 'is not an effort to combat terrorism, but a mere fig-leaf to undermine Islam itself'. While presenting a generally sympathetic account of the institutions, Moosa critiques the narrow scope of their curricula, which focus heavily on the sunnah (practice) of the Prophet Muhammad as revealed in the hadith literature and issues like gender segregation and bodily purity. The system of instruction is not monolithic, being informed by the Prophet Muhammad's often-cited statement that differences (*ikhtilaf*) between believers are a blessing. The problem, Moosa suggests, is that interpretative flexibility, while acknowledged in theory, is trumped in practice by the search for *authenticity*. 'Often it turns out that practitioners wedded to the authority of the canonical law schools are unable to unshackle themselves from the methodology they acquired and feel bound to uphold the authority of the past.'[5] The future of madrasas, he concludes,

> is hobbled by the inability of madrasa communities to make informed decisions about the complex world they inhabit. Trapped in an ideological bind, hesitant about the merits of Western knowledge production and its potential synthesis with the Islamic knowledge tradition, madrasas are unable to harness their full intellectual strength to make a meaningful contribution to broader society.[6]

We may conclude from Moosa's study – which has ramifications far beyond South Asia – that Saudi funding of madrasas is not in itself a source of extremism, but rather a fixing of the epistemological status quo in a world of fast-moving intellectual, technological and social change. As Meijer indicates, the concentration on purity and religious knowledge in madrasas places their alumni at a disadvantage when addressing the world outside of the madrasa, and it is the shock of this encounter that sometimes leads to radicalization.

Following the Mecca siege and Shiite disturbances in Qatif inspired by the Iranian revolution, King Fahd devoted himself to intensifying the Wahhabi mission both at home and overseas, seeking to bolster the legitimacy of his family by appropriating the authority of Islam through his role as Custodian of the Two Holy Shrines. Vast sums were spent on expanding the mosques in Mecca and Medina, along with Quran schools, libraries, madrasas and a major enterprise for printing the Quran.

A particular focus was on *da'wa* (evangelism) overseas, both to strengthen the Al Saud's claim to legitimacy as rulers of the Hejaz and to divert religious energies from internal critique of the regime. According to one estimate, the kingdom spent some $70 billion on Islamist missionary work in the period between 1979 and 2006.[7] The two decades between 1982 and 2002 saw the construction of some 1,500 Saudi-funded mosques, 210 Islamic centres, 202 colleges and 2,000 schools in the US, Canada, France, UK, Russia, Germany, Switzerland, Australia, Belgium, New Zealand, Spain, Italy, Bosnia, Croatia, Hungary, Japan, South Korea, Thailand, Burundi, Fiji, Kenya, Cameroon, Uganda and Brazil. Muslim-majority countries that benefited from Saudi mosque funding included Afghanistan, Algeria, Pakistan, Egypt, the Palestinian Territories, Jordan, Lebanon, Yemen, Indonesia, Malaysia and Bangladesh in addition to mixed Muslim and Christian countries such as Nigeria.

European cities with Saudi-funded Islamic centres included Brussels, Geneva, Madrid, London, Edinburgh, Rome, Zagreb, Lisbon, Vienna, Aachen, Munich, Budapest, Malmö and Malaga. Thanks to the complicity of host governments, and local municipalities – not to mention the interests of local contractors who benefited from them – Islamic centres, mosques and schools funded by Saudis have met with little opposition. The only significant exceptions have been in Switzerland where new minarets were banned after a referendum in 2009 and Norway where the government endorsed the arctic city of Tromsø's decision to reject a Saudi-funded mosque unless the kingdom rescinds its ban on non-Muslim public worship.

The amount of ideological leverage delivered by Saudi Arabia's *da'wa* programme may be hard to assess as individuals who attend Saudi-funded mosques for personal prayers, Friday prayer and Muslim festivals need not necessarily be affected by Wahhabi values.

Nevertheless, there is considerable evidence of the damage to Islamic diversity that is driven by petrodollars distributed by the Saudi kingdom. James Dorsey estimates that the Saudi kingdom's spending on supporting ultra-conservative strands of Islam, including Wahhabism, Salafism and Deobandism, across the globe up till 2016 ranged from $70 billion to $100 billion.[8]

According to Krithika Varagur the Saudi Ministry of Islamic Affairs, Dawah [evangelism] and Guidance has a staff of over 9,500 people with the remit to oversee religious diplomacy in some two dozen countries in Europe, Asia, Africa, the Middle East, Australia and the US. In 2017 it had an operating budget of more than $1.8 billion. Foreign activities reported by its overseas offices include:

> TV, radio, newspaper and magazine content; as well as courses, lectures, missionary and conversion activities, preaching, prison visits, seminars, camps, preaching tours ... and distributing Qurans, Quran commentaries, pamphlets and cassettes in both Arabic and in translations. For the Islamic year 2016-17 [1437–8 AH] its activities included sponsoring 22,146 conversions to Islam, 16,644 seminars, 43,303 preaching tours and 373,454 classes or lectures around the world.[9]

Beyond the ministry lie what Varagur calls the 'Big Three' charities – the Muslim World League, World Association of Muslim Youth and the International Islamic Relief Organization – whose annual budgets are estimated in the tens of millions. Funds have also been raised through less well-known charities, some of them connected to terrorism or religious violence. One she highlights as having been particularly notorious was the Al-Haramain Islamic

Foundation founded in 1988 which spent around $50 million a year on printing books and establishing mosques and schools, with forty offices in the kingdom and more than 100 overseas, in Asia, Africa and the Balkans. Prior to 9/11, she writes, Al-Haramain operated a centralized system according to which none of its subsidiaries could receive funding without the personal approval of the director Sheikh Aqil ibn Abd al-Aziz al-Aqil:

> Through this central command Al-Haramain has been linked to an all-star list of terrorist groups including Jemaah Islamiyah in Indonesia, Al-Ittihad Al-Islami in Somalia, Lashkar-e-Taiba in Pakistan, Chechen rebels [in Russia] and of course, Al Qaeda. From 2004 to 2010 the UN recommended its assets be blocked due to its Al Qaeda affiliations, but this proved incredibly difficult to enforce.[10]

With the charity's offices constantly opening and closing, and frequent changes of name (at least ten in the case of Kosovo), it became impossible for the UN to keep track. Other difficulties in tracing sources of funding that emerged after the 11 September attacks include the paperless *hawala* system of money transfers based on personal trust which Varagur sees as 'one reason why Saudi charities, even ones that were fairly official or state-endorsed, so frequently became embroiled with terror finance'.[11]

In research visits to Indonesia and Nigeria as well as Kosovo, Varagur found consistent patterns of anti-Shia and anti-Sufi proselytization. In Indonesia, known traditionally for its eclectic and syncretistic forms of Islam containing Hindu and animist elements, she traced the personal and institutional links between the bombers who killed more than 200 people – mostly Australian tourists – at Paddy's Pub on the island of Bali in October 2002, organized by the al-Qaeda-affiliated Jemaah Islamiyah. Four of the bombers were graduates of the Saudi-endowed Ngruki boarding school in central

Java, part of a broader outreach of Saudi-sponsored evangelism centred on LIPIA, a branch of the Imam Muhammad ibn Saud University in Riyadh.[12] As she states 'Saudi fingerprints are all over the Salafi-jihadist networks of Indonesia and directly contributed to Indonesia's most traumatic terror attack ever.'[13] In Indonesia the Salafist network based on the Ngruki school became known as an 'Ivy League for jihadists'. It coalesced around two Indonesian veterans of the Afghan jihad, Abdullah Sungkar and Abu Bakr Ba'asyir, who were part of the long-established diaspora of Yemenis from the Hadhramaut valley (from which the bin Laden family also originates). At one point the pair avoided arrest by travelling to Saudi Arabia on forged passports where they met the geocentrist scholar Ibn Baz, who counselled them to visit and remain in Peshawar from where they could easily rejoin the Afghan jihad.[14]

Sungkar died in 1999 before the Bali bombing, while in 2020, when Varagur's report appeared, Ba'asyir was eighty-one years old and still in jail. But the jihad in Indonesia was far from dead. In May 2018 three different families were involved in the bombing of three churches and a police station at Surabaya in East Java, killing fifteen victims and thirteen of the attackers, one of them an eight-year-old girl. The jihadist group responsible, Jamaah Ansharut Daulah, had radicalized themselves watching videos of beheadings by ISIS in Iraq and Syria. Their operational leader was Saiful Munthohir, an alumnus of a group that had pledged allegiance to ISIS. Its spiritual leader Aman Abdurahman, who had studied for seven years at LIPIA, had been jailed in 2010 as an accessory to the Bali bombing but remained influential behind bars through his widely circulated cassettes. He allegedly planned the Surabaya attack before going to prison, giving his blessing to Munthohir and his circle. In 2018 he was sentenced to death for inspiring the Surabaya attacks.

In Nigeria, the diverse population of Muslims mainly in the northern regions has belonged to Sufi orders such as the Tijaniyya and Qadiryya. Saudi outreach encouraged consolidation, with King Faisal pioneering 'Islamic solidarity' (*al-tadamun al-islami*) as a principle of Saudi foreign policy.[15] From the early 1960s Faisal cultivated the premier of the Northern Region, Ahmadu Bello, with grants approaching $250,000 per year to promote proselytization, mainly through the Jama'atu Nasril Islam (Society for the Support of Islam) headed by Abubakar Gumi, a Nigerian scholar who had worked as a Hajj official in Mecca. Gumi established operations in Nigeria for the Muslim World League. Gumi dispensed its funds at his discretion, gaining more traction after Bello was assassinated in a violent military coup in 1966, the first of several lasting till 1999. His successor as governor allowed Gumi more leverage, including free access to the media. 'Gumi used his platform to attack Sufis more vociferously, using open air sermons, radio, television and cassette tapes that are still circulated in Kano markets today.'[16] In 1978 Gumi, through his protégé Ismail Idris, created another group known locally as Izala based on the Hausa initials of the Society of Removal of Innovation and Re-establishment of the Sunnah (prophetic custom). Varagur, who visited Nigeria for her 2020 report, writes:

> Although Izala was always led by and staffed by Nigerians, its agenda had every mark of the Wahhabi mission. It was founded to eradicate Sufi practices, so-called polytheism (*shirk*), and unnecessary innovations (*bidah*) from Nigerian Islam ... Izala preachers were energetic and straightforward. They relied on Ibn Abd al-Wahhab's Book of Tawhid, the key text of Wahhabism, but spoke in demotic Hausa. Izala attacked various local religious practices like visiting graves, carrying charms, using holy water, divination, claiming to see Allah in dreams

and visions, and the veneration of Sufi saints. Its preachers even discouraged eating meat slaughtered by Sufis.[17]

Before he died in 1992 at age sixty-nine, Gumi gave popular sermons in Kaduna denouncing anyone reciting the Tijaniyya prayer as an 'unbeliever' — a manifestation of *takfir* that landed some of his followers in jail. One of them, Sheikh Abdullahi Garangawa, a graduate of Medina who preached in Kano, told Varagur that he was detained ten times by police and briefly held twice in jail. But by the time he returned to Nigeria after a five-year period studying sharia law at the University of Medina (1991–6) 'Izala had gone mainstream', changing its approach from anti-Sufi polemics to promoting implementation of sharia, a move that would prove highly, if disastrously, successful.

Since 1999, when democratic forms were restored in Nigeria after years of autocratic military rule, some 50,000 people are reported to have been killed in sectarian and ethnic violence. 'Restoration of the sharia' as promoted by Salafis became a catchword in the north, where newly elected parliaments with large Muslim majorities demanded 'restoration' of Islamic sharia law, as applied in early colonial times. Restoration was described as the 'dividend from democracy'. A sharia-based penal code was introduced in Zamfara, Kano, Sokoto and nine other states or governorates. In colonial times sharia included the death penalty for Muslims who participated in 'pagan' (that is, traditionalist) religious rites. A Muslim accused of murdering a Christian could be freed by the court if he swore his innocence on the Quran.

Nigerian Muslims are defensive about outside criticism of sharia punishments. Thus the Southern Council for Islamic Affairs said in a statement: 'Islam and Shari'a are inseparable. No amount of black mail ... will stop Muslims from the pursuit of their fundamental human rights to practice their religions in full, without dictation, as to which aspect of their faith should or should not be observed.'[18]

The issue, of course, is highly controversial and contentious. In Muslim-majority states, Muslim norms, such as sex segregation in schools and a ban on alcohol, are being imposed on Christians and other non-Muslims. Yet in the absence of a Nigerian Supreme Court ruling declaring sharia constitutional, judges are reluctant to impose sharia penalties, such as amputation for theft. In 2007 the Bauchi State Shariah Commission asked the newly elected governor to ratify forty-three amputations and death penalties for adulteries, sodomy and so on, passed by the state's sharia court since 2003. The issue was clearly subject to official embarrassment not least because Nigeria is, in theory at least, a fully secular state. Johannes Harnischfeger, a German academic, states that it is 'almost impossible to access court files, and the authorities do not provide reliable information'.[19]

Gunnar Weimann, a researcher attached to the German embassy in Abuja, identified a number of cases where floggings for sexual misdemeanours and amputations for theft had been carried out.[20] He pointed out, however, that public embarrassment had been a powerful restraining force. Three Nigerian women sentenced to death by stoning were acquitted on appeal after massive publicity campaigns. In the case of Safiyya Hussain, a widow accused of having a lover outside of marriage, in Spain alone 600,000 people signed an Amnesty International petition, Pope John Paul II urged Catholics to pray for her, while the mayors of Rome and Naples declared her an honorary citizen of their cities. Sentenced in October 2001, she was acquitted on appeal in March 2002.

The issue of sharia law in Nigeria is particularly problematic, as it is a religiously mixed society with significant minorities living in majority areas. While the northern states are largely Muslim, there are substantial Christian minorities. The same goes for the mainly Christian south, where substantial numbers of Muslims are located. Authorities differ on the overall proportion of Christians and Muslims. According to the World Christian Encyclopedia, Christians form an overall majority, but the *Economist* and CIA put the Muslims ahead, with 50 per cent against 40 per cent Christians (with the balance of 10 per cent being animists or adherents of traditional religions). Harnischfeger sees religious populism as dangerous, not least because of the ethnic and social tensions it articulates.

> What looks like a national conflict that splits the 140M Nigerians into two camps, appears, on close inspection, as a series of local conflicts in which very different actors are involved. In Kano and other cities of the far North, Christian migrants from the South, mostly Igbo and Yoruba, have clashed with Muslim Hausa-Fulani who use the Islamization campaign to assert their ancestral rights over the economically successful 'settlers'.[21]

Further south, in the so-called Middle Belt, where Hausa-Fulani settlers compete with the indigenous non-Muslim population over the dwindling supply of land, calls for restoration of sharia amount to an assertion of political supremacy. 'In this context', Harnischfeger comments, 'religion is attractive not as a resource for peace, but as a means for mobilizing for violent conflict. Political Islam, with its claim to enforce religious laws, is well placed to mobilize for the defense of land and to assert political dominance.'[22]

The most catastrophic outcome of Saudi proselytizing in Africa has been the group known as Boko Haram, the cognomen given by Nigerian media to the Salafist group calling itself Jama'at Ahl-Als? Sunnah li-Dawa wa'l Jihad – 'Group of the People of the Sunnah for Preaching and Jihad'. Although it pledged allegiance to ISIS in 2015, according to Varagur the group, which became notorious for kidnapping schoolgirls, 'existed for six years as a nonviolent fundamentalist group and only turned violent in 2009' when its founder Muhammad Yousuf was interrogated and executed by the police after a clash with the military, in which some 1,000 people were killed.

Yousuf had been a protégé of Jafar Adam, a charismatic preacher granted a scholarship to the Islamic University of Medina after winning a Quran-recitation contest in Kano in 1988. After returning to Kano, Adam joined Izala and attracted a large following 'for his charismatic sermons and debates' with Shia and Sufi leaders. He preached from core Wahhabi texts, which enthralled his listeners, by explaining them in colloquial Hausa. In the 1990s Adam was installed at a new mosque in Maiduguri, capital of Borno state. Here he created a new group separate from Izala, which he called Ahl al-Sunnah ('People of the Sunnah'). The group considered itself more purely Salafist, less tainted by the political mainstreaming of Izala. Adam's star student, Muhammad Yousuf, was chosen to lead the Ahl al-Sunna's youth wing in Maiduguri but, like his former mentor, soon broke with the parent group for being insufficiently Islamic.

After establishing a centre in Maiduguri named after Ibn Taymiyya he published a foundational manifesto consisting mainly of citations from Saudi Salafi texts. Yousuf sheltered briefly in the Saudi kingdom while being investigated for his extremist rhetoric, but this did not prevent him acquiring thousands of followers across north-eastern states and neighbouring countries including Niger, Chad and Cameroon. The leader who took over, Abu Bakr Shekau, was no fan of the Saudi kingdom. In a video filmed in 2015 he denounced the Saudi state as being in a 'state of unbelief, because it is a state that belongs to the Saudi family and they do not follow the Prophet ... Saudi Arabians, since you have altered Allah's religion, you will enter hellfire!'[23]

Since 2020 when Varagur's report was published the circles of jihadist violence in Africa have been widening with deadly attacks on traders bringing goods to countries bordering the Sahel, the semi-arid region bordering the Sahara, where the writ of national governments such as that of Ghana, based in the relatively wealthy Atlantic littoral, is challenged by jihadists from the less populated northern areas. As the *Financial Times* reported in January 2024 'Governments across west Africa and their international allies are seriously discussing whether the Islamist groups wreaking havoc in the Sahel ... would expand into the relatively peaceful countries on the coast such as Benin, Ghana, Togo and Ivory Coast.'[24] It would certainly be wrong to attribute the political disorder and volatility of Sahel countries such as Burkina Faso, northern Mali and Niger (former colonies of France where French forces were recently withdrawn under populist pressures) wholly or even mainly to ideological penetration by Islamists rooted in the Salafist discourse promoted by Saudi organizations.

A major reason for the collapse of government authority in the fragile Sahel states was NATO's decision, backed by Britain and France, to support the rebels who overthrew the Libyan ruler Muammar al-Qadhafy in 2011. Rather than contributing to the stability of the oil-rich North African state, the NATO action contributed to its breakdown, with knock-on effects in the Sahel state where Libya had been dominant. Nevertheless, the Salafist agenda originally promoted by Saudi *da'wa* has been the beneficiary of ill-advised Western responses to the events that overthrew Qadhafy in 2011. As Varagur makes plain in her report, the 'Boko-Haram' ideology – which has spread throughout numerous groups in the Sahel region – 'directly springs from the Salafi corpus spread by Saudi-educated Nigerian preachers'.[25]

As Dorsey noted in his 2016 paper 'Creating Frankenstein', Saudi largesse, estimated at $70 billion to $100 billion, has 'funded mosques, Islamic schools and cultural institutions and social services, as well as the forging of close ties to non-Wahhabi Muslim leaders and like-minded ultra conservative Muslim worldviews into an influential force in Muslim nations and communities across the globe'. Christopher Hill, a former US assistant secretary of state for Southeast Asia, argued that it would be wrong to accuse Saudis of exporting terrorism directly. 'What they have done', he corrected, 'is to encourage their own radicals – a natural by-product of Wahhabism … to commit their terrorist acts elsewhere. As the radicals leave, so does Saudi money which funds their terrorist activities. The estimated 2,500 Saudis who joined ISIS [from 2015] was the group's second largest contingent.'[26]

The most devastating outcomes of sectarian conflict seeded if not encouraged by the Saudi kingdom have been in Afghanistan and Pakistan, two countries with rich pluralistic cultures embracing a variety of religious traditions and ethnicities. Both have been subjected to a type of religious homogenization comparable with the original Wahhabi onslaught in Arabia. Anti-Shiism was fundamental to this process.

Pakistan, founded in contradistinction to Hindu-majority yet secular India, had problems accepting the diversity of Muslim traditions even before General Zia-ul-Haq introduced his Islamization programme between 1978 and 1988. After the 1979 Iranian revolution, Zia, fearing the export of Shia-based radicalism, drew closer to Saudi Arabia, encouraging the funding of Salafist and Deobandi mosques along with the promotion of the Arabic language. With the development of the anti-Soviet jihad in Afghanistan the 'influx of sectarian, anti-Shiite Wahhabi materials grew exponentially', putting Pakistan's Shia minority as well as the country's Sufi traditions under increasing pressure. Radical spin-offs from the process of 'Wahhabization' included Sipah-e-Sahaba and an even more radical faction Lashkar-e-Jhangvi, a group that was banned for promoting sectarian violence after killing a group of Iranian air force cadets on an official visit to Pakistan. Lashkar-e-Jhangvi, banned in the US as a terrorist organization, was implicated in the 2007 assassination of former prime minister Benazir Bhutto and is suspected of playing a role in the 2009 grenade attack on the visiting Sri Lankan cricket team.

Both groups have publicly called for the killing of Shia in Pakistan who comprise between 10 and 15 per cent of the population. Between 1999 and 2003, according to a 2015 report by the Minority Rights Group, 'around 600 Shia were killed as a result of extremist violence' with some 500 doctors fleeing the country 'as a result of the assassination of 50 of their colleagues in Karachi alone'. Since then, the situation has got even worse. In 2011 militants sent an open letter to the mainly Shia Hazara community in Quetta, capital of Baluchistan, which numbers in the region of 600,000. The letter stated that 'all Shia are worthy of killing' and that Pakistan would be their graveyard.[27]

The letter heralded a new phase of violence, aimed at Shia professionals and officials, as well as pilgrims visiting holy sites and festivals. The echoes of the Wahhabi attacks on Iraq in the 1800s are clear. The Hazaras, as will be shown below, are particularly vulnerable, as many tend to be ethnically distinct from Pashtuns, having been descended from the Mongolian Tartars who invaded India in the thirteenth century CE. But Shias of all ethnicities have been exposed to neo-Wahhabi attacks. In May 2015, more than forty members of the Nizari Ismaili community (followers of the Aga Khan) were killed when a group of gunmen boarded a bus in Karachi. Several militant groups, including Tehrik Taliban Pakistan, Jundullah and the Islamic State, claimed to have perpetuated the slaughter. A spokesman for Jundullah said the victims had been infidels and threatened more attacks against Shias, Ismailis and Christians.

The predicament facing minorities in neighbouring Afghanistan has been even more precarious. The Taliban movement, which emerged after the Soviet withdrawal, was largely Pashtun in ethnicity and Deobandi in religious orientation. Its founding father Sami ul-Haq was the son of a Deobandi cleric and former senator who founded a madrasa in the town of Akora Khattak on the Indus River around 60 km east of Peshawar. In a book published in 2015 he insisted that the Taliban provided good government, Osama bin Laden was an 'ideal man' and that al-Qaeda had never existed. As Dorsey has written, madrasas such as his can provide education for the poor and marginalized in the absence of quality. They can be seeds of jihadism, both spiritual and activist:

> Deobandis, like Wahhabis and Salafis, advocate theological conservatism and oppose liberal ideals and values, and like its theological cousins, run the gamut from those who are apolitical and focus exclusively on religion, to militant Islamists who empathise with jihadists and see seizure of power as the way to implement the Sharia and change social behaviour. These various ultra-conservative sects, irrespective of their attitude towards politics and violence, benefit from the fact that with the government's failing to invest in quality public education, madrassas have turned into institutions of rote learning for the poor. These madrassas evade conveying understanding of the Quran, and are a far cry from the institutions of religious and scientific learning in the first centuries of Islam that produced intellectuals, scholars and scientists.[28]

Before it was overthrown in the US invasion following the attacks on New York and the Pentagon in September 2001, the Taliban government had only been recognized by Saudi Arabia, Pakistan and the UAE. It held most of the country until overthrown by the

US-led invasion in December 2001 that followed the attacks on New York and Washington. The visually impaired Taliban leader Mullah Omar had refused to extradite Osama bin Laden to the US, arguing that to do so would be a violation of Islamic rules of hospitality. Both Mullah Omar and bin Laden escaped the US invasion. Omar died in Quetta in 2013. Bin Laden was finally 'executed' in his hideout in Abbottabad, Pakistan, by a group of US Navy SEALS in May 2011.

The insurgency launched by the Taliban against the NATO-led International Security Assistance Force and elected governments of Hamid Karzai and Ashraf Ghani proved successful, despite the presence of well-armed and well-equipped forces from the US, Britain and other countries. It culminated in the fall of Kabul in August 2021 and the chaotic and ignominious retreat of Western forces that resembled the fall of Saigon in 1975.

The Taliban – named from the madrasa students who dominated its ranks – had roots in the anti-Soviet jihad that was funded by the American CIA and Saudi Arabia through Pakistan's Inter-Services Intelligence agency, much of which had been 'radicalized' – or staffed with ultra-conservative operators – during the regime of Zia-ul-Haq. Many of the students originally forming the Taliban had acquired experience of 'asymmetrical warfare' against the Soviets, with knowledge of the landscapes – physical, ethnic and social – that served them well when fighting foreign troops of the International Security Assistance Force and of the Afghan army, which was being painfully constructed by the Karzai and Ghani governments. Ideologically they were driven by a combination of Pashtun tribalism (as distinct from nation-building approaches espoused by commanders such as the Uzbek Abdul Rashid Dostum and the charismatic and liberal-minded Tajik Ahmed Shah Masoud), with a style of ultra-patriarchal religiosity based on a combination of the Pashtunwali (the Pashtun tribal code which sees women as totemic and tradable vehicles of tribal honour) and a version of the Deobandi doctrine sharpened by the activist imperatives urged by Islamist thinkers such as Sayyid Qutb and Abu Ala al-Maududi.

Dorsey sees transformed Deobandi activism, supported by Saudi *da'wa*, as crucial not just for the Taliban (whose leading commanders, including Mullah Omar and Jalaluddin Haqqani, were trained in Deobandi madrasas) but to globalized Islamism generally. He cites the Pakistani economist and author Professor Akbar Zaidi:

> As Pakistan's economy and politics have moved towards West Asia, and away from an Indian history and past, its various Islams have also been influenced by these trends. Pakistan's version of Deobandi Islam is affected by Saudi Wahhabism, and hence it becomes difficult to argue that these madrassas are still in any sense Deobandi ... Islam, even Pakistani and Afghani Islam, is now globalised, Wahhabised, as well as affected by geopolitical influences, which have a far-reaching impact on local and domestic Islam.[29]

Dorsey's paper contains a highly plausible account, written by a US diplomat based in Lahore, that describes the recruitment process whereby impoverished families may be drawn towards fundamentalist outlooks. He cites a 2008 cable from Bryan Hunt, a US diplomat stationed in Lahore, Pakistan, who reported that 'financial support estimated at nearly US $100 million annually was making its way to (conservative) Deobandi and Ahl-e-Hadith clerics in the region from "missionary" and "Islamic charitable" organisations in Saudi Arabia and the United Arab Emirates, ostensibly with direct support from those governments'.

According to Hunt the funding tends to 'exploit poverty' in marginal areas, such as southern Punjab or towns such as Multan and Bahawalpur, which become recruiting grounds for militant groups. He reports that the Gulf funding has spawned a network that exploits growing poverty in these areas, enabling *da'wa* missionaries to recruit children into the growing Deobandi and Ahl-e-Hadith madrasa network, from which they are 'indoctrinated into jihadi philosophy, deployed to regional training/indoctrination centres, and ultimately sent to terrorist training camps in the Federally Administered Tribal Areas (FATA)'. In detailing how the Saudi funds are put to work, Hunt reports:

> the local Deobandi or Ahl-e-Hadith maulana (religious scholar) will generally be introduced to the family through these (charitable) organisations. He will work to convince the parents that their poverty is a direct result of their family's deviation from 'the true path of Islam' through 'idolatrous' worship at local Sufi shrines and/or with local Sufi Peers. The maulana suggests that the quickest way to return to 'favour' would be to devote the lives of one or two of their sons to Islam. The maulana will offer to educate these children at his madrassa and to find them employment in the service of Islam. The concept of 'martyrdom' is often discussed and the family is promised that if their sons are 'martyred' both the sons and the family will attain 'salvation' and the family will obtain God's favour in this life, as well. An immediate cash payment is finally made to the parents to compensate the family for its 'sacrifice' to Islam. Local sources claim that the current average rate is approximately Rs 500,000 (approximately US$ 6,500) per son.[30]

Hunt's report to his bosses in Washington did not detail how much of this money showered on Deobandi mosques and madrasas in Pakistan ended up with the Taliban. But it is difficult to believe that in the mountainous regions of West Pakistan where Pashtun and other tribal systems bestride the Durand Line (an artificial border of 2,611 km devised by a British imperial administrator in 1890 to separate the Indian Raj from notionally independent Afghanistan) no Saudi largesse has reached the Taliban. In an email to *New York*

Times correspondent Carlotta Gall, Prince Turki al-Faisal, who directed Saudi intelligence for more than twenty-four years, stated, 'When I was in government not a single [Saudi] penny went to the Taliban', adding that 'stringent measures [were] taken by the kingdom to prevent any transfer of money to terrorist groups' at a time before the Taliban had taken power.

Writing in 2016, however, Gall pointed to a wealth of data challenging Prince Turki's claim. Although the kingdom 'officially, if coolly supported the American mission and the Afghan government and even sued for peace in clandestine negotiations on their behalf', the country was also backing the Taliban insurgents. 'Over the years, wealthy Saudi sheikhs and rich philanthropists have also stoked the war by privately financing the insurgents.' She cites a former Taliban finance minister who explained how he travelled regularly to Saudi Arabia over the years, ostensibly to perform the Hajj, but also to raise cash from wealthy donors. Citing the distinguished professor Vali Nasr, a former State Department advisor, she states that the Taliban had also been allowed to raise even more millions by the extortion of '"taxes" by pressing hundreds of thousands of Pashtun guest workers in the kingdom and menacing their families back home'.

The gist of Gall's article – which proved to be prophetic – was that the Saudis were playing a double game by tacitly supporting the Taliban while pretending to back their US ally in supporting the Afghan government. 'Playing multiple sides of the same geopolitical equation', she concludes, 'is one way the Saudis further their own strategic interests ... But it also threatens to undermine the fragile democratic advances made by the United States in the past 15 years, and perhaps undo efforts to liberalize the country.'[31]

The same ambivalence might be seen when considering Saudi *da'wa* in the United States itself. Much of the data about Saudi outreach in US mosques, for example, may be anecdotal. As Eleanor Doumato has stated, 'there is very little documentation as to the nature and extent of Saudi influence' in the United States, and she questions the methodology of a 2005 report published by the Center for Religious Freedom (CRF) with the provocative title *Saudi Publications on Hate Ideology Invade American Mosques*.

In her testimony to the US Senate, the report's author Nina Shea quoted from her own study, stating that:

> Wahhabi extremism is more than hate speech; it is a totalitarian ideology of hatred that can incite to violence. The fact that a foreign government, namely Saudi Arabia, has been working to mainstream within our borders such hate ideology demands our urgent attention ... The Saudi textbooks and publications described in the Center's report could ... pose a serious threat to American security and to the traditional American culture of religious toleration and freedom.[32]

Doumato points out, however, that 90 per cent of the texts cited in the report were in Arabic, with the rest divided among English, Urdu, Chinese and Tagalog (one of the major languages spoken in the Philippines). Yet according to a 2004 survey by Zogby International and Project MAPS (Muslim Americans in the Public Square), people of Arab ethnicity constitute only 26 per cent of the American Muslim population compared with 34 per cent from South Asia, 20 per cent who are African American and 7 per cent who are of African origin.

Not unreasonably, Doumato questions any impact such 'hate literature' might have, especially as, according to surveys conducted in 2003 and 2006, English is the language of the Friday sermon (*khutba*) in 97 per cent of American mosques. Arab Americans, moreover, tend to be less religiously observant than South Asians and African Americans. A survey in 2000 of around half the 1,200 mosques in the United States determined that there were some 69,000 mosque-attending Muslims of Arab ethnicity, compared with 160,000 South Asians and 136,000 African Americans.[33]

Regardless of its aims and methods – Doumato concludes – 'What the report reveals, albeit inadvertently, is not a conduit for successful proselytism among American Muslims, but the failure of the Saudis and the Saudi Ministry of Islamic Affairs to be credible advocates for a Saudi version of Islam that would appeal to American Muslims.'[34] A more plausible view of the inefficacy of Wahhabi proselytizing in the US cited by Doumato comes from a 2007 Pew Research sample of more than 1,000 Muslims residing in the US, including immigrants. It found that American Muslims were 'decidedly American in their outlook, values and attitudes', and that they tended to 'reject Islamic customs by larger margins than Muslim minorities in Western European countries, and that they are religiously and ethnically diverse, socially conservative and politically liberal'.[35]

None of this means that anecdotal materials should be ignored. My personal knowledge, though limited, may not be insignificant. When teaching at the University of California, San Diego, in 2000, I acted *faux-naif* and asked one of my students, a pious young woman of Afghan heritage, if she would be joining her family in observing the *mawlid* – the Prophet's birthday which is celebrated throughout the Muslim world but banned in Saudi Arabia because the Wahhabi mullahs regard it as *shirk* (idolatry). 'No way!' she indignantly replied. The imam of her mosque in downtown San Diego, she added helpfully, was doing his best to discourage *mawlid* celebration, but they still had some way to go. In retrospect it appeared that the imam in question may have been none other than Anwar al-Awlaki, the US-born jihadist and al-Qaeda propagandist killed in a drone strike in Yemen authorized by President Obama in September 2011, the first US citizen to have been victim of a targeted assassination by a US president (his sixteen-year-old son was killed in a subsequent strike, and his eight-year-old daughter died in a commando raid ordered by President Trump in 2017). According to records obtained by the FBI, Awlaki spent almost five years as the imam of the al-Ribat mosque in San Diego from 1996–2000, where he had a 'following' of between 200 and 300 people: perhaps my student was one of them! Two of the 9/11 hijackers, Khalid al-Mihdhar and Nawaf al-Hazmi, are believed to have attended the mosque in early 2000. After the 9/11 attacks, witnesses told the FBI that Awlaki had a close relationship with the hijackers.

While it would be difficult to attribute blame directly for Awlaki's Salafist teachings on Saudi Arabia, the curriculum of the King Fahd Academy in London provides an irrefutable textual source for a type of anti-Western radicalization similar to materials Nina Shea found in Arabic-language materials in American mosques. Among their findings in 2006, MacEoin and his researchers (all of them Muslims) found a first-grade textbook with a section on *al-wala' wa'l-bara'* ('loyalty and disavowal') in which 'Muslims are asked to avoid any sort of engagement with non-believers, such as attending their celebrations, showing happiness "on their festivals", offering them sympathy or condolences, cooperating in artistic activities like singing, dancing, theatre, and taking part in sports'.

> As for participating with them in their lawful celebrations, or in their tragedies, or in offering them sympathy and condolences during calamities, the right way is the impermissibility of congratulating them or offering them condolences, as many of the scholars have conclusively ruled. The reason for this is that closeness to them will result, and then love towards them will become firm because of treating them with esteem. It is forbidden because of these dangers. It is also forbidden to greet them before they greet you, or to give way to them on the road.[36]

Other types of 'imitating the unbelievers' in the syllabus include references to 'that which they call art, like singing and playing instruments, dancing, acting, and establishing theatres and movie theatres which are visited by those who have lost their sense of righteousness, and do not take life seriously'. Students are also urged to disregard sports which 'distract them from remembering Allah and being obedient to Him'.[37]

Following the Policy Exchange exposé which attracted considerable media attention in Britain, the curriculum changed radically. After 2015 the King Fahd Academy adopted the International Baccalaureate programme that encourages critical thought and is used by several highly regarded institutions containing Muslim students, such as the Aga Khan Academies in Mombasa, Kenya, and Hyderabad, India, both of which I visited in 2010 and 2017. In 2017 Ofsted, the independent agency concerned with maintaining educational standards in England and Wales, gave King Fahd Academy a mediocre report, stating there was need for improvement in the quality of teaching, learning and assessment, as well as in the personal development and behaviour of pupils. On humanities and world religions, however, it found that the teaching was 'strong', with teachers 'enthusiastic' and learning activities 'probing'. In particular it singled out the statement of a pupil who told the inspectors that 'Islam teaches tolerance'. Almost two decades after the attacks of 9/11, there were signs that the impact of Wahhabi-style outreach was softening. In May 2023, however, the school closed for good to the dismay of teachers and parents who had not been given adequate warning. As the school's sole source of funding came from the Saudi government, its closure bore the hallmarks of Crown Prince MBS.

Such a picture may be consistent with the 'taming of the Wahhabi ulama' and reform-minded Islamists in Saudi Arabia mentioned above. Domestically, Saudi clerics have been subject to increasing pressures from the state as they lose their leverage over society. There appear to have been complex processes at work in this area as the dynasty sought to harness the radical momentum of Islamism when it regarded it as being in its interest, while repressing it when it was not.

Broadly speaking, the three decades prior to the 1990s were a time when the ideology of the Sahwa – the movement of Islamic awakening – developed around what Lacroix calls the 'close affinities' between the Wahhabi tradition and ideas of Sayyid Qutb. Afghanistan was crucial, with the regime encouraging ulama to recruit volunteers for the anti-Soviet jihad. Thousands travelled to Pakistan, to return battle-hardened and often radicalized, after the Soviet withdrawal. As Toby Jones of the International Crisis Group observes, 'The legacy of the jihad, particularly the belief that Islam was a powerful political tool that had vanquished a global superpower had a profound impact, leading to well-known consequences such as the radicalization of Osama bin Laden and his adherents.'[38]

The momentum towards radicalization crested with the invasion of Kuwait by the Iraqi dictator Saddam Hussein in 1990 and the Saudi government's decision to permit the presence of US and coalition troops on its soil. Chief Mufti Ibn Baz's two fatwas – the first of which authorized the stationing of non-Muslim troops including Americans in Saudi Arabia in 1990, and the second authorizing war against the Muslim state of Iraq in 1991 – were highly controversial, not least because earlier in his career, Ibn Baz had been briefly imprisoned by Ibn Saud for objecting to an American mission that was looking for water.[39] The presence of more than half a million American troops supplemented by smaller contingents of British, French and Italian forces along with an influx of 1,500 foreign reporters and television crews – with stories about female soldiers driving trucks or frying bacon in the holy land – created a crisis of legitimacy for the regime. Its fragility was exposed by a well-planned and-executed attack with a truck-bomb on a building housing American servicemen that killed nineteen Americans and one Saudi national in al-Khobar in 1996. While initially the regime tried to persuade the US that Shiite militants backed by Iran were responsible, the evidence was insufficient to persuade the Clinton administration to accuse Iran directly, and contrary evidence pointing to links between al-Qaeda and domestic hostility to the US presence proved more convincing.

Dissenting clerics had openly challenged the lawfulness of King Fahd's decision to invite foreign troops into the kingdom as well as Ibn Baz's endorsement. In sermons that were taped and distributed on cassettes and pamphlets, leading clerics such as Dr Safar al-Hawali, dean of the Islamic College at the Umm al-Qura University in Mecca, and Salman al-Awdah of the Imam Muhammad ibn Saud University in Riyadh (an associate of Yousuf al-Uyairi who had been arrested and tortured after the al-Khobar bombing) not only questioned the legitimacy of inviting foreign troops, but pointed to the corruption and incompetence of a regime that had spent billions of dollars importing foreign defence equipment without having the capacity to use it.

While not a member of the Muslim Brotherhood, al-Awdah, who had studied with Ibn Baz, was clearly influenced by the discourse of Hasan al-Banna, Sayyid Qutb and the Syrian Brotherhood scholar Muhammad Surur Zayn al-Abdin. As al-Rasheed explains, the Gulf War, with its international media onslaught, gave increased global coverage to debates that had long been maturing inside the kingdom, intensifying 'what had already been fermenting in Sa'udi society, namely the increasing polarization over issues related to the country's rapid modernization and close relationship with the West, and the incompatibility with Islam of this close relationship'.[40]

In 1994 the regime arrested both preachers and detained them for five years, releasing them in 1999. The experience seemed to have chastened them to a certain degree, and in the aftermath of 9/11, with Saudi Arabia again under the international spotlight, the regime found it politic to use their popularity to try to boost its legitimacy. As Jones remarked in March 2005, members of the Sahwa played an ambiguous role as 'both supporters and critics of the regime – a remarkable accomplishment considering both the short leash given by the ruling family to dissenters as well as some of the critics' personal history of anti-regime political activism'.[41]

In the turbulence generated by the Anglo-American invasion of Iraq – based on false claims that the Iraqi leader Saddam Hussein was threatening the West with 'weapons of mass destruction', the Sahwa clerics were soon outflanked by more radical voices. In May 2003, six weeks after the American-led invasion of Iraq, insurgents attacked three residential compounds housing foreigners in Riyadh killing twenty-six people, some of them Westerners but also many Saudis and Arabs who lived there too. Some of the residents worked for the Vinnell Corporation, a US defence contractor involved in developing Saudi weapons systems and training its security forces. It was clear that the suicide bombers had inside knowledge. After attacking the guards of the heavily protected compound, they knew how to operate the switches of the main gate before 'driving at breakneck speed with a bomb weighing nearly 200 kilograms to the most densely inhabited part of the complex'.[42]

The next attack, in November 2003, on another Riyadh compound, was even more disturbing for the regime and for the millions of foreigners residing in the kingdom, as most of the victims were Muslims. According to the official Saudi account, suicide bombers drove into the compound and blew themselves up killing seventeen workers and injuring more than 100. They were said to have targeted a compound of minor importance housing Arabs because the Western-occupied compounds were too well guarded. Bradley, however, finds the official explanation thoroughly unconvincing. There was no 'announcement that members of the security forces had died in the attack, despite reported gun battles, both before and after the explosions, between Saudi and private security forces defending the compound and those terrorists determined to destroy it'.[43]

On other occasions when security forces had suffered casualties, Saudi television would carry live reports of the families of 'martyrs' being visited by the interior minister Prince Nayef ibn Abd al-Aziz. In this instance, no such visits were broadcast. Bradley, citing opposition sources, concludes that the attackers did not blow themselves up, but detonated the car bomb by remote control, enabling them to escape. Later, in its version of events, an al-Qaeda website claimed that one suicide bomber did die – having been (like Juhayman al-Utaybi) a member of the National Guard. As Bradley suggests, this would 'mean that the infiltration of security forces by al-Qaeda had reached the point of them being able to secure close cooperation in actually carrying out the attacks'.[44]

Moreover, contrary to official accounts admitting that the attackers had worn police uniforms and had used police cars, the reality appeared that they had used a vehicle with special-forces markings. Bradley concludes that even if senior Saudi officials were serious in hunting down al-Qaeda and its operatives, the implementation was ineffective 'because the campaign against al-Qaeda was being conducted against the will of the rank and file, many of whom sympathized with al-Qaeda's goals'.[45]

In the next major attack in May 2004, the second to have afflicted the eastern oil city of al-Khobar, the killers went from house to house in the gated compound, separating Muslims from non-Muslims. Twenty-two people, mostly foreigners, were killed, some by having their throats cut, others being tied up and dragged behind cars. After a brief gunfight, the security forces apparently let three of the attackers escape through the tight police cordon, indicating that, as in Riyadh, there was probably a level of collusion. After this attack in al-Khobar and a similar event in the port city of Yanbu, there were unconfirmed reports of mass resignations by Americans employed by Saudi Aramco.

The massive security crackdown that followed these attacks seems to have held, with loyal security forces seizing stockpiles of weapons and making hundreds of arrests. The arrests extended to three al-Qaeda sympathizers, Sheikhs Nasr al-Fahd, Ali al-Khudayr and Ahmed al-Khalidi, who had pronounced *takfir* on Muslims refusing to join the global jihad. The three subsequently appeared on Saudi television and renounced their support for militancy. Thereafter, the Sahwa sheikhs were intimidated but not entirely silenced. The 'surge' in Iraq, when US troops fought an insurgency against mainly Sunni rebels in the cities of Falluja and Ramadi west of Baghdad, placed a huge strain on the relationship between the Saudi regime and its American allies, with statements, petitions, chat rooms and internet discussion boards calling for Saudis to join the jihad in Iraq where their Sunni brethren were being 'exterminated' by *rawafid* 'rejectionists' (that is, Shia) allied to the Western 'crusaders'.

In November 2004, twenty-six religious scholars, including the Sahwa cleric Salman al-Awdah, issued a fatwa endorsing Saudi and Muslim support for the insurgency, yet falling short of directly calling on Saudis to join the jihad in Iraq as *fard ayn* (individual duty).[46] The clerics did not exhort Saudis or Muslims from outside Iraq to travel there to fight the Americans, although they did vaguely encourage 'our Muslim brothers to stand by their brothers in Iraq by ... supporting them as much as possible'. Nevertheless, as Jones points out 'while it was not an endorsement of al-Qaeda, it was also not a reflection of a moderate political position' as it demonstrated 'that both jihad and other violence were justified within certain boundaries and especially against the U.S. and its interests, a position constituting a real dilemma for the royal family'.[47]

More radical voices, such as al-Awdah's former associate Yousuf al-Uyairi, condemned the Sahwa sheikhs for working with client governments allied to infidels and for linking their 'corrupted local practices with the globalized forces of the enemy', thereby betraying the Sahwa programme's 'transformative potential'. In particular al-Uyairi accused al-Awdah of giving in to the state and having submitted to realpolitik, acquiescing merely in the 'modification' rather than the execution of their *manhaj* (revolutionary programme) which had become corrupted and weakened in consequence.[48]

For anyone conversant with Western political discourses from revolutionary Marxists to Irish republicans, the timbre of these polemics may sound familiar – absolutism versus pragmatism, ultimate goals deferred to enable existing structures to survive. A particular character, though, lies in what might be called the flawed universalism of much of the Sunni discourse – its insistence of seeing Islam's 'universal mission' to change reality in terms that explicitly exclude the Shia tradition. The sectarian dynamic of Sunni radicalism attained its fullest expression in Abu Musa al-Zarqawi, killed by a US air strike in 2006, and his successors who came to form the so-called Islamic State under Abu Bakr al-Baghdadi, its self-proclaimed 'caliph', that straddled the border of Iraq and Syria after the outbreak of the Syrian civil war. Like Zarqawi, they were violently sectarian in outlook, pronouncing *takfir* on Shias and others who rejected their sectarian outlook.

In 2015 Prince Turki al-Faisal, the former Saudi intelligence chief who had been his country's ambassador to both the US and the UK, produced a widely circulated paper that sought to exonerate the

Wahhabi tradition from any association with ISIS and their bloodthirsty anathemas.

> These heretics, or *khawarij* as they are known in Islam, have destroyed revered sites of worship and contemplation in the name of 'destroying idols', including millennia-old sites of civilization. They have collectively judged and sentenced to death all Muslims who disagree with them, Sunni and Shia, for being blasphemers. For those of us Muslims who follow the traditions of the Salaf and the teachings of Imams Ahmad bin Hanbal and Abdul Wahhab, our ideals of self-improvement through personal struggle to overcome (or 'jihad'); our reverence for our righteous ancestors, the salaf al-salih, have been hijacked.[49]

However, any thought of religious inclusiveness implied in the prince's message defending Wahhabism needs to be contrasted with the anti-Shia thrust of the statement, signed by thirty-eight clerics including Safar al-Hawali and shown on Saudi Islamist websites. Although it fell short of calling for a jihad, it stated that Sunni Muslims in Iraq were being murdered and marginalized by Shiites backed by Iran and the US-led forces.

> We direct this message to all concerned about Shi'ites in the world: the murder, torture and displacement of Sunnis ... is an outrage ... Muslims must stand directly without Sunni brothers in Iraq and support them by all appropriate, well-studied means ... Muslims generally should be made aware of the danger of the Shi'ites. Clerics and intellectuals should not stand [with] hands folded over what is happening to their Sunni brothers in Iraq; all occasions should be used to expose the Shi'ite practices ... What has been taken by force can only be taken back by force.[50]

Hostility to Iran, abetted by America and especially by the neo-conservatives who regarded Iran as a threat to American Middle Eastern interests and had never forgiven the Iranians for holding their diplomats hostage in 1979–80, gave the regime a platform it could share with the Wahhabi clerics, enabling it to face down opposition from more liberal-minded elements. The latter included the Committee for the Defense of Legitimate Rights and later Movement for Islamic Reform in Arabia led by the exile Sa'ad al-Faqih from London. In 2008, according to a leaked US diplomatic cable, King Abdullah repeatedly exhorted the US to 'cut off the head of the snake' by launching military strikes to terminate Iran's nuclear programme in order to prevent it from converting nuclear energy to military use.

King Abdullah's hopes may have been frustrated by the 'Iran Nuclear Deal' or Joint Common Plan of Action (JCPOA) jointly signed between Iran and the United States, France, Russia, the United Kingdom, China, Germany and the European Union. It was not surprising that in 2017 his half-brother King Salman, who came to the throne on Abdullah's death in January 2015, warmly welcomed President Trump's decision to withdraw from the deal. Saudi Arabia and its Gulf allies professed alarm that the ending of UN sanctions on Iran that formed part of the deal would make it easier for the Islamic Republic to help its Shia co-religionist in Bahrain and allied sectarian forces in Syria and Yemen.

There were also internal dynamics at work in the kingdom's pursuit of an explicitly anti-Shiite policy. As al-Rasheed avers, in the wake of the 'Arab Spring' uprisings that led to the overthrow of the Mubarak regime in Egypt, the Ben Ali regime in Tunisia and lit the fuse of the civil war in Syria, the adoption of a Sunni policy of 'sectarianism' – or, more precisely, of deliberate 'sectarianization' – became 'a pre-emptive counter-revolutionary strategy that the Saudi regime deployed to exaggerate religious differences and hatred, and prevent the development of national non-sectarian politics'. The strategy, which has been highly successful, makes it virtually impossible for Sunni and Shia to 'create joint platforms for political mobilization'.[51]

In March 2011 a 'Day of Rage' announced on Facebook and other social media, that would echo the massive street protests in other Arab capitals, fizzled out when people received anonymous text messages conveying 'dire warnings of huge fines, loss of nationality and expulsion from the country' for anyone taking part. The failed protests in Riyadh followed weeks of demonstrations in Qatif, where police had fired on mainly Shiite protestors. While these Shia protests were initially inspired by the Arab Spring, they were focused less on demands for democracy than on improved conditions for the Saudi Shia, who were seen to be supporting their co-religionists in neighbouring Bahrain, where the ruling Sunni family, the al-Khalifas, preside over a Shia majority. After weeks of sit-ins and protests at the Pearl Roundabout in Manama the Saudis sent troops across the causeway to disperse the demonstrators and 'restore order' in Bahrain. For any Saudis thinking of taking part in the Day of Rage, the message was clear. As al-Rasheed explained:

> By constructing calls for demonstrations on the 'Day of Rage' ... as a Shia conspiracy against the Sunni majority with the objective of spreading Iran's influence in the Sunni homeland, the regime deepened sectarian tension and undermined efforts to mobilize the youth in various cities, including those where the Shia live ... Sectarian discourse proved to be successful in suppressing the Bahraini pro-democracy movement ... This allowed the Saudi regime to send strong signals not only to its own politically agitated Shia minority, many of whom have religious, social and kinship ties with the Bahrainis, but also more

importantly to the Sunni majority inside Saudi Arabia. The regime compelled its Sunni majority, long brought up on a sectarian discourse that denounces the Shia as heretics, to consider their government as a protector against Shia conspirators and foreign agents allegedly acting in the name of Iran, a rival regional power.[52]

The message was reinforced in January 2016 with the execution of forty-seven men – one of the larger bulk executions at the time. Forty-three had been convicted for the attacks attributed to al-Qaeda in the Arabian Peninsula in the early 2000s, but four were from the Shia minority, including the prominent Sheikh Nimr al-Nimr, an outspoken critic of the regime but no terrorist. While he was not a mainstream figure in the Shia religious establishment, he had a considerable following among the youth, and though he did not explicitly call for a Shia uprising, he did little to discourage it, hinting that he might support Iran in the event of it deciding to intervene to support the Saudi Shia.

According to a 2008 cable released by WikiLeaks, a US official who spoke with al-Nimr reported that his private remarks were consistent with his disregard for the Saudi government, his support of foreign intervention on behalf of the Saudi Shia and their 'inference that the Sheikh at the very least will not denounce the idea of violent uprising ... [S]ome local analysts ... believe that al-Nimr would not hesitate to join Iranian agents in a possible uprising.'[53]

The execution of al-Nimr was defended by the British government, who claimed that due process had been observed. It was applauded by Sunni commentators, including Jamal Khashoggi, who said it sent 'a clear message to anybody who wants to overthrow the government. Al-Nimr openly called for the overthrow of the [Saudi] system and allegiance to Wilayit al-Faqih [Iran's supreme leader]. That amounts [to] treason [in] any democratic country. It is not about his view as a Shia; it's about his call to overthrow the government and swear allegiance to a foreign leader.'[54]

Khashoggi's justification chimed in with that attitude of most Saudis who regard Shiite citizens as potentially disloyal. As Paul Aarts and Carolien Roelants put it 'although Shi'ites never tire of explaining that their loyalty to the Saudi state has never been in doubt', and the great majority, including the so-called 'reformists' (*islahhiyun*) follow the guidance of the non-political Iraqi Grand Ayatollah Ali al-Sistani as their *marja* or the 'source of emulation', 'the notion prevails among Saudi Sunnis that it is impossible by definition for Shi'ites to be loyal to the state.'[55]

The killing of al-Nimr produced riots in Tehran, and in Mashhad, Iran's second most populous city, the Saudi consulate was burned down. These consequences were entirely predictable: encouraging nationalist-sectarian feeling among the kingdom's Wahhabi-Sunni majority was exactly what the regime wanted. As Jones observed, 'the execution, both its timing and that it happened at all, was very calculated' at a time of falling oil prices and when the war against Houthi rebels in Yemen was going badly (see Chapter 1). 'One way to deflect attention away [from the war] is to find a way to sustain ideological commitment to the campaign. The Saudis have never really developed a coherent kind of nationalism, but they sure have gotten traction out of anti-Shi'ism.'[56]

Anti-Shiite sentiment found further expression in the mass execution of thirty-seven alleged 'terrorists' in April 2019. While the state-run news agency said the men had been executed for 'their adoption of extremist, terrorist ideology and forming terrorist cells to corrupt and disturb security, spread chaos and cause sectarian discord', at least thirty-three of the victims belonged to the Shia minority.

In June 2019 when the French edition of this book went to press these tensions rose dramatically, producing a real danger of armed conflict in the Gulf. After sabotage attacks on four oil tankers passing through the Strait of Hormuz in May and June, Saudi Arabia and the UAE issued stern warnings to Iran, despite the Islamic Republic's strong denial of responsibility. In an interview with the Saudi-owned newspaper *Asharq al-Awsat*, within hours of the second attack, the Saudi crown prince directly accused the Iranian regime of sabotage, and said that while his country did not want war, 'We will not hesitate to respond to every threat against our sovereignty, our people, our territorial integrity and our vital interests.'[57] President Donald Trump endorsed this position, claiming the attacks had 'Iran written all over [them]', a position echoed by the British foreign secretary Jeremy Hunt, who was standing as a candidate to succeed Theresa May as Conservative prime minister. But others were much more cautious. António Guterres, the UN secretary general, called for an independent investigation. 'It's very important to know the truth and it's very important that responsibilities are clarified. Obviously that can only be done if there is an independent entity that verifies those facts.'[58]

In a country where many are brought up to believe that Shiites spit in their food, making it difficult for Sunni and Shia to eat together, or that it is 'unclean to shake hands with a Shi'ite making a ritual ablution necessary',[59] sectarian nationalism offers an ideal way of deflecting people from addressing the deeper structural problems of economic inequality and urban anomie that will be considered in the next chapter.

8
Arms and Benefits

In Francis Ford Coppola's *Godfather* film trilogy, Michael Corleone, played by Al Pacino, rids his Mafia family of rival dons after the death of his father Don Vito, played by Marlon Brando, rising to become leader of the Mafia 'family' before eventually ending his days as a sad and lonely figure consumed with guilt over the murder of his brother Fredo. At age thirty-nine, MBS has a long way to go before fully fitting the *Godfather* scenario, but there can be little doubt about his Corleone-style progression. The bright younger son of a doting father, he supplanted his older half-brothers, becoming at twenty-four the private aide to his father, who was governor of Riyadh. When in 2011 Prince Sultan bin Abdal-Aziz, the long-serving defence minister, died, Salman replaced him in defence, with MBS as his trusted advisor. Then in June 2012 Prince Nayef, the hard-line interior minister and crown prince, died, to be succeeded by Salman as next in the gerontocratic progression. In January 2015 King Abdullah died, enabling Salman to become king. The situation required some deft, Corleone-style footwork, on the part of father and son, as the 'dons' belonging to a rival faction – namely the sons of King Abdullah – still had power and influence.

In November 2017 a number of wealthy Saudis, including eleven of Mohammed's princely cousins, were arrested for 'corruption' and incarcerated in the gilded luxury of the Ritz-Carlton hotel in Riyadh until they handed over assets MBS claimed had been obtained illegally. US president Donald Trump endorsed the crackdown in one of his celebrated tweets: 'I have great confidence in King Salman and the Crown Prince of Saudi Arabia, they know exactly what they are doing. Some of those they are harshly treating have been "milking" their country for years!'

This may not have been a *Godfather*-style shoot-out, but its effects were not dissimilar, and violence was certainly employed. At least seventeen detainees were taken to hospital after suffering from physical abuse and one of them, Major General Ali al-Qahtani, is reported to have died in custody, his neck apparently twisted, and his body badly swollen along with other signs of abuse, according to one witness cited by the *New York Times*.

The detainees included two of the kingdom's most powerful men, Miteb bin Abdullah, son of the late King Abdullah and head of the National Guard, and Alwaleed bin Talal, billionaire financier known globally for his stakes in Twitter and Apple, Citigroup and News Corp. General Qahtani was an aide to Prince Turki bin Abdullah, a son of the late King Abdullah and a former governor of Riyadh, and he had probably been tortured for information about his boss. Both Miteb and Turki were relieved of their posts and held in the Ritz-Carlton along with Alwaleed, son of the 'red prince' Talal bin Abd al-Aziz, who had been passed over for the throne for his liberal leanings. Alwaleed, who built up his own investment fortune, has been ranked as one of the world's wealthiest men.

In November 2017 *Forbes* magazine placed him at number forty-five in its global listing of the world's billionaires with a net worth of $18.7 billion, but the news of his arrest immediately wiped nearly $2 billion off the value of his principal asset, a 95 per cent share in Kingdom

Holding which owns stakes in a broad swathe of companies in Europe, the US and Saudi Arabia, including Citigroup, Twitter and the Four Seasons hotel management chain, owners of the luxury George V hotel in Paris.[1] Following Alwaleed's arrest, the CEO of Kingdom Holding released a puzzling statement that the 'Kingdom of Saudi Arabia is in full confidence with Kingdom Holding Company (KHC) ... as [it] pursues its investment strategy and global business operations'. A Saudi analyst working for a different company interpreted the statement as a sign that operations at Kingdom Holding would continue normally, making it unclear if the corruption allegations levelled at Alwaleed were tied to Kingdom Holding or were 'solely related to the arrested Prince and the other accused people'.[2] Alwaleed is said to have been released after handing over assets worth $6 billion.[3]

Like most other detainees, Alwaleed kept silent about his detention and the financial penalty he suffered. Exceptionally, his younger brother Khaled expressed outrage, and was immediately locked up.[4]

Although the Saudi government claimed that its investigations into alleged corruption 'were conducted in full accordance with Saudi laws' and that 'all those under investigation had full access to legal counsel in addition to medical care', it refused to specify any of the charges, citing privacy laws. Even after detainees were released it refused to clarify who was found guilty or innocent, making it impossible to determine how much of the process was 'driven by personal score settling'. While it may be a considerable time before the extent of private score-settling can be known for sure, it is clear that the main thrust of the operation was a purge of princes and retainers belonging to King Abdullah's branch of the family. Detainees included Khaled al-Tawijeri, King Abdullah's chief of the royal court who was ousted on Salman's accession, Fawaz Alhokair, who owned the kingdom's franchises of Zara, Banana Republic, Gap, Nine West and Topshop as well as dozens of other stores, and Salah Kamel, an elderly businessman from the Red Sea port city of Jeddah.

According to press reports, Miteb bin Abdullah, former head of the Saudi Arabian National Guard (SANG), the powerful 200,000-strong tribal militia and security force and successor to the Ikhwan, was released after three weeks in custody when he agreed to pay more than $1 billion in a settlement. The SANG had been under the command of Abdullah and his sons since the early 1960s. With its network of tribal militias, it was an important source of power for the Abdullah faction. Other sons of the late king who were detained included Prince Turki bin Abdullah who had been trained as a fighter pilot in Britain and the US before briefly serving as governor of the Riyadh province during his father's reign and acting as CEO of the multi-billion-dollar King Abdullah charitable foundation. Part of the crown prince's motive was evidently to force the late king's children to 'return' billions of dollars they considered to be their lawful inheritance.

In August 2023 Prince Turki, who had been accused of graft over the construction of the city's metropolitan railway, was sentenced to seventeen years in prison.[5] Two of the late king's other sons, Prince Faisal bin Abdullah, former head of the Saudi Red Crescent Authority, and Prince Mishaal bin Abdullah, a former governor of Mecca province, were briefly detained after they complained about the death of General Qahtani, who is said to have been 'in the peak of health' when arrested. By January 2019 when the campaign ended officially (though several detainees including Prince Turki remained in custody) the government claimed – without mentioning names – those 318 individuals had been summoned as suspects or witnesses, and that eighty-seven had confessed to charges and reached financial settlements that included the forfeiture of real estate, companies, cash and other assets.

Altogether, the government claimed to have 'reached settlements' worth more than $106 billion in the crackdown on 'corruption', with $13 billion in cash. The seizure of relatively little cash was explained by the fact that detainees tended to keep most of their money abroad, where the government could not take it without a substantive legal process. Most of the seized assets were in domestic real estate holdings or shares of companies, which the government was expected to liquidate over time.

In the case of one company, however, the crown prince's acquisition required an external legal process as it was registered in Dubai. Soon after his rise to power in 2015 he expressed an interest in buying MBC, the Arab world's largest media company which owns a range of satellite television stations beaming shows like *The Voice* and *Arabs Got Talent* into millions of homes. MBC inevitably has considerable leverage over Arab public opinion. While the company's owners and most of its board were arrested, the crown prince and his associates needed the services of two British firms, the accountants PricewaterhouseCoopers (PWC) and the law firm Clifford Chance. It does not stretch the *Godfather* scenario far to suggest a parallel between the role of PWC and Clifford Chance to that of Michael Corleone's *consigliere*, the lawyer and fixer Tom Hagan, played by Robert Duvall in *Godfather II*. As the *New York Times* reported laconically, 'Neither firm publicly raised any concerns that the sellers had been detained by the buyer.'[6]

In launching the campaign against 'corruption' that so impressed President Trump, MBS did not make his own claims to austerity, increasing the impression that the project was less about corruption than his own bid for wealth and power. In many societies – and especially where the state is regarded less as the defender of the public weal than the source of patronage – the conspicuous display of wealth is an essential attribute of power. In appropriating or reducing the wealth of the Abdullah foundation, MBS was not just taking the family's money but reducing the family's power.

According to the same logic, his own conspicuous consumption – exemplified by the purchase of a Russian billionaire's yacht, *Serene* (€500 million), or the replica 'Chateau Louis XIV' nestling in forested park between Versailles and Marly-le-Roi (€275 million) or the purchase (through a princely intermediary) of Leonardo's *Salvator Mundi*, the world's most expensive painting, for €450 million – indicates not so much purchases of luxuries as statements of power and authority that show other members of the family who is now in charge of the state.

There are, of course, precedents for displays of this kind within the Saudi family. Prior to the rise of MBS, its most powerful and conspicuous member was Prince Bandar bin Sultan, the long-serving ambassador to Washington and one of the regime's key fixers. Significantly, his daughter Princess Reema has now succeeded him in that all-important post.

As an outstanding example of what might be called 'caste-prejudice' operating in the House of Saud, the egregious and charming Bandar, son of the defence minister and crown prince Sultan bin Abdal-Aziz, who died in 2011, could never be considered for the throne. His mother was an illiterate servant or 'concubine' from the Asir region who Prince Sultan made pregnant when she was only sixteen. Bandar was initially sent to live with her in Asir, excluded in effect from the family, until taken up by Prince Sultan – and his grandmother Hussa – who recognized his keen intelligence. A dossier held by Britain's Ministry of Defence summed him up as having 'lots of charm and dash; speaks excellent English … The son of the minister of defense by a negress. His father at first neglected him because of his dark skin, but later recognized his qualities.'[7]

Impressively Bandar rose to become one of the world's most accomplished diplomats working at the heart of power. He served as the kingdom's ambassador to the United States from 1983 to 2005 before becoming secretary general of the National Security Council (2005–15) and director of its intelligence agency (2012–14). As a long-serving envoy in the US capital he was dean of the diplomatic corps throughout President Bill Clinton's presidency from 1993, a position he continued to hold under President George W. Bush.

Bandar had spent time at Britain's Royal Air Force College in Cranwell and the US Maxwell Air Force Base in the 1960s and flew military aircraft until 1977 when he injured his back in a crash. Having served as his country's military attaché, in 1983 he became the Saudi ambassador when Ronald Reagan was president. As the Saudi king's personal envoy, the prince dealt with – according to David Ottaway of the *Washington Post* – 'five US presidents, ten secretaries of state, 11 national security advisers, 16 sessions of Congress, an obstreperous American media, and hundreds of greedy politicians'.[8] No Arab ambassador – perhaps no ambassador – has come close to matching Prince Bandar's influence in the American capital. According to Bruce Reidel, a former CIA analyst, Bandar was 'probably the most effective ambassador in Washington ever'. Not only was he highly regarded by every president, he made sure that he was indispensable to both sides: in Ottaway's words, 'at once the king's exclusive messenger and the White House's errand boy'.[9] The journalist Susanne Koelbl, who met him in January 2018 before the Khashoggi murder, tells us that those who know him describe him as a 'dazzling personality: he is attentive and kind, loyal and funny and particularly clever' as well as being a 'brilliant raconteur'. But he is also an aficionado of Machiavelli, whose outlook he embraced when doing an MA in international politics at Johns Hopkins in Baltimore: he can be a 'dangerous manipulator, a daredevil who becomes menacing, brutal, even destructive' in pursuit of the kingdom's policies.[10]

A few days after 9/11, which he watched on a bank of television screens in his office, Bandar helped arrange to get some members of the bin Laden family out of the United States, a move that was made under the supervision of the FBI. It caused widespread consternation, with sources in the US media claiming a cover-up, as the bin Ladens had been spirited out of the country before anyone could have the opportunity to interrogate them or explore any links they might have with the hijackers. A 'hawk' on the issue of Saddam Hussein's Iraq, which he regarded as a continuing threat to the Saudi oilfields, it was reported that in advance of the 2003 US invasion of Iraq Bandar was shown details of the war plans by George W. Bush – before they were shown to the US secretary of state Colin Powell, even though Powell was his personal friend. Bandar was certain that Saddam would never forgive or forget his defeat in the first Gulf War, and that any talk of compromise or containment was futile. According to Bandar, though many European and Arab countries were saying publicly that they opposed a military effort to topple Saddam, they were saying something different in private. Given his high-level contacts in the West and beyond, his view would have carried much weight.

In 2005 Bandar resigned early as ambassador for 'personal reasons', arriving conveniently in Riyadh a few weeks before the death of his uncle King Fahd, an event that elevated his father Sultan to be next in line for the throne. The new King Abdullah, whose mother had belonged to the powerful Shammar tribe, was seen as an 'outsider' by many in the royal family, whose inner group of full brothers (including Fahd, Sultan, Nayef, Salman and Ahmed) were sons of Abd al-Aziz's wife Hussa bint Al Sudairi (1900–69). The Al Sudairi brothers – widely known along with their immediate progeny as the

Al Fahd – used to dine with their mother on a daily basis prior to her death. History does not record what she told 'her boys' on those occasions, but they formed a powerful faction inside the family, and the choice of Sultan as crown prince was clearly aimed at balancing family factions, ensuring that the new king had support from his half-brothers. When he had moved to Riyadh as a boy, Bandar is said to have been very close to Hussa. Who can tell what insights she imparted to her much-loved grandson?

The White House hailed Bandar as a close and steadfast friend of the US and a 'tireless advocate for close ties, warm relations and mutual understanding'.[11] Bandar's critics, however, see him as an evil genius and terrorist godfather linked to jihadist activities and right-wing, reactionary causes. In the 1980s he siphoned millions of dollars to the Nicaraguan Contras engaged in a terror campaign to overthrow the left-wing Sandinista government. While direct links between the prince and the 9/11 hijackers have never been established, the release in 2016 by the Obama administration of twenty-eight pages that had been kept out of the official report into the atrocity on grounds of national security revealed a financial trail to the prince's wife.

Additionally, an address book belonging to Abu Zubaydah, a senior member of al-Qaeda captured in a raid by Pakistani forces in 2002, contained unlisted phone numbers for a bodyguard at the Saudi embassy as well as a company entrusted with the management of the prince's private property in Aspen, Colorado. 'Both of those numbers were unpublished, so they had to have gotten into Zubaydah's phone book through a personal contact who knew what those numbers were and what they represented', said former senator Bob Graham, co-chair of the congressional commission that compiled the dossier.[12]

The money trail connected the prince's wife Princess Haifa

al-Faisal (a daughter of King Faisal and sister of Princes Turki and Saud) with Osama Bassnan, a former employee of the Saudi government's Educational Mission in Washington, who was living in San Diego in September 2001. Bassnan's wife was said to be suffering from 'health problems' for which she received cheques totalling some $74,000 from Princess Haifa, as well as at least one directly from Bandar himself. Bassnan lived across the street from two of the 9/11 hijackers, Nawaf al-Hazmi and Khalid al-Mihdhar, who were on the American Airlines plane that crashed into the Pentagon.

After checking the bank details, the FBI determined that some of the cheques for Bassnan's wife were passed on to another Saudi national called Omar al-Bayoumi, thought to be a member of Saudi intelligence charged with monitoring the views and activities of Saudi students in America. Bayoumi had direct ties to the two terrorists, having helped find them an apartment in San Diego in 2000, one year before 9/11, and even signing their lease.[13]

According to the FBI, several of the cheques made out to Mrs Bassnan were passed on to Mrs Bayoumi. Spokespeople at the Saudi embassy said it was not unusual for wealthy Saudis like Princess Haifa to help fellow nationals with money, and Bandar and his wife were known for both their generosity as well as their lavish lifestyles. Despite Bayoumi's association with the hijackers, the FBI concluded that Bayoumi did not have 'advance knowledge of the terrorist attacks' or 'knowledge of al-Hazmi's and/or al-Mihdhar's status as al Qaeda operatives' or that 'the assistance provided by al-Bayoumi to al-Hazmi and al-Mihdhar was [given] wittingly'.[14]

In September 2021, on the twentieth anniversary of 9/11, the Biden administration allowed the FBI to begin releasing some of the documents that had been withheld from public scrutiny on grounds of national security. The US government had come under pressure from lawyers acting for some of the families of the victims of 9/11 who were suing the Saudi government for providing financial and logistical support for the hijackers, charges which the Saudi government had consistently denied. After some families made it known that President Biden and the first lady would not be welcome at memorial events unless some classified files were released, the president issued an executive order instructing government agencies to review, declassify and release more information. Among the first documents released by the FBI was one that showed that despite their earlier conclusion that Bayoumi did not have prior knowledge of the attack, its agents had continued to investigate possible ties between him and the two hijackers as recently as 2016.

When originally questioned by the FBI in 2003 Bayoumi claimed that he had met the two hijackers casually at a restaurant in Los Angeles, an encounter that was purely accidental. However, the document released by the FBI in September 2021 states that his account was 'directly contradicted by eyewitness statements', including one by a named witness, Caisin bin Don. The latter's account suggests a pre-arranged encounter, with Bayoumi placing himself visibly in the restaurant's front window and signalling the two men to join him at his table. The FBI document notes that another witness who met the hijackers at a convenience store in northern Virginia also claimed it had been a 'chance meeting' in a uniquely similar fashion to the way Bayoumi described his 'chance meeting' with Hazmi and Mihdhar in Los Angeles.

As Devlin Barrett, a journalist specializing in security matters, stated in the *Washington Post*, the document 'contains significant redactions, but nevertheless shows that FBI officials were sceptical of claims by various witnesses that Saudis in the United States who met with the two hijackers did so accidentally through chance encounters'.[15] The FBI investigators were also interested in Fahad al-Thumayri, a former official at the Saudi consulate in Los Angeles who also served as an imam at the King Fahad Mosque in the Los Angeles suburb of Culver City. According to FBI sources, in 2004 the Saudi consul wanted to fire a consul employee for storing and distributing extremist literature, but Thumayri and his colleague Muhammad Muhanna used their influence with the Saudi government to retain the individual, referred to as PII in the redacted document.

PII's claim that they never knew or discussed 9/11 at the mosque is directly contradicted by FBI sources which state that after the attacks on New York and the Pentagon PII would offer the greeting 'Isn't it great that our brothers are fighting?', while a different source 'whose reporting proved reliable in the past' advised that this individual 'was very vocal against Christians, Jews and enemies of Islam'.

Neither this document, nor the previous release of the twenty-eight pages provides unequivocal evidence of official Saudi government involvement in the September 2001 attacks. In its 2004 report, the 9/11 Commission, while acknowledging that Saudi Arabian individuals and charities had long been considered 'primary sources of al-Qaeda funding', rejected the idea that Saudi officials had assisted the attacks, finding 'no evidence that the Saudi government as an institution or senior Saudi officials individually' funded the terrorist group, a conclusion repeatedly proclaimed by the Saudi embassy as further details emerged from the vast volume of partly declassified documents held by the FBI and other agencies.

The September 2021 document was no exception. 'The Kingdom has always advocated for transparency surrounding the September 11 tragedy', said an embassy statement, adding that 'no evidence has ever emerged to indicate that the Saudi government or its officials had previous knowledge of the terrorist attack or were in any way involved in its planning or execution. Any allegation that Saudi Arabia is complicit in the September 11 attacks is categorically false.'[16]

At this writing, however, victims' families are far from satisfied with this exoneration and can be expected to hope that claims of Saudi involvement would be sustained by the release of further documents. Terry Strada, whose husband died in the North Tower, speaking for the 9/11 Families United group, said: 'Now the Saudis' secrets are exposed and it is well past time for the kingdom to own up to its officials' roles in murdering thousands on American soil.'[17] The path of litigation will doubtless endure for decades. A key question will focus on the extent to which any foreknowledge of the 9/11 plot, or assistance given to the hijackers by Saudi officials, employees or charities were known in the higher reaches of power. While the government's claim that 'rogue operators' were responsible for Khashoggi's assassination in Turkey may have failed to convince investigators from the CIA and the United Nations (as we saw in Chapter 1), the murder of nearly 3,000 people of many nationalities (including sixty-seven British citizens) on American soil presents a far more complex situation.

The 11 September atrocity occurred at a time when King Fahd had been incapacitated by a stroke and power was divided, not to say contested, between the two branches of the family represented by the Al Fahd and the rival clan led by Crown Prince Abdullah. At that juncture, the top-down authoritarian control now exercised by MBS through his coterie of praetorians was clearly absent. Indeed, this was the time when Osama bin Laden, son of one of the family's most conspicuous beneficiaries as a builder of highways, palaces and restorer of Islam's holiest mosque, was able to publicly challenge the monarchy from a position of privilege in a manner that would have been unthinkable two decades later. But to prove that the kingdom was institutionally implicated in the attack on its closest ally by its most prominent enemy remains a formidable legal challenge whatever new documents come to be declassified.

Another – more sinister – thought is the role Bandar may have had in 'framing' Saddam Hussein for 9/11. We know for sure that the attack on New York and the Pentagon was used by the neo-conservatives in the younger Bush administration, especially Vice President Dick Cheney and Defence Secretary Donald Rumsfeld, as the excuse to 'go after' Saddam Hussein, even though there was absolutely no evidence linking the Iraqi dictator to the attacks on the Twin Towers and the Pentagon. From Bandar's perspective, however, the American attack on Iraq in 2003 was a positive outcome of his diplomatic manoeuvrings, enhanced by his proximity to George W. Bush. The immediate threat to the Saudi oilfields that so worried him was relieved by the Iraqi dictator's overthrow.

Bandar's return to Riyadh, where he headed the National Security Council and served as director of intelligence, coincided with the popular insurgencies known as the 'Arab Spring' which led to the overthrow of the Mubarak regime in Egypt, the Ben Ali regime in Tunisia and the Qadhafy regime in Libya. In Bahrain where the Sunni al-Khalifa family rules over a Shia-majority population, the Saudi government was so alarmed by the protests that they sent more than 1,000 troops from the National Guard, along with Sunni contingents from Jordan, the UAE and Pakistan, across the causeway to Manama, the capital. By 2014 some 5,000 Saudi and Emirati forces along with 7,000 American troops were positioned less than 16 km from the Pearl Roundabout, the centre of the protest movement.

In the case of Syria, Saudi intervention was less overt. Claims by Bandar's critics need to be treated with caution, not least because the processes by which the Saudis make their foreign policy decisions are so opaque. While outsiders cannot be privy to the inner workings of the system, there can be little doubt that Bandar had enormous 'clout' especially during the years 2012–14 when he was director of Saudi intelligence. In the case of Libya, for instance, Bandar is said to have helped finance al-Qaeda-linked extremists who attacked the

US consulate in Benghazi after the NATO intervention in Libya, killing the US ambassador J. Christopher Stevens in September 2012. In Egypt he may well have been behind the military coup by General Abd al-Fattah al-Sisi, a former military attaché in Riyadh, who overthrew the Muslim Brotherhood government of Mohamed Morsi in August 2013.

As we saw in Chapter 1, Saudi backing for the clampdown against the Brotherhood contrasted with the decades of support the mainstream Islamist movement received during the reign of King Faisal. It also seemed to contradict the support the Saudis and other Gulf emirates provided to Islamist rebels fighting the Assad regime in Syria after the civil war broke out in 2011. Prior to the civil war, Bandar had been influential in tilting US policy against Iran, joining with Cheney, the deputy national security advisor Elliott Abrams and other neo-conservatives in promoting what would become a de facto Saudi alliance with Israel.

The rationale he offered the Americans was that the kingdom's strategic embrace of Israel would weaken the leverage Iran had gained after the war in Iraq, where the US invasion in 2003 had produced a government that reflected the country's Shia majority. The new US strategy was a major departure from the second Bush administration's policy of encouraging 'moderate' Shia forces in Iraq. With the Americans now regarding Shia Iran and Alawi-dominated Syria as sources of instability in contrast to the 'moderation' prevailing in Sunni-dominated states, the stage was set for the 'sectarianization' of the conflict in Syria in the wake of the Arab Spring. Bandar followed the Wahhabi clerics underpinning his regime in regarding Shias as irreconcilable infidels. In British intelligence circles he is seen as the evil genius behind the ill-considered Saudi and Gulf support for the 'moderate' Sunni rebels in Syria who would rapidly morph into the fanatical ISIS caliphate.

In 2016 Sir Richard Dearlove, the former head of the British Intelligence Service MI6 and former master of Pembroke College Cambridge, revealed an ominous conversation he had with Bandar even before the 9/11 atrocity. 'The time is not far off in the Middle East, Richard, when it will be literally "God help the Shia". More than a billion Sunnis have simply had enough of them.'[18] Bandar's anti-Shia fulminations were consistent with those of the Saudi King Abdullah who urged the United States to 'cut off the head of the snake' by launching military strikes to destroy Iran's nuclear programme, according to a US diplomatic cable exposed by WikiLeaks.

A copy of the cable sent in April 2008 and published by the *New York Times* showed the Saudis feared Shiite Iran's rising influence in the region, particularly in neighbouring Iraq following the establishment of a Shia-majority government. As the conflicts in Iraq and Syria unfolded, with ISIS announcing its caliphate and symbolically bulldozing the ditch that divided Syria and Iraq, Bandar's prediction began to look chillingly plausible.

As Patrick Cockburn noted in the *Independent*,

> In Mosul, Shia shrines and mosques have been blown up, and in the nearby Shia Turkoman city of Tal Afar 4,000 houses have been taken over by Isis fighters as 'spoils of war'. Simply to be identified as Shia or a related sect, such as the Alawites, in Sunni rebel-held parts of Iraq and Syria today, has become as dangerous as being a Jew was in Nazi-controlled parts of Europe in 1940.[19]

As Cockburn relates, the former British intelligence chief:

> does not doubt that substantial and sustained funding from private donors in Saudi Arabia and Qatar, to which the authorities may have turned a blind eye, has played a central role in the Isis surge into Sunni areas of Iraq. He said: 'Such things simply do not happen spontaneously.'

This sounds realistic since the tribal and communal leadership in Sunni majority provinces is much beholden to Saudi and Gulf paymasters and would be unlikely to cooperate with Isis without their consent.[20]

In the same remarkable talk, delivered at the Royal United Services Institute, a London think-tank founded in 1831 by the Duke of Wellington, Dearlove pointed to the contradiction in Saudi policy noted above. On the one hand, the Saudis believed that they possessed 'a monopoly of Islamic truth' leading them to be 'deeply attracted towards any militancy which can effectively challenge Shiadom', particularly with regard to Iran. Such a policy was exemplified by support for Sunni rebels in Syria and for the Sunni insurgencies in Iraq that surfaced in the wake of the US invasion where an elected government, however flawed and corrupt, was a more adequate reflection of that country's Shia majority than the Sunni-dominated regime of Saddam Hussein. Beyond the Middle East, as former secretary of state Hillary Clinton noted in a December 2009 cable published by WikiLeaks, Saudi Arabia 'remains a critical financial support base for al-Qa'ida, the Taliban, LeT [Lashkar-e-Taiba in Pakistan] and other terrorist groups' notorious for attacks on Shias.[21]

Domestically, however, as Clinton noted, the Saudi government saw al-Qaeda and its affiliates as a mortal threat to their rule. In his lecture, Dearlove highlighted the extent of Saudi schizophrenia by relating how, soon after 9/11, he visited the Saudi capital Riyadh with the British prime minister Tony Blair. He recalled the then head of intelligence Prince Nawwaf bin Abd al-Aziz 'literally shouting' at him across his office: '9/11 is a mere pinprick on the West. In the medium term, it is nothing more than a series of personal tragedies. What these terrorists want is to destroy the House of Saud and remake the Middle East.' As Cockburn remarks, 'in the event, Saudi

Arabia adopted both policies, encouraging the jihadis as a useful tool of Saudi anti-Shia influence abroad but suppressing them at home as a threat to the status quo'.[22]

That policy has now unravelled, not least because of Bandar's ill-considered support for the Sunni insurgents in Syria and Iraq. As Emma Sky, a British academic who served as an advisor to the US forces in Iraq, stated in February 2019 as the last ISIS enclave was collapsed before Kurdish–Syrian troops helped by US and Russian air strikes, the US-led Iraq war had succeeded in basically changing the regional balance of power in Iran's favour, enabling Iran to 'grow more powerful and to develop land corridors across Iraq and Syria and up against Israel's borders'. The Syrian civil war, she explained, had been the catalyst.

> When the Assad regime had come under such opposition internally, Iran then started supporting the regime and the Saudis and Gulf countries started supporting the opposition groups. And in that struggle Iran, Russia and Assad had come out as the winners ... Syria had seen the confluence of the Arab Spring and the rise in Iranian influence. The old social contract that we saw in the Middle East whereby regimes promised security and jobs and the price was no political freedom, that contract is really frayed. Governments are no longer able to provide those opportunities. You have rapidly rising and growing populations, and the price of oil has come down.[23]

Bandar's masterplan of overthrowing the Syrian government in favour of Sunni Islamists clearly failed, and its unintended consequence was a rise in the very Shiite power he had hoped to contain. Political failure was matched by military ineptitude. In the end the rag-bag forces of the disparate groups of supposedly moderate Sunni rebels proved no match for the Machiavellian way that Assad turned the tide against them, unleashing the jihadists he held in his prisons to destroy them in an unholy alliance with Iranians, Russians, Americans and Turks.

Bandar's role in this despicably unheroic conflict, where regimes have tended to use war and the military not for defence of frontiers, society or 'people', but to preserve the privilege of family *asabiyya*, is characteristically opaque. The use of chemical weapons is a case in point. While the US, Britain and France, as well as the Arab League, accused the Assad regime of using chemical weapons that killed more than 350 people, most of them civilians, in the Ghouta suburb of Damascus in August 2013, some people in the rebel area interviewed by journalists claimed that the casualties had been caused by rebels of the Saudi-supported Jabhat al-Nusra group who bungled their handling of the dangerous toxins. 'When Saudi Prince Bandar gives such weapons to people, he must give them to those who know how to handle and use them', warned a female rebel fighter cited in one report.[24]

The claim that Sunni rebels were behind the attacks was challenged by US, British and French intelligence. The latter concluded that the attack 'could not have been ordered and carried out by anyone but the Syrian government'. It said 'the launch zone for the rockets was held by the regime while the strike zone was held by the rebels', and that at the time commanders feared a wider attack on Damascus from the opposition. The investigative journalist Seymour Hersh, however, famed for his exposés of official cover-ups from the My Lai massacre in 1969 to the abuses by US troops of Iraqi prisoners in the Abu Ghraib prison in 2004, produced evidence that the sarin gas in the Ghouta attacks came from rebels, not the regime.

The key to Hersh's challenge to the official narrative was the analysis by Theodore Postol, a professor of technology and national security at the Massachusetts Institute of Technology, who reviewed UN photos of the spent rocket canisters used in the attack with a group of his colleagues. They concluded that the large-calibre rocket shown in the pictures was an improvised device likely to have been manufactured locally. Postol and his colleague Richard Lloyd concluded that the range of such a rocket could not have been much more than 2 kilometres, whereas the official narrative attributing the sarin attack to government forces required a minimum of 9.

While weight of media coverage in the US and the West generally continued to place the blame on the Assad regime, the Obama administration conspicuously failed to act on the president's threat that by using chemical weapons Bashar al-Assad had crossed a 'red line' that would justify an attack on Syria similar to the US attack on Iraq in 2003.

As Hersh narrates:

> The proposed American missile attack on Syria never won public support and Obama turned quickly to the UN and the Russian proposal for dismantling the Syrian chemical warfare complex. Any possibility of military action was definitively averted on 26 September when the administration joined Russia in approving a draft UN resolution calling on the Assad government to get rid of its chemical arsenal. Obama's retreat brought relief to many senior military officers … The administration's distortion of the facts surrounding the sarin attack raises an unavoidable question: do we have the whole story of Obama's willingness to walk away from his 'red line' threat to bomb Syria? He had claimed to have an iron-clad case but suddenly agreed to take the issue to Congress, and later to accept Assad's offer to relinquish his chemical weapons. *It appears possible that at some point he was directly confronted with contradictory information: evidence strong enough to persuade him to cancel his attack plan and take the criticism sure to come from Republicans.*[25]

Bandar's team, it need hardly be added, took a different view of the Ghouta attack, with one of them telling Koelbl 'we showed the Americans irrefutable proof' that it was Assad's force that had been responsible. It may be significant, however, that in Koelbl's narrative it wasn't the prince himself who made this statement, but a 'close confidant of Prince Bandar's who ha[d] hitherto followed our conversation in silence'.[26]

Similar doubts attach to the alleged use of chlorine gas dropped by Assad's forces from helicopters in the rebel-held suburb of Douma in February 2019. A leaked report by an expert from the Organisation for the Prohibition of Chemical Weapons in The Hague stated that 'The dimensions, characteristics and appearance of the cylinders, and the surrounding scene of the incidents, were inconsistent with what would have been expected in the case of either cylinder being delivered from an aircraft.' It said instead that manual placement of the cylinders in the locations that investigators found them in is 'the only plausible explanation for observations at the scene'. Photographs of the victims of this attack were circulated around the world as evidence against the Syrian government and were used to justify air strikes by the US, UK and France. The main rebel group on the ground at the time was Jaysh al-Islam, a previous recipient of Saudi support. At that point they had nothing to lose and everything to gain by staging a false flag attack in a last-ditch attempt to get NATO powers to intervene against the Syrian government.[27]

While the truth behind Bandar's possible Saudi engagement with chemical weapons cannot be determined with certainty, the prince's involvement in arms sales to the Saudi kingdom is well established and documented. Early in his career as ambassador, he secured the purchase of AWACS surveillance aircraft by the kingdom in the teeth of Israeli and congressional opposition that annoyed the powerful Israeli lobby concerned with Saudi obstruction (as they saw it) of the peace process between Israel and the Palestinians.

A request for advanced F-15 fighter jets and Lance surface-to-surface missiles for Saudi Arabia stalled in Congress, and in February 1985 the US president Ronald Reagan abandoned it. Bandar and his father Prince Sultan turned instead to Reagan's friend, the British prime minister Margaret Thatcher. Within months they had negotiated the al-Yamamah ('The Dove') arms deal, a multi-billion-pound package of forty-eight British-built Tornado jets, plus a host of extras including twenty-four planes for an 'air defence role' and thirty Hawker trainer aircraft. It was Britain's biggest-ever arms contract, worth initially £15 billion, soon to be increased to around £20 billion in a deal that allowed for spare parts, upgrades in hardware, support equipment and additional Tornados.

The al-Yamamah deal – the largest export contract ever signed by the UK government – was in line with Britain's strategic view that defending the Gulf monarchies, including Saudi Arabia, was vital to its interests. Britain's strategy was not confined to defending the Saudi kingdom and its former protectorates of Bahrain, Kuwait, Qatar and the UAE from external attack. The strategy included countering 'hostile influence and propaganda within the countries themselves'.[28] In the case of Bahrain this had long meant protecting the Sunni elite against the demographic challenge of the Shia majority; in the case of Saudi Arabia it meant helping the ruling family against internal enemies. While the Yamamah deal provided lucrative jobs for the workers in Lancashire employed by British Aerospace (BAE), it also proved to be the source of lucrative offerings for members of the Al Saud family.

As Chas Freeman, US ambassador to Riyadh from 1989 to 1992, explained to the journalist Mark Hollingsworth, al-Yamamah became a 'huge commission-generating machine' with a large proportion of BAE's hardware and spare parts sold at a high premium or 'friendship price'. The difference was distributed in pay-offs to Saudi defence officials, intermediaries and, according to Freeman, 'members of the royal family'.[29] As Hollingsworth explains, the Saudis paid for aircraft with oil. Around 600,000 barrels of crude a day were sold to BP and Shell, to be refined and sold on the open market, with the proceeds paid into a trust account in London held by the British government with BAE as the custodian and the Saudis as the beneficiary. The account could then be drawn upon by BAE as the aircraft were delivered. As Freeman observed:

> This in effect was a general slush fund for the Saudi Ministry of Defence. They could debit anything they wanted against this account and BAE would do the procurement. It was not subject to public scrutiny in either country. And it was not part of the Saudi defence budget ... The fact is that if you have a potentially limitless trust fund that you can buy anything you want from with no one the wiser, no matter how honest or patriotic your instincts might be, the temptation for abuse is large.[30]

One need hardly add that Bandar, his father, the defence minister Prince Sultan, and close relatives were the main beneficiaries of the 'off-budget' commissions, thought to amount to around 30 per cent of the contract's overall value. When in 2004 details were leaked to the British press, readers of the *Guardian*, *Sunday Times* and other papers learned how one travel agent had spent £60 million supplying Saudi royals and dignitaries with chartered yachts in Cannes, lavish trips to Hawaii, suites and whole floors of the world's top hotels and luxury cars – including the gift to one princess of a new Rolls Royce limousine that was flown across the Atlantic in a specially chartered jet.

With the documents made public, Ministry of Defence police and the Serious Fraud Office (SFO) began an official investigation into charges of corruption. In November 2004 the SFO made two arrests, with BAE claiming that it welcomed the investigation, believing it 'would put these matters to rest once and for all'.[31] In the meantime BAE started negotiations with the Saudi government for delivery of a batch of Eurofighter Typhoons that were jointly produced by Britain, Germany, Italy and Spain after France dropped out of the project.

According to the BBC, the project was worth £6 billion with 5,000 jobs at stake in the manufacturing countries, but other sources put the figure higher at £10 billion and 50,000 jobs. In June 2007 the BBC's investigative *Panorama* programme claimed that BAE Systems 'paid hundreds of millions of pounds to the ex-Saudi ambassador to the US, Prince Bandar bin Sultan'.[32] On 6 December, Prince Bandar, now Saudi Arabia's national security advisor, met with officials of the British Foreign Office, having spent a week in Paris discussing a possible French alternative with officials including President Jacques Chirac.

In London, Bandar met with Prime Minister Tony Blair and other officials. We can infer the outcome of the meeting from a personal memo Blair sent to the government's chief law officer, the attorney-general Lord Goldsmith. The prime minister said that if the BAE investigation continued there would be a 'real and immediate risk of a collapse in UK/Saudi security, intelligence and diplomatic co-operation, which was likely to have seriously negative consequences for the UK public interest in terms of both national security and the UK's highest priority foreign policy objectives in the Middle East'.[33]

The director of the SFO, Robert Wardle, received the same message from Britain's ambassador to Saudi Arabia, Sir Sherard Cowper-Poles, who told him that 'British lives on British streets would be at risk' if the investigation continued. While the Organisation of Economic Co-operation and Development (OECD) Convention on Combating Bribery, to which Britain is party, prohibits the decision to drop investigations into corruption from being influenced by considerations of national economic interest or the potential effect upon relations with another state, it does not explicitly exclude grounds of national security. On 14 December 2006, Goldsmith announced that the investigation had been discontinued on grounds of public interest and national security. In his declaration to Parliament he denied the decision had been made on commercial grounds.

> All relevant agencies were clear about the crucial importance of UK-Saudi co-operation in the fight against terrorism and the damage to UK interests – and, potentially, UK lives – if that co-operation were withdrawn. Having been advised of the risk to national security if the SFO investigation continued, the director of the SFO concluded that it was not a risk that could properly be taken in the public interest.

When challenged by the economist Lord (Maurice) Peston he denied any considerations other than national security.

> Lord Peston: Everybody knows that you cannot do business in these countries without bribery and corruption. The problem is not whether everybody knows that but that nobody seems to be able to prove it. What advice are Ministers prepared to give to British companies that want to export to the relevant countries, but cannot get through without bribing the relevant people? Are we to give up all these markets on the grounds of being holier than thou or do we just still keep our heads in the sand and pretend that nothing wrong is happening?
>
> Lord Goldsmith: I do not accept the premise of the question. It is very important to make it clear that dropping this case – which was not an entirely comfortable decision, as I said in my letter to the noble Lord – does not mean that we are backing off in any way from our commitment to tackling international corruption. On the contrary, I am clear that we should redouble our efforts. I have told the director of the SFO

that he should vigorously pursue current investigations, including a number of other cases against BAE.[34]

At a European Union summit in Brussels, Prime Minister Tony Blair claimed that in stopping the inquiry he had put to one side the effect on 'thousands of British jobs and billions of pounds worth for British industry' that might have put Britain in conflict with international law. 'Our relationship with Saudi Arabia is vitally important for our country in terms of counter-terrorism, in terms of the broader Middle East, in terms of helping in respect of Israel and Palestine. That strategic interest comes first.'[35] Delivery of the first two Eurofighter Typhoon aircraft (of seventy-two purchased by the Saudi air force) took place in June 2009.

While results from the attorney-general's campaign against corruption appeared less than visible, his exhortation for the doubling of efforts appears to have been taken to heart in Britain's Ministry of Defence (MoD) which continued to maintain quarterly payments to Prince Bandar after the SFO investigation had been terminated. Documents that came to light after a court case in March 2023 prove that the payments were made via the MoD which would 'instruct' one of its officials 'to take the necessary action' to task British Aerospace 'to make the payment'. The payments included the funding of Prince Bandar's private jet.[36]

While the MoD acknowledged that the BAE payments to Bandar were 'made according to agreements between the British and Saudi governments', that it was for the Saudis to decide how the funds were to be spent, and that talk of corruption was only 'conjecture',[37] arms manufacturers – and their thousands of employees and subcontractors – were not the only beneficiaries of the MoD's off-balance-sheet payments. Some people living amid the bucolic charms of Oxfordshire and the splendours of the Rocky Mountains were also able to benefit from Bandar's lavish spending, with his property portfolio including a British stately home and an American ranch. Glympton Park is an eighteenth-century country house with a 1,000-hectare estate complete with a village and church near Blenheim Palace, home of the dukes of Marlborough. He was able to visit his property by special arrangement with the Royal Air Force, which allowed him to land his private jet – a 375-seater Airbus A340 painted in the blue and white livery of the Dallas Cowboys, his favourite American football team – at Brize Norton, a nearby military airbase. The property has now been sold to the king of Bahrain and his son for a reported £120 million, making Bandar a substantial profit as he bought the property for £8 million from a disgraced Australian financier before spending an estimated £42 million on refurbishments that included a full-scale replica of an English public house.[38]

Bandar's American properties included two ranches near Aspen, Colorado, and a fifteen-room mansion which he sold – at a considerable loss – in 2012, after the price had been reduced from $135 million to $49 million. Bandar, it need hardly be added, was far from being the only prince to benefit from the al-Yamamah 'commission-generating machine'.[39] In addition to Bandar's father Prince Sultan, his brother-in-law Turki bin Nasser (husband of Sultan's daughter Noura) benefited massively as head of the Saudi air force. In 1988, soon after the second contract (al-Yamamah 2) was signed, BAE hired Turki's British friend, a former RAF wing-commander, Tony Winship, with a remit to 'pay for anything that Prince Turki, his family and demanding entourage desired: houses, sports cars, accommodation in luxury hotels, yachts, cash, prostitutes, gambling trips, trips in private jets, medical bills, unlimited restaurant meals and flights'.[40]

By the late 1990s the slush fund had grown tenfold from £300,000 per year to £3 million. London hotels and their staff were among the leading beneficiaries: a visit of several days from Prince Turki and his staff produced more than £80,000 in bills, plus £2,200 in tips (all paid for by BAE). A few days at a health farm cost more than £30,000. As Hollingsworth and Mitchell relate:

> Despite owning houses in Barcelona, Riyadh, Dhahran, Beverly Hills and Sussex Square, near Hyde Park [in London], Prince Turki felt the need to stay at the most luxurious hotels at BAE's expense – Maxim's in Paris (£62,000), Carlton Tower [London] ($49,000), Caesar's Palace [Las Vegas] (£46,000) and New York Plaza (£240,000).[41]

In an interview he gave to the American television *Frontline* programme in September 2001 Prince Bandar was remarkably brazen about the rake-offs, acknowledging that corruption was an inevitable adjunct of arms purchases and other aspects of modernization in Saudi Arabia.

> If you tell me that building this whole country, and in spending $350 billion out of $400 billion that we misused or got corrupted with $50 billion, I'll tell you: 'Yes, so what?' But I'll take that any time ... We did not invent corruption, nor did those dissidents, who are so genius, discover it. This has happened since Adam and Eve. It's human nature. You know what? I would be offended if I thought we had a monopoly over corruption.[42]

His statement may seem ironic, but it was not entirely frivolous. As a concept corruption is culturally loaded. The definition adopted by Transparency International, the anti-corruption organization, is 'the abuse of entrusted power for private gain'. 'Grand corruption', it states,

> consists of acts committed at a high level of government that distort policies or the central functioning of the state, enabling leaders to benefit

at the expense of the public good ... Political corruption is a manipulation of policies, institutions, and rules of procedure in the allocation of resources and financing by political decision makers, who abuse their position to sustain their power, status and wealth.[43]

When applied to the Kingdom of Saudi Arabia this definition, though accepted internationally, entails some obvious difficulties. One of them is the distinction between private gain and the public good, based on the assumption that corruption occurs when the former gains at the expense of the latter, with the latter usually identified as the state. Yet in Saudi Arabia, as in other Gulf principalities, the family *is* the state. There may be formal divisions between private and public realms, but these are often ignored in practice, not just because of individual moral lapses but rather because the interests of tribe and family transcend those of the public domain. The point was put rather brutally by Mohammed Abdullah Khilewi, a Saudi diplomat at the United Nations who defected in 1994 and was granted asylum in the United States.

> If a poor guy steals a chicken to feed his starving family, they cut off his hand. If a prince steals billions, it's okay. Some members of the Saudi royal family see the country as though it were their private property. They treat the Saudi people as their slaves. As the old joke goes, Saudi Arabia is the only family-owned business with membership in the United Nations.[44]

'Corruption' may be seen as transgression because it violates or blurs the boundaries between the public and the private realms. But, as many scholars have argued, the public/private distinction grew out of 'European medieval political theology and became fundamental to the ideological and bureaucratic structures of modern states and markets'.[45] Capitalism and the corporate institutions which accompanied its rise in the West – including parliamentary assemblies and other institutions of representative government – contain a distinct type of cultural patterning that is directly traceable to certain Christian ideas and institutions. Attempts to export them or to impose them on the non-Western world have not always been successful.

Marxists and post-Marxists who are disinclined to grant autonomy to religious ideas, seeing in them a reflection, rather than a source, of the configurations of power and authority, have tended to underplay the distinctively Christian component of the post-Christian West where the private/public division is sustained in law, if not always in practice. Yet the narrative of Western Christianity is fundamental to the way this distinction evolved. As Ernst Kantorowicz argued in *The King's Two Bodies* (1957) – his classic study of medieval political theology – the modern corporation and the corporative structures that issue from it largely derive from the mystic personhood of Christ that came to be physically embodied in the church as an institution. He shows that from the twelfth century CE the idea of the church as the mystical body of Christ was replaced by the corporative concept of the two bodies of Christ.

> One, a body natural, individual and personal (*corpus naturale, verum, personale*); the other a super-individual body politic and collective, the *corpus mysticum*, interpreted as a *persona mystica*. Whereas the *corpus verum* through the agency of the dogma of transubstantiation and the institution of the feast of Corpus Christi, developed a life and a mysticism of its own, the *corpus mysticum* proper came to be less and less mystical as time passed on, and came to mean simply the Church as a body politic or, *by transference, any body politic of the secular world.*[46]

According to Kantorowicz the emerging group structures of secular life – towns, cities, guilds and so forth – acquired public legal recognition as 'bodies' parallel with and comparable to the church. At a political level a distinction was made between the mortal person of the king and the eternal institution of the crown. Under charters from the king (or sometimes the bishop) the city also acquired its own *corpus mysticum*, its fictional identity which allowed the group personality of the organism to transcend the sum of its individual component parts. In due course the greatest of artificial persons became the state. Where sovereignty is contested by the people, the mystic body is vested typically in an assembly, whose members represent parts of the body politic. Thus in a republic the mystic body of the crown may be transferred to 'the people' – not as an aggregate of individuals, but as a fictionalized abstraction.

In regions where dynastic power prevails over other systems of government, while reinforcing itself bureaucratically through a system of institutional patronage, the lines dividing family and state are blurred, to say the least. Indeed, *dawla*, the Arabic word generally used for 'state', can also mean 'dynasty' in a way that resonates with the Khaldunian paradigm mentioned in Chapter 3: the verbal root d-w-l from which *dawla* derives conveys the notion of turning, rotation and change. It seems consistent with a world of shifting territories and ephemeral political constellations rather than the sociologist Max Weber's model of a community claiming a monopoly of the use of violence within a designated patch of territory.

The ideology of the Saudi state is ambiguous, not to say contradictory. It presents itself as a force for modernization that celebrates its achievements in technology, modern health facilities and education. As al-Rasheed explains:

> The state glorifies its efforts in these fields. To celebrate the Saudi National Day (usually on 23 September) the Ministry of Information places advertisements in local and international newspapers informing

readers about the number of schools, hospitals, airports, factories and ports built under the auspices of the Al Saud. Similarly, the relative political stability of the regime has impressed outside observers in a region that has experienced turmoil, civil wars, coups and revolutions.[47]

At the same time these signal achievements, which are largely due to the oil that gushes from the Eastern Province that Ibn Saud conquered in the early twentieth century, are thematically linked to dynastic power and success. State narratives marking the centenary of modern Saudi rule in 1999 'demonstrated how the state shares with its population a preoccupation with genealogy'.[48] While the state fosters a cult of personality around Ibn Saud as founder of state and nation, people outside the dynasty were invited to abandon their own descent in favour of a universal *umma* (Muslim community) – making the dynasty itself the focus of allegiance. The 'Protestant work-ethic' famously noted by Weber is conspicuous by its absence.

In mirroring the dynastic system on which the state is constructed, the culture of dependency in Saudi Arabia, as elsewhere in the Gulf, relies above all on individual patronage. Under the *kafala* (sponsorship) system, foreign workers and businesses require Saudi sponsors before they can obtain visas. The system allows foreigners to run businesses established in the name of the Saudi sponsor in exchange for a fee, enabling the Saudi partner to 'earn money while doing nothing'.[49]

Writing in 2012, House stated that 'private sector business employs roughly nine expats for every one Saudi' – contributing to the massive quantity of foreign workers (with 6.2 million employed in the private sector in 2009 against around 1 million Saudis) and adding massively to Saudi unemployment. Programmes of 'Saudization' come up against the perennial issue of training versus competitiveness, with businessmen arguing that having to train Saudis rather than hiring skilled foreign workers will reduce their company's productivity and ability to compete internationally.

Rather than being a separate sphere based on Kantorowicz's 'fictional personhood' whereby the church as a corporate body was transformed into the state, the public domain is the product of two different aetiologies. One, which we examined in Chapter 6, issues from *hisba* – the ruler's duty to 'enjoin the good and forbid the evil', a function performed by the vigilantes of the *mutaween* or 'religious police'. The other function of the state – or rather the public domain – issues out of Saudi family largesse, as by-product of the rentier state. As an oil-rich monarchy, Saudi Arabia, like other Gulf monarchies, has a rentier economy: until recently there has been no general taxation, which means that there is no foundational social contract based on the reciprocity between the people and their rulers.

As the 2004 UN *Arab Human Development Report* explained, taxation makes a government:

> subject to questioning about how it allocates state resources. In a rentier mode of production, however, the government can act as a generous provider that demands no taxes or duties in return ... The hand that gives can also take away, and the government is therefore entitled to require loyalty from its citizens invoking the mentality of the clan.[50]

In his 2016 *Economist* interview, MBS made it clear that while there might be value-added taxes (VAT) on individual goods, general taxation was out of the question.[51] For all the bluster about modernization, there are no plans to alter what is basically a rentier system of government by largesse.

Although increasing cohorts of Saudis have been able to enjoy the benefits of wealth and modernization, with the state providing a cradle-to-grave umbrella of welfare provision, including fine modern hospitals and schools, this provision, as in other oil-rich states, is a function of largesse rather than rights. Marwan Muasher, former foreign minister of Jordan, has explained the implications for the Gulf as a whole:

> The region's large oil reserves, and the Arab countries' influence over the price of oil since the 1970s, have proved as much a curse as a blessing … In oil-rich countries, the government made use of its oil income to act as a general provider for its people. Rather than encourage a culture of self-reliance or private sector–led growth, oil state governments fostered a culture of dependency. Citizens came to depend on their rulers to deliver jobs, services, and favors without supplying in return the productivity necessary to develop the economy. Even worse, as governments did not need to raise taxes from their citizens for income, their authoritarianism was more difficult to challenge. The political culture they developed was one of 'no taxation, no representation'.[52]

A political culture built on the distribution of largesse is also conditioned by nepotism and favouritism. As I aim to show in the next chapter, it is the ultimate expression of what Americans like to call 'family values'.

9
Family Values

The Basic Law of Government decreed by King Fahd in 1992 states that Saudi Arabia is a 'sovereign Arab Islamic state' with a monarchical system of government where 'rule passes to the sons of the founding King Abd al-Aziz Al Saud and to his children's children'. According to Article 5, the 'most upright' of these sons and grandsons should receive the allegiance – *baya* – of the people – including his siblings – in accordance with the principles of the Holy Quran and the tradition of the Prophet. The king chooses the crown prince and can relieve him of his duties by royal decree. Article 6 states that 'citizens are to pay allegiance to the King in submission and obedience, in times of ease and difficulty, fortune and adversity'.[1]

As al-Rasheed comments, this article was a 'clear response to the Gulf crisis and the opposition that followed' the stationing of infidel US troops in the peninsula. 'The focus on the Saudi royal family [was] interpreted here as a reinforcement of the right of the Al Saud to rule at a time when the voices of opposition had succeeded in creating an atmosphere in which this could no longer be taken for granted.'[2] In addition to establishing a Consultative Council whose members are chosen by the king from 'scholars and men of knowledge' (a category that may include scientists or technocrats), the

Basic Law invokes the 'role of family as the kernel of Saudi society'. Article 9 states:

> The family is the nucleus of Saudi society. Its members shall be raised and adhere to the Islamic creed which calls for obedience to God, his messenger and those of the nation who are charged with authority; for respect and enforcement of law and order; and for love of the motherland and taking pride in its glorious history.[3]

Al-Rasheed sees polygamous marriage as central to the process by which the Saudi *dawla* or state embedded itself in society:

> Thanks to polygamy the ruling group was able to widen its control over important rivals, tribal nobility and religious circles when those were turned into wife-givers. Important sections of society became dependent on the state/ruling lineage for their survival. The Al Saud elevated those with whom they intermarried to the rank of royal affines, (in-laws), a status that masked their loss of autonomy and bargaining power. As previous rivals became the maternal kin of important princes and future kings, they lost their ability to challenge Saudi rule. The royal court consisted not only of genuine allies, but also of previous enemies turned into maternal kin.[4]

The adoption of 'family' as a public value often has reactionary or ultra-conservative associations. Readers may recall that under France's Vichy government during the Second World War, the republic's revolutionary motto of *Liberté, Egalité, Fraternité* was replaced by *Travail, Famille, Patrie*. As Samin suggests, the invocation of family in Article 9 involves an implicit rejection of liberalism within a 'kinship-based or non-individualistic ethos of nationhood',[5] where the 'purposeful rejection of the individual as the basic unit of value in the Saudi political system moves in harmony with the Saudi state's discourse concerning its exceptional nature and origins'.[6]

The structures of tribal patriarchy are echoed through a myriad of reflective forms: 'Being a respectable Saudi means mimicking the prestige of the royal lineage in miniature – for example by producing a family tree.' While 'informal networks of power and patronage' remain central to the workings of the system, the state has reinforced these structures by 'formalizing kinship mechanisms for the purposes of domination and control'.[7] As Caroline Montagu noted in her 2015 paper for the British think-tank Chatham House, the state's focus on tribalism has led to an increasing sense of regional and tribal identity, with growing interest in family lineages. As one of her interviewees put it: 'People are suddenly doing their family trees and looking for their origins. Their family lineages are being revived and they have family *diwaniyyat* (receptions) every week with all the family who can come.'[8]

A significant issue here is the relationship between state and family. It is important to recognize that 'family' in Muslim societies may have a different character from the 'family' as understood in those regions of Western Europe that created what we now call 'the West'. In the Islamic world not only is polygyny (one man with up to four wives) permitted: first cousins are allowed to marry in accordance with the teachings of the Quran – a doctrine that enables patriarchal families to circumvent the inheritance rights of women by making cousin-marriage virtually mandatory. The contrast with Western culture is significant. Although Roman law had allowed marriage between first cousins, in medieval times the Catholic church not only banned marriage between first cousins, but extended the ban to the 'seventh canonical degree' (that is, sixth cousins) 'producing a vast range of people, often resident in the same locality, that were forbidden to marry'.[9]

The contrast between Western Europe and the Islamic heartlands of Arabia could not be greater. Indeed, the historic distinction between 'in-marriage' and 'out-marriage' is one of the most critical factors in analysing cultural and political differences between Western and Muslim societies and in charting their respective historical trajectories. In Saudi Arabia, for example, rates of consanguineous marriage (to a second cousin or closer) are very high (57.7 per cent in Riyadh, 51 per cent nationally). There are, of course, significant consequences for health – with high rates of infant mortality (18.5 per cent per thousand in 2005) and inherited disorders such as diabetes, with 1.5 million Saudis either having or being carriers of the beta-thalassemia trait. Cousin marriage reinforces the patriarchal family, enabling it to keep females as tradable commodities between families, while allowing males to exercise control over the property that women inherit under Islamic law.

At the same time, where women cannot travel without a male guardian – and have only very recently been permitted to drive at all – cousin marriage may offer a degree of protection, as a woman's father or brothers will be close relatives whose sense of honour demands that she be treated with respect. Under the guardianship system, however, Saudi women have the legal status of minors. All must have a male 'guardian' – usually a father or husband, but sometimes a son or uncle – whose permission they need to obtain passports and mobile phones, travel, pursue certain medical procedures or even access their bank accounts. The rules extend even to foreign women who marry Saudis. They are unable to take their children to another country in the event of divorce, as occurred in the case of an American woman married to a Saudi man who was unable to return with her daughter to the United States after their divorce.[10]

As explained in the previous chapter, the boundaries separating state institutions and family are far from clear and often breached. The Al Saud family, moreover, is a royal family like no other: there are literally thousands of them, descending from the twenty-two wives Ibn Saud had while technically observing the sharia requirement of four wives – maximum – at any one time. He was 'father to the nation' in more than a metaphorical sense. In the context of a tribal society, these prudential intermarriages had the benefit of binding together a number of different groups at a time when Ibn Saud was merely the head of a coalition of tribes who founded the modern kingdom in 1932 after he invaded the Hejaz, with its holy cities, Mecca and Medina. The trouble was that up until very recently his descendants all expected their emoluments. According to the US security specialist Anthony Cordesman, writing in 2002:

> It is almost certain ... that there are over 5,000 males who can claim some kind of title as a 'prince' in the Saudi royal family and well over 80 younger princes who have significant status as ranking members of the 'next generation' and thus have some claim to power. Some estimate the total number of 'princes' goes over 10,000 and the figure could easily reach 20,000 by 2020, although only a fraction are descendants. There are obvious limits as to what the Kingdom can or should pay members of the Saud family as these numbers increase, particularly because so many adult princes have shown they can make no claim to public funds except by accidents of birth.[11]

The scale of this burden can be gauged from a classified cable sent by Wyche Fowler, US ambassador to Saudi Arabia, to his government in November 1996, exposed by WikiLeaks. Fowler reported that members of the Al Saud family receive stipends ranging from $270,000 a month for more senior princes to $8,000 'for the lowliest member of the most remote branch of the family'. The system is calibrated by generation, with surviving sons and daughters of Ibn Saud receiving between $200,000 and $270,000, grandchildren around $27,000, great-grandchildren around $13,000 and great-great-grandchildren the minimum $8,000 per month.

According to the US embassy's calculations, in 1996 the budget for around sixty surviving sons and daughters, 420 grandchildren, 2,900 great-grandchildren and 'probably only about 2000 great-great-grandchildren at this point' amounted to more than $2 billion, with the stipends providing 'a substantial incentive for royals to procreate' since – in addition to bonuses received on marriage for palace construction – a royal stipend begins at birth. One minor prince, according to a Saudi source, had persuaded a community college in the US state of Oregon to enrol him even though he had no intention of attending classes: his principal goal in life was to have more children so he could increase his monthly allowance.[12]

In addition to the stipends, senior princes have tended to enrich themselves via 'off budget' programmes that 'are widely viewed as sources of royal rake-offs' according to Fowler. The largest of these, according to the cable, was thought to relate to the holy shrines of Mecca and Medina – around $5 billion annually – and the Ministry of Defence's strategic storage project, worth around $1 billion. Both were highly secretive and 'widely believed to be a source of substantial revenues for the king' – at that time King Fahd – 'and a few of his full brothers'.[13] Other ways the princes obtained money included borrowing from banks without paying them back (Saudi banks have since been reluctant to lend to royals unless they have proven repayment records) and using princely 'clout to confiscate land from commoners, especially if it is known to be the site for an upcoming project and can be quickly sold to the government for a profit'.[14]

King Abdullah, whose ten-year rule between 2005 and 2015 was seen as a period of modest reform, curbed some of these excesses by stopping handouts to family members going on holiday and discouraging them from using the national airline as a 'private jet service'. As Karen Elliott House writes, 'this plethora of princes is so large and so diverse that little if anything links them except some Al Saud genes ... Collectively, they increasingly are viewed by the rest of Saudi society as a burdensome privileged caste.'[15] Although, thanks to another aspect of tribalism, even being an Al Saud doesn't guarantee great privilege: sons and grandsons of Ibn Saud whose mothers don't belong to elite Arabian lineages are considered ineligible for the throne.

Saudis may regard themselves as 'citizens', but in reality they are subjects according to any constitutional understanding of the term. Under the rentier system prevailing in the Gulf they owe allegiance to their king in exchange for such benefits as he chooses to provide for them: they do not enjoy full citizens' rights. As Montagu points out, 'the kingdom has no formal democratic process, but has some traditional representation and consultation mechanisms, chiefly through the traditional meetings, or *majalis*.'[16] The *majalis* are the regular but informal open-house sessions held by senior members of the community, princes, businessmen, tribal and religious leaders, and in some cases professionals such as doctors or engineers. They are 'essential loci for discussion, rumor, chat and gossip, and also for the informal presentation of petitions'.[17] While such

> meetings have served as the social 'glue' of the kingdom, they serve the clientelism or vertical structure of Saudi society while serving as channels for people to make their views known and to raise suggestions, grievances or other topics. They have functioned less well in terms of the horizontal integration of people from different backgrounds and areas of expertise.[18]

Given the absence of constitutional rights, it appears to be charitable organizations that provide for a degree of 'horizontal integration' involving people from different backgrounds in common non-profit enterprises. Nora Derbal, a scholar who spent a decade researching a variety of Saudi associations and non-governmental organizations, writes:

> Despite the boundaries imposed by the authoritarian state through an intrusive and narrow legal framework, social activists have been able to carve out spaces of autonomy under the umbrella of charity. Within charitable organizations Saudis and non-Saudis in Saudi Arabia have been able to develop agency and to engage in a self-empowered manner. Charity work generates social status, networks, meaning of life and fulfilment, sometimes an income and always access to a social world outside the realm of the family. Charity is a social space in which change – for example in gender relations or in relations between citizens and migrants – has been and continues to be negotiated and practiced.[19]

One of the lesser-known associations Derbal explored in her research was a community of hikers who contribute to charity out of their fees.[20] The Hikers camp in the arid hillsides near Jeddah has young men and women mingling without segregation, with the women changing from the all-black *abayas* into modest but 'comfortable hiking gear'. After venturing up the terrain's barren slopes they relax for convivial evenings with a barbecue (that is notably alcohol-free despite the Hikers' models in two US non-profits, Toastmasters International and the Hash House Harriers who describe themselves as 'drinkers with a walking problem').[21] The BBQ is chastely followed by 'music and marshmallows' with everyone 'invited to stay, to engage in all-night conversations and to share and discuss ideas for social causes that the group could support'.[22]

In contrast to many Saudi youngsters who live at home before marriage and are prone to diverting themselves by sitting on couches and playing with electronic devices, the Hikers emphasize the values of 'positive thinking, self-confidence and self-esteem' in accordance with the outlook of American self-help books that do well in the kingdom. They 'critically distanced themselves from promoting Islam and would not want to be religious'.[23] When Derbal hiked with them in the years between 2010 and 2020 this may have seemed avant-garde, but as she observes:

> Many of the activities that the Hikers promoted and that were considered risky and against dominant social norms less than a decade ago – such as the mingling of unrelated young Saudi men and women, concerts, entertainment and the participation of women in outdoor sports events – are today considered 'the new normal' of public social life in Saudi Arabia ... Change has occurred in areas that many had assumed to be essential parts of Saudi culture: gender segregation, the condemnation of music, little tolerance for the arts, and the powers of the 'religious police' (*mutawwa*), among others. Today young Saudi men and women can go for hikes around Riyadh and afterward enjoy an evening of barbecue, music and mingling, all without fear of the *mutawwa*.[24]

Charity is enjoined in the Quran, with prayer and the obligation of *zakat* (purifying dues) often coupled and mutually reinforcing. In the classical narratives the Prophet Muhammad lost both his parents when very young, and the faithful are especially enjoined to secure a place in paradise by looking after orphans. Groups such as YIG (the Young Initiative Group) and the Hikers organize events such as 'Breakfast with Our Orphans', while the Hikers 'invited orphans on their hiking trips and to other social activities, particularly during Ramadan'.[25] One Jeddah charity includes foundlings or children of unknown parents in its remit, many of them having been abandoned at mosques or other public places. Jeddah social workers attribute the rising number of foundlings (with some 500 new children a year) to 'growing poverty among Saudis and to the social discrimination associated with an illicit relationship' in a country where 'sexual intercourse outside of marriage is considered a crime (*zina*) which places the children of such encounters in a limbo'.[26]

Regardless of a child's appearance (with many of the foundlings or orphans seen by Derbal having African or Asian appearances) they will be registered as Saudi citizens, a remarkable loophole in the country's rigid nationality law which only grants the automatic right of citizenship to children of Saudi fathers. Saudi nationality, however, does not eradicate the stigma of orphanhood when 'genealogy remains one of the key facets of Saudi identity' and where tribalism remains salient, even though the tribe 'no longer refers to a lifestyle or occupation, but to a social network of kinship, loyalty and identity'. As Derbal observes, 'For most Saudi citizens descent and bloodlines continue to play an important role in identity construction but also in matters of everyday life such as marriage' where filiation (descent) 'entitles a child to maintenance from their father and qualifies them as an inheritor', with orphans and foster children lacking inheritance rights.

The stigma suffered by young orphan women in several Gulf countries including Saudi Arabia persuades some of them to dress in the *buya* style (from the English word 'boy') that subverts the prevailing 'hegemonic model of femininity'. *Buyas* wear short hair, men's shorts and soccer strips, while adopting a masculine walking gait.[27]

Despite the kingdom's vast riches, the charities she observed confront a growing problem of poverty. 'Few countries in the world experience a disparity in wealth as extreme as that which exists in Saudi Arabia.'[28] Derbal sees the growing wealth gap as challenging the 'rentier state' assumption common to Gulf monarchies whereby the authoritarian oil-rich states 'buy their citizens' acquiescence through strategic investment in hydrocarbon revenues into welfare and high living standards'. The growing disparities of wealth, rarely discussed in the popular literature, were sharpened by the devastating floods that took hold in Jeddah on the eve of the Hajj in November 2009. While the prosperous north of the city was barely affected, neighbourhoods in the south and east were devastated, with jerry-built houses crumbling, bridges and power lines collapsing, and buses and cars swept away by torrents of mud. Flood relief became a catalyst for the social engagement of youngsters of both genders she details in her book.

The finding in her research that she found most surprising in numerous interviews

> was a general lack of reference to Saudi Arabia's clerics and religious authorities. While some charity organizations might invoke a religious edict (*fatwa*) of a specific senior religious official in the written representation of their practices (in order to justify the use of zakat money, for example), clerics did not appear as a source of orientation or authority in the conversations I had with social activists and philanthropists (especially not those with women).[29]

While some of her interlocutors would invoke passages from the Quran and sayings attributed to the Prophet Muhammad, interpreting their meanings in relation to a particular situation, others invoked more broadly the 'importance of generosity and charity in tribal culture'. Derbal concludes that given 'charity is a universal phenomenon, one that often accommodates and interacts with other discourses and practices such as Islamic ethics or tribal solidarity', 'access to Islam' on the part of volunteers 'rested immediately with the individual believer rather than being mediated through the religious authorities'. This crucial insight suggests the surfacing of a trajectory not dissimilar to that observed in the post-Christian world where, as Anglican scholar Don Cupitt famously argued, old doctrines of supernatural redemption are translated into a 'practical struggle to create a society that realizes the full moral and religious potential of each one of its members'.[30]

The non-profit welfare associations and charity foundations she explored have proliferated since the year 2000 while coming under closer government supervision. On ascending the throne in 2015, King Salman issued a decree turning welfare associations into NGOs, enabling them to fall within the purview of the international Financial Action Task Force established by the OECD to combat money laundering, a remit that was expanded after 9/11 to monitor terrorist financing. The founders of new NGOs or civil society organizations must deposit the sum of 5 million riyals (€1.2 million) into the foundation's account or register assets in its name that yield annual revenues of SR500,000 (€123,000), a requirement 'that effectively render[s] foundations a privilege of the economic elite'.[31] Derbal sees the regulations as increasing the leverage of the Saudi national state:

> Under the new laws the operational activities of civil society organizations remain circumscribed and threatened by vague expressions in the regulations that allow them to be misused according to the interpretative standpoint of the government ... The regulations explicitly forbid any civil society organization from an international organization from engaging in activities outside of Saudi Arabia – or receiving a representative from an international organization unless it has written permission to do so from the ministry [of Social Affairs]. The limitations illustrate the extensive regulative and monitoring powers of the government's bureaucratic apparatus.[32]

All NGOs and civil society organizations must be registered with, and approved by, the government within limited mandates. As Montagu suggested, other associational life is 'difficult, often illegal, often "virtual" and often banned'. Even cultural groups such as Hatun al-Fassi's well-known Sunday Club had to be registered and submit a schedule of their discussions. Meetings are illegal except in the case of registered associations, permitted cultural groups or 'meetings that the government would like to go 'under the radar'. Montagu's interviewees reported a lack of consistency in applying the rules, with associations caught in a 'Catch-22' scenario: 'It is said to be increasingly difficult to have any groupings that are unregistered, but it is often impossible to register.'[33] The effect of the restrictions, however, was generally 'to prevent people meeting for most social, cultural, socio-political, human rights purposes, or any other forms of contact' with the result that the locus of association was now in the 'virtual space' of the social media, especially Facebook, Twitter, WhatsApp and YouTube. As one Saudi journalist explained to Montagu:

> The government also monitors the virtual world and uses it as a tool of government policy. The government has its people in the Twittersphere; government officials, posing as ordinary people, often oppose ideas on Twitter. However, if the government were to try to shut it down it would be disastrous because people have got used to talking on it and having their own voices and exchanging ideas with no restraints.[34]

Saudis can officially make their feelings public by submitting petitions to the king, with several groups urging political reforms. As Montagu stated,

> petitions have long been a channel – although not necessarily an effective one – for Saudi citizens to demand government change and reform. Notable petitions have included 'Towards the State of Rights and Institutions', the 'Free Youths Coalition', and the 'Saudi Revolution', the 'Jeddah YouTube Letter to the King', the 'Islamic National Party', the 'Saudi Women's Revolution', and, from the Islamist standpoint, the 'Statement of a Call for Reform'.[35]

The main demands within the petitions are respect for human rights, freedom of expression, constitutional monarchy, transparent elections, social justice, an end to discrimination, an independent judiciary and ending of corruption, and for women to have full rights as citizens. In the 2000s, campaigners for a constitutional monarchy were dealt several blows with ten lobbyists arrested after ninety-nine pro-reformers signed a petition entitled 'Milestones on the way to constitutional monarchy'.[36]

The arrest of petitioners is an obvious disincentive in a country where the climate of fear is pervasive. Simon Valentine, a British academic who spent four years in the kingdom teaching English, says that 'meeting and talking with Saudis one soon perceives the fear that lurks behind the smiles, the sense that people are constantly aware of being watched, censored and condemned'.[37] Pascal Menoret, an anthropologist who formed close relationships with the young male tearaways he describes in his brilliant ethnographic essay *Joyriding in Riyadh* (2014), reports that surveillance, repression and eventually torture are realities that shape everyday life and deeply modify people's interactions with each other – and with the anthropologist or field worker.

> This is a country where 12,000 to 30,000 political prisoners and prisoners of opinion rot in overcrowded, violent jails; a country where repression is organized by security forces that report to a handful of senior princes, out of the reach of an abrupt, arbitrary judicial system; a country where physical punishment, torture and the threat thereof, in the absence of transparent and fair procedures, are the alpha and omega of the judiciary and the ultima ratio of political acquiescence.[38]

Saudi Arabia has no written constitution or written penal code, claiming that its laws are based only on the Quran and the sunnah (the teachings and practice of the Prophet). Those accused of political offences are often sentenced by the Specialized Criminal Court, set up to try terrorism-related cases, which routinely denies defendants the most basic fair-trial guarantees, including the right to a lawyer, and passes sentences in closed proceedings. Authorities continue to hold prominent rights activists in prolonged incommunicado detention, completely cut off from their families and the outside world. According to the now disbanded Saudi Civil and Political Rights Association, one in every 600 Saudis is in jail because of their opinions or political activities. Since the whole judicial system is based on confessions extracted under torture or the threat of torture, it is physical violence, not the Quran, that is the 'true foundation of the law'.

Viewed through any kind of lens, social, cultural or economic, the kingdom is one of the world's most repressive polities. On the rankings devised by Freedom House, a US-funded NGO, America's leading ally in the Arab world occupies the bottom percentile (5.8 per cent) in terms of political rights and civil liberties, belonging with Syria, North Korea, Somalia and the Central African Republic in the category designated 'the worst of the worst'. As we saw in Chapter 5, executions are conducted in public, and are not infrequent, with sickening examples circulating on YouTube.

In 2016 the kingdom executed 146 people, including a mass execution of forty-seven men on 2 January; forty-three of these were reported to have been associated with al-Qaeda attacks in the 2000s, but four were members of the country's Shia minority, including the prominent cleric Nimr al-Nimr, an outspoken critic of the regime, certainly, but no terrorist. In April 2018 there were reported to be at least thirty-eight Shia men awaiting execution. On 12 March 2022 there was the execution of eighty-one men, the largest mass execution for decades with the total of 196 executed that year representing a substantial increase, despite promises to curtail death penalty use, according to Human Rights Watch.

The following year was almost as harsh, with one single month (August) averaging a rate of four executions per week. Some of the death penalties have been meted out for drug offences, despite repeated promises to limit executions where the death penalty is not mandated under sharia law. Some appear overtly political. According to Amnesty International, in July 2023 the Specialized Criminal Court sentenced Mohammed al-Ghamdi to death 'solely for tweets' criticizing the authorities.

The 2016 protests in Sheikh al-Nimr's hometown of Awamiya led to a siege by the Saudi authorities, with tensions flaring over plans to demolish the historic district, which the government claimed was being used by armed insurgents. At least a dozen people are said to have been killed in the protests, and many young men went into hiding to avoid checkpoints at all the town's exits. One of the protestors Yussuf al-Mushaikhass (aged forty-two) was executed in July 2017 along with three other men after being found guilty by the Specialized Criminal Court for offences including 'firing at a police station in Awamiyya twice, resulting in the injury of a policeman', 'armed rebellion against the ruler' and 'participating in riots'.

His family only found out that he had been executed afterwards, when they saw a government statement read on TV. According to Amnesty International the court's decision was largely based on 'confessions' obtained under torture. In the days after Nimr's execution, social media – whether spontaneous or engineered by the government – produced a response indicative of widespread approval, with '900,000 anti-Shia slurs against 30,000 anti-Sunni slurs recorded across the Arabic Twittersphere'.[39]

Initially, in the aftermath of the Arab Spring when Saudi youth, like others, were enlivened by prospects for change, the 'Twittersphere' may have served as a refuge for free expression, a trend that was rapidly eroded as 'Twittertrolls' employed by the government hit back at any suggestions of disloyalty. Koelbl estimates that a good half of bots on Twitter are government-generated 'fakes'.[40] Controlling social media – even partially – has obvious advantages for the regime. Saudi Arabia has the highest number of active Twitter/X users in the Arab world: 2.4 million, or more than double the number in Egypt, a country whose population is three times larger. The mastermind behind the trolling operation is thought to have been MBS's infamous fixer Saud al-Qahtani who was sacked from his jobs and 'disappeared' from public visibility after his role in the Khashoggi murder was exposed but appears to have been restored to grace (see Chapter 1).

In August 2017 al-Qahtani launched a 'blacklist' asking the Twitter community to tag the names of people who did not support the blockade of Qatar. As the Gulf analyst Quentin de Pimodan explains, the trolling system al-Qahtani headed, as chairman of the board of directors of the Saudi Federation for Cyber Security and Programming, engaged academics and specialists working for think-tanks close to the Emirati and Saudi leadership. MBS was boosted as a visionary and a thoroughly modern figure: talking points focused on how he was the same age as the majority of Saudi citizens, was tech-savvy, had an entrepreneurial mindset and so forth. Only a few people had the temerity to question the feasibility of the country building a $500 billion city in the desert when the Aramco initial public offering had yet to occur, that the King Abdullah Economic City was facing major difficulties and that plans for privatization advocated by the McKinsey consultancy behind Vision 2030 have a questionable record in the Gulf.

The talking points they address, de Pimodan suggests, have been 'reshaping realities, diverting criticisms toward other topics, bullying journalists and analysts who questioned some plans and reforms'. Activists are threatened, academics mocked and only in a few cases are the issues they raise addressed. 'According to this particular Saudi Twitter community', he says, 'the leadership was beyond reproach and the Saudis were living the dream.' If anyone raised questions about the proposed Aramco initial public offering, the plans for solar power or any other issues that might challenge official narrative, 'a massive counter narration' would occur on Twitter, denouncing the anonymous sources used by journalists. The official authorities would follow suit with statements in more measured diplomatic tones.

Opinion manufactured and 'shared' on Twitter and other platforms may be the least obnoxious of the electronic tools the regime uses to sustain its control over society in the age of 'fake news'. A more menacing type of control involves the use of malware (malicious software) against opponents. Two months after Khashoggi's murder, in December 2018, a friend of Khashoggi's, Omar Abd al-Aziz, a Saudi exile living in Canada, filed a lawsuit against NSO, an Israeli software company registered in Cyprus. An investigation published by the University of Toronto's Citizen Lab had revealed that Abd al-Aziz's and Khashoggi's phones had been hacked using the NSO's malware known as Pegasus, which is only sold to governments. 'The hacking of my phone played a major role in what happened to Jamal, I am really sorry to say', Abd al-Aziz told the US broadcaster CNN. 'The guilt is killing me.'[41]

Pegasus hacks a smartphone by sending it a fake message, such as notice of a package delivery or urgent news about a family member. If the recipient clicks on the link, the system installs sophisticated malware on the device that can go undetected and send information back to those doing the spying. Abd al-Aziz shared with CNN more than 400 messages he had exchanged with Khashoggi. Many concerned their plan to create a digital activism project called 'cyber bees', aimed at documenting Saudi human rights abuses in short films that could be easily shared online. The messages were explicitly critical of MBS.

In November 2018 the Israeli daily *Haaretz* reported that the NSO group had offered the Saudi government an advanced version of the software, Pegasus 3, 'an espionage tool so sophisticated that it does not depend on the victim clicking on a link before the phone is breached'. According to the paper, representatives of the group met with Abdullah al-Malihi, a close associate of Prince Turki al-Faisal, former head of Saudi Arabia's intelligence services, and Nasser al-Qahtani, a top Saudi businessman close to the crown prince, in June 2017 in Vienna. After a number of subsequent meetings between al-Malihi and al-Qahtani and 'officials of Israeli companies in which other Israelis were present ... an agreement was made to sell the Pegasus 3 to the Saudis for $55 million'.[42]

As Nicholas Wright explained in *Foreign Affairs* – the journal of the American Council on Foreign Relations – the new information technologies are a gift to authoritarian regimes, enabling 'high levels of social control at a reasonable cost'.

> Governments will be able to selectively censor topics and behaviors to allow information for economically productive activities to flow freely, while curbing political discussions that might damage the regime. China's so-called Great Firewall provides an early demonstration of this kind of selective censorship.[43]

Wright suggests that people will know that the omnipresent monitoring of their physical and digital activities will be used to predict undesired behaviour, even actions they are merely contemplating.

> In order to prevent the system from making negative predictions, many people will begin to mimic the behaviors of a 'responsible' member of society. These may be as subtle as how long one's eyes look at different

elements on a phone screen. This will improve social control not only by forcing people to act in certain ways, but also by changing the way they think.[44]

These subtle forms of high-tech social control may not work for everyone, given the differences in status and economic opportunity that prevail in the kingdom today. Menoret's young interlocutors, many of them members of the kingdom's displaced Bedouin tribes, found that Riyadh 'had little to offer if one was not closely connected to the royal family' or part of the oil-rent distribution networks controlled by them. They saw the Saudi capital as a 'selective El Dorado where only a handful became rich, while the majority of residents, parsimoniously financed by the state or their employer, struggled to cover astronomic housing, transport and living costs'.[45] For all the brazen affluence of princely palaces, the low-income areas of Riyadh 'match the ghettos, banlieues, *problemområde* and *favelas* of other cities and testify to the fact that, in liberal societies as in those systems that are described as "authoritarian", political power is equally based on economic violence'.[46]

Menoret shows the way an atomised society is perpetuated by the control of public space:

> Riyadh was a gigantic suburb where families and individuals lived scattered in individual houses and small apartment buildings, far away from each other but under the surveillance of the state ... Saudi Arabia was one of the rare Muslim majority countries where, for fear of political mobilization, mosques were closed outside of prayer times. Malls were not more welcoming, and private security companies filtered out and chased bachelors and members of the lower classes. Even streets were repulsive and pedestrian-unfriendly; large and busy, deprived of shade, difficult to cross, their asphalt nearly melting under a scorching sun, they were abandoned to cars, trucks and taxis.[47]

In this sexually segregated society, where marriage is seen as a calming influence, unmarried men are 'feared as unruly and disruptive' but, as House points out, most of the 40 per cent of unemployed Saudi men under the age of twenty-four who would like to marry can't afford the bride price. In a patriarchal society in which a majority of marriages are arranged, a woman's sexuality and reproductive capacity is 'family' property, a commodity to be exchanged or traded, rather than being an aspect of her individual identity or selfhood. Virginity is not just prized but fetishized: as the Egyptian writer Mona Eltahawy puts it in *Headscarves and Hymens*, 'Our hymens are not ours; they belong to our families.'[48] In 2008 Carol Fleming, an American married to a Saudi, estimated the average middle-class dowry at 70,000 Saudi riyals (about US$18,660) for a virgin and SR20,000 (about US$5,330) for a non-virgin (that is, widowed or divorced woman), sums far beyond the reach of many young men. Menoret witnessed the consequences, spending many hours with frustrated young men whose idea of fun was to drive cars at 150 mph, 'drifting' into high-speed arabesques in parking lots and highways, or slaloming through traffic using a skilful combination of handbrake and steering wheel.

Car drifting, imported from Japan, is now an official sport in Dubai and the Saudi kingdom, with Red Bull as a sponsor, but the illicit version is strictly forbidden, with fines of 10,000 riyals (more than €2,300) and two months' jail for offenders. The newly asphalted roads of Riyadh's expanding grid – a city that has grown from a population of 300,000 in 1970 to 6 million today – provide perfect spaces for drifters as they wait for the urban expansion that will enrich their owners in the course of time.

Like the monarchs of early modern Europe, the Saudi kings have bought loyalty, or rewarded their courtiers and members of their family, by giving out grants of land for future development. Land speculation was far from being confined to urban areas. The greed of the ruling family – and the sycophantic army of speculators that followed in its wake – was responsible for a massive ecological disaster as the country used its aquifers for wholly unsuitable agriculture. As Elie Elhadj, a Syrian banker and agronomist who worked as CEO for a major Saudi bank in the 1990s, has demonstrated, the kingdom 'squandered tens of billions of dollars on the fruitless quest to make the desert bloom and, in so doing, wasted the nation's finite water inheritance without regard to posterity'.[49]

In the early 1980s, as petrodollars flooded its economy, the government – aided by an army of technical 'experts' – decided to invest in agriculture using 'fossil water' from non-renewable aquifers. Anyone flying over the country – even at 10,000 metres – can still see the circular fields (many of them now brown) created by the pivot-irrigation systems installed in the regions of Riyadh and Qatif. Thanks to massive investment, Saudi Arabia increased its wheat production by almost thirty times, from 142,000 tonnes in 1980 to 4.1 million in 1992, increasing its arable land fourteen-fold from 67,000 hectares in 1980 to almost a million in 1992. The massive investment and subsidies produced wheat at a cost of around $500 per tonne compared with the world price of $120, adding to the budget deficit that peaked at $130 billion between 1984 and 1992.

According to Elhadj, liquidity became so tight that the government had to delay (default) for a few years in honouring its financial obligations to thousands of contractors, suppliers and farmers. The original amounts were eventually paid, without interest, in the form of medium-term government bonds. By 1996 most of the new wheat-growing areas had been abandoned – 650,000 hectares out of 857,000. The venture is best described as an example of ecological lunacy: given the high rates of evaporation in the searing desert sun the quantity of water needed to irrigate one hectare of land is twice to three times the quantity needed in temperate zones. Between 1980 and 1999, a gargantuan quantity of water – 300 billion cubic metres equivalent to six years' flow of the River Nile into Egypt – was wasted in this way, two-thirds of it non-renewable.

As in the case of Israel, 'making the desert bloom' has a powerful emotional appeal in a region where agricultural land is sparse. As Elhadj remarks, somewhat caustically,

> Desert agriculture is not an intuitive choice for an economist. However, food independence has a nationalistic appeal, conveying a message of control over the country's own political and economic destiny ... Propagated in the national discourse as a well-planned strategy to insulate the country from the risk of a possible wheat boycott by oil-consuming, food producing countries, desert irrigation was turned into a sacrosanct belief.[50]

While this may have sounded like good propaganda, the motives were largely financial. As Elhadj points out,

> the early participants in desert agriculture were investors, not farmers. They were absentee owners with little or no experience of farming. The premise of high financial returns from government subsidies [for] wheat growing enticed some of the country's richest business families, mainly from the Riyadh and Qassim regions, to undertake the risk of the new adventure ... While food independence and settlement of the Bedouins might have played a role in the Saudi government's drive toward food self-sufficiency, the early business investors became engaged in the adventure purely to enrich themselves.[51]

'The policy', he concludes, 'has been hugely beneficial to the Saudi entrepreneurs and to the foreign suppliers and their local Saudi sponsors.' It represents an 'extreme case of a politically determined ecological policy' with the 'negative tendencies of [a] poorly informed elite enjoying rentier economic circumstances'.[52]

The collapse of the wheat experiment may have hurt some investors, but it has not arrested the rampant growth of urban real estate and its value. In Riyadh the Al Saud family was given the nickname al-Shubuk – 'the fences' – for the hundreds of miles of wire they planted in the desert to keep intruders out of their properties, while waiting for the city's sprawl to reach them. As Menoret found, there was an improbable community of interest between developers and car drifters, with developers constructing 'miles of straight asphalt that the drifters used as a playground, far away from people's eyes, private security guards and police patrols'.[53] Whenever the builders arrived and constructed new boulevards of suburban villas along with speed bumps and police stations, the drifters would move on to the next undeveloped site.

Among his community of outsiders, Menoret saw signs that the flouting of Wahhabi strictures is not confined to billionaire princes with their holiday compounds in Marbella, Tangier or Aspen. Escaping 'the strict behavioral and spatial order promoted by the state', 'boys and girls and boys and boys flirted from car to car on select avenues' in outlying parts of Riyadh, 'throwing their phone number to each other on scraps of paper, texting each other or following the other's car'. Alcohol was easy to find, 'provided that you had the right contact and a car to get there'. A colourless local hooch made from dates, known as *al-kuhul al-watani* or 'national alcohol', was widely available, and when kept in water bottles was undetectable to visual inspection. After picking it up from your dealer 'you would mix the alcohol with non-alcoholic beer and quickly reach inebriation. As Saudis would say, what's prohibited is highly desirable.' In these circles at least the pressure of religious control was clearly diminishing.[54]

This could be to MBS's advantage as he seeks to update the Saudi economy. Most of Menoret's tearaways are likely to remain among those left behind, but for others there are opportunities: 200,000 young Saudis are now studying on scholarships overseas, and 45,000 students have now graduated from the world's largest all-female university. Saudi religious textbooks – which as recently as 2014 were imported into Mosul by notorious *Daesh* or Islamic State for use in schools, thanks to their hard line on infidels and dissidents – are now being modified to acknowledge examples of the Prophet Muhammad's kindness to Jews. But whatever superficial modernization ensues, the Saudi state still depends for its legitimacy on its long-standing accommodation to the Wahhabi faith. It is largely because of Saudi-funded evangelism that the violently anti-Shia Salafist movements inspired by Wahhabi ideology – from Islamic State to the al-Qaeda affiliate formerly known as Jabhat al-Nusra – are still spreading through the world, a trend that may paradoxically accelerate following the loss of IS's last territorial enclave on the Syria–Iraq border.

On his visit to the kingdom in May 2017, President Trump commended MBS's Vision 2030 as 'an important and encouraging statement of tolerance, respect, empowering women and economic development'. But most of his speech, given in the presence of fifty leaders of Muslim-majority states, was devoted to condemning extremism. In rhetoric worthy of any village imam or mullah, he proclaimed: 'A better future is only possible if your nations drive out the terrorists and extremists. Drive. Them. Out. Drive them out of your places of worship. Drive them out of your communities. Drive them out of your holy land and drive them out of this earth.'[55]

Trump's hosts no doubt found it pleasing that he bracketed Iran and Hezbollah – two Shia-based entities – with Islamic State and al-Qaeda as the primary causes of extremism in the region echoing the paranoid formulations of MBS (see Chapter 1). He made no reference to the fact that during the course of his visit to one of the world's most tyrannical and theocratic states – the first country to be so honoured by his administration – Iranians were going to the polls in a general election that would have been unthinkable in the Saudi kingdom. The outcome saw Hassan Rouhani, a moderate leader keen to ease the Islamic Republic's isolation, chosen to serve a second term as president. In August 2021, however, Rouhani was succeeded by the hard-line cleric Ebrahim Raisi, an ally of Supreme Leader Ali Khamenei, following an election opposition sources regarded as rigged.

President Trump's decision to unilaterally withdraw from the Joint Comprehensive Plan of Action (JCPOA), the 'Iran nuclear deal' negotiated by Secretary of State John Kerry under his predecessor Barack Obama, and his sponsorship of the Abraham Accords between Israel and two leading Gulf states (UAE and Bahrain) led to a growing polarization between a so-called Axis of Resistance led by Iran and its mainly Shiite allies (including the Assad regime in Syria, Hezbollah in Lebanon, the Houthi movement in Yemen plus the Sunni Hamas resistance movement in Gaza). Despite the Biden administration's attempt to revive the JCPOA, the geopolitical shift represented by the 'Axis of Resistance' on one side and the US and its allies on the other seemed set to maintain its momentum, with Iran becoming a leading supplier of weaponry for Russia in its war with Ukraine.

Will the challenge of Iran – a flawed democracy, no doubt, but nonetheless a system that allows for shifts in political direction in a constitutionally ordered manner – succeed in galvanizing the Saudis into adopting political change? From both his public statements and his actions it is clear that MBS is rooting for change in the exercise of power, but not its distribution, as we were reminded in the *Godfather* showdown at the Ritz-Carlton hotel described in Chapter 8.

It seemed clear, however, that for all his public statements announcing his endorsement of more moderate versions of Islam that MBS implausibly claimed prevailed in the kingdom prior to the 1979 Islamic revolution in Iran, this was no liberal coup that would lead to a more open society. The religious police may have been curbed, gender mixing less severely enforced and women allowed to take the wheel. But under the pretext of fighting terrorism, hundreds of clerics, intellectuals and Islamic thinkers have been detained. According to al-Rasheed, 'many of those detained are not radical Islamists ... Moderate Islam will not emerge in Saudi Arabia under a repressive regime whose foundation is based on purging theological differences and criminalizing the Muslim "other"'.[56]

While MBS's grab for power and attempt to eliminate rivals in anticipation of his ageing father King Salman's demise (or abdication on grounds of ill health) may appeal to his contemporaries, the foreign policy initiatives he appeared to be pushing with his mentor MBZ and his new friend Jared Kushner were proving counterproductive. His Corleone-style intervention in Lebanon, where he tried to force the resignation of Prime Minister Saad Hariri during the latter's visit to Riyadh, backfired at first. Hariri formally rescinded his resignation in December 2017, temporarily dashing Saudi hopes that his departure would open the way for an Israeli invasion aimed at eliminating Iran's powerful ally, Hezbollah, from its pivotal position in the Lebanese government – an aim that motivated Israel's attack on Lebanon in autumn 2024.

The subsequent initiative cooked up by MBS and Kushner appeared equally unpropitious. According to the *New York Times* the Saudis tried to break the deadlock in the Middle East peace process by pressuring Mahmoud Abbas, the Palestinian president, to agree to a Palestinian state with limited sovereignty and non-contiguous territories whose capital would be Abu Dis, a suburb of Jerusalem now separated from the city by Israel's separation barrier.[57] Under this plan the Israelis would keep the vast majority of West Bank settlements, while the Palestinian refugees would abandon any right of return for themselves or their descendants.

When Abbas visited Riyadh, according to the report, he was subjected to pressure similar to Hariri's. If he refused to accept these terms, he would be pressured to resign, to make way for someone who would. While, as the *New York Times* writers suggested, the plan reflects both the inexperience of MBS and Kushner, as well as a possible desire to curry favour with the US president, any chances of it gaining traction were wrecked by Trump's decision to recognize Jerusalem as Israel's capital, a move that proved too much for the ageing monarch. Other things apart, a Palestinian capitulation along the lines devised by MBS and Kushner would have handed Iran a massive propaganda boost in its claim to be arch-defender of Palestinian rights. Israel's war in Gaza, however, following the Hamas attack in October 2023 appears to have changed the calculus.

In the short term, MBS's *Godfather*-style of leadership seemed as likely to backfire as his foreign policy efforts in Yemen, Lebanon and Palestine. According to well-placed commentators, the extrajudicial arrest of his fellow princes had scared off foreign investors, extinguishing his plans for the Aramco initial public offering which has now been placed on hold indefinitely, crippling his hopes for reform. For Western leaders, the Khashoggi murder and the scrutiny it produced – and especially the opinion of CIA chief Gina Haspel that MBS ordered the killing – made for a degree of embarrassment.

Despite the international outcry caused by the war in Yemen and the Khashoggi murder, MBS chose to 'brazen it out' by attending the G20 summit of wealthy countries at Buenos Aires in Argentina, where he was overheard talking to President Macron of France. The Élysée Palace said the two leaders had a five-minute exchange on the sidelines of the summit in which Macron conveyed a 'very firm' message to the prince over the killing and the need to find a political solution for the situation in Yemen. Snatches of the conversation were captured on audio before either leader was aware of it. As reported by the *Guardian*, the conversation proceeded as follows:

'I do worry. I am worried ... I told you' says Macron.

'Yes, you told me,' the prince says. 'Thank you very much.'

'You never listen to me.'

'No, I listen, of course,' replies Prince Mohammed, smiling broadly after apparently becoming aware of the TV crew.

'Because I told you. It was more important for you,' Macron says, and gives a tight smile, before turning away from the camera to speak further to the prince. Macron then says something inaudible, to which the Saudi leader says: 'It's OK. I can deal with it.'

After another indecipherable segment, Macron says: 'I am a man of my word.'[58]

While the British prime minister Theresa May claimed she had 'strong words' for the prince, insisting there should be 'full accountability' for the murder, President Trump, his staunchest ally, appeared more ambivalent, with his hawkish national security advisor, John Bolton, telling the press that there had been no room for a meeting in the president's schedule. By contrast the crown prince's meeting with President Putin of Russia appeared super-friendly, with 'high-five' hand-slapping and warm body language, while in the photograph shared with President Xi Jinping of China both appear smiling and cheerful. The mood was indicative of the shift in geopolitical momentum noted above.

After the G20 summit, MBS travelled east to be warmly received by rival South Asian leaders, Pakistan prime minister Imran Khan and Indian prime minister Narendra Modi. When a few Pakistani journalists put up Khashoggi's image on their social media displays they received calls from their employers to take them down, and most of them complied. MBS received the treatment usually accorded to heads of state: air force jets escorted his plane when it entered Pakistani air space, red carpets were rolled out on landing, children greeted him with bouquets larger than themselves, 3,500 doves were released and a fleet of SUVs (specially hired for the occasion as the government had sold all its luxury limos as part of an austerity drive) followed the two leaders in their open landau. As Mohamed Hanif, the Pakistani novelist, noted somewhat caustically,

> Prince Mohammed won over lots of Pakistani hearts when, after a plea from Mr. Khan, he announced the release of more than 2,000 Pakistani prisoners from Saudi jails. Nobody questioned the merits of a justice system in which a prince can release thousands of prisoners because he is in a good mood. How many can he jail when he is having a bad day?[59]

MBS's visit to India was less spectacular, but he nevertheless had the distinction of being personally met at the airport by Prime Minister Narendra Modi at a time of heightened tension with Pakistan. Just before his visit, Pakistan-based militants of the 'Army of Muhammad' had succeeded in killing forty Indian soldiers serving in Indian-controlled Kashmir, and Pakistan shot down two Indian air force jets and captured one of the pilots in a standoff that brought two nuclear armed powers to the brink of war. Dispelling any suspicions that the Kashmiri militants had been the beneficiaries of Saudi funding, MBS's visit to the two South Asian powers appears to have been salutary, as shortly after his departure from India Imran Khan released the pilot as a gesture that had the effect of de-escalating tensions.

MBS's visit to China, where he received all the honours due to a head of state from President Xi Jinping was less dramatic but nevertheless indicative of Saudi Arabia's global shift. There were the usual statements about mutual investments in economic developments, but on the scandal of Muslim detentions – the thousands of Uighurs incarcerated in 're-education' camps in their homeland of Xinjiang – the young man expecting to be Guardian of the Two Sacred Shrines and future leader of the Umma was impressively silent. China is Saudi Arabia's biggest trading partner, with imports of hydrocarbons and related materials valued at $46 billion in 2018. The opportunity for Saudi investment in the world's largest economy with a gross domestic product of $25 trillion, and the opportunities for Chinese investment in Arabia looked rosy despite a downturn in the Chinese and global economies. With China there would be no quibbles about war crimes in Yemen, human rights abuses at home or the murder of a US-based journalist. As Yang Jiechi, a senior Chinese official, was telling the Munich Security Conference a few days before MBS's arrival in Beijing, 'China respects human rights. The ethnic groups in China are all working together.'[60]

On his return to Saudi Arabia in February 2019, MBS performed the functions of 'deputy king' while his father was absent in Egypt. Two important appointments he made in that capacity were making his full brother Khalid deputy minister of defence (only 'deputy' because MBS himself holds the portfolio) and the daughter of Bandar bin Sultan, Princess Reema, Khalid's successor as the king's ambassador in Washington DC. As Saudi Arabia's first ever female envoy she has an unusual string of qualifications. Having been brought up mainly in the US during her father's long tenure as envoy, Princess Reema has a bachelor's degree in museum studies and an impressive business record as CEO of Alfa International, described as a 'leading luxury retail corporation that, among other pursuits, operates the Harvey Nichols store in Riyadh'.

While her fellow diplomats may wonder if managing an upmarket retail store is an ideal qualification for addressing the increasing difficulties between the Saudi kingdom and its US ally in the face of growing hostility in Congress, the princess's appointment sent an important signal to the world. As noted by Bloomberg News, the decision to pick the daughter of 'Bandar Bush', the long-serving Saudi envoy in Washington, suggested that the government was trying to soften its image at a time of tense relations with Congress over the murder of Khashoggi as well as 'outrage over the arrest of women activists and Yemen's humanitarian crisis'. Fawaz Gerges, an astute observer of Middle Eastern affairs, thought the appointment 'represents a new beginning, trying to polish the image of Saudi Arabia and reinforce the image of the king and his son as reformers. They're trying to address concerns and the critics of the kingdom in the United States.'[61]

At the same time, it showed the Saudis – and other family members – that the Al Sudairi or Al Fahd faction of the family was as determined as ever to remain in control of the sprawling dynastic system. The elevation of Khalid to the defence ministry sent a rather different message, telling the world that the ambassador who had reassured Khashoggi that he would be safe if he collected his divorce papers from the Saudi consulate in Istanbul was now in control of the kingdom's armed forces.

By early March 2019, however, there appeared to be a last-minute obstacle in the path to absolute power being forged by the ambitious sons of Salman against the family consensus. The glitch came from inside the king's own entourage. It appears that during his visit to Egypt the ageing monarch was warned by one of his advisors that his son might be plotting against him. Suspecting that some of his security staff might be in league with the crown prince, he or his advisors appointed a new security team. They also dismissed the

Egyptian security personnel who were guarding him, suspecting that these agents might be acting for President Sisi with the aim of unseating Salman.

A new team of loyalist guards was flown in from Saudi Arabia. The apparent rift between father and son was underlined when – contrary to the usual protocol – the crown prince was not among the guests who greeted the king at the airport on his return to Riyadh. A power struggle appeared to be in course, between some of the old king's supporters and the 'Young Turks' surrounding MBS. At this writing (in February 2023), the 'Young Turks' appeared firmly in charge. There remains the remote possibility, however, that after King Salman's departure through death or abdication, there still could be one final, gerontocratic shuffle sideways down the line of the sons of Ibn Saud. Prince Ahmed ibn Abd al-Aziz (born in 1942, the same year as President Joe Biden) is the most senior prince to have refused to make his *baya* to MBS. He remains, with Salman, the 'last of the Sudairies'. Unsurprisingly, since March 2020 he has been detained by his nephew for 'plotting to overthrow the government'. In May 2022 Prince Ahmed's eldest son Abdulaziz joined a royal delegation to the UAE, a gesture seen as signalling family unity after the years of factional discord while MBS built up his power, making a palace countercoup seem less probable.[62]

10
Terraforming Arabia

Terraforming Mars is a board game considered suitable for anyone over the age of twelve. It has players, representing rival capitalist corporations, who compete in 'terraforming' the red planet, making it habitable by increasing its temperature, levels of oxygen and the size of its oceans. Players gain points by laying down tiles representing oceans with sea creatures or forests with small animals and predators or building fantastic cities in the barren planet's landscape. The winner is the one who has most tiles on the board when the 'terraforming process' has been completed. An enthusiastic games reviewer explains that there are lots of ways to win. 'It's the kind of game that rewards strategic planning, but occasionally requires you to completely revise your tactics.'[1]

The game had yet to be invented when Mohammed bin Salman was a small boy, but there can be little doubt that he would have enjoyed it had it been available. As the eldest child of the brood that Salman bin Abd al-Aziz shared with his second wife Fahdah bint Falah al-Hithlain, daughter of the leader of the belligerent Ajman tribe, Mohammed had received a far more indulgent upbringing than his older half-brothers who had been sent for education abroad. As Bradley Hope and Justin Scheck explain:

While the older [half]-brothers were establishing their careers, adolescent Mohammed seemed aimless. He had a habit of daydreaming during family events, a tendency some mistook for absentmindedness. On vacation to Marbella or elsewhere, he and his younger brother Khalid would go off exploring or scuba diving. He'd spend hours playing video games, including the Age of Empires series where you build armies and conquer enemies, and indulging a love of fast food. Salman still brought professors and writers around and hosted weekly seminars, but his requests that Mohammed study or read books rather than play video games seemed more like nagging than the strict orders the prince used to issue to his older sons.[2]

Neom, Mohammed's brain-child on the Red Sea Coast opposite the Egyptian resort of Sharm el-Sheikh, is a visionary enterprise. The name is a hybrid combining the Greek *neo* ('new') and the Arabic *mustaqbal* ('future'). In an article in *Le Monde* Aureliano Tonet and Margherita Nasi suggested that the original inspiration was a science fiction film *Guardians of the Galaxy* (James Gunn 2014) which became Mohammed's favourite movie after he had watched it on a plane.[3] The prince hired the film's set designer Olivier Pron who assembled a team of special-effects artists to work on the project. The team were encouraged to let their imaginations roam through the spirals of Galaxy Hollywood without technological or budgetary constraints.

Given the daunting landscape of north-west Arabia where Neom is now breaking ground, the board game where players seek to 'terraform' the Arabian desert seems a plausible model. But instead of individual players, aged twelve and upwards, acting as 'a money-driven corporation, desperate to cash in on the terraforming project being completed on Mars' (as our games reviewer has it), there are real corporations with real shareholders in this game including the

Boston Consulting Group (BCG), Oliver Wyman and McKinsey and Company.

The showpiece of Neom is The Line, a steel and glass structure with parallel 500-metre mirror wall facades (a height just short of the World Trade Center in New York that collapsed when the planes crashed into them on 11 September 2001). The walls are separated by a 200-metre gap that is supposed to be filled by shrubs and trees and cascading terraces with plants and ponds. Posters and videos on display at an exhibition devoted to the project at the Abbazia di San Gregorio in Venice, which I visited in June 2023, revealed enticing vistas with unveiled females and their partners picnicking in a fantasy cityscape of scrubland and concrete artfully framed with shade and light. Images purporting to show The Line from high altitude have a silver streak shafting without any kink or bend, from its extrusion on the rocky Red Sea Coast to its termination in the inhospitable Arabian desert.

An introductory poster explains that The Line will transverse three distinct ecological zones: coastal desert, Precambrian mountains and Palaeozoic upper valley. Its agenda of 'radical sustainability' will require 100 per cent renewable energy enabling the production of food using 'sustainable water desalination'. It purports to offer 'a sustainable urban model for several million inhabitants' with the preservation of nature a priority. This linear city, we are told, will be able to save 95 per cent of nature while connecting the three ecological zones with a single linear backbone, creating a mixed-use community with 'exceptional liveability' in five-minute neighbourhoods with zero cars and zero road infrastructure where everyone has access to nature.

The more practical model of The Line is said to have been devised – post-galactically as it were – by veteran American architect Thom Mayne (born in 1944), winner of the 2005 Pritzker Architecture

Prize with Morphosis, the studio he co-founded in Los Angeles in 1972. Significantly, Mayne and his colleagues have no experience of working in Muslim environments – in marked contrast to the late Tom Payette, designer of the impressive and brilliantly executed Aga Khan hospital in Karachi. Before designing this hospital, Payette – at his client's request – visited numerous sites from Spain to Pakistan to evaluate different styles of Islamic architecture. His remit was to learn how qualities of Muslim living as well as architecture could be incorporated into the university hospital's design.

It might not be too outlandish to describe Mayne's linear vision as 'Islamically illiterate' in terms of its aesthetic as well as its social vision. Nothing could be further from The Line as envisaged by its proponents than, say, iconic Islamic cities such as Samarkand in present-day Uzbekistan or Baghdad prior to its destruction by the Mongols in 1258. In creating Baghdad in 762 CE, Abu Jafar al-Mansur, the second Abbasid caliph, built a walled circus with a diameter of more than 2.5 km topped by a green dome more than 50 metres high that dominated the surrounding flatlands, a marvel in its time but on a human scale allowing comfortable access to houses, shops and government offices.

As the city spread beyond its original walls to the east bank of the River Tigris, the two halves were linked by a bridge of boats. Bin Salman's linear city, by contrast, is based on the implausible prospect of transforming the desert environment using billions of cubic metres of desalinated water. Mayne has explained that in their presentation for the concept he and his colleagues showed the Saudis a 'conceptual map that took New York apart' enabling them to 'develop the scale that broke down socially into communities that had personalities' giving 'people opportunities to live in very different environments like you would in London or Manhattan'.[4]

In awarding the contract to Western designers oblivious of Muslim contexts, MBS and his apparatchiks demonstrated either ignorance of the aesthetic and cultural traditions prevailing in the Muslim world, or, more probably, the disdain for them that his clan exhibited when they destroyed the Ottoman fabric of Mecca.

As Alpa Depani, a UK-based architect, wrote in her review in the *Architects' Journal*, in the Abbazia exhibition, despite its videos, posters and impressive displays alongside three-dimensional models 'showing carpets of green and improbably mature trees growing abundantly in dark crevices', actual details seemed scarce. The exhibition gave little detail about the rapid-transit infrastructure people would need to navigate the linear city of 9 million people along an artificial canyon 170 km long but only 200 m wide. 'The Line does not so much ignore the failure of post-war "streets in the sky" urbanism to consider how people move and their innate anxiety about separation from the ground plane, as set fire to it.'[5]

In lieu of providing detail about the project's feasibility, the exhibition intersperses the videos and models with placards filled with faux-professional verbiage aimed at impressing non-initiates. In this zero-gravity world, we are informed, 'a language of verticality and multi-level landscape creates a fine-grain urban texture, enabling a matrix that organizes both public and private programs into a dynamic, vibrant and liveable city with easily-accessible daily needs'. The 'tapestry of spaces', a strategic arrangement of bridges and plug-ins traversing the urban canyon, promises to 'reduce urban travel time, improving liveability and quality of life'.

While details of transportation are vague, with no indication of how The Line's promised 9 million citizens living along its 170-km axis will interact to form actual human communities, we are simply told they will benefit: a placard in bold lettering displaying trees and waterfalls proclaims the 'UBIQUITOUS PUBLIC REALM' created by the 'network of parks' that weave through The Line's urban environment, enabling a 'cohesive and interconnected green network that aids the mitigation of heat, the provision of clean air and access to natural light to improve residents' well-being'. This is certainly a radical departure from traditions of Saudi living. As Susanne Koelbl, a German journalist who lived in Riyadh and other Saudi cities, states in her book *Behind the Kingdom's Veil*, 'Saudis believe public spaces are uncontrollable, sinful, and should be avoided whenever possible.'[6]

According to a TV documentary shown on the Discovery Channel and approved by the Saudi government, The Line will be divided into 140 modules, each of them 800 m long and housing 80,000 people. The first five modules will each be developed by a different studio, picked from 'a playing field of 20'. The film features interviews with architects from six studios, led by Mayne's Morphosis and other global practices including Cook Haffner, Pei Cobb Freed, HOK and OMA. But in an article in the online architectural journal *Dezeen*, a spokesperson from HOK said that while the practice had been engaged in the early stages of the design, it was no longer participating in the project.

In the documentary, the crown prince strikes a note of defiance. 'They say a lot of projects in Saudi Arabia can't be done. They're too ambitious. They can keep saying that and we can keep proving them wrong.' Lead architect Thom Mayne echoes the prince's can-do optimism, saying, 'I can't think of anybody that wouldn't want to be part of this project. It's going to be, without question, the most extraordinary piece of work that begins in the first quarter of the 21st century.'

A more revealing comment comes from Sir Peter Cook, eighty-six, founder of the Cook Haffner studio which also contributed to the design. 'I think higher than 500 meters', he told the *Architects' Journal*, 'is a bit stupid and unreasonable and all our engineer friends will tell you this'. Fifty metres would be 'quite agreeable, high enough, nice view, easy to get up and down'. In all likelihood – Cook thought – the structure 'would eventually reach 50 metres in height' at best.[7] In the documentary Cook is more tactful, if ambiguous: 'If it succeeds it will be a new Babylon, so to speak. And if it doesn't succeed it will be an interesting phenomenon.'[8]

In an interview with *Dezeen*, Tarek Quddumi – Neom's executive director for urban planning – explained that 'residents will be able to travel along The Line at high speed, enjoying access to the entire city at a fraction of what is needed in current cities of similar size. Once off the mobility system', he added without giving details of the type or method of transport, residents would find themselves in 'five-minute communities' within 'walking distance of all their daily needs, with unparalleled access to nature'. In contrast to modern 'flat cities', The Line would be organized in a 'vertical and three-dimensional way' with self-shading and natural ventilation 'enabling constant cooling of the public realm'.

Nature, according to Quddumi, would be accommodated with 'terrestrial animals and waterflows' moving 'through curated corridors on the ground plane'. Birds that fly at different heights would have their 'designated nature corridors ... designed in combination with the right glass treatment, ceramic frit, glass transparency and reflective factors'. A zero-carbon city, The Line would compensate for the emissions caused in the course of construction by carbon offsetting and carbon sequestration. 'Irrespective of its physical stature', it would demonstrate that 'the world has the human capacity, the technology and the commitment to revolutionise our current way of life'.[9]

In viewing the displays at the Abbazia di San Gregorio in Venice I was reminded of two very non-Islamic models. Rather than echoing the Hanging Gardens of Babylon as suggested by Peter Cook, I thought of Fritz Lang's movie *Metropolis* (1927), a masterpiece of German Expressionism, where the futurist city with its stadiums, skyscrapers and sky-born turnpikes dominates the upper levels offering comfort and convenience to its bourgeois residents while toilers in the vast engine rooms driving the system are reduced to human robots. In this respect, the Hollywood-inspired vision of the young MBS (who was never schooled in America in his formative years) and that of the ageing Thom Mayne seemed to coincide: an outdated early-twentieth-century vision of what might constitute urban 'architecture' in the twenty-first century.

The other image that came to mind was of the fantasy castles built by King Ludwig II in Bavaria. Ludwig, who inherited the throne in 1864 at the age of nineteen on the death of his father Maximilian II, was the most passionate advocate of Wagner's visionary music-theatre. Without Ludwig's financial support it is doubtful if the great composer (a hero to Adolf Hitler, but during his lifetime in constant flight from his creditors) would have been able to complete the *Ring* cycle, *Parsifal* or even *Tristan and Isolde*, not to mention the celebrated opera house he created at Bayreuth.

Ludwig's fascination with Wagner, amounting to an obsession, virtually bankrupted the Bavarian treasury along with his personal fortune. The castles he built or refurbished at Neuschwanstein, Linderhof and Herrenchiemsee were inspired by his love of Wagnerian myth and his fascination with France's *ancien régime* Bourbons. Neuschwanstein – the Gothic-Romanesque folly commanding a peak above the fir-covered slopes of the Pollat River – is the inspiration for Disneyland's kitschy replica, the Sleeping Beauty Castle, while Herrenchiemsee, modelled on the Palace of Versailles, was Ludwig's homage to Louis XIV, with the Linderhof based on the Trianon in tribute to Marie Antoinette and the 'religious cult' he confessed to holding in her memory.[10]

The construction of Ludwig's castles bankrupted the Bavarian treasury and led to the king's removal on grounds of insanity in a palace plot headed by his uncle, followed by his probable suicide by drowning in 1886. But after a century and a half, Ludwig's fantasy castles are now among the top tourist attractions and currency earners in Germany.

Could The Line – if completed – have a comparable impact on the Kingdom of Saudi Arabia? In their analysis of the project, two architectural critics Loup Calosci and Olivier Namias speculate about the costs using the model of the World Trade Center in New York destroyed by the mainly Saudi hijackers on 11 September 2001. Yamasaki's Twin Towers, then the tallest in the world, cost $900 million in 1973, equivalent of $62 billion in 2023. According to their calculation, at 170 km long The Line is equal to 2,468 World Trade Centers placed end to end. Does a figure of $15 trillion, they ask, far beyond the $500 billion currently earmarked by MBS, 'give a more realistic idea of the project's costs, or will the economies of scale, notably on the facades, lower the bill'?

It should also be noted, they comment, that unlike the World Trade Center The Line is under construction in virgin desert, while the former benefited from New York's existing infrastructure. Moreover, the World Trade Center did not have gardens on every floor and was 100 m lower in height than the proposed linear skyscraper. The Line, they conclude, along with other planned projects 'could rapidly exhaust the most well-stocked wallets, even those of the oil kings'.[11] Their scepticism was already being vindicated as this book went to press, when Bloomberg reported that the project had been scaled back to house 300,000 people instead of the 1.5 million originally claimed for 2030, with only 2.4 kilometres of the planned 170 kilometres completed.[12]

Their scepticism is together reinforced by a report in the *Wall*

Street Journal in February 2024 that the public investment fund (PIF) tasked with paying for The Line and a host of other 'megaprojects' has seen its cash levels fall from $60 billion in December 2020 to around $15 million since September 2023, requiring the country to make massive borrowings at a time when interest rates were rising and the price of oil remains moderate.[13] Of course the seepage of cash and cost of borrowing are hardly a problem for a country holding the world's largest reserves of hydrocarbons, estimated at 255.2 billion barrels at the close of 2020, along with 5.4 trillion cubic metres of natural gas.[14] Saudi Aramco's initial public offering (IPO) in 2019 raised a record $25.6 billion through the sale of 3 billion shares – a mere 1.5 per cent of the company's value – that increased to $29.4 billion after the selling of 450 million additional shares.[15]

The IPO in December 2019 may have failed to meet expectations – MBS having claimed that the company was worth $2 trillion, whereas the markets considered $1.5 trillion more realistic. With the listing failing to meet the transparency requirements of stock exchanges in London and New York it landed on the Riyadh Tadawul stock exchange at $29.4 billion, the largest public offering at that time. In September 2023 there were reports that the company was planning to sell additional shares worth up to $50 billion. Given the volume of investments planned by MBS and his government, the cash would certainly be needed.

By mid-2023 videos were circulating showing that ground had been broken at the start of The Line's construction, with images of steel reinforcements littering the desert along with videos showing giant cranes in action, speeded-up bulldozers and even load-bearing helicopters. Many experts – following Sir Peter Cook – remained sceptical about the project's viability. Human rights campaigners pointed to the human cost in addition to Neom's vastly underestimated $500 billion price tag. The Line and its surrounding developments (including a luxury marina for yachts and a fancy coastal resort) are located in the territory of the Huwaitat tribe, a region that crosses the boundaries of southern Jordan, north-west Saudi Arabia and the Sinai Peninsula, now part of Egypt.

The Huwaitat came to international prominence in the British-supported Arab revolt against the Ottomans during the First World War. Their leader, Sheikh Auda Abu Tayi, played by Anthony Quinn alongside Peter O'Toole in David Lean's epic film *Lawrence of Arabia* (1967), was instrumental in taking the port of Aqaba from the Ottomans, enabling Britain and its allies to provide the support that would culminate in the fall of Jerusalem and Damascus in 1917. The Huwaitat were the vanguard of the Arab revolt that ended the Ottoman Empire, leading to the installation (under British auspices) of Hashemite kingdoms in Iraq and Transjordan. This may be one reason that as the likely future leader of the Al Saud, long-time dynastic rivals of the Hashemites, MBS has been more than happy to tribally cleanse the Huwaitat from their ancestral territories in the Tabuk region he now controls.

As a volunteer for Oxfam and Save the Children Fund, in 1959 I myself worked with the Huwaitat during a period of drought, bringing them food such as flour, dates and pulses with the help of the Jordanian army. They were a dignified and friendly people, proud of their heritage. They struck me as being culturally assured to a remarkable degree. When I accompanied Sheikh Khalaf and his friend in a small private plane piloted by a wealthy Oxfam donor, the two Huwaiti men who had never been airborne before were unfazed by the experience and immediately took to counting the number of goat-hair tents of their people as we flew over outlying territories.

Unsurprisingly, the tribal cleansing of the Huwaitat, abetted by three Western consultancies – BCG, Oliver Wyman and McKinsey – which signed multi-million-dollar contracts with the Saudi PIF, the agency driving the Neom project, does not feature in the expensive promotional material displayed in the Abbazia or on the Discovery Channel documentary. In 2020, around 20,000 Huwaitis were forced to leave their homes.

One of their campaigners, Abdal Rahim al-Huwaiti, was killed in what Saudi officials claimed was a shoot-out with security forces. Other Huwaitis, according to activists, were detained for spreading anti-displacement leaflets and refusing to sign relocation documents. More than a dozen Huwaitis are reported to have been abducted by Saudi security forces and held incommunicado. In October 2022 it was reported that three tribal members – Shadli, Ibrahim and Ataullah – had been sentenced to death for their resistance, though at this writing there has been no confirmation that the sentences have been carried out. Around the same time some Huwaiti leaders were shown on Saudi television pledging allegiance to the Al Saud.

The mass displacement of the indigenous Huwaitis, for which a complaint has been lodged at the United Nations, is not the only downside to a project that may come to discredit not only the Al Saud and its leadership but the architects and Western consultants who devised and promoted it. After images of the project were released in 2022, several planning authorities expressed scepticism. Philip Oldfield, who heads the built environment school at the University of New South Wales in Sydney, told *Dezeen* that the carbon costs used in construction would 'overwhelm any environmental benefits'.

In the same issue, Marshall Brown, director of the Urban Imagination Center at Princeton, pointed to the 'physical and environmental phenomena that would have to be dealt with to achieve the incredibly minimal and singular character' of the images shown in the models and drawings.[16] Wilhelmus Maas of the Rotterdam studio MVRDV and director of The Why Factory, an urban think-tank, doubts that any finished structure will bear much resemblance to the images displayed online or at the Abbazia. The Line's double-bar profile, he said, 'doesn't make sense in terms of variety, in terms of wind pressure, in terms of keeping cold air in'. But he was positive about the overall concept. 'I love deserts and I do see the necessity to develop them so that ultimately rain comes back to those places, so I think it's crucial to work on that.'[17]

The most strident critique came from Adam Greenfield, an architectural writer. He quoted J. Robert Oppenheimer, the American physicist regarded as the father of the atomic bomb, who famously explained the appeal of working on atomic weapons for a scientist: 'When you see something that is technically sweet, you go ahead and do it.' Greenfield points out that Neom and The Line are being planned at a time when temperatures in the Arabian desert are increasing dangerously. Before their recent displacement, the Huwaitat had learned over centuries how to navigate extremes of heat, but even for them a projected increase in both land surface temperatures and wet-bulb temperatures by 6°C and 4°C, respectively, could be daunting.

Bearing in mind the appalling conditions suffered by mainly South Asian construction workers prior to the 2022 football World Cup in Qatar, when some 4,000 are estimated to have died, the prospects for a new generation of imported workers must be bleak. A 2022 paper by a team of environmentalists cited by Greenfield argues that the projected rise in temperatures in the Arabian Peninsula poses 'significant risks on human survivability unless strict climate mitigation takes place'.[18]

Greenfield sees a parallel between Oppenheimer's hubris, brilliantly portrayed by Cillian Murphy in Christopher Nolan's Oscar-winning film, and architects such as Thom Mayne who are queuing up to join the exciting prospect of Neom and The Line. Whereas normally architects find themselves hedged by planning and commercial issues, such as floor area ratios and thousands of other conditions, with the normal city 'a roiling pit of contention crammed with fractious constituencies' each of which demands its say, architects working for MBS may find, like Oppenheimer, that working on the project is indeed 'technically sweet'.

'Along comes someone who encourages you to dream big, assures you that whatever you imagine can and will be built, and best of all, offers you a fat purse for sharing the contents of your beautiful mind with the world.'[19] Echoes of 'mad King Ludwig's castles' are compelling, though one may doubt if any of the 'beautiful minds' MBS has lured to the Kingdom of Saudi Arabia will measure up to the genius of Richard Wagner.

While The Line is the boldest and most discussed item in the bonanza of the crown prince's visionary projects, many others both included in Neom and outside the north-west region appear to be showering architects, engineers and designers with Saudi largesse. As with The Line, the promotional materials are dazzling. The most egregious (and least plausible) is a mountain resort planned for Trojena in the Neom area, topped by a crystalline tower of more than 300 m with tapering columns of glass designed by the Zaha Hadid studios in London, with the German studio LAVA as master planners. Neom is reported to have already committed $5 billion to build a dam at the base of the resort to provide water for the artificial snow.[20]

Prospective visitors are told that the resort, called Collective Retreats, has sixty open-air guest rooms and meeting places. It will offer a 'full array of year-round outdoor activities including skiing and snowboarding, high altitude training and paragliding, mountain biking, hiking and water sports, as well as culture-forward programming around film, art, music and food'. Paragliding may be plausible, though landing may be a challenge in the rugged terrain, but an outdoor ski resort some 50 km from Aqaba, one of the hottest corners on earth, seems pure science fiction. Even the latest model snow cannons require ten times the energy of a domestic oven as well as 10 litres of water a second.[21]

Artificial snow machines requiring large quantities of water and energy, now in growing use in Alpine and other ski areas as the snowline recedes, are under increasingly critical scrutiny. As early as 2006 a study by the OECD predicted that two-thirds of the Alpine ski areas were in jeopardy while warning against the use of snow cannons because of their impact on water supplies and local ecosystems.[22]

Saudi Arabia is largely dependent on desalinated water requiring vast amounts of energy to produce, whether by old-fashioned thermal methods of heating and condensation, or the more recent reverse osmosis, whereby sea water is pumped through a complex series of membranes at molecular level using seventy times atmospheric pressure.[23] Both methods will have used serious amounts of energy even before the snow-making process. Yet snow machines are currently being tested with a view to making Trojena ready for the Asian Winter Games in 2029, an event that seems barely less probable than holding the Olympics on Mars.

We may doubt along with Sir Peter Cook and other architects that The Line will finally reach the monumental scale displayed in its promotional materials, in the nature-friendly vision promoted in expensively commissioned videos and exhibitions, and we may take a sceptical glance at the thought of ski-slopes in the neighbourhood of Aqaba. Other projects planned or already underway seem less implausible. Even if uncompleted they will leave monumental footprints on the Arabian landscape along with attendant human benefits.

Roshn, a branch of the PIF, has a target of building 400,000 houses with a view to increasing home ownership to up to 70 per cent by

2030. According to *Dezeen*, in 2023 6,000 homes have already been built, with another 27,000 under construction. The project entails building 850 mosques, 2,400 schools and the planting of a million trees. The PIF has two tourist projects on the west coast – the Red Sea and Amaala – as well as a ring-shaped hotel on stilts, a hotel among the sand dunes to be served by an airport – one of the world's largest – designed by Foster and partners. Although after the murder of Khashoggi Lord Foster resigned from the advisory board of Neom, work on his winning design for the airport continues.

Foster's decision to design this airport along with several others was strongly criticized by the campaigning group Architects Climate Action Network (ACAN) which stated that 'based on Saudi Arabia's reputation for human rights abuse, slavery and deaths in construction, working on projects there which are not critical would be unethical' and contrary to the Royal Institute of British Architects' Professional Code of Practice. In the face of the climate emergency, ACAN concluded, 'it doesn't make sense to build more airports let alone an airport of this scale'.[24] However the RIBA's Professional Code of Practice did not prevent its incoming president Chris Williamson from making a slightly shamefaced defence of his studio's work on Neom's high-speed rail links. He decided to work on the project after consultations with others working in the region as well as the UK government, whose official guidance describes the Saudi kingdom as a 'key UK government trading partner'.[25]

Foster's engagement with the Saudi kingdom is not limited to airports. In March 2024, the *Architects' Journal* reported that the partnership was designing a 'megatall skyscraper' reaching a height of 2 km on a site near Riyadh's international airport which Foster is currently refurbishing. If completed the tower would be the world's tallest building, dwarfing the current record holder, the 828-metre-high Burj Khalifa in Dubai.[26]

Another of the 'giga-projects' the studio has designed has been described as 'the world's first fully immersive experiential marine life centre' at the Amaala resort on the Gulf of Aqaba. The partnership's alluring promotional image displays a series of glass-reinforced concrete structures moulded to echo the shapes of the coral reefs that adorn this coast. While Red Sea coral appears unusually able to resist rising ocean temperatures due to its high salinity, the reefs are currently endangered by pollution, mass tourism and over-fishing from the Egyptian side of the gulf where the resort of Sharm el-Sheikh is located.[27] The centre will have a sub-aqua level enabling visitors to view coral in one of the world's largest man-made reefs through a large suspended demi-spherical tank filled with local marine life, along with what are described as 'augmented reality experiences' and undersea tours in submersible vehicles. In October 2022 it was reported that the bulk earthworks had been completed and that excavations had begun below the surface.

A more ambitious project than the Red Sea tourist developments, with the marinas, manicured islets and beaches designed to lure wealthy tourists, is the Oxagon, a large octagonal structure, half of it an artificial island on the Red Sea Coast of the Neom area, which promises to be the world's largest floating structure. The project also includes a terminal for cruise ships and an oceanographic research centre. The futurist city, promoted in glossy videos, will have water-filled squares linked by canals, with both residential areas and an industrial complex containing 'the world's first integrated port and supply chain ecosystem'. According to MBS, 'Oxagon will be the catalyst for economic growth and diversity in Neom and the Kingdom further meeting our ambitions under Vision 2030'.[28]

One may hope that Oxagon will avoid the ecological disaster of the artificial islands on the coast of Dubai in the Persian Gulf, where, according to the environmental news service Mongabay, 'dredging and redepositing of sand from seafloor clouded the waters with silt, damaging the marine habitat, burying coral reefs, oyster beds and subterranean fields of sea grass, threatening local marine species and others dependent on them for food.'[29] Some of Dubai's artificial islands shaped as palm trees or, more bizarrely, as the map outlines of modern countries are still struggling to find investors, with those yet to be occupied by humans now colonized by marine animals such as sea snakes.

Not all the kingdom's ongoing projects, however, belong in the realm of Hollywood-inspired fantasy. A $63 million restoration programme of historic Diriyah, the Al Sauds' original capital with the iconic mudbrick city of At-Turaif, a UNESCO World Heritage Site since 2010, has now been completed to a standard that a world-class Islamic art historian regards as excellent, with the adjacent area with parks and restaurants a place where families gather after sundown. King Salman's Park in Riyadh, with 11 square kilometres of green space irrigated using recycled city water, is on the way to becoming the world's 'largest urban park'. The site includes a 110-metre-high pyramid designed by the late Catalan architect Ricardo Bofill. The Murabba district of Riyadh, dominated by a 400-metre-high cube filled with 2 million square metres of shops, may well achieve its aim of becoming the star attraction of the Saudi capital's downtown area containing '100,000 residential units, 9,000 hotel rooms, 980,000 square metres of shops and 1.4 million square metres of office space'.[30] Qidiyya, a family-friendly amusement park of 367 square kilometres and forty minutes from Riyadh, promises record-breaking roller-coaster rides, including the world's longest, tallest and fastest, as well as sports arenas, concert halls and a golf course named after Jack Nicklaus.

In the frenzy of development that will soon outflank Dubai's Quasi-Manhattan, the kingdom's second city, Jeddah, has not been neglected, with a vast new residential development funded by the PIF along with a stadium designed by GMP Architekten (Germany), an opera house designed by Henning Larsen (Denmark) and oceanarium by the US studio SOM. The fine old city known as the Balad is now being restored with spaces for art initiatives.

Its crowning glory, the Jeddah Tower, was at 1,000 metres the world's tallest building until overtaken by Foster's proposed Riyadh tower – almost 180 metres higher than the Burj Khalifa and more than three times taller than London's tallest building, the Qatari-owned Shard designed by Renzo Piano. Construction of the Jeddah Tower, begun in 2014, was suspended after just sixty-three of the planned 254 storeys had been built when its principal investors Prince Alwaleed bin Talal and Bakr bin Laden (Osama's half-brother) were arrested for money laundering and corruption in the Ritz-Carlton coup (see above, p. 197). Building was resumed in 2023 after a five-year hiatus during which a skeleton of hollow rooms surrounded by giant orange cranes served as a concrete reminder of Prince Alwaleed's temporary fall from grace.

Some of this surge in development, much of it funded by the PIF under the crown prince's control, is part of the strategy to enable economic development after the world weans itself off oil. The overall plan, Vision 2030, is to transform the nation into a modern and vibrant society by diversifying its economy away from oil.[31] The economic goals are ambitious. According to Bloomberg the country is aiming to become a 'global supply chain hub' and create new industries such as electric vehicles and pharmaceuticals both to meet local demand and for export. In October 2023 the PIF was reported to have partnered with the Saudi Electricity Company to start an infrastructure company to service electric vehicles. There was speculation that the PIF could buy the Shanghai-based Human Horizons Group that makes electric vehicles in China.[32] Investment decisions in this area are not just commercial but have wide-ranging strategic implications. As Karl Maier writes for Bloomberg, 'In a world bristling with upheaval, the transition to EVs is already reshaping economies and global alliances. China is well ahead of the game, holding more than 80 per cent of the world's lithium-ion battery capacity.'[33]

Consistent with this strategic pivot, the crown prince is investing in developing the country's copper mines – estimated at containing between 1 per cent and 5 per cent of the world's reserves of a metal essential for electrification – while a local company, Tamgo, has signed an exclusive deal to market hydrogen fuel cells with AFC Energy, the world's leading producer, to generate 'clean electricity'. The Saudi energy minister, the crown prince's older half-brother Prince Abdulaziz bin Salman, has stated that the country plans to use its uranium, also claimed to be between 1 and 5 per cent of the world's total, to build up its nuclear power industry and diversify its energy sources. The announcement raised obvious concerns about the possibility of a nuclear arms race in the region should the JCPOA agreed between Iran and permanent members of the UN Security Council plus Germany in 2015 fail to prevent the Islamic Republic from producing weapons-grade material.

A less contentious part of the kingdom's plan to wean itself off oil involves the development of solar energy. In February 2023, two local companies in the PIF portfolio agreed to build the world's largest solar power plant at al-Shuaibah in the Mecca province. With sunshine even more plentiful than oil in the Saudi kingdom and with a generating capacity of more than 2,000 megawatts, Shuaibah may soon overtake the current record holder at Ouarzazate in the Moroccan Sahara, which has a current capacity of 580 megawatts, sufficient to power a city the size of Prague.[34]

The PIF has a target to develop 70 per cent of the kingdom's renewable energy by 2030, a key factor in its mandate to invest at least US$40 billion annually in the domestic economy. There is no certainty, however, that this goal can be achieved, despite recent surges in the price of oil. In November 2023 the PIF was said to be worth US$650 billion but had been losing money, declaring losses of $11 billion in 2022 compared with a profit of $19 billion in 2021.[35] In February 2024, according to the *Wall Street Journal*, its cash levels had fallen by about three-quarters, to about $15 billion, the lowest since December 2020.[36]

While energy diversification may seem a relatively distant goal, and the kingdom is unlikely to achieve its target of net-zero carbon emissions by 2060, tourism could promise a quicker way of generating revenues free of hydrocarbons.[37] Much is being made of the potentialities of the AlUla Oasis in the north-west in the vicinity of Mada'in Saleh, also known as al-Hijr. Mada'in Saleh is the second city after Petra (now in Jordan) created by the Nabatean kingdom that flourished from the late third century BCE until annexed by the Romans in 106 CE.

In 2008 UNESCO awarded it World Heritage status as 'a major site of the Nabatean civilization' containing an ensemble of tombs and monuments cut into the local sandstone that bear 'outstanding witness to important cultural exchanges in architecture, decoration, language use and the caravan trade' linking the Indian Ocean and the Mediterranean.[38] While the monumental façades of Mada'in Saleh are less impressive than those of Petra in neighbouring Jordan, with its iconic sandstone façades, gorges and caves, the region offers impressive touristic potential.

The AlUla websites show brilliantly staged pictures of 'adrenaline-pumping activities' such as rock-climbing on the sandstone cliffs, monumental art works created in the sandscapes or 'panoramic walks' along the streets of AlUla old town, where Western-attired couples can 'walk the streets of history … along the world's largest hand-painted carpet' beneath a funky panoply of lights. Daylight pictures show vast natural sculptures created by wind and water where a pair of sandstone towers called the Dancing Rocks merge 'into a single sculpture that seems to sway in unison as if it were an intimate couple alone on the dance floor' – an image that might recall a romantic visit by the website's scribe to the Arches National Park near Moab, Utah, but hardly evocative of the Quranic Thamud, whose people were destroyed for rejecting the Prophet Saleh after whom the Nabatean city was named.

Most of the presentations which seem alien to the traditional Saudi zeitgeist have the cultural hallmarks of Western consultancies. To repeat a phrase from the reviewer of Terraforming Mars quoted above, today's players engaged in terraforming the terrain of north-west Arabia certainly include 'money-driven corporations, desperate to cash in on the terraforming project'. Just as the notorious Scramble for Africa in the nineteenth century was driven by competition between rival European powers, the twenty-first-century Scramble for Arabia has been driven in part by competition between rival consultancies, namely the McKinsey corporation and the Boston Consulting Group (BCG).

As one of the few Saudi princes not to have been educated, at least partly, in the West, MBS seems to have been unusually dazzled by the hard-selling pitch of the consultancy corporations. Early in 2016, a year after the death of King Abdullah, a delegation from the Saudi royal court arrived in Washington to interest American businesses and arms manufacturers in opportunities in the kingdom. According to Walt Bogdanich and Michael Forsythe, the delegation's tour guides in the US capital – agents from McKinsey and its chief rival BCG – actually 'outnumbered the Saudis', with the consultants taking notes during the meetings. Four years later McKinsey filed a late disclosure notice to the US Justice Department under the

Foreign Agents Registration Act, showing that they were not just consulting, but representing Saudi interests in the US.

McKinsey was working with the Saudi government to strengthen its diplomatic outreach, helping set up what became the Saudi Center for International Strategic Partnerships, which McKinsey said was 'an entity whose purpose would be to help manage and improve Saudi Arabia's relationships with numerous countries around the world'.[39]

These were the best of times for the planetary consultants. As the authors state, 'the young prince was enamoured of them' believing 'he needed their expertise to turn his big dreams into reality' including Neom, his city of the future.[40] The lobby of the Ritz-Carlton in Riyadh 'was full of McKinsey men', with regular appearances of Managing Partner Dominic Barton. 'Even the taxi drivers could identify individual consultants and their firms.'[41] In 2017 McKinsey announced it had bought Elixir, a local consulting company, in a rare acquisition driven by the lure of Elixir's local contacts and ties to the planning ministry. 'So ingrained was McKinsey into the kingdom's affairs that the planning ministry became known as the Ministry of McKinsey.'[42]

The company's payroll in the kingdom ballooned to 140 people, adding almost 50 per cent to its staff in the region. The authors, citing a former employee, state that the Elixir consultants were 'so close to the Saudi ministries that they're often indistinguishable from government employees'. According to another former consultant this proximity upended the traditional relationship between consultant and client whereby – at least in theory – consultants spoke 'hard truths to their clients'. They recalled that Ian Davis, a former McKinsey managing partner, told new employees they should see themselves rather as modern-day 'courtiers and viziers'.[43]

The entrepreneur Peter Thiel who made billions from the Paypal payments system he developed with Elon Musk takes a dim view of

McKinsey at this time. As he explained to the English philosopher John Gray, it was 'a real thing in 1985 in the United States. If you hired a consultant, they actually helped improve your company, because the companies were badly run.' But 'at this point McKinsey is a total racket, it's just all fake ... McKinsey is not going to be anything other than a super corrupt, fake racket in 2023'.[44]

McKinsey is far from being the only consultancy to benefit from Saudi largesse. Their rival BCG had long cultivated MBS as advisors to his foundation MiSK whose stated aim is 'to cultivate and encourage learning and leadership in youth for a better future in Saudi Arabia'.[45] Although both consultancies had worked on projecting an oil-free future for the kingdom, avoiding mass employment by investing in areas such as mining, tourism and finance, it was BCG not McKinsey that was instrumental in devising the prince's Vision 2030, the masterplan involving Neom and related projects. Concerns about collapsing oil prices and possible cuts in fuel subsidies raised the spectre of civil unrest in a new Arab Spring, always a worry for the region's authoritarian regimes.

A third consultancy that enters the picture is the London-based SCL Group, better known through its subsidiary Cambridge Analytica, 'notorious for influencing elections across the globe for any candidate willing to pay its fees'.[46] The initial aim, say the authors, 'was to conduct focus groups across the kingdom asking people how they would feel if the price of oil increased'. But the work went well beyond the traditional McKinsey remit of providing advice to companies about saving money and improving efficiency.

A former executive involved in the work is quoted as saying: the purpose behind it was 'to reduce the risk of unrest'. Given that the kingdom's population is one of the youngest in the world with one of the highest levels of engagement with platforms such as Instagram, Twitter (now X) and Facebook, the consultants forged a technique known as 'sentiment analysis' whereby social media posts are mined for keywords, 'allowing companies to measure attitudes about their products'. As the authors explain:

> The Saudis latched onto the fact that sentiment analysis had potential way beyond determining how people felt about their pizza delivery experience. In a country like Saudi Arabia, where it seemed everyone was chatting on Facebook, Instagram, or Twitter, it could be used by the government to take the public's temperature and smoke out influential malcontents.[47]

The political role of Western consultancies in sustaining autocracies and outsourcing diplomacy is disturbing enough, but their cultural footprint has also been considerable, as shown in their approach to tourism and sport. As Koelbl writes in her penetrating study of the kingdom:

> If MBS gets his way, the religions of the future will be nationalism, entertainment, tourism and sport. It's a future of amusement parks, innovative industries, five-star hotels, and modern mega-cities – all powered by renewable energy. And if you believe the crown prince this glittering future will offer fantastic opportunities for entrepreneurs and investors.[48]

The crown prince's enthusiastic young followers, with help no doubt from internet bots manufactured or relayed by the intelligence services, may welcome the revolutionary change in the tone of public discourse after centuries of Wahhabi restrictions. As Sergei Guriev, an economist, and Daniel Treisman, a political scientist, explain in their book *Spin Dictators*, modern dictators like Xi Jinping of China and MBS add 'spin' to the traditional repertoires of fear and repression, 'using hackers and trolls to dominate social networks' – a method that serves to 'track dissidents online' while promoting their global images.[49] But there is a danger that language devised by

Western consultants to lure investors may be underestimating the possibility of push-back or backlash if planeloads of tourists succumb to the alluring promotions displayed on the Neom websites.

The appeal of AlUla provides an interesting example. The impression of a sales pitch aimed at the upper end of the Western tourist market (or, more precisely, well-heeled global elites most of whom reside in the Global North) is reinforced by alluring images of the AlUla Wellness Center, where visitors may improve their breathing techniques in a 'full moon sound bath' before one of the Mada'in Saleh's Nabatean temples as well as having counselling sessions with Ashley Turner, a famous Californian therapist and yoga instructor. Yoga aficionados may benefit from 'daily sensory-based experiences' led by global experts featuring 'yoga, meditation, sound healing, fitness and more' with fit-looking people doing their exercises before retiring for 'four days and nights of shared experiences and workshops' at a special 'couples retreat' in the Hidden Valley.

Opinions of contemporary Muslim scholars towards the practice of yoga may vary, but that of the respected Hanbali scholar Sheikh Muhammad Saleh al-Munajjid who studied with the eminent Abd al-Aziz ibn Baz is unequivocal, condemning it as a form of idolatry 'based on lies and charlatanry' that may appeal 'to simple minded people who are weak in faith'. Some yoga postures imitating animals (one might note the familiar 'lion' posture, though he does not mention this specifically) detract from human dignity including 'adopting nakedness and resting on all fours'. He also criticizes the tendency of yoga practitioners to encourage a vegetarian diet 'for which Allah has not revealed any authority'.

The learned sheikh's fatwas — his online responses to believers' questions — do not bear the authority of the Saudi state. The popular website IslamQA, which he launched in 1996, is banned in the kingdom as only the Dar al-Ifta' — the official religious establishment – is authorized to issue fatwas. But there can be little doubt that traditional scholars would share Munajjid's hostility to yoga. As a student of his mentor, Ibn Baz, who as grand mufti presided over the Dar al-Ifta' till his death in 1999, has noted, while Saudi Arabian muftis (scholars authorized to issue fatwas) have been relatively open and liberal in permitting modern technological innovations, 'in the realms of social norms (e.g., ritual, the status of women) they maintain a "Puritanical" Wahhabi approach'.[50]

While the Fritz Langian vision of Neom and The Line may be accommodated under the category of technical modernization, the promotion of yoga would seem to impinge on mufti territory. The fact that it features in state-sanctioned promotional material raises a significant question. We may assume that this material, with its cascade of tourist-speak clichés, has been approved at the highest level. Does this mean that Wahhabi puritanism is being abandoned?

The answer may be obvious to hard-liners opposed to the prince's reforms, such as Sheikh Badr al-Meshari, a popular preacher in Riyadh with more than half a million followers on X, formerly Twitter, who was arrested in July 2023. But mainstream clerics under the newly centralized judiciary are likely to accept that there will be an exceptional jurisdiction in the country's special economic zones, including Neom and the Red Sea Project. Here commercial laws will be based on international rather than local standards, with more relaxed social norms, including the possibility of serving alcohol.[51]

A less contentious and potentially more productive dimension of Vision 2030 than tourism builds on indigenous creative forces that already exist in the Saudi art scene. Way back in 2003, long before the rise of MBS and before the Anglo-American invasion of Iraq that overthrew the Baathist dictator Saddam Hussein, Stephen Stapleton, a British artist and cultural entrepreneur, joined with two leading Saudi artists Abdulnasser Gharem and Ahmed Mater in founding Edge of Arabia, an artist-led organization, with the aim of encouraging 'grassroots cultural dialogue in Saudi Arabia and between Saudi Arabia and the Western world'.[52] Notable exhibitions included the Future of a Promise at the 2011 Venice Biennale and the 2012 London exhibition #cometogether. As Rebecca Anne Proctor and Alia al-Senussi state:

> Despite the conservative shroud that still lay over Saudi society, arts organizations, galleries, patrons and artists were finding ways to create and show art within a climate of restriction. The art, in many ways, was born from the restrictions – freedom of expression was found through a conceptualist language, through signs and metaphorical symbolism.[53]

Predating the top-down cultural revolution now presided over by MBS, Edge of Arabia was the harbinger of a new dawn not just in the arts but also social behaviour. As Stapleton explained in 2023:

> The Saudi artist we exhibited as part of Edge of Arabia between 2008 and 2018 put critical thinking at the centre of their practice; they expressed a tension and a conflict that was an honest reflection of the society they were trying to change. That language doesn't feel as relevant now, mainly because of the significant changes that are taking place in Saudi's cultural sector. When you have 500,000 people dancing at a festival on the outskirts of Riyadh, all expressing themselves in a way not publicly seen before in this country, the darker psychological symbols – of fear, of conflict – which were so evident in the best Saudi art of my generation don't make as much sense as they used to.[54]

Iwona Blazwick, former director of London's Whitechapel Gallery who now chairs AlUla's 'Valley of the Arts' (*wadi al-fann*), is overseeing the installation of site-specific works in an area of more than 40 square kilometres. The Royal Commission for AlUla was established in 2017 to safeguard and celebrate the desert landscape with its impressive rock formations. The area has featured a number of large-scale installations by contemporary artists from around the world, including Desert X, a project originally held in southern California.

Its co-curator, the Brazilian Marcello Dantas, sees the show as celebrating the 'virginity of this landscape in people's minds … a new interpretation of a very ancient place with a forgotten history'. One of its most striking installations, by the Kuwaiti artist Monira al-Qadiri, is composed of large-scale bronze sculptures inspired by meteorite fragments found by Ibn Saud's friend Harry St John Philby when he crossed the Empty Quarter in 1932. There are planned installations that three international artists – James Turrell, Michael Heizer and Agnes Denes – will share with two leading Saudi artists Ahmed Mater and Manal Al Dowayan.

Although Mater and Al Dowayan are celebrated for Arab and Islamic themes (Mater's representations of the Ka'ba as a giant magnet drawing in metal filings was shown at the Hajj Exhibition in the British Museum in 2012), the engagement with Turrell, famed for his works celebrating light and space, with Heizer, a specialist in monumental structures, and with Denes, best known for her artificial 'green' mountains, conveys a much greater sense of universality than the somewhat passé modernism of The Line. Al Dowayan, who would represent her country at the 2024 Venice Biennale, curated the *Oasis of Stories*, an installation at AlUla featuring drawings made by the local population, including schoolchildren, farmers and disabled people.[55] Blazwick sums up her vision: 'Art is art. It is not instrumentalist wherever it happens, whether in America, Russia or China.'[56]

Two other Gulf monarchies, Qatar and the UAE, have spent vast sums of money in developing the 'soft power' of culture and tourism. As Proctor and al-Senussi suggest, 'the vast and expensive cultural missions of both Gulf powers … underline a quest for cultural dominance and diplomacy in a region that had hitherto never been known for its art but just for its oil and conservative brand of Islam'. By contrast, they argue:

> Saudi Arabia is mobilizing its own cultural resources and artists, of which there are a greater number due to the country's larger population ... What is taking place in Saudi Arabia at state level is new. The Kingdom wants its own artists to engage in conversations with the international art world taking place, through art exhibitions and events in the Kingdom that mix Saudi and international artists, as well as abroad.[57]

According to Chris Dercon, former director of Tate Modern in London, 'the Saudi art scene is one of the strongest emerging movements in the Middle East, with young, intelligent grassroots artists coming from very different classes of Saudi society, with training in different fields.'[58] While like Qatar and the UAE it has been importing big-name Western art brands, such as a recent deal with the Beaubourg (Centre Pompidou) in Paris to develop a new museum in AlUla, 'it is at the same time striving to enhance its already established grassroots art scene' alongside its ancient and modern heritage.[59]

The idea of using culture to wean Saudi society off oil predates the ascendancy of MBS. In 2008, on the seventy-fifth anniversary of Aramco, King Abdullah announced his intention to build a centre for arts, culture, science and technology to enable people to access the 'knowledge economy', a project completed in 2017 with the construction of the King Abdulaziz Center for World Culture or 'Ithra' (enrichment) at Dammam, around 25 km from the iconic Dhahran oil well. The centre's monumental profile, designed by the Norwegian architect firm Snøhetta, is said to have been inspired by the shapes of ocean-washed pebbles lying on nearby beaches, though its huge bulbous forms cladded in corrugated metal piping evoke the organic contours of a whale or other sea creature rather than inert pieces of stone. The interior of 100,000 square metres comprises a host of cultural facilities, including an auditorium, cinema, library, museum and an exhibition hall filled with preserved animals and sea creatures, with an animated surround decorated with rocks and scintillating shoals of fish.

Exhibitions advertised on Ithra's website include Net Zero, featuring works by Saudi and international artists which 'express the spirit of sustainable creativity and whose artistic practices maintain a professional focus on sustainability and global warming'. Visitors with children may visit the Sustainability Studio in Ithra's Lush Gardens, where they can enjoy interactive and fun activities such as scientific experiments and arts and crafts that promote the concept of preserving the environment using 'nature itself for a green and sustainable future'.

This aspect of Ithra's vision may not yet be aimed at the present. Beyond the captions of its websites there remain questions about the Saudi kingdom's actual commitment to 'sustainability'. At the Cop 28 environmental summit in Dubai in December 2023, Mary Robinson, former president of Ireland and chair of The Elders, the organization of retired global leaders founded by Nelson Mandela, berated the Saudis and other oil-producing states for undermining efforts to wean the world off fossil fuels. The Saudis, she said, along with other oil-producing countries were taking the 'climate talks hostage' by weakening demands for the tough measures needed to hold the planet within the 1.5-degrees-Celsius warming threshold.[60] After the conference's final text had been agreed she stated:

> At Cop 28 transparency, equity and climate justice have been undermined by misleading language, false solutions and game-playing. Furthermore, the final agreement lacks the critical financial keys to

unlock the trillions of dollars needed for any just transition. Without providing the necessary means for implementation we doom those countries on the frontiers of the climate emergency to failure.[61]

The Saudi energy minister Prince Abdulaziz bin Salman (MBS's elder half-brother) demonstrated the accuracy of Robinson's comments when he told a Riyadh forum that the global efforts demanded of nations in the final text, including 'transitioning away from fossil fuels in energy systems', were options rather than requirements. Stressing the differences in wording between 'transitioning away from' fossil fuels and the 'phasing out' of fossil fuels contained in earlier drafts that had been urged by a coalition of developed and vulnerable nations, he likened the final text to an 'a la carte menu'. Stressing the inclusiveness, or semantic ambiguity, of 'transition' he said: 'there are people that are transitioning because they want to change their energy mix like us and there are those who believe that they should transition away because they don't want to use fossil fuels.' One climate specialist, Tom Evans, described the prince's framing as 'incredibly misleading':

> The text is very clear that these are global efforts – that means everyone, including Saudi Arabia, signed up to transitioning away from fossil fuels, it's not a pick and mix ... The only choice a country like Saudi Arabia now has is whether to continue denying the international consensus that the fossil fuel era is coming to an end or instead step into the fold and play its part in the energy transition.[62]

Whether or not one agrees with Mary Robinson's critique of the Saudi engagement at Cop 28, 'jumpstarting' a creative economy using the country's oil revenues while they last could well make strategic sense. The funding may come from the state, but, as Proctor and al-Senussi point out, the seeds of the creative sector were sown decades ago when there was little government support, through networks of individuals and businesses that were already functioning and profitable. Saudi artists acknowledge that there are constraints. As one of them put it,

> they are used to operating with the 'censor inside'. They have learned the art of metaphor and symbolism and embrace it wholly, and in their belief, it does not detract from the message they are trying to convey. Their art cannot be labelled as 'propaganda' as its artistic creation is not propelled by the state, even if its financial production and support is.[63]

Creative arts have thrived under Chinese and Soviet communism, as in Tsarist Russia, as well as in the Islamic Republic of Iran. There is no rubric stating that human creativity can only flourish in democratic spaces. But the display of Saudi art patronage, however impressive, could have unintended political consequences. Can the project of enabling new opportunities for the creative arts be confined to the cultural sphere while insulating autocratic power from art's transgressive, questing energy? Proctor and al-Senussi cite a statement by Prince Badr bin Abdullah bin Mohammed bin Farhan (a princeling close to MBS who 'fronted' his purchase of Leonardo's *Salvator Mundi* at Christie's, New York, for $450 million in 2017). After being appointed the Saudi kingdom's first minister of culture in 2018 he stated that 'Art and culture are transformative and by that we mean they have the power to change things.' The authors underline the prince's belief that 'creative practice through art and cultural activities could diversify the economy – rescuing it from diminishing oil resources' in order to 'change society and ultimately preserve the regime'.[64]

History, however, may well reveal the opposite. Top-down enlightenment (or what Abdulnasser Gharem a leading Saudi artist calls a 'harsh enlightenment') could help sow the seeds of revolution, as happened in France under Louis XVI.[65]

An even greater challenge for the regime, and indeed the whole of Saudi society, may issue from sport. In November 2023 it became clear that Saudi Arabia would be likely to host the 2034 FIFA World Cup – a tournament of forty-eight nations and the world's most watched and talked-about football event – when Australia dropped out of the bidding. After announcing its bid, the kingdom received the immediate backing of the Asian Football Confederation, and as there were no other bidders it was more than likely that FIFA would confirm the venue officially in 2024.

The decision will come as no surprise to enthusiasts of the 'beautiful game'. From early 2023 the sports pages of newspapers were filled with stories about the astonishing sums of money being paid to lure international stars to the kingdom. Big names reported to have signed for the kingdom's leading competition, the Saudi Pro League, included Karim Benzema, winner of the 2022 Ballon d'Or award for best player in the world – lured from Real Madrid – and Chelsea star midfielder N'Golo Kanté. Both of them signed for the Saudi team al-Ittihad. Cristiano Ronaldo, five-time winner of the Ballon d'Or, moved to al-Nassr from Manchester United, along with Liverpool's Sadio Mané, while Liverpool's captain Jordan Henderson signed for al-Ettifaq.

By the middle of 2023, clubs in the Saudi Pro League, owned by the PIF and essentially controlled by the crown prince, were reported to have spent nearly $500 million on fees, 'catapulting them among the biggest spenders in global football'.[66]

Not all the superstar footballers had to move, or play in the kingdom. The Argentine superstar Lionel Messi, arguably football's greatest living exemplar, winner of eight Ballons d'Or, scorer of 100 international goals and according to *Forbes* magazine the world's highest-paid athlete with earnings of more than $150 million in 2018, only has to visit the kingdom without actually playing there.

The *New York Times* says his contract as a tourism ambassador indicates he could receive around $25 million over three years for doing 'little actual work, a few commercial appearances, a handful of social media posts, and some all-expenses paid vacations to the kingdom with his family and children'.[67] The only requirement is that he shares images of these visits with his vast social media following, estimated at 400 million people. Crucially, according to the contract, he is not permitted to say anything that might 'tarnish' the country's image.

Critics inevitably accused the kingdom of 'sportswashing', of manufacturing global support through figures such as Ronaldo and Messi that would divert attention from the litany of human rights abuses documented by organizations such as Amnesty International and Human Rights Watch. A spokesman for the Saudi embassy in Washington argued that claims of 'sportswashing' reeked of 'ethnocentricity': the kingdom's sport agenda, he insisted, had been driven 'with Saudi Arabia and its citizens – not Westerners – in mind'.[68] The crown prince himself, in a rare interview, said he 'did not care' about sportswashing accusations. His aim was to make his country a sporting superpower to boost tourism and wean it off oil in line with Vision 2030. 'If sport washing is going to increase my GDP by way of 1% then I will continue doing sport washing', he told Fox News. Asked how he felt about the term he replied: 'I don't care ... I'm aiming for another 1.5% [GDP]. Call it whatever you want. We're going to get that 1.5%.' 'When you want to diverse an economy you have to work in all sectors: mining, infrastructure, manufacturing, transportation, logistics.' Part of this, he explained, was tourism which had increased from 3 per cent of GDP to 7 per cent. Sport which used to be only 0.4 per cent was now 1.5 per cent.[69]

Achievement in sport would raise Saudi Arabia's profile in the 'international pecking order' while improving public health in a society which, though 70 per cent of the population is under thirty-five, suffers from chronically high rates of obesity and diabetes.[70]

Despite widespread comments about sportswashing, the appearance of international football stars in the kingdom was far from being a novelty initiated by MBS. In 1978, before the crown prince's birth, the Brazilian star Roberto Rivellino was accorded a hero's welcome when he arrived on the supersonic Concorde jet to play for al-Hilal. Although the pro-Western shah had yet to be overthrown by the Islamic revolution in Iran, Gulf football rivalry was already evident, with Saudi rulers unhappy about having to accept that Iran was the only Middle Eastern country to qualify for the 1978 World Cup. Football is hugely popular in the Middle East and North Africa, as in most other regions, and has deep organic roots.

As the Norwegian scholar Dag Henrik Tuastad notes, football has been 'a uniquely popular arena for social expression' in the Saudi kingdom, especially since the 'Arab Spring' upheavals of 2010–11, when football became a 'space for a form of social revolt' where young people, usually controlled by the patriarchal system, could 'bond together and get together outside of the family chains'. Al-Ittihad, based in Jeddah, is often seen as 'the people's club' whose fans hail from the Hawsawi clan with West African Hejazi roots, while the al-Wahda team has red and white colours inspired by the Indonesian flag, a nod to people from the East Asian archipelago who settled in the Mecca region.[71] In a country without national elections, football contains an exceptional democratic element. In 2012, for example, Prince Nawaf bin Faisal, grandson of King Fahd, was obliged to step down as president of the Saudi Football Association after the national team failed to qualify for the 2014 World Cup in Brazil. His successor, elected by the Saudi football federation, was Ahmed Eid al-Harbi, a former Saudi national goalkeeper. Another royal forced to step down was Faisal bin Turki in 2013 when a video circulating on YouTube showed him running off the pitch after rudely shoving aside a security official.[72]

While the lure of Saudi money may be part of the reason why international stars are drawn to the kingdom, James Dorsey, the leading authority on football politics in the region, suggests there may be deeper cultural reasons. Muslim players in Europe are often subject to racist abuse, especially in former communist countries, where players with African roots may be subject to banana gestures or monkey chants. He suggests that high-profile transfers of Muslim players such as Real Madrid's Benzema, Chelsea's N'Golo Kanté and Kalidou Koulibaly, Lens's Seko Fofana, Lyon's Moussa Dembélé and Manchester City's Riyad Mahrez may be explained in part by European culture wars that fuel anti-Muslim and anti-black sentiment, with observant Muslims such as Benzema feeling more comfortable in the Land of the Two Shrines (Mecca and Medina) where fasting is observed during Ramadan and daily prayer times accommodated. In Europe and other Western countries, they may not only face racist taunts but may feel pressured to accommodate homosexual or transgender values they regard as contrary to their faith.

A broader question that arises in the context of Saudi Arabia is the relation between football and Islam. Some Arab commentators, not necessarily Islamist ones, see Western sports as a legacy of colonialism: 'The Middle East may be free of its colonial overlords', said Ali al-Salim, an Emirati investor and commentator, in reference to the Saudi acquisition of Newcastle United and the UAE's purchase of Manchester City, 'but its populations remain captives of European materialism, including English football clubs.'[73] The grand mufti of Saudi Arabia Muhammad ibn Ibrahim al-Sheikh, in office till his death in 1969, forbade the institutionalization of soccer on the grounds that organizations such as leagues, associations and governing bodies conflicted with Islamic values of equity and justice. 'The nature of the game' he warned 'sparks fanatical partisanship, troubles and the association of hate and malice' that contravene Islamic notions of 'tolerance, brotherhood, rectification and purification of hearts and sews resentment, grudges, and discord' among winners and losers.[74] A treatise on football by a Salafist writer Sheikh Mashhoor bin Hasan al-Salman cites numerous arguments against soccer by authorities including Abd al-Aziz ibn Baz before concluding, on balance, that 'football training is in the realm of the permissible, as we do not know of any proof that prohibits it.' The Prophet is cited as stating that 'the strong believer is better and more beloved by Allah than a weak believer'.[75]

Militant clerics, however, were much less nuanced. After the Anglo-American attack on Iraq in 2003 a prominent Kuwaiti Salafist, Hamid bin Abdullah al-Ali, issued an online fatwa widely circulated on jihadist forums regretting that the Umma was watching the 2006 World Cup matches while forgetting 'massacres, killing and violation of honour. Ask yourselves what goal you want to shoot? I ask God to honour Islam and Muslims, that he humiliates polytheism and the polytheists and destroys the enemies of religion.'[76]

A British Islamist website, banned in 2006, stated that soccer promotes nationalism as part of a 'colonial crusader scheme' aimed at dividing the Umma and causing Muslims to stray from a

> unified Islamic identity. The sad fact of the matter is that many Muslims have fallen for this new religion, and they too carry the national flag. Football has become one of the destructive hoes which our enemies are using in order to destroy the Islamic Ummah [while] encouraging other nations to do the same.[77]

The relation between sport and religion raises the question as to whether sport itself is a form of religion, or substitute. The question has exercised scholars of religion, especially in the US where intensity of devotion to events such as the Major League Baseball championships is sometimes seen as transcending religious enthusiasms. Paul Tillich, the influential protestant theologian, defined religion as a 'state of being grasped by an ultimate concern, a concern which qualifies all other concerns as preliminary', concerns, he suggested, that may in themselves contain answers to the meaning of life.[78] Given that notions of God, the divine or the supra-empirical may be absent from some traditions regarded as religious, such as Buddhism, Tillich's notion of 'ultimate concern' – a subjective idea predicated on a person's opinion or cultural outlook – allows that transcendence does not necessarily include an omnipotent all-important supernatural creator such as proclaimed in the Abrahamic traditions of Judaism, Christianity and Islam. Sociologists building on the work of Emile Durkheim, who saw the sacred as an expression of human collectivity, identify religious features in sport that are not just metaphorical. Harry Edwards has identified some of them:

> Sport has a body of formally stated beliefs accepted on faith by great masses of people ... Sport also has its 'saints' – those departed souls who in their lives exemplified and made manifest the prescriptions of the dogma of sport ... Sport also has its ruling patriarchs, a prestigious group of coaches, managers and sportsmen who exercise controlling influence over national sports organizations ... Sport has its 'gods' – star and superstar athletes who ... wield great influence and charisma over the masses of fans ... Sport has its shrines – the national halls of fame and thousands of trophy rooms and cases ... Sport also has its 'houses of worship' spread across the land where millions congregate to bear witness to the manifestations of their faith.[79]

Catherine Albanese, a scholar of religion, adds that sporting rituals, like religious rituals, create an alternative 'world of meaning complete with its own rules, boundaries, dangers and successes' on playing fields, as in sacred spaces, where people take on their assigned roles, 'often wearing special symbolic clothing to distinguish them from non-participants'. As with religious rituals, the goal of sporting activity is contained within the activity itself, in which people may engage because of its inherent meanings or pleasures.[80] One might add to Albanese's analysis that the drama of sport is commensurate with religious narratives – or, more precisely, with those of the Abrahamic traditions that establish a moral balance that tilts between the ultimate destinies of salvation and damnation. A winning goal or penalty takes both scorer and team to heaven, with hell – or relegation – the cost of defeat.

In recognizing the extent to which sport – especially football – can be a substitute religion, ultra-conservatives such as Aal al-Shaikh and Ibn Baz, and the jihadists who follow their reasoning, point to an important divergence between mainstream cultures and the jihadist fringe. As Dorsey demonstrated in his thesis, militant clerics who support groups such as the Taliban in Afghanistan, Boko Haram in Nigeria or the Shabbab in Somalia, while often recruiting followers from soccer clubs, denounced the 2006 World Cup as a plot aimed at corrupting Muslim youth from jihad, making it a 'cultural invasion worse than military war because it seizes the heart and soul of the Muslim'.[81]

The same rationale makes it attractive to rulers wishing to wean their youth off jihadist ideas by encouraging loyalty to national teams. In this respect, the jihadists who condemn sporting enthusiasm for fostering feelings of national identity at the expense of the universal Islamic Umma may not be misguided. It is precisely for this reason that Gulf autocrats such as the Qatari rulers and MBS are embracing sport – and especially soccer – as an alternative quasi-religion.

Football, as evidenced by the Saudi bid to host the 2034 World Cup, is an obvious substitute for Wahhabi Islam, as both a source of international legitimacy and an outlook commanding national allegiance. But there are several other sports in the frame. The most controversial has been golf, where the Saudi-owned LIV Golf – an upstart fifty-four-hole tournament signified by its Roman numerals – merged with America's main professional golfing body, the PGA Tour, after offering leading players hundreds of millions of dollars to switch their allegiance. While most professional golfers capitulated to a deal that former US president Donald Trump, whose golf courses host LIV events, regards as 'beautiful and glamorous' by bringing extra prize money into the sport, critics see the move as a blatant example of sportswashing.

Two US senators, Elizabeth Warren and Ron Wyden, both of them liberal-minded Democrats, condemned the proposed merger as the 'Saudi regime's latest attempt to sanitise its abuses' in a public letter to the US Justice Department. Honourable resisters to the financial inducements offered to professional golfers included the Irish master Rory McIlroy and the American Tiger Woods who is reported to have turned down a mind-boggling $800 million to join the Saudi scheme prior to the merger. After the merger, McIlroy said he felt betrayed and let down by the PGA, while Woods felt 'frustrated' by the agreement.[82]

Sarah Leah Whitson, executive director of DAWN (Democracy for the Arab World Now), told the *Guardian*, 'This is a merger in name only. This is really about the Saudi government throwing a premium at PGA Tour that they obviously found too overwhelmingly tempting to resist.' She saw it as a form of insurance, a way of preventing 'what happened in the wake of Khashoggi's murder in 2018 when US investors pulled more than a billion dollars from the Saudi stock market and cut their business deals' with the kingdom.[83]

The Saudi government now has stakes in American businesses and sporting institutions, British clubs such as Newcastle United as well as a plan to host a Formula One Grand Prix each season at a new racetrack under construction near Jeddah, which will replace the current Jeddah Corniche Circuit where the Saudi Arabian Grand Prix has been held since 2021. Observers view these sporting developments as making it much more difficult and costly for businesses to repeat the withdrawal of investments from the kingdom that happened in 2018.

Will 'sportswashing' be a strategy for overcoming commercial Western concerns about working conditions and human rights abuses? The example of Qatar, the only Wahhabi-majority state other than Saudi Arabia, is instructive. Widespread exposés in the Western media about conditions faced by immigrant workers may have annoyed the Qataris, but they did not stop the 2022 World Cup. It was widely seen as a global success, being the first occasion when an Arab Muslim country hosted the world's greatest sporting occasion.

A report in the *Guardian* that 6,500 immigrant workers had died in work-related accidents between 2011 and 2020 was strongly disputed by the Qatari government, which eventually admitted to a much smaller figure of between 400 and 500 deaths in the building of the competition's eight new stadiums. Qatari spokespeople, however, pointed out that in the construction boom that followed the award to the Gulf state only 2 per cent of workers were employed on the stadiums, with the majority working on other projects such as the Doha subway system. In 2013 the International Trade Union Confederation estimated that 4,000 workers would have died by the time that the tournament would begin in November 2022. According to data released by the Qatari government, some 12,400 immigrant men had died between 2011 and 2020, a figure the Indian authorities regarded as consistent with the size of Qatar's immigrant population, estimated at 2.5 million in 2020.

Le Monde, however, pointed out that men aged between twenty and fifty made up almost half this figure despite that before arriving in Qatar they had been required to undergo health checks to detect any existing medical conditions. A detailed analysis based on official figures of deaths in 2020 found that 25 per cent of the immigrants who died in Qatar were aged between twenty and forty, compared with 10 per cent of Qatari nationals. Most immigrant deaths (60 per cent) were of men under fifty-five, with 20 per cent aged between thirty-five and forty-four. With temperatures exceeding 40 degrees Celsius in summer and up to 30 degrees during the winter months, working conditions were dangerous, to put it mildly.

A 2019 study in the medical journal *Cardiology* noted a strong correlation between high temperatures and 'cardiovascular events' recorded among Nepalese workers in Qatar. 'The pronounced mortality from cardiovascular events during hot season is most likely due to intense heat stress' said the researchers, who estimated that around 35 per cent of fatal cardiac arrests could have been prevented by better protecting workers from heat. Dr Dan Atar, a professor of cardiology at Oslo University Hospital and co-author of the study, stated: 'these workers are recruited in their countries partly for their good health, yet hundreds of them die every year in Qatar.'[84]

The response of Qataris to these exposés ranged between nuanced acceptance and outright rejection. A study by the Carnegie Endowment for International Peace acknowledged that the huge influx in foreign workers consequent on the award had 'placed a heavy burden on the government, which introduced a series of reforms aimed at improving working conditions'. These included regulating the entry, exit and residence of expatriates, establishing a Workers Support and Insurance Fund, and adopting a minimum wage and mandatory health insurance for all residents and visitors. But beyond bureaucratic tinkering in the face of working in intense heat without adequate safety measures, the government's response seemed trifling.

More significant was the response of the Qatari public. While Qatar, like its Arab Gulf neighbours, is a tribal autocracy, it has the unique distinction of enjoying a relatively free press, with Qataris less constrained in voicing criticism of official policies than the subjects of other rulers in the region. According to the Carnegie researchers, 'in Qatar, as in many Arab countries, the Western human rights discourse' advocating for more 'just, humane and pluralistic' social policies is regarded as 'purely ideological' and lacking balance.

Many Qataris, especially the young and well educated, see the human rights concerns as stemming from a 'traditional orientalist mentality which views Eastern peoples as inferior' to occidentals. Although some countries previously hosting the World Cup had been criticized for human rights violations, Qataris felt that the criticism of their country levelled by organizations such as Human Rights Watch and Amnesty International was unduly harsh. According to this perspective, Western human rights discourse over 'discriminatory issues affecting women's independence in marriage, study, work and travel' or LGBTQ+ rights was duplicitous and self-serving.

Qatar had prided itself on its diplomatic approach even before the October 2023 Gaza crisis when the emirate was the primary actor in negotiating a pause in Israeli hostilities in exchange for the release of Israeli hostages captured by Hamas and Palestinian prisoners held by Israel in December 2023. In the build-up to the 2022 World Cup, it had taken an emollient line on LGBTQ+ issues. Before the tournament began, the emir, Sheikh Tamim bin Hamad al-Thani, announced that fans from the LGBTQ+ community would not face discrimination and would be welcome so long as they respected the country's culture, principles and values.

This 'don't ask don't tell' position recalled the similar position adopted in the US armed forces under President Bill Clinton. It proved insufficient, however, to satisfy the human rights advocates, including some football enthusiasts for whom LGBTQ+ rights had become totemic. For example, though the French team were the defending champions, most of the major cities such as Paris, Lille and Marseille declined to broadcast matches on giant public screens, while sixteen Australian players went so far as to broadcast a video publicly attacking Qatar's human rights record, from the abuse of migrant workers to the plight of LGBTQ+ people in a state where homosexuality is punishable by up to seven years in prison. When FIFA banned players from wearing rainbow-coloured 'OneLove' armbands on the pitch, a major row erupted with German players covering their mouths in the team photo of their first match with Japan. Qatar's foreign minister, Mohammed bin Abdul Rahman al-Thani, expressed a view widely held in his country when telling readers of the *Frankfurter Allgemeine Zeitung* that they had been misinformed about human rights issues while their 'government has no problem with us when it comes to forging energy partnerships or making investments'. To underline his point, within a month of his interview in November 2022 the Qatar public investment fund announced an investment of €2.43 billion in the German energy company RWE, becoming its largest shareholder.[85]

In the case of Qatar, 'sportswashing' seems to have worked. In the moral calculus of East–West relations, demand for energy by consumers in the industrialized Global North will surely continue to trump concerns over working conditions and human rights in the Global South. In Gulf countries, including Saudi Arabia, both the rulers and their subjects who have benefited immeasurably from the sale of hydrocarbons can agree that accusations about human rights violations and the conditions facing immigrant workers involve hypocrisy and double standards on the part of gas-guzzling Western consumers, especially when issues such as LGBTQ+ rights are given prominence. In the past, the Quranic ban on homosexuality (*liwat*) tended to be honoured in the breach.

To guarantee the chastity of women as honour-bearers of the patriarchal family, pederasty, though not discussed, was tolerated. As the Iranian-born sociologist Janet Afary has written 'beardless boys, not yet being men, could be penetrated without losing their essential manliness'.[86] But in an era when Enlightenment values and cardinal cultural differences between tradition and modernity have become critical fault-lines, the issue of gay rights raises highly contentious feelings. All the Abrahamic traditions, not just Islam, are affected, with polarizing debates among priests, rabbis and imams over questions such as the rights of gay people and homosexual unions. Demands by activists that sexual behaviours deemed to contradict religious teachings be recognized and celebrated rather than 'swept under the carpet', as in the past, pose a cultural challenge to all religious orthodoxies, including those endorsed by the Russian Federation, where LGBT advocacy groups face being banned as 'extremist organisations'.[87]

On a second issue relating to the 2022 World Cup in Qatar uncovered by the Carnegie researchers, the picture was significantly different, with a clear lack of consensus between the ruling elites and their subjects. The Carnegie Endowment research into the 2022 World Cup suggests that 'normalization' with the Jewish state would be less than universally popular. When the Qatari government authorized direct flights between Tel Aviv and Doha for the tournament, the news was greeted with 'widespread opposition among nationals and residents' with a rare protest movement, Qatari Youth Opposed to Normalization, issuing public statements condemning the move. At the start of the tournament crowds waved pro-Palestinian banners, with Moroccan fans waving Palestinian flags in a show of solidarity as they celebrated their country's victory over Spain.

As Hind al-Ansari wrote in her report for the Carnegie Endowment, 'The overwhelming support for Palestine displayed by Arab crowds in Doha presents both a set-back and reality check for the US Department of State, which hoped that direct flights between Qatar and Israel would "bolster people-to-people ties and economic relations."'[88]

The Abraham Accords fostered by the United States offered the prospect of normalization between the Gulf states, including – it was hoped – Saudi Arabia and Israel. By the time of the 2022 World Cup, two Gulf states – the UAE and Bahrain – had signed the accords recognizing Israeli sovereignty and entailing full diplomatic relations, followed by Morocco and Sudan. As well as promising Israel commercial opportunities in the oil-rich states, supporters had hoped that popular perceptions about Israel would improve not just in signatory states but throughout the Arab world. Qatar did not sign the accords, despite trading with the Jewish state since 1996. But it enjoyed unusual de facto diplomatic relations with Israel as the Arab state that hosted the leadership-in-exile of Hamas, the faction that had ruled the Gaza Strip, the sliver of Palestinian land adjoining Egypt that Israel evacuated in 2005, when some of the settlers who had been there since 1967 were forcefully evicted by the Israel Defense Forces (IDF).

After Hamas took control of Gaza in 2007 it became engaged in a complicated *pas de deux* with Israel, whereby successive governments, mostly led by Benjamin Netanyahu, exploited Hamas militancy to undermine the authority of the Palestinian Authority (PA), officially controlled by the nationalist Fatah organization under its ageing president Mahmoud Abbas. Under the 1993 Oslo accords, the PA was supposed to govern the occupied West Bank and contribute to Israeli security by restraining armed resistance.

Despite military operations against Hamas following rocket attacks from Gaza in 2012, 2014 and 2021, critics pointed out that successive Israeli governments approved moves to ease pressure on Hamas with periodic prisoner releases, the transfer of funds from Qatar and increasing numbers of permits allowing Gazans to work in Israel. Mediation by senior Qatari figures with Hamas played a vital role in these displays of strategic theatre whose effect was to divide Palestinian public opinion, allowing Netanyahu to claim he had 'no one to talk to', while focusing on threats from Iran and its Lebanese ally Hezbollah.[89] As the Israeli commentator Zvi Bar'el explained in *Haaretz*:

> The rift between Fatah and Hamas was the pillar on which Netanyahu built his policy, [as] he explained to every mediator who sought to advance the peace process. The key questions were 'Can Abbas control Hamas?' and 'Can he fight Hamas terror?' As long as there was no affirmative answer to those questions, he argued, there is no reason to hold negotiations with the Palestinian Authority because it doesn't represent the entire Palestinian public.[90]

A broader part of the Israeli strategy was the 'normalization' of the Abraham Accords, building on earlier peace treaties with Egypt and Jordan, with the biggest prize of all, normalization with Saudi Arabia, a much-anticipated step.

The brutal Hamas attack that killed some 1,200 Israelis and other nationals including civilians, women and children and captured 240 hostages on 7 October 2023 was aimed, among other things, at preventing further moves towards 'normalization'. The US president Joe Biden was explicit about this, stating that 'One of the reasons Hamas moved on Israel … [was] they knew I was about to sit down with the Saudis. Guess what? The Saudis wanted to recognize Israel.' The message was repeated in more nuanced language by Secretary of State Antony Blinken who told CNN that he wouldn't be surprised if part of the motivation for the attack 'may have been to disrupt efforts to bring Saudi Arabia and Israel together'.[91]

The Saudis had always insisted that normalization with Israel wouldn't take place until tangible steps had been taken to resolve the Palestine issue leading towards a resumption of the neglected peace process and a two-state solution based on Israel's 1967 borders. Given the current composition of the Israeli government, including ministers of the ultra-right Kahanist movement, who can reasonably be described as 'Judaeo-fascists', a deal between Saudi Arabia and the current Israeli government brokered by the US has always seemed problematic. But it was not impossible given the reality of US military leverage over Israel, the possibility of a change of administration in Jerusalem (publicly advocated by Senator Chuck Schumer, America's highest-ranking elected Jewish official), and the fact that as an unelected autocrat MBS can exercise foreign policy directly without having to answer to public opinion.

When the Trump administration helped orchestrate the Abraham Accords with Bahrain and the UAE, Saudi Arabia sent out unambiguous signals. As David Rundell, a former US ambassador to Riyadh, pointed out, 'Riyadh implicitly supported the deal by allowing Saudi journalists to write op-eds praising it.' It was unlikely the deal would have materialized 'had the Saudis strongly objected'.[92] Less than three weeks before Hamas's murderous attack, MBS himself was telling Fox news, 'every day we get closer' in the negotiations with Israel.

The 7 October attack put paid to any such hopes, at least for the foreseeable future. The Saudis have no feelings of solidarity with Hamas or the Muslim Brotherhood – indeed they were instrumental in helping the coup that overthrew the elected Muslim Brotherhood government of Mohamed Morsi by General Abd al-Fattah al-Sisi, a former military attaché in Riyadh, in 2013. It is not unreasonable, moreover, to suggest that MBS authorized the murder of Khashoggi *because* of his Muslim Brotherhood links.

As Koelbl points out, Khashoggi's political ideology was close to that of the Brotherhood which looked for a democratic transformation framed by Islamic law, an outlook seen as threatening by all the region's authoritarian rulers.[93] But given popular support for Palestinians, not just in the Middle East but even in the United States, where after the Israeli invasion of Gaza a growing cohort of young people showed support for them, Saudis could not be seen to be standing aside while the IDF pulverized Gaza. The humanitarian catastrophe, with more than 40,000 people killed, is seen by Israel's critics as heralding a new *nakba* (catastrophe) that could vastly exceed the original exodus of Palestinians in 1948. There were indications, at this writing, that Washington may have been preparing to use its financial leverage to oblige Egypt, Iraq, Yemen and Turkey to accept up to 2 million Palestinian refugees in exchange for the aid those countries receive from the US.[94] Any such US plan, which would be strongly resisted by Egypt, would leave Saudi Arabia on the sidelines. As Gregory Gause observed, 'Riyadh has an interest in ending the fighting and making progress towards a peaceful settlement of Israeli-Palestinian issue but has few levers that it can or will use to advance that goal right now.'[95]

Despite the crisis in Gaza where Palestinians, a third of them children, were dying in their thousands, MBS had been trying to reassure the world that in the Kingdom of Saudi Arabia business was carrying on as usual. Even in late October 2023, while images of Israeli bombing were making Gaza look like Dresden in 1945, the Saudi government proceeded with its annual Future Investment

Initiative conference known as 'Davos in the Desert' attended by leading global investors, including Jamie Dimon of JPMorgan, Jane Fraser of Citigroup and around '6,000 other business titans'.[96] The aim was clearly to show that MBS could be a 'reliable economic partner' in the current unstable conditions. He was 'not a disrupter' brandishing the oil weapon, as happened after the 1973 Yom Kippur War.[97]

It was far from clear when this book went to press if this strategy would work. While the Houthis in Yemen were threatening international shipping by launching drone attacks on cargoes destined for Israel or beyond in solidarity with Hamas, the movement's ally Hezbollah was sending rockets into the northern Israeli settlements from southern Lebanon, displacing more than 60,000 people inside Israel's border, threatening a wider regional war involving Israel and the Islamic Republic of Iran. The 'Axis of Resistance' supported by Iran was seen in Israel and by its Western allies as increasingly menacing, while in the West Bank territories Israeli settlers, unleashed by the IDF, were killing Palestinians with impunity. Israeli troops, exhibiting the same level of paranoia and the dysfunctional command shown after the initial attack of 7 October when many Israeli soldiers and civilians were killed by 'friendly fire', even managed to shoot three Israeli hostages who had escaped from Hamas waving a highly visible makeshift white flag, as well as an off-duty soldier who had shot two Arab assassins at a Jerusalem bus stop.

The presence of US aircraft carriers in the eastern Mediterranean was intended to deter any move by Hezbollah's ally Iran in the event of further escalation. Yet while the Iranian leadership made it clear that they had not been party to the Hamas attacks, there was no certainty that the crisis in Gaza, with its mounting toll of deaths, could be prevented from spiralling beyond the Israel–Palestine theatre. Egypt, Israel's closest regional ally after the suppression of the Morsi government in 2013, feared being destabilized socially and politically in the event of an exodus of more than a million Palestinians into the Sinai Peninsula, where the Sisi regime had been working with Israel to suppress Hamas and its jihadist allies, allowing the Netanyahu government to continue avoiding peace talks with the Palestinians and to maintain the Israeli policy of settlement expansion in the West Bank.[98]

A further danger of escalation was emerging in the Red Sea where the US and its British ally responded to attacks on international shipping by the Houthis by mounting air strikes on sites in Sanaa, Taiz, the port of Hodeidah and other military targets. While US and British spokesmen, including President Biden, claimed the action was essential to secure free passage for international shipping following a UN Security Council resolution condemning the Houthi attacks and that it was unconnected to the war in Gaza, most European governments dissociated themselves from the US–British counter-strikes on the grounds that they undermined diplomatic efforts to resolve conflicts in both Yemen and Gaza. At the United Nations, the Chinese delegate said, 'The last thing we need at this stage is reckless military adventurism' while the Saudi foreign ministry expressed 'great concern', calling for 'self-restraint and avoiding escalation'.[99] As the Qatari prime minister Sheikh Mohammed bin Abdul Rahman al-Thani told the BBC, 'the strikes will inflame the conflict ... creating a high risk of further escalation and expansion. We prefer diplomacy over a military resolution, and we believe we shouldn't just focus on those small conflicts [such as the Red Sea crisis] but we should focus on the main conflict in Gaza, for as soon as that is de-fused, I believe everything else will be de-fused.'[100]

The strikes against the Houthis, launched by Britain and the US, raised concerns among Gulf rulers who, however authoritarian, felt the need to respond to both domestic and global outrage generated by the Dresden-like images of Gaza and the suffering of Palestinians. To worldwide demonstrations calling for a ceasefire in Gaza, already planned before the military strikes, were added new calls for ending the conflict in Yemen.

The war in Gaza was releasing feelings that had long been present outside of official channels as thousands of people, many of them young, took to the streets in cities all over the globe. As Vijay Prasad commented, Israel had launched eight bombing campaigns against Gaza since 2006 along with other repressive measures including the separation barrier or 'apartheid wall' in Jerusalem and the occupied West Bank, but none of these measures had 'evoked the kind of response from around the world as this violence that began in October 2023'.[101]

The sheer scale of the military violence unleashed on Gaza, with nearly 2 per cent of the population killed and more than 95 per cent displaced, was far beyond that 'seen in any contemporary war, neither in Iraq (where the US disregarded most of the laws of war) nor in Ukraine (where the death toll of civilians is far smaller despite the war now lasting two years)'. One consequence of the mass protests has been to persuade the government of South Africa to level a charge of genocide against the government of Israel at the International Court of Justice at The Hague. In its filing, the South African government documented numerous atrocities along with statements by Israeli officials calling for a 'Second Nakba' or 'Gaza Nakba' with citations of Israeli ministers using racist language such as the statement by former defence minister Yoav Gallant that 'we are fighting human animals'.

The eighty-four-page filing by South Africa and Israel's response were widely reported in international press and media. This is not the place to analyse the legal content of the South African charges that have been dismissed as 'without merit' by the US State Department and have triggered accusations of 'blood libel' by Israeli ministers evoking antisemitic tropes from medieval Europe. The salient point raised by Prasad is how the global protests against war in Gaza, and Israel's backing (if somewhat nuanced) by its Western allies, reflect a shift in the global consciousness, marking 'a rapid decline in the legitimacy of the West' including the NATO countries in the view of the Global South, as indicated by the accusations of genocide levelled by South Africa.

The shifting dynamics of global power have not gone unnoticed in Riyadh. When President Xi Jinping of China visited the Saudi capital in December 2022 he was treated with fulsome honours (unlike Secretary Blinken) with a purple carpet after his plane had been escorted by Saudi jets streaming the green and white colours of the kingdom's national flag. In November 2023, the kingdom signed a landmark deal with China enabling it to accept the Chinese currency in payment for oil, an arrangement similar to that of China's largest oil-trading partner Russia.

Since 1974, the kingdom has traded oil exclusively in US dollars. While the initial deal is relatively small (around $7 billion), it is a harbinger of the future where global trading in the Chinese currency has been rising rapidly, tripling since 2021. Trading in the renminbi enables China and Russia to avoid any sanctions imposed by the US through its leverage of the dollar. Given the deteriorating relationship between the US and China, the primary destination for Saudi exports by value and with Saudi Arabia being China's second-largest oil supplier after Russia, the kingdom has clearly been insuring itself against possible dollar sanctions.

On the political front, the kingdom's pivot away from its Western allies was evident in the apparent reconciliation between Saudi Arabia and Iran brokered by China, leaving the US on the sidelines. Saudi Arabia's re-orientation, seen by some as a 'paradigm shift', may be firmed up geopolitically when it becomes a member of the so-called BRICS group of emerging markets led by China with the aim of shaking up the Western-dominated global order. The kingdom will join the existing acronymic members (Brazil, Russia, India, China, South Africa) along with Iran, the UAE, Argentina, Egypt and Ethiopia. According to the Chinese leader, the doubling of the group marks a historic expansion, a new starting point that 'will bring vigour to the BRICS cooperation mechanism and further strengthen the force for world peace and development'. Lula da Silva, Brazil's president, said the expansion meant the group would now represent 46 per cent of the world's population and an even greater share of its economic output. Its first enlargement for more than a decade was seen as a boost for Beijing that could 'counter Western dominance over international institutions and affairs'.[102]

The prospects for a reorganized and hopefully more equitable global order in a world dominated by China and BRICS may lie some way in the future. Additional to the uncertainty of escalation in the region following the Gaza war, Saudi Arabia currently faces a reduction in oil prices due to recession in China, the lowering of demand through the increasing electrification of terrestrial transport in the industrialized world and increasing hydrocarbon production in the US. Although MBS's half-brother, the oil minister Prince Abdulaziz bin Salman, has cut Saudi output by a million barrels per day (bpd) since 2022, these measures failed to raise the price per barrel above $77, way below the level needed for MBS's ambitious plans for Vision 2030. With the US currently producing 13 million bpd compared with Saudi's 9 million bpd, analysts suggest the Saudis would need to make further cuts in output to compete with higher levels of US production. This could still push the cost of Saudi crude down to less than $60 per barrel, the price on which US producers were planning to sell their oil.

Given MBS's ambitious plans for Saudi Arabia, a widening of the Israel–Gaza war into a broader regional conflict involving Iran would be disastrous. An 'Abrahamic peace' with the Jewish state as hoped for by the United States would provide him with a much-needed bonus. As Rundell states:

> It would improve Saudi Arabia's relations with its most important security partner, the United States – and reduce opposition [to relations with Israel] among the Saudi public. What's more peace would strengthen Saudi Arabia's hand against Iran which since the 1979 Iranian revolution has challenged Saudi leadership in the Muslim world and sought to extend its influence in Lebanon, Iraq, Syria, and Yemen. Despite the recent Saudi Iranian rapprochement, Saudi and Israeli leaders still share many reasons to resist Iran's pursuit of regional hegemony and nuclear weapons.[103]

A problem facing MBS, however, is the level of pro-Palestinian sentiment in his country, despite the wish he shares with other Gulf rulers and Israel to see the end of Hamas. As Dennis Ross, the veteran US official engaged in decades of tortuous Arab–Israel peace negotiations, wrote in the *New York Times* just after the Hamas attack:

> over the past two weeks when I talked to Arab officials throughout the region whom I have long known, every single one told me that Hamas must be destroyed in Gaza. They made it clear that if Hamas is perceived as winning it will validate the group's ideology of rejection, give leverage and momentum to Iran and its collaborators and put their own governments on the defensive.[104]

Ross's statement makes it clear that for the United States and its allies in the Gulf, including Saudi Arabia, the geopolitical stakes are high, a factor that explains the Biden administration's endorsement of Israel's devastating attack on Gaza, despite strong and increasingly critical reservations about civilian casualties. Given that Saudi Arabia, unlike Qatar, lacks a relatively free press and that virtually all vehicles of opinion including social media are subject to government control or manipulation, it may be more plausible to infer the existence of support for Palestinians from the degree of official repression, rather than attempting an independent assessment of public views.

According to the London-based Arab Digest, an independent news site, 'Any kind of public expression of pro-Palestinian sentiment in the kingdom, whether a tweet, post or video, is liable to lead to immediate arrest' with religious scholars telling people they should stop discussing Gaza. 'Leaders', they say, 'know the issue better than you', a clear reference to MBS though he is not mentioned by name. 'Electronic flies' controlled by Saud al-Qahtani, puppet master of the Khashoggi butchery, energetically promote pro-Israeli accounts of the war, with media figures known to support MBS appearing on Israeli television. Yet a rare poll published by the Washington Institute for Near East Policy in December 2023 found that 90 per cent of Saudis think that Arab countries should sever all ties with Israel 'in protest against its military action in Gaza'.[105] At this writing, the prospects for MBS's plans for normalization with Israel do not seem hopeful. However, Israel's destruction of the Hezbollah command structure by means of booby-trapped devices in September 2024, the assassination of its leader Hasan Nasrallah, the bombing of Beirut and invasion of southern Lebanon could reopen the prospect of Saudi–Israeli normalization by weakening Iran and its Shiite allies in Yemen and Lebanon. Shortly after the IDF launched their offensive in the southern city of Rafah, despite the US administration's warnings about civilian casualties, a 'precision bomb' aimed at two Hamas commanders set fire to a crowded camp of displaced Palestinians, killing dozens of people, including children. International outrage was barely mitigated by the government's claim that this was a 'tragic accident', by the US government's claim that Israel had not in this instance crossed a White House 'red line' in its infliction of casualties, or by the displays on Israeli television and social media of right-wing Israelis happily comparing the Gaza conflagration to the Lag Ba'Omer bonfire night taking place at that time, when Jews remember the Bar Kochba rebellion against the Romans.[106]

The crown prince's worst fear, according to the Arab Digest, is that having put all his eggs in one basket, 'he could see the Israelis somehow manage to lose the war'.[107] Despite America's support for Israel, this seems more than probable if by 'winning' the Israelis expect to achieve the elimination of Hamas militarily, politically and ideologically. At the start of the war the US defence secretary Lloyd Austin publicly warned Israel that it risked 'strategic defeat' in Gaza if it failed to protect the civilian population. At this writing, Israel's action, conducted in anger and without a clear 'political horizon', had fully realized Austin's warning. There was every probability that following the ever-rising toll of Palestinian deaths resulting from starvation and bombing in Gaza and attacks by Israeli settlers in the West Bank, and an Israeli incursion into Lebanon, the rejectionist ideology espoused by Hamas would not only persist but eventually re-emerge even stronger after its military capacity had been depleted or even destroyed.

The Israeli government's folly in pursuing an unattainable total victory rather than settling for a 'deal', as urged by most international actors other than the US and its British acolyte, whereby remaining hostages would be released in exchange for Israeli-held Palestinian prisoners and a permanent ceasefire, threatened a strategic defeat not only for Israel but for MBS, who had invested so much political capital in the prospect of 'normalization'.

In May 2024, the US announced it had reached a 'near final' set of arrangements for a bilateral deal with the kingdom that would serve to boost its defences against Iran while providing American help for Saudi Arabia's civilian nuclear infrastructure and increasing ties with its tech industries. The crown prince confirmed the arrangements stating on X (formerly Twitter) that 'the semi-final version of the draft strategic agreements' between the two countries was 'almost being finalized'. Both the Saudis, and Democrats in the US Congress had made it clear, however, that the landmark trade and defence agreement should be predicated on US acceptance of a two-state solution, long sought by the Saudis, to the conflict in Palestine.[108]

Despite the much talked about revival of the two-state solution in Israel–Palestine, the obstacles remained formidable, though not insuperable. Some critical voices, not just Palestinian supporters, challenged the demonization of Hamas in the Israeli and Western media when the terrorists who broke out of Gaza were reported to have decapitated babies and raped Israeli women in an orgy of violence. Early reports indicated that Hamas operatives themselves, along with the Israelis, were taken by surprise by the ease with which they breached the Gaza security fence, allowing not just the more extreme faction of Islamic Jihad to join the attack on Israelis, but an undisciplined rabble of chancers. Chaos was rampant on both sides on the night of 7 October 2023.

The American investigative reporter Max Blumenthal, son of Sidney Blumenthal, a former aide to President Bill Clinton, produced a detailed account, citing Israeli sources, indicating that many of the casualties at Kibbutz Be'eri attacked by Hamas on the morning of 7 October were actually victims of 'friendly fire' by the IDF. His report cites an Israeli woman Yasmin Porat who told Israeli radio that the IDF 'undoubtedly killed' numerous Israeli non-combatants during gun battles with the Hamas terrorists on 7 October.

While *Haaretz* initially dismissed Blumenthal as a 'conspiracy theorist', the Israeli daily later quoted an Israeli police report revealing that an IDF helicopter, arriving at the scene of the massacre following a 'rave', fired at the terrorists and apparently also hit some of the revellers at the Nova festival near Kibbutz Ra'im, 364 of whom were killed. Ms Porat, the Israeli woman who survived the massacre and escaped after being held by Hamas gunmen, told Israeli radio that the IDF had 'undoubtedly' killed numerous Israeli non-combatants during gun battles with the Hamas terrorists. 'They eliminated everyone including the hostages', she stated referring to Israeli special forces. The Hamas gunmen, she said, had treated them humanely. 'Their objective was to kidnap us to Gaza, not to murder us.'[109] Reports of 'friendly fire' casualties suffered by Israelis gained recognition in February 2024 when the army announced an investigation into the killing of a dozen Israeli hostages – including a pair of twelve-year-old twins – at a house in Kibbutz Be'eri where they had been taken captive by Hamas terrorists. Rather than negotiate with the terrorists, who demanded safe passage back to Gaza in exchange for releasing the hostages, the commander in charge of the operation, Brigadier General Barak Hiram – who regularly toughened his troops by making them watch animal killings in slaughterhouses – ordered a tank to fire at the house, killing the hostages along with their captors.[110]

It will doubtless take years before a full account of the 7 October atrocity will be publicly available. However, any verdict showing that the Israeli response was not only disproportionate – with the Palestinians, mostly non-combatants and children, outnumbering the 1,200 Israelis killed on 7 October at a ratio of more than thirty Palestinians for one Israeli killed – but motivated by extremist elements in the Israeli government seeking the 'ethnic cleansing' of the Gaza strip would be embarrassing, not to say highly damaging, for MBS's normalizing agenda.

The more nuanced approach of the Qataris, who had avoided joining the Abraham Accords while keeping their channels with Israel open, offered a better prospect for Arab–Israeli engagement than MBS's quest for full 'normalization'. With Qatar acting as the leading broker behind the release of hostages in November 2023 in exchange for a one-week cessation of hostilities, humanitarian relief in Gaza and the release of 130 Palestinians held by Israelis, the Qatari emir Tamim bin Hamad al-Thani emerged as a more significant player on the international stage than MBS, despite the miniscule size of his territory compared with that of Saudi Arabia. As Tzachi Hanegbi, Israel's national security advisor, tweeted (in English): 'I'm pleased to say that Qatar is becoming an essential party and stakeholder in the facilitation of humanitarian solutions. Qatar's diplomatic efforts are crucial at this time.'[111]

The *Times of Israel* explained that unlike his Gulf neighbours the Emir Tamim isn't worried about an uprising or challenge to his rule from political Islamists. 'Instead, he hosts Islamist terror groups including Hamas alongside a trade office for Israel and thousands of American troops at the al-Udeid base, from which the United States routinely carries out operations in the region.' Yet, as the paper pointed out, there can be no doubt that the emir's sympathies lie with the Palestinians. His foreign ministry 'solely' blamed Israel for the slaughter on 7 October and has never condemned the Hamas atrocities. Yet, paradoxically, 'his sway over Hamas' might be the only hope for Israeli families desperate 'for a reunion with their abducted sons, daughters, grandparents and other loved ones'.[112]

As a diplomatic player, Qatar punches far above its weight and, unlike Israel, Saudi Arabia and the UAE, prefers not to use military force to resolve disputes. In contrast to MBS and his mentor MBZ, who also feels threatened by the Muslim Brotherhood (despite the patronage it received from Crown Prince and later King Faisal during the Nasser era), the Thanis have continued to tolerate, even patronize, the Brotherhood which Riyadh classified as a terrorist organization in 2014 after the Saudi-sponsored overthrow of Morsi the previous year. The Qataris had been propping up Morsi's government with loans of $5 billion in 2012–13 plus a grant of $500 million. Though not constitutionally answerable to an electorate, they see themselves as friends of democracy and are powerful advocates for universal education, with Education City in the capital Doha holding branch campuses of six US universities. The emir's mother, the formidable Sheikha Moza bint Nasser, regarded as 'one of the world's most glamorous women', chairs the Arab Democracy Foundation and has served as a UNESCO special envoy for basic and higher education as well as being a UN advocate for sustainable development goals.[113] It hardly needs adding that misogynistic accounts in the Saudi, Emirati and Egyptian media portray her as a 'power-hungry manipulator of weak men'.[114]

In contrast to the Saudis, the Qataris can be seen as benign dictators with strong Enlightenment views. Far from persecuting the Muslim Brotherhood, the Thanis have employed them in senior positions without appearing bothered that they would subvert their rule. As David Roberts writes, Qatar's support for the Brotherhood is 'unencumbered by any notion that it would be stoking a revolutionary problem for itself', allowing a level of freedom that is unusual – if not entirely unique – in the Middle East.[115] The TV show on Al Jazeera hosted by the Brotherhood's leading scholar the late Sheikh Yousuf al-Qaradawi reached some 60 million viewers across the Arab world, while its various broadcasts featuring Saudi dissidents or disputes within the ruling family have constantly irritated Riyadh.[116]

As a state with a relatively small territory and tiny population (around 300,000 indigenous nationals) enjoying levels of per capita income comparable to Monaco and Liechtenstein, the Qataris do not fear a popular uprising. Any threats to their wealth, as one of the world's largest producers of natural gas with 30 per cent of the global market, are more likely to issue from a regional conflict involving Iran and Saudi Arabia. Their relations with the Islamic Republic of Iran, a state detested and feared by other Gulf states, has a material interest in the undersea North Field petroleum deposits shared by both countries.

There is no love lost between Saudi and Qatari dynasties. The emir's father Sheikh Hamad bin Khalifa, who abdicated in favour of his son in 2013, accused the Saudis of plotting against him in 1995 in a failed attempt to prevent him replacing his own father. Sheikh Hamad's disdain for the Al Saud dynasty became public after a leaked phone call with the Libyan ruler Muammar Gaddafi around 2002, when he 'trash-talked' the monarchy in Riyadh, predicting its imminent collapse and acknowledging that 'he was actively promoting' its destabilization through various channels.[117]

Ideological sympathies as well as dynastic rivalries are engaged in this rivalry. Although the Muslim Brotherhood founded in Egypt in 1928 draws its support from mainly Sunni countries, the inspiration for the Shia-based Iranian revolution that overthrew the pro-Western shah in 1979 was partly inspired by the Brotherhood's leading intellectual Sayyid Qutb (1906–66). Qatar enjoyed excellent relations with Tunisia during the brief tenure of the Brotherhood-linked Ennahda party led by Rachid al-Ghannouchi. The latter's son-in-law Rafik Abdessalem, former head of research at the Al Jazeera centre in Doha, served as Tunisia's foreign minister from 2013–15. At a time when many Western governments view the Muslim Brotherhood as a terrorist organization, Qatar can be seen as bearers of what might be styled a modern Islamic enlightenment, where changes in discourses internal to Islam are enabled and given traction.

Qatari support for the Brotherhood and its activist Hamas offshoot is in marked contrast to the Saudi scenario sponsored by MBS. Andrew Hammond, one of the most perceptive observers of the country, describes his approach as 'defanging' not 'dethroning' Wahhabism. He points out that MBS's aim has been levelled primarily at the Sahwa or 'left-oriented' group represented by prestigious scholars such as Safar al-Hawali and Salman al-Awdah, preachers inspired by the Muslim Brotherhood, who began 'advocating for a more equitable relationship between ruler and ruled in the 1990s, aimed at making society more, not less Islamic, according to their utopian vision'. As Hammond explains, the movement's discourse evolved in critical ways during the early 2000s, 'producing the political reformism of al-Awda that moved beyond the traditional pietistic concerns of Wahhabism to endorse the popular movements' known as the Arab Spring from 2011.

This is clearly the trend that Riyadh dreads utterly, which explains why al-Awdah and other leading preachers of this persuasion are either in exile or on death row. But it does not mean that Wahhabism is dead. Far from it: although MBS, as Hammond explains, has been praised by state ulama as a modernizer (*muhaddith*) and renewer (*mujaddid*) the key underpinnings of the Saudi state endorsed by the religious establishment 'have not changed one iota: protests are banned, political parties are banned, and public petitions regarding government policy are banned'.[118]

Through their media and preaching activities, the clerics are still dominated by Nejdi Hanbalis who are either from or close to the family of Ibn Abd al-Wahhab. Although the religious police have been abolished, the Wahhabi scholars are still tasked with policing what the government calls 'ideological security' (*al-amn al-fikri*) with the ruler 'still framed ideologically as *wali al-amr* – the Islamic guardian of the state whose responsibility for its affairs is a trust from

God that entails creating the protective conditions for securing the Muslim's faith and salvation'.[119]

A reformist Islam that is democratically friendly is clearly the biggest dread of the current Saudi regime, an outlook exacerbated by dynastic disdain for the Qataris. They regarded Jamal Khashoggi as a threat because he was a Brotherhood fellow traveller with a high public profile. As Koelbl suggests, following David Ignatius, he was murdered because, as a prominent journalist, 'he may have had enough influence to trigger a hashtag protest in Saudi Arabia' setting off an 'uprising against the monarchy over social media'. But he was also a victim of dynastic rivalry. An article in the *Washington Post* a few weeks after his murder exposed his links with the Qatar Foundation chaired by Sheikha Moza.

According to the *Post*'s own story, text messages between Khashoggi and Maggie Mitchell Salem, a one-time aide to US secretary of state Madeleine Albright, and an executive at the foundation, show that Ms Salem

> at times shaped the columns he submitted to the Washington Post, proposing topics, drafting material and prodding him to take a harder line against the Saudi government. Khashoggi also appears to have relied on a researcher and translator affiliated with the organization, which promotes Arabic-language education in the United States.[120]

Not surprisingly, the Saudi-owned *Arab News* made hay with the revelation, suggesting that Khashoggi's involvement with the foundation risked breaching the *Post*'s editorial guidelines as published on its website:

> A reporter or editor ... cannot accept payment from any person, company or organization that he or she covers. And we should avoid accepting money from individuals, companies, trade associations or

organizations that lobby government or otherwise try to influence issues the newspaper covers ... We avoid active involvement in any partisan causes – politics, community affairs, social action, demonstrations – that could compromise or see to compromise our ability to report and edit fairly.[121]

The article commented:

Although nothing in the current revelations suggests that Khashoggi accepted payment from Qatar, the mere fact that his columns and articles were suggested, researched and translated by an affiliated [sic] with the Qatari government which since the mid-nineties has been at odds with Saudi Arabia, many observers are likely to question their integrity and whether or not they reflected Jamal's views or those of the Qataris.[122]

Arab News concluded with the government's official line that Khashoggi was 'killed by a team of Saudi agents who according to the kingdom's investigations were ordered to negotiate his return but ended up killing him instead.' Since then, the Saudi government has charged a number of officials with the murder.[123] No names were given, but even if they had been the masterminds Saud al-Qahtani would not have been among them. Eventually, eleven 'suspects' were reported to have been tried for murder. All were found guilty with five of them sentenced to death. All were pardoned. Jamal Khashoggi's son Salah appears to have been satisfied with the verdict. The *Washington Post* reported that all Jamal's sons received multi-million-dollar homes and five-figure monthly payments as compensation for the killing of their father – a settlement in line with Islamic law whereby the families of victims have the choice of settling for blood money.[124]

Although he was officially suspended from the royal court, allegedly by order of the king, al-Qahtani the puppet master was never prosecuted, and rumours of his death by poisoning turned out to have been exaggerated. In 2019 a Saudi court cleared him of any charges connected with the assassination. Though barred from the United States, by 2021 he was said to be making a come-back, with social media posts praising him as 'hero', 'patriot' and 'leader'. Several included photo tributes, while others 'have showcased videos of him posing with Prince Muhammad'. As MBS's chief torturer and enforcer in his rise to power, al-Qahtani's cyber skills and hacking capabilities are evidently too valuable to be dispensed with. A senior Gulf official is quoted as saying: 'There is no question that al-Qahtani is back. The question is, did he ever really leave?'[125]

At this writing (January 2024), the international rehabilitation of al-Qahtani's boss also appears complete. US president Joe Biden, who on coming to power in 2020 had wanted to treat him as a 'pariah', was reported to have given MBS a 'hearty handshake' at the Group of 20 summit in New Delhi.[126] In June 2023 he was shown at the Elysée Palace towering over President Emmanuel Macron on his second official visit to the French capital. There was even talk of a state visit to the United Kingdom. Those who might ask if King Charles would want to be photographed shaking hands with a man designated by the CIA as a murderer might be reminded that his mother, the late Queen Elizabeth, had no problem shaking hands with the former IRA terrorist Martin McGuinness.

Realpolitik may rule in affairs of state, with bigger questions involving truth and justice left hanging in the air. But what of Jamal Khashoggi? To date, no forensic traces of his remains have been found. Were they destroyed in the Saudi consul's barbecue in Istanbul or repatriated along with the bone-saw when the hit squad returned to Saudi Arabia?

In an era when social media may incline even hard-headed sceptics towards conspiracy theories, anonymous gossip circulating in the cybersphere should be treated with the utmost caution. But a Saudi blogger who calls himself Mujtahid (Interpreter) should not be dismissed out of hand. In a series of tweets relayed by the Arab Digest, Mujtahid describes the crown prince as a 'Machiavellian and narcissistic psychopath' who enjoys psychologically, even physically, torturing people. His only hobby is video games, in which he has invested billions, as well as trolling through Twitter and other feeds.

Since the war in Yemen that started in 2014, he has tended to spend a significant portion of his time on his luxury yacht *Serene* where he is 'rumoured' to keep Khashoggi's fingers or even his head, brought to him as trophies after the killing. It is here that Leonardo da Vinci's *Salvator Mundi* is also said to hang. While Mujtahid's account could be based on the idlest of gossip (the story of Khashoggi's severed fingers appeared in the UK's *Daily Mirror* in December 2018 having been leaked by Turkish intelligence soon after the murder), other details Mujtahid reveals about MBS's habits and personality do not seem implausible.

Except for when he has an important meeting or special event, says Mujtahid,

> MBS has a disorganised daily schedule which means that his life is in a state of constant chaos ... The prince is reportedly a habitual user of stimulants, and so has no specific time when he likes to go to bed. He can sleep any time, day or night, although not without sleeping aids, and when he does sleep no one dares wake him, so his sleep can last for a long time, sometimes all day. Then when he awakes, he immediately starts ingesting stimulants and energy drinks again and again and so the cycle repeats. No one can predict how long he sleeps again, whether a few hours or several days, depending on what he takes and how he feels at any given moment. Saudi officials try to accommodate his behaviour as best they can. Meetings at all levels have no specific times or duration.

They can start at dawn, noon or midnight and last for ten minutes, ten hours, or several consecutive days. Sometimes MBS calls a meeting and then goes to sleep and ignores it which means no one else can leave until he wakes up. This can take 10 hours or more. Other times after waiting twelve hours they receive a message saying his highness will not attend and they have to reschedule – and woe betide any minister or functionary MBS finds asleep when he does awaken or has made an excuse and left.[127]

Erratic timekeeping is characteristic of narcissistic dictators oblivious to the schedules or needs of their subordinates. One is reminded of Stalin in the late 1940s when he would summon aides for meetings or to watch movies late at night. It is also a demonstration of power at its most raw: as every corporate executive knows, keeping people waiting is a way of demonstrating one's superior authority. In October 2023, MBS kept US secretary of state Antony Blinken waiting for several hours for a meeting that was 'presumed to happen in the evening but which the crown prince only showed up for the next morning'.[128] This was a violation of protocol amounting to insult for the most senior diplomat of the kingdom's oldest ally at a time of heightened international conflict.

The killing of Khashoggi with which this book began is a scandal whose ramifications are far from being spent. With the Middle East entering a new period of turmoil after the Hamas attack of 7 October 2023, it is far from clear that the kingdom, and its investors, will benefit from MBS's cherished hopes for 'normalization' in line with the Abraham Accords. At the United Nations, the US, despite reservations about the slaughter and starvation of Palestinians, has held firmly to the Israeli narrative that Hamas is an organization of evil terrorists that must be destroyed utterly. The inherent contradiction in this agenda, demanding the wholescale destruction of an organization that must also be bargained with to secure the release of hostages it is still holding, appears to have escaped a government bent on revenge that uses mass starvation as a weapon of war. The great majority of the world community, however, including President Biden, whose peace plan in June 2024 proposed a trade between hostage release and a ceasefire that could become permanent, takes the more nuanced view of the conflict in line with the Qataris. During the 2024 US presidential election campaign, the Democratic candidate, Vice President Kamala Harris, took a similar view. However, the overwhelming victory of her Republican rival Donald Trump opens the prospect of an even more brutal realignment of forces in the region, with closer collaboration between the intelligence networks of Saudi Arabia and its Gulf allies and an Israeli state dominated by ultra-nationalists, in repressing protests against the ethnic cleansing – not to mention genocide – of Palestinians in Gaza and the occupied West Bank.

Hamas is a reality, however brutal, and its power is something that needs to be engaged with. Paradoxically, it may be the pragmatic realism of the Qataris, rather than the brutal militarism of the Israelis, that has saved the lives of some hostages in the present crisis, as many Israeli families have come to realize.

As Shivshankar Menon, a former foreign minister and security advisor to the Indian government, stated in a perceptive article in *Foreign Affairs*, 'choosing to meet violence with violence is a choice'. When Pakistani terrorists landed by sea in Mumbai in November 2008 and went on a rampage in hotels, cafés and a train station, killing at least 174 people and injuring more than 300, the government of Manmohan Singh opted not to 'undertake an overt military strike on terrorist camps in Pakistan' but responded to the atrocity 'through diplomatic and covert channels'. The United Kingdom took a similar approach when challenged by IRA atrocities on the

British mainland during the 1970s and 1980s (although members of its security forces were involved in illegal killings).

In November 2023, following pressure from the international community and hostage families, diplomatic channels through Qatar were deployed, enabling the first batch of 105 hostages, including children and elderly people, to be released in exchange for Palestinians held in Israeli prisons. Israelis, of course, insist that it was only military pressure on Hamas that made such releases possible. But this is highly disputable: in 2011 Gilad Shalit, an Israeli soldier captured by Hamas in June 2006 and held in Gaza for more than five years, was exchanged for more than 1,000 Palestinian and Arab Israeli prisoners following 'back-channel' deals between Mossad – the Israeli spy agency – and Hamas commanders.

Given that precedent – overseen by Israeli prime minister Benjamin Netanyahu – it is hardly far-fetched to assume that a deal with a much more favourable exchange rate than Shalit's one Israeli for more than 1,000 Palestinians could have been secured for the release of all the 130-odd surviving hostages in exchange for Palestinians held by Israel. The difference in 2023 was that Netanyahu's government – a volatile coalition including Bezalel Smotrich (finance minister) from the Religious Zionist party and Itamar Ben-Gvir (security minister) from the ultra-right Otzma Yehudit (Jewish Power) party – threatened to bring down the government if it were seen to be 'soft' on Hamas and the Palestinians. In an interview broadcast in February 2024 Smotrich was explicit: bringing home the remaining 134 captives held by Hamas was 'less important' than the destruction of their captors.

Menon's South Asian model of restraint suggests that given the existence of Qatari channels, an alternative strategy should at least have been tried from the start, saving thousands of non-combatants' lives.

Sadly, Jamal Khashoggi is no longer with us to share his views on the Hamas atrocity or Israel's disproportionate response. But despite his family's acceptance of blood money, he will not be forgotten in his homeland, in the cultural consciousness of his compatriots, or in the world at large. When public political discourse is banned or controlled by the state, non-verbal communication can still flourish, especially if it conveys ambiguities.

In June 2019 visitors to the Basel art fair in Switzerland were invited to enter 'The Safe', an installation by Saudi artist Abdulnasser Gharem. 'The Safe' is a room-sized white box beneath a pale-yellow awning. The interior walls — with only one person permitted to enter for one minute at a time — recall the padded cells of a prison or mental institution. One side is dominated by the Saudi flag displaying the sword and *kalima* (the Muslim credo that there is only one God and Muhammad is His prophet). At the end of the room, set on a steel table, there are some two dozen rubber stamps that visitors are invited to impress on the padded wall. The stamps display messages in Arabic and English, such as 'the difference between the terrorist and the martyr is the media coverage'.

But it's the steel table that grabs the attention. With its trolley-wheels, sink and curving tap, it is the type of table to be found in any city morgue. It can easily be read as a non-explicit reference to the butchery suffered by Khashoggi, authorized by the ruler of the kingdom whose religious banner dominates the space above.

Gharem, whose work commands six-figure sums in the international market, is a former lieutenant-colonel in the Saudi army. In interviews, he always stresses that his work is 'not about taking sides'. In the dysfunctional realm of MBS's kingdom, 'The Safe' is a fitting symbol of cruelty and repression. But the fact that the artist continues to reside and work in the kingdom signals a significant message of hope.

Acknowledgements

Unholy Kingdom originated as an article in the *London Review of Books* several months before the murder of Jamal Khashoggi drew international attention to Saudi Arabia's Mafia-style operations. Mary-Kay Wilmers and Daniel Soar commissioned and edited the original article. The late Eric Hazan of La Fabrique saw the potential for expanding it into a book, and I am especially grateful for his encouragement and meticulous editing of the French version that appeared in 2019 before the lockdowns caused by Covid-19. Etienne Dobanesque, who translated the original English text, and Jean Morisot and Thalie Barnier of La Fabrique did vital work checking many facts and references that feature in this expanded and updated English version. David Commins read the English version and made useful comments. Patrice Gujet and Nicholas Ward-Jackson kindly hosted me in Paris and Venice. Others who helped by giving advice or suggestions did not wish to be named. I would like to thank them all with the proviso that the views expressed in this book are my own and that any factual errors are my responsibility.

Notes

1. Murder in Istanbul

1. Jonathan Rugman, *The Killing in the Consulate*, Simon & Schuster, 2019, p. 107.
2. Ibid., p. 91.
3. Ibid., p. 131.
4. Ibid., p. 175.
5. Ibid., p. 177.
6. Madawi al-Rasheed, 'The Saudi lie', *London Review of Books*, vol. 41, no. 6, 21 March 2019.
7. Heather Timmins, 'What does the US owe Jamal Khashoggi?', *Quartz* (19 October 2018).
8. Mark Mazzetti and Ben Hubbard, 'It wasn't just Khashoggi: a Saudi prince's brutal drive to crush dissent', *New York Times* (17 March 2019).
9. Mark Mazzetti, 'Saudi operatives who killed Khashoggi received paramilitary training in US', *New York Times* (22 June 2021).
10. Madawi al-Rasheed, *The Son King: Reform and Repression in Saudi Arabia*, Hurst, 2020, pp. 89–90.
11. 'Young prince in a hurry', *Economist* (9 January 2016).
12. Andrew England and Simeon Kerr, 'Saudi Arabia: how the Khashoggi killing threatens the prince's project', *Financial Times* (22 October 2017).
13. Simeon Kerr et al., 'The Saudi prince uses "Davos in the Desert" to woo world's top investors', *Financial Times* (27 October 2017).
14. Ibid.
15. 'Interview with Muhammad bin Salman', *Economist* (6 January 2016).
16. Paul Roberts, 'Gates Foundation cuts ties with Saudi charity over journalist's murder', *Seattle Times* (2 November 2018).
17. Walt Bogdanich and Michael Forsythe, 'How McKinsey has helped raise stature of authoritarian governments', *New York Times* (15 December 2018).

18. David D. Kirkpatrick et al., 'The wooing of Jared Kushner: how the Saudis got a friend in the White House', *New York Times* (8 December 2018).
19. Nicholas Kristof, 'Jared and the Saudi crown prince go nuclear', *New York Times* (2 March 2019).
20. Kirkpatrick et al., 'The wooing of Jared Kushner'.
21. David Rohde, 'Is Trump trying to bully America's intelligence agencies into silence?', *New Yorker* (31 December 2019).
22. Reuters (23 October 2018).
23. Mark Landler, 'Despite evidence on Khashoggi, Trump sticks with the crown prince. Why?', *New York Times* (18 November 2018).
24. David E. Sanger, 'Candidate Biden called Saudi Arabia a "pariah." He now has to deal with it', *New York Times* (25 February 2021).
25. Rugman, *The Killing in the Consulate*, p. 182.
26. Gardiner Harris, Eric Schmitt, Helene Cooper and Nicholas Pandos, 'Senators, furious over Khashoggi killing, spurn president on war in Yemen', *New York Times* (28 November 2018).
27. David D. Kirkpatrick, 'The kingdom and the Kushners: Jared went to Riyadh. So did his brother', *New York Times* (21 March 2019).
28. Rugman, *The Killing in the Consulate*, p. 182.
29. Editorial Board, 'Saudi Arabia's threadbare cover-up of Khashoggi's killing unravels further', *New York Times* (8 February 2019).
30. *Human Rights Council Forty-First Session 24 June–12 July 2019 Annex to the Report of the Special Rapporteur on Extrajudicial, Summary or Arbitrary Executions: Investigation into the Unlawful Death of Mr Jamal Khashoggi*, United Nations, 2019, pp. 56–7.
31. David D. Kirkpatrick and Nick Cumming-Bose, 'Saudis called Khashoggi "sacrificial animal" as they waited to kill him', *New York Times* (10 June 2019).
32. Stephanie Kirchgaessner, 'Top Saudi official issued death threat against UN's Khashoggi investigator', *Guardian* (23 March 2021).
33. Tarek Cherkaoui and Michael Arnold, *Chronicle of a Death Foretold: The Jamal Khashoggi Affair and Turkish–Saudi Relations*, TRT World Research Centre (October 2018), p. 18.
34. Ibid.
35. Ibid., p. 6.
36. Saudi Arabia social media statistics 2024, globalmediainsight.com.
37. Al-Rasheed, *The Son King*, p. 15.
38. Khaled M. Abou el-Fadl, 'Saudi Arabia is misusing Mecca', *New York Times* (12 November 2018).
39. Ibid.
40. CBS, *60 Minutes* (19 March 2018).
41. 'Crown Prince Mohammed bin Salman talks to TIME about the Middle East, Saudi Arabia's plans and President Trump', *Time* (8 April 2018).
42. Talmiz Ahmad, 'An execution that inflames sectarian cleavages across West Asia', *Wire* (India) (5 January 2016).

43 Chiara Pellegrino, 'Mohammed bin Salman and the Invention of Tradition', Oasis International Foundation (19 June 2018), p. 3.
44 Abdullah Alaoudh, 'Saudi Arabia is slowly killing my father', *New York Times* (30 December 2020).
45 Stéphane Lacroix, 'Saudi Arabia and the limits of religious reform: religion and diplomacy', *Review of Faith and International Affairs*, vol. 25, no. 2, 2019; James M. Dorsey, 'Saudi religious moderation: how real is it?', BESA (6 June 2019).
46 Rugman, *The Killing in the Consulate*, p. 72.
47 Barbara Plett Usher, 'Saudi Prince Turkey al-Faisal on Saudi–US relationship', *BBC News* (13 January 2019).
48 Rugman, *The Killing in the Consulate*, p. 45.
49 Jamal Khashoggi, 'The expanding Shiite crescent', *Al Arabiya* (16 June 2013).
50 Ben Hubbard, 'Channel in Bahrain goes silent after giving opposition airtime', *New York Times* (2 February 2015).
51 Hugh Miles, *Al Jazeera: How Arab TV News Challenged the World*, Abacus, 2005, p. 53.
52 Petra Marquardt-Bigman, 'Jamal Khashoggi was a victim of Saudi terror. He was also a keen supporter of Palestinian terrorism', *Haaretz* (21 October 2018).
53 Al-Rasheed, *The Son King*, p. 74.
54 'Crown prince receives George Tenet Medal from CIA director', Saudi Press Agency Riyadh (10 February 2017).
55 Richard Sokolsky and Aaron David Miller, 'Saudi Arabia's new crown prince is a bumbling hothead', *Politico* (29 June 2017).
56 Ben Hubbard, 'Dialogue with Iran is impossible, Saudi Arabia's defense minister says', *New York Times* (2 May 2017).
57 Arnold and Cherkaoui, *Chronicle of a Death Foretold*, p. 14.
58 Vali R. Nasr, 'A Saudi Murder Becomes a Gift to Iran', *New York Times*, 12 November 2018.
59 Shmuel Sandler, 'BESA Center Perspectives paper no 1,841', 8 December 2020.
60 Ibid.
61 Karen DeYoung and Missy Ryan, 'US declares Saudi crown prince immune from Khashoggi killing lawsuit', *Washington Post* (18 February 2022).
62 Karen Elliott House, 'Biden may regret releasing report on Khashoggi murder', *Harvard Gazette* (27 February 2021).

2. The Wahhabi Mission

1 David Commins, *The Wahhabi Mission and Saudi Arabia*, I. B. Tauris, 2006, pp. 17–18.
2 Mohamed Ed Husain, *The House of Islam: A Global History*, Bloomsbury, 2018, p. 64.
3 Commins, *Wahhabi Mission*, p. 21.
4 Cole M. Bunzel, *Wahhabism: The History of a Militant Islamic Movement*, Princeton University Press, 2023, pp. 104–5.
5 Madawi al-Rasheed, *A History of Saudi Arabia*, 2nd ed., Cambridge University Press, 2010, p. 15.

6   Ibid., pp. 18–19.
7   Ibid., p. 28.
8   Ibid.
9   Ibid., p. 19.
10 Commins, *Wahhabi Mission*, p. 29.
11 Ibid.
12 Ibid., p. 30.
13 Ibid., p. 63.
14 Ibid.
15 Ibid., p. 64.
16 Ibid., p. 65.
17 Ibid., p. 68.
18 Ibid., p. 69.
19 Ibid., pp. 69–70.
20 Ahmad Dallal, *New Cambridge History of Islam*, vol. 6, Cambridge University Press, 2020, p. 115.
21 Commins, *Wahhabi Mission*, p. 11.
22 Ibid., p. 119.
23 Dallal, *New Cambridge History of Islam*, p. 115.

3. Ibn Saud: Founder of a Kingdom

1   Leslie McLoughlin, *Ibn Saud: Founder of a Kingdom*, Macmillan, 1993, p. 162.
2   Ibid., p. 12.
3   Harry St John Philby, *The Heart of Arabia: A Record of Travel and Exploration*, Constable, 1922, p. 101.
4   McLoughlin, *Ibn Saud*, p. 90.
5   Ibid., p. 192.
6   Ibid., p. 25.
7   Robert Lacey, *The Kingdom: Arabia and the House of Sa'ud*, Hutchinson, 1981, p. 72.
8   McLoughlin, *Ibn Saud*, p. 29.
9   Ibid., p. 30.
10 Ibid., p. 31, n. 21.
11 Commins, *Wahhabi Mission*, p. 82.
12 Ali Yousuf, (trans.), *The Holy Quran*, Goodwork Books, 2022, p. 266.
13 Yves Lacoste, *Ibn Khaldun: The Birth of History and the Past of the Third World*, trans. David Macey, Verso, 1984, p. 106.
14 Ibid., p. 103.
15 Commins, *Wahhabi Mission*, p. 85.
16 Lacey, *The Kingdom*, p. 145.
17 Commins, *Wahhabi Mission*, p. 84.
18 McLoughlin, *Ibn Saud*, p. 43.
19 Lacey, *The Kingdom*, p. 146.

20 Commins, *Wahhabi Mission*, p. 85.
21 Aziz al-Azmeh, *Islams and Modernities*, 2nd ed., Verso, 1996, p. 147.
22 Ibid., p. 151.
23 Ibid.
24 Commins, *Wahhabi Mission*, p. 85.
25 Hafiz Wahba, *Arabian Days*, Arthur Baker, 1964, p. 129.
26 Quoted in Lacey, *The Kingdom*, p. 185.
27 McLoughlin, *Ibn Saud*, p. 50.
28 Ibid., p. 51.
29 Commins, *Wahhabi Mission*, p. 86.
30 Ibid., p. 89.
31 Lacey, *The Kingdom*, p. 209.
32 Ibid.
33 Lacey, *The Kingdom*, p. 213.
34 Madawi al-Rasheed, *A History of Saudi Arabia*, p. 69.
35 Malise Ruthven, 'Terror: the hidden source', *New York Review of Books* (24 October 2013).
36 Al-Rasheed, *A History of Saudi Arabia*, p. 101.

4. Petroleum and Patriarchy

1 Anthony Sampson, *The Seven Sisters: The Great Oil Companies and the World They Made*, Hodder & Stoughton, [1975] 1981, p. 106.
2 'Seven wells of Dammam', *Aramco World*, vol. 14, no. 1, January 1963.
3 Frank Jungers, *The Caravan Goes On: How Aramco and Saudi Arabia Grew Up Together*, Medina Publishing, 2013, p. 22.
4 James Barr, *Lords of the Desert: Britain's Struggle with America to Dominate the Middle East*, Simon & Schuster, 2018, p. 108.
5 Sampson, *The Seven Sisters*, pp. 110–11.
6 Elizabeth Monroe, *Philby of Arabia*, Ithaca Press, 1973, p. 222.
7 Ibid., p. 224.
8 Sampson, *The Seven Sisters*, p. 112.
9 Ibid., p. 114.
10 McLoughlin, *Ibn Saud*, p. 165.
11 Ibid., p. 167.
12 Sampson, *The Seven Sisters*, p. 115.
13 Laurence Grafftey-Smith, *Bright Levant*, John Murray, 1970, p. 167.
14 Barr, *Lords of the Desert*, p. 108.
15 Ibid., p. 119.
16 McLoughlin, *Ibn Saud*, p. 172.
17 Sampson, *The Seven Sisters*, p. 115.
18 Ibid.
19 US Cable 22 06RIYADH8921 A, November 2006, WikiLeaks.

20. McLoughlin, *Ibn Saud*, p. 188.
21. Ibid., p. 192.
22. US Cable 22, WikiLeaks.
23. Ibid.
24. Thomas Devaney, 'Virtue, virility, and history in fifteenth-century Castile', *Speculum*, vol. 88, no. 3, 2013, p. 744.
25. David Holden and Richard Johns, *The House of Saud*, Macmillan, 1981, pp. 217–18.
26. Barr, *Lords of the Desert*, p. 30.
27. McLoughlin, *Ibn Saud*, p. 34.
28. Ibid., p. 49.
29. Ibid., p. 73.
30. Ibid., p. 117.
31. Ibid., p. 118.
32. Harry St John Philby, *Arabian Jubilee*, John Day, 1952, p. 99.
33. Abdul Rahman Munif, *Cities of Salt* [*mudun al-milh*], trans. Peter Theroux, Jonathan Cape, 1988, p. 134.
34. Ibid., p. 199.
35. Ibid., p. 214.
36. Ibid., p. 287.
37. Jungers, *The Caravan Goes On*, p. 51.
38. Ibid.
39. Toby Matthiesen, *The Other Saudis: Shiism, Dissent and Sectarianism*, Cambridge University Press, 2015, p. 68.
40. Jungers, *The Caravan Goes On*, p. 62.
41. Matthiesen, *The Other Saudis*, pp. 68–9.
42. Ibid., p. 69.
43. Lacey, *The Kingdom*, p. 388.
44. Karen Elliott House, *On Saudi Arabia: Its Peoples, Past, Religion, Fault Lines and Future*, Knopf, 2013, p. 119.
45. Ibid., pp. 120–1.
46. Ibid., p. 120.
47. Andrew Hammond, 'Reordering Saudi religion: MBS is defanging Wahhabism, not dethroning it', *Maydan* (20 September 2021).

5. Managing the Ulama and Mismanaging the Hajj

1. UN General Assembly, 63rd session, 46th plenary meeting, 12 November 2008, digitallibrary.uk.org, A_63_PV.46-ENpdf, p. 6.
2. Paul Wood, 'Life and legacy of King Fahd', *BBC News* (5 August 2005).
3. Al-Rasheed, *A History of Saudi Arabia*, p. 265.
4. House, *On Saudi Arabia*, p. 235.
5. Ibid.
6. Ibid., p. 237.

7. Thomas Hegghammer and Stéphane Lacroix, 'Rejectionist Islamism in Saudi Arabia: the story of Juhayman Al-Utaybi revisited', *International Journal of Middle East Studies*, vol. 39, 2007, pp. 103–22: 107.
8. Ibid., p. 122.
9. Yaroslav Trofimov, *The Siege of Mecca: The Forgotten Uprising in Islam's Holiest Shrine and the Birth of al-Qaeda*, New York, 2008, p. 69.
10. Ibn Kathir, *Signs before the Day of Judgment*, trans. Huda Khattab, Dar al-Taqwa, 1992, p. 90.
11. Trofimov, *The Siege of Mecca*, p. 222.
12. Matthiesen, *The Other Saudis*, p. 103.
13. Not to be confused with Prince Bandar bin Sultan, former Saudi ambassador to Washington.
14. Trofimov, *The Siege of Mecca*, p. 198.
15. Matthiesen, *The Other Saudis*, p. 113.
16. Ibid.
17. Madawi al-Rasheed, 'Sectarianism as counter-revolution: Saudi responses to the Arab Spring', in Nader Hashem and Danny Postel (eds), *Sectarianization: Mapping the New Politics of the Middle East*, Hurst, 2017, pp. 143–58.
18. Commins, *Wahhabi Mission*, p. 115.
19. Ibid.
20. Ibid.
21. Ibid., p. 119.
22. Ibid.
23. Ibid., p. 121.
24. John R. Bradley, *Saudi Arabia Exposed*, Palgrave Macmillan, 2005, pp. 136–7.
25. Mustafa Akyol, 'Islam's tragic fatalism', *New York Times* (23 September 2015).
26. Ibid.
27. Ziauddin Sardar, *Mecca the Sacred City*, Bloomsbury, 2014, p. 230.
28. Nicolai Ourussoff, 'New look for Mecca gargantuan and gaudy', *New York Times* (29 December 2010).
29. Sardar, *Mecca the Sacred City*, p. 342.
30. Khaled Abou el-Fadl, 'Saudi Arabia is misusing Mecca', *New York Times* (12 November 2018).
31. Ibid.
32. Ibid.

6. Conflicting Currents

1. Commins, *Wahhabi Mission*, p. 110.
2. Roel Meijer (ed.), *Global Salafism: Islam's New Religious Movement*, Hurst, 2009, p. 10.
3. Ibid.
4. Ibid., p. 13.
5. Ibid., p. 19.

6 Henri Lauzière, *The Making of Salafism: Islamic Reform in the Twentieth Century*, Columbia University Press, 2015, p. 67.
7 Gudrun Krämer, *Hasan al-Banna*, One World, 2010, p. 51.
8 Stéphane Lacroix, *Awakening Islam: The Politics of Religious Dissent in Contemporary Saudi Arabia*, trans. George Holoch, Harvard University Press, 2011, p. 41.
9 Lawrence Wright, *Looming Tower*, Penguin, 2007, pp. 79–80.
10 Malise Ruthven, *A Fury for God*, Granta Books, 2002, pp. 202–3.
11 Lacroix, *Awakening Islam*, p. 45.
12 Krämer, *Hasan al-Banna*, p. 20.
13 John Calvert, *Sayyid Qutb and the Origins of Radical Islamism*, Hurst, 2018, p. 99.
14 Martin Kramer, 'The Salience of Islamic Antisemitism', London Institute of Jewish Affairs, October 1995.
15 Ronald Nettler, *Past Trials and Present Tribulations: A Muslim Fundamentalist's View of the Jews*, Oxford Pergamon Press, 1987, p. 49.
16 Ibid., pp. 86–7.
17 Ibid., p. 76.
18 Adolf Hitler, *Mein Kampf*, trans. James Murphy, Hurst and Blackett, 1939, p. 256.
19 Nettler, *Past Trials*, p. 78.
20 Hitler, *Mein Kampf*, p. 273.
21 Ibid., p. 272.
22 Olivier Roy, *The Failure of Political Islam*, trans. Carol Volk, Harvard University Press, 1994.
23 Kramer, 'The Salience of Islamic Antisemitism'.
24 *Al-Hadith wa'l-thaqafa al-Islamiyya* [Prophetic Tradition and Islamic Culture], 1st Grade High School, King Fahd Academy, London, 2005.
25 'Investment in Saudi Arabia's health sector continues to rise as the government addresses long-term challenges', oxfordbusinessgroup.com.
26 Theodosius Dobzhansky, 'Nothing in biology makes sense except in the light of evolution', *American Biology Teacher*, vol. 35, no. 3, 1973, pp. 125–9.
27 'Teaching evolution in the Middle East', nielsenlab.org (25 February 2016).
28 Ibid.

7. A Sectarian Outreach

1 Alex Alexiev, 'Tablighi Jamaat: jihad's stealthy legions', *Middle East Quarterly*, vol. 12, Winter 2005.
2 Xavier Ternisien, 'Les quatre principes familles de l'Islam militant', *Le Monde* (25 January 2002).
3 Denis MacEoin, *The Hijacking of British Islam: How Extremist Literature Is Subverting Mosques in the UK*, Policy Exchange, 2007, p. 22.
4 Ebrahim Moosa, *What Is a Madrasa?*, Edinburgh University Press, 2015, p. 218.
5 Ibid., p. 192.
6 Ibid., p. 219.

7. MacEoin, *The Hijacking of British Islam*, p. 26.
8. James M. Dorsey, 'Creating Frankenstein: the impact of Saudi export of ultra-conservatism in South Asia', Social Science Research Network (29 July 2016).
9. Krithika Varagur, *The Call: Inside the Global Saudi Religious Project*, Columbia Global Reports, 2020, pp. 35–6.
10. Ibid., p. 40.
11. Ibid., p. 41.
12. Ibid., p. 60.
13. Ibid., p. 70.
14. Ibid., p. 71.
15. Ibid., p. 95.
16. Ibid., p. 97.
17. Ibid., p. 98.
18. Johannes Harnischfeger, *Democratization and Islamic Law: The Shariʿa Conflict in Nigeria*, University of Chicago Press, 2008, p. 41.
19. Ibid., p. 35.
20. Gunnar J. Weimann, *Islamic Criminal Law in Northern Nigeria: Politics, Religions, Judicial Practice*, University of Amsterdam Press, 2010.
21. Harnischfeger, *Democratization and Islamic Law*, p. 37.
22. Ibid., p. 239.
23. Varagur, *The Call*, p. 105.
24. Aanu Adeoye, 'The Islamist insurgents threatening West Africa', *Financial Times* (22 January 2024).
25. Varagur, *The Call*, p. 101.
26. Dorsey, 'Creating Frankenstein', p. 2.
27. 'Shia and Hazaras in Pakistan', Minority Rights Group, 2018, minorityrights.org.
28. Dorsey, 'Creating Frankenstein', p. 5.
29. Ibid., p. 11.
30. Ibid., pp. 10–11.
31. Carlotta Gall, 'Saudis bankroll Taliban even as king officially supports Afghan government', *New York Times* (6 December 2016).
32. Eleanor Abdella Doumato, 'Saudi Arabian expansion in the United States: half-hearted missionary work meets rock-solid resistance', in Madawi al-Rasheed (ed.), *Kingdom without Borders*, Hurst, 2008, pp. 301–19: p. 309.
33. Ibid., p. 312.
34. Ibid., p. 311.
35. Ibid., p. 319.
36. MacEoin, *The Hijacking of British Islam*, p. 52.
37. Ibid.
38. Toby Craig Jones, 'The clerics, the Sahwa and the Saudi state', *Strategic Insights*, vol. 4, no. 3, 2005.
39. Bernard Heykal et al. (eds), *Saudi Arabia in Transition*, Cambridge University Press, 2015, p. 130.

40 Madawi al-Rasheed, *A History of Saudi Arabia*, Cambridge University Press, 2002, p. 166.
41 Jones, 'The clerics, the Sahwa and the Saudi state'.
42 John R. Bradley, *Saudi Arabia Exposed*, Palgrave Macmillan, 2005, p. 113.
43 Ibid.
44 Ibid., p. 114.
45 Ibid.
46 Madawi al-Rasheed, 'The minaret and the palace: obedience at home and rebellion abroad', in al-Rasheed, *Kingdom without Borders*, pp. 199–217: 214.
47 Jones, 'The clerics, the Sahwa and the Saudi state'.
48 Roel Meijer, 'Yousuf al-Uyairi and the transnationalisation of Saudi jihadism', in al-Rasheed, *Kingdom Without Borders*, p. 233.
49 *Asian Affairs* journal weblog (25 September 2015).
50 Saeed Shehabi, 'The role of religious ideology in the expansionist policies of Saudi Arabia', in al-Rasheed, *Kingdom Without Borders*, p. 192.
51 Al-Rasheed, 'Sectarianism as counter-revolution: Saudi responses to the Arab Spring', in Hashemi and Postel (eds), *Sectarianization*, pp. 143–58: p. 143.
52 Ibid., p. 145.
53 Dania Akkad and Linah Alsaafin, 'US thought Nimr's allegiances lay with Iran: Wikileaks', *Middle East Eye* (2 January 2016).
54 'Reactions to Saudi execution of prominent Shia cleric', *Middle East Eye* (2 January 2016).
55 Paul Aarts and Carolien Roelants, *Saudi Arabia: A Kingdom in Peril*, Hurst, 2015, p. 98.
56 Cited in Max Fisher, 'The cold war between Saudi Arabia and Iran that's tearing apart the Middle East, explained', Vox (4 January 2016).
57 'MBS accuse l'Iran d'être responsible de l'attaque de pétroliers en mer d'Oman', *Le Monde* (16 June 2019).
58 Patrick Wintour, 'UK joins US in accusing Iran of tanker attacks as crew held', *Guardian* (14 June 2019).
59 Aarts and Roelants, *Saudi Arabia*, p. 95.

8. Arms and Benefits

1 Igor Bosilkovski, 'Saudi billionaire Alwaleed bin Talal's network takes a hit after news of his arrest', *Forbes* (6 November 2017).
2 Ibid.
3 Susanne Koelbl, *Behind the Kingdom's Veil: Inside the New Saudi Arabia under Crown Prince Mohammed bin Salman*, Mango, 2020, p. 207.
4 Ibid.
5 Stephen Karlin and Katie Paul, 'Future Saudi king tightens grip on power', Reuters (6 November 2017); Ajil Financial Services Company Qatar (2 August 2022).

6. Ben Hubbard et al., 'Saudis said to use coercion and abuse to seize billions', *New York Times* (11 March 2018).
7. David Leigh and Rob Evans, 'Prince Bandar', *Guardian* (7 June 2007).
8. 'Prince Bandar bin Sultan: larger-than-life diplomacy', *Economist* (6 November 2008).
9. Ibid.
10. Koelbl, *Behind the Kingdom's Veil*, pp. 179, 185.
11. Leigh and Evans, 'Prince Bandar'.
12. Jennifer Rizzo, 'Prince and the "28 pages"', CNN (5 August 2016).
13. Tim Golden and Sebastian Rotella, 'The Saudi connection: inside the 9/11 cast that divided the FBI', *New York Times Magazine* (23 January 2020, updated 3 September 2021).
14. Rizzo, 'Prince and the "28 pages"'.
15. Release of FBI Electronic Communication dated 4 April 2016, Pursuant to Executive Order 14040 § 2(a) (3 September 2021); Devlin Barrett, 'FBI releases 9/11 investigation document that scrutinized Saudis', *Washington Post* (12 September 2021).
16. Barrett, 'FBI releases 9/11 document'.
17. Ibid.
18. Patrick Cockburn, 'Iraq: how Saudi Arabia helped ISIS take over the north of the country', *Independent* (13 July 2014).
19. Ibid.
20. Ibid.
21. Ibid.
22. Ibid.
23. Emma Sky, *Today*, BBC Radio 4 (11 February 2019).
24. Dale Gavlak and Yahya Ababneh, 'Syrians in Ghouta claim Saudi-supplied rebels behind chemical attack', Mintpress News (29 August 2013).
25. Seymour M. Hersh, 'Whose sarin?', *London Review of Books*, vol. 26, no. 10, 22 May 2014. Emphasis added.
26. Koelbl, *Behind the Kingdom's Veil*, p. 191.
27. Peter Hitchens, 'Strange news from the OPCW in the Hague', *Mail Online* (17 May 2019); Caitlin Johnstone, 'Confirmed: chemical weapons assessment contradicting official Syria narrative is authentic', *Information Clearing House* (17 May 2019).
28. Mark Hollingsworth and Sandy Mitchell, *Saudi Babylon*, Mainstream, 2005, p. 153.
29. Ibid., p. 161.
30. Ibid., p. 160.
31. 'SFO to investigate BAE contracts', *BBC News* (3 November 2004).
32. BBC *Panorama* (7 June 2007).
33. J. Rosenberg, 'SFO director good man in a bad world', *Daily Telegraph* (31 July 2008).
34. Hansard online (18 January 2007), cols 778, 779.
35. 'Blair defends Saudi probe ruling', *BBC News* (15 December 2006).
36. David Pegg and Rob Evans, 'MoD paid millions into Saudi account amid BAE corruption scandal', *Guardian* (8 March 2024).
37. Ibid.

38 Rupert Neate, 'Saudi prince sells Cotswolds estate to king of Bahrain for £120m', *Guardian* (5 April 2021).
39 Hollingsworth and Mitchell, *Saudi Babylon*, p. 160.
40 Ibid., p. 162.
41 Ibid., p. 165.
42 Ibid., p. 115.
43 Transparency International website, transparency.org.
44 Mohammed al-Khilewi, 'Saudi Arabia is trying to kill me', *Middle East Quarterly*, September 1988, pp. 66–77.
45 Sarah Muir and Akhil Gupta, 'Rethinking the anthropology of corruption', *Current Anthropology*, vol. 59, suppl. 18, April 2018, p. 85.
46 Ernst Kantorowicz, *The King's Two Bodies: A Study in Medieval Political Theology*, Princeton University Press, [1957] 2016, p. 206. Emphasis added.
47 Al-Rasheed, *A History of Saudi Arabia*, p. 12.
48 Ibid.
49 House, *On Saudi Arabia*, p. 166.
50 United Nations Development Programme, *The Arab Human Development Report 2004: Towards Freedom in the Arab World*, UNDP, 2005, pp. 41, 171.
51 'Transcript: interview with Muhammad bin Salman', *Economist* (6 June 2016).
52 Marwan Muasher, *The Second Arab Awakening and the Battle for Pluralism*, Yale University Press, 2014, p. 19.

9. Family Values

1 'The Basic Law of Government', shura.gov.sa.
2 Al-Rasheed, *A History of Saudi Arabia*, p. 172.
3 Nadav Samin, 'Parricide in the kingdom', in al-Rasheed (ed.), *Salman's Legacy*, Hurst, 2018, pp. 197–213: 210.
4 Al-Rasheed, *A History of Saudi Arabia*, p. 219.
5 Samin, 'Parricide in the kingdom', p. 210.
6 Ibid., p. 211.
7 Ibid., p. 200.
8 Caroline Montagu, 'Civil society in Saudi Arabia: the power and challenges of association', Royal Institute of International Affairs, 2015, p. 15.
9 Jack Goody, *The Development of the Family and Marriage in Europe*, Cambridge University Press, 1983, p. 56.
10 Ben Hubbard, 'American woman, divorced from Saudi husband, is trapped in Saudi Arabia', *New York Times* (5 March 2019).
11 Anthony H. Cordesman, 'Saudi Arabia enters the 21st century', Center for Strategic and International Studies, Washington DC, 30 October 2002, p. 13.
12 Richard Brenneman, 'Wikicable on rampant Saudi royal corruption', richardbrenneman.wordpress.com.
13 Ibid.

14 Ibid.
15 House, *On Saudi Arabia*, p. 125.
16 Montagu, 'Civil society in Saudi Arabia', p. 3.
17 Ibid., p. 25.
18 Ibid., p. 24.
19 Nora Derbal, *Charity in Saudi Arabia*, Cambridge University Press, 2023, p. 296.
20 Ibid., p. 252.
21 Ibid., p. 250.
22 Ibid., p. 245.
23 Ibid., p. 293.
24 Ibid., p. 291.
25 Ibid., p. 234.
26 Ibid., p. 226.
27 Ibid., p. 231.
28 Ibid., p. 29.
29 Ibid., p. 305.
30 Don Cupitt, *Sea of Faith*, BBC, 1984, pp. 362–3.
31 Derbal, *Charity in Saudi Arabia*, p. 272.
32 Ibid., p. 274.
33 Montagu, 'Civil society in Saudi Arabia', p. 22.
34 Ibid., p. 20.
35 Ibid., p. 11.
36 Ibid., p. 10.
37 Simon R. Valentine, *Force and Fanaticism: Wahhabism in Saudi Arabia and Beyond*, Hurst, 2015, p. 29.
38 Pascal Menoret, *Joyriding in Riyadh: Oil, Urbanism and Road Revolt*, Cambridge University Press, 2014, p. 21.
39 Alexandra Siegel, 'Does Twitter bridge the Sunni-Shiite divide or make it worse?', *Washington Post* (7 January 2016). Cited in Nader Hashemi and Danny Postel (eds), *Sectarianization: Mapping the New Politics of the Middle East*, Hurst, 2017, pp. 13–14.
40 Koelbl, *Behind the Kingdom's Veil*, p. 39.
41 Nina dos Santos and Michael Kaplan, 'Jamal Khashoggi's private WhatsApp messages may offer new clues to killings', CNN (4 December 2018).
42 Amos Harel et al., 'Israeli cyber firm negotiated advanced attack capabilities sale with Saudis, Haaretz reveals', *Haaretz* (25 November 2018).
43 Nicholas Wright, 'How artificial intelligence will reshape the global order', *Foreign Affairs* (10 July 2018).
44 Ibid.
45 Menoret, *Joyriding in Riyadh*, p. 53.
46 Ibid., p. 17.
47 Ibid., p. 54.
48 Mona Eltahawy, *Headscarves and Hymens*, Faber and Faber, 2015, p. 109.
49 Elie Elhadj, 'Saudi Arabia's agricultural project: from dust to dust', *Middle East Review of International Affairs*, vol. 12, no. 2, June 2008, pp. 29–37.

50 Ibid., p. 34.
51 Ibid., p. 35.
52 Ibid.
53 Menoret, *Joyriding in Riyadh*, p. 64.
54 Ibid., p. 137.
55 'Full Donald Trump speech in Saudi Arabia May 21st 2017', YouTube, 21 May 2017.
56 Madawi al-Rasheed, 'Can the Saudi crown prince transform the kingdom?', *New York Times* (10 November 2017).
57 Anne Barnard et al., 'Talk of a peace plan that snubs Palestinians', *New York Times* (3 December 2017).
58 Julian Borger, '"I am worried": Macron's chat with Saudi prince captured at G20', *Guardian* (1 December 2018).
59 Mohamed Hanif, 'A happy marriage between God and budget deficits', *New York Times* (19 February 2019).
60 Jochen Bittner, 'Is there an upside to Brexit?', *New York Times* (6 March 2019).
61 Abbas al-Lawati and Donna Abu-Nasr, 'Saudi prince shows grip on power, names first female U.S. envoy', Bloomberg News (23 February 2019).
62 Aziz el Yaakoubi and Ghaida Ghantous, 'Saudi crown prince signals family unity as succession looms', Reuters (20 May 2022).

10. Terraforming Arabia

1 Ruth Gaukrodger, 'Terraforming Mars board game review' (4 August 2022), space.com.
2 Bradley Hope and Justin Scheck, *Blood and Oil: Mohammed bin Salman's Ruthless Quest for Global Power*, Simon & Schuster, 2020, pp. 20–1.
3 Aureliano Tonet and Margherita Nasi, 'Neon, le rêve hollywoodien de Mohammed Ben Salman pour l'Arabie saoudite', *Le Monde* (10 February 2020).
4 Tom Ravenscroft, 'The Line architects explain Saudi mega city in Discovery Channel documentary', *Dezeen* (18 July 23).
5 Alpa Depani, 'Venice's NEOM exhibition is an ageing starchitect fantasia', *Architects' Journal* (1 June 2024).
6 Susanne Koelbl, *Behind the Kingdom's Veil: Inside the New Saudi Arabia Under Crown Prince Mohammed bin Salman*, Mango, 2020, p. 101.
7 Gino Spocchia, 'The Line architect Peter Cook questions Saudi desert city's buildability', *Architects' Journal*, (26 May 2023).
8 Tom Ravenscroft, 'The Line architects explain Saudi mega city in Discovery Channel documentary'.
9 Interview with Lizzie Cook, *Dezeen* (11 August 2022).
10 Wilfred Blunt, *The Dream King*, Hamish Hamilton, [1970] 1984, pp. 96, 117.
11 Loup Calosci and Olivier Namias, 'Mohammed Ben Salmane, le prince des villes nouvelles', *AMC*, no. 318, November 2023.

12   Tom Ravenscroft, 'This week Saudi Arabia scaled back The Line megacity', *Dezeen* (13 April 2024).
13   Eliot Brown and Chelsey Dulaney, 'Megaprojects in the desert sap Saudi Arabia's cash', *Wall Street Journal* (20 February 2024).
14   Shoshanna Delventhal, 'What is Saudi Aramco? Its history, IPO and financials', *Investopedia* (27 March 2022, updated 19 May 2024), investopedia.com.
15   Ibid.
16   Nat Barker, 'Sustainability and liveability claims of Saudi 170-kilometre city are "naïve" say experts', *Dezeen* (8 August 2022).
17   Ibid.
18   Adam Greenfield, 'All those complicit in Neom's design and construction are already destroyers of worlds', *Dezeen* (2 November 2022); Sarah Safieddine et al., 'Present and future land surface and wet bulb temperatures in the Arabian Peninsula', *Environmental Research Letters*, vol. 17, no. 044029, 2022.
19   Greenfield, 'All those complicit'.
20   Brown and Dulaney, 'Megaprojects in the desert sap Saudi Arabia's cash'.
21   Tristan Kennedy, 'The "absurd" project to reintroduce snow at an abandoned Lake Como ski resort', *Daily Telegraph* (9 November 2023).
22   Jon Ungoed-Thomas, 'Mounting concern over environmental cost of fake snow for Olympics', *Guardian* (6 November 2021).
23   Henry Fountain, 'The world can make more water from the sea, but at what cost?' *New York Times* (25 October 2022).
24   Will Ing, 'Fosters + Partners to design six-runway "aerotropolis" in Saudi Arabia', *Architects' Journal* (1 December 2022).
25   Tom Ravenscroft, 'Incoming RIBA president defends work on Neom', *Dezeen* (19 August 2024).
26   Richard Waite and Gita Spocchia, 'Foster + Partners behind plans for 2 km-tall Saudi tower', *Architects' Journal* (4 March 2024).
27   Jenny Goss and Vivian Yee, 'The Red Sea's coral reefs defy the climate-change odds', *New York Times* (19 November 2022).
28   Naida Hakirevic Prevljak, 'OXAGON, world's largest floating industrial complex unveiled', Offshore Energy (17 November 2021).
29   Tina Butler, 'Dubai's artificial islands have high environmental cost', Mongabay (23 August 2005).
30   Tom Ravenscroft, 'Everything you need to know about Saudi Arabia's 14 "giga projects"', *Dezeen* (19 September 2023).
31   Rebecca Anne Proctor and Alia al-Sanussi, *Art in Saudi Arabia*, Lund Humphries, 2023, p. 9.
32   'Saudi Arabia's PIF in talks to inject $250M into Chinese car maker', *Al-Monitor* (7 November 2023).
33   Karl Maier, 'The race for electric cars drives new global rivalries', Bloomberg (8 November 2023).
34   Nicki Shields and James Masters, 'Morocco in the fast lane with the world's largest concentrated solar farm', CNN (16 July 2019).

35 'Saudi Arabia's sovereign wealth fund declares $11bn loss in 2022', *Middle East Eye* (11 July 2023).
36 Brown and Dulaney, 'Megaprojects in the desert sap Saudi Arabia's cash'.
37 'Saudi Arabia launches world's largest solar-power plant', *Economist Intelligence* (11 July 2023).
38 UNESCO World Heritage Convention, Hegra Archaeological Site, whc.unesco.org.
39 Walt Bogdanich and Michael Forsythe, *When McKinsey Comes to Town*, Allen Lane, 2022, pp. 246–7.
40 Ibid., p. 247.
41 Ibid.
42 Ibid., p. 244.
43 Ibid., p. 248.
44 John Gray, 'John Gray and Peter Thiel: life in a postmodern world', *New Statesman* (17 January 2024).
45 Bogdanich and Forsythe, *When McKinsey Comes to Town*, p. 248.
46 Ibid., p. 251.
47 Ibid., p. 252.
48 Koelbl, *Behind the Kingdom's Veil*, p. 87.
49 Daniel Treisman and Sergei Guriev, *Spin Dictators: The Changing Face of Tyranny in the 21st Century*, Princeton University Press, 2022, pp. 26, 163.
50 Muhammad al-Atawneh, *Wahhabi Islam Facing the Challenges of Modernity: Dar al-Ifta in the Modern Saudi State*, Brill, 2010, p. xvi.
51 Rory Jones, 'Alcohol-free Saudi Arabia plans champagne and wine bars at Neom', *Wall Street Journal* (17 September 2022), p. 25.
52 Proctor and al-Senussi, *Art in Saudi Arabia*, p. 35.
53 Ibid., pp. 35–6.
54 Ibid., p. 72.
55 Rawaa Talass, 'Fusing contemporary with ancient: DesertX opens in Saudi Arabia's AlUla', *Art Newspaper* (13 February 2024).
56 Proctor and al-Senussi, *Art in Saudi Arabia*, p. 64.
57 Ibid., p. 49.
58 Ibid.
59 Ibid.
60 George Lee, 'Mary Robinson played big part at COP28 summit in Dubai', RTE (17 December 2023).
61 'Mary Robinson reacts to final COP28 agreement', The Elders (13 December 2023).
62 Joe Lo, '"A la carte menu": Saudi minister claims Cop28 fossil fuel agreement is only optional', *Climate Home News* (10 January 2024).
63 Proctor and al-Senussi, *Art in Saudi Arabia*, p. 87.
64 Ibid., p. 39.
65 Ibid., p. 65.
66 'Saudi Arabia is spending a fortune on sport', *Economist* (10 August 2023).
67 Karim Zidan and Tariq Panja, 'Lionel Messi, Saudi Arabia and the deal that paid off for both sides', *New York Times* (18 June 2023).

68. Ibid.
69. Paul MacInnes, 'Mohammed bin Salman says he will "continue doing sport washing" for Saudi Arabia', *Guardian* (21 September 2023).
70. James M. Dorsey, 'A successful Saudi sports blitz takes more than money', Substack (5 July 2023).
71. Ali Humayun, 'Saudi Arabia, football and faith's role in a revolution', *Athletic* (3 August 2023).
72. James M. Dorsey, 'The Turbulent World', Substack (5 August 2023).
73. Dorsey, 'A successful Saudi sports blitz'.
74. James M. Dorsey, *Soccer: Moulding the Middle East and North Africa*, PhD thesis, University of Utrecht, Netherlands, 2016, p. 99.
75. Ibid., p. 98.
76. Dorsey, *Soccer*, p. 174, n. 629.
77. Dorsey, 'Mistakes regarding Friday Salat and the threat against abandoning it', in *Soccer*, pp. 100, 174, n. 630.
78. Paul Tillich, *Shaking the Foundations*, SCM Press, 1948, p. 6.
79. Harry Edwards, *Sociology of Sport*, in Shirl J. Hoffman (ed.), *Sport and Religion*, Human Kinetics, 1992, pp. 7, 261–2.
80. Ibid., pp. 7–8.
81. Dorsey, *Soccer*, pp. 76, 123, n. 626.
82. Ewan Murray, 'Tiger Woods frustrated by controversial Saudi framework agreement without tours', *Guardian* (28 November 2023).
83. Chris Stein, 'Saudi leader trying to avoid "pariah" status with LIV-PGA merger, says campaigner', *Guardian* (28 June 2023).
84. Gary Dagorn and Iris Deroeux, 'Qatar 2022: pourquoi il est très difficile d'estimer le nombre de morts liés aux chantiers de la Coupe du monde', *Le Monde* (15 November 2022).
85. RWE press release Doha and Essen, 1 October 2022.
86. Malise Ruthven, 'Divided Iran on the eve', *New York Review of Books* (2 July 2009).
87. Steve Rosenberg, 'Russian court bans "LGBT movement"', *BBC News* (30 November 2023).
88. Hind al-Ansari, 'The World Cup and normalization: a reality check', *Sada*, Carnegie Endowment (26 January 2023).
89. Steve Hendrix and Hazem Balousha, 'Netanyahu and Hamas depended on each other', *Washington Post* (23 November 2023).
90. Zvi Bar'el, 'Israel's new Hamas-Gaza concept is doomed to fail just like the last one', *Haaretz* (13 October 2023).
91. 'Hamas attack aimed to disrupt Saudi-Israel normalization, Biden says', Reuters (21 October 2023).
92. 'Why MBS wants peace with Israel: Saudi Arabia would quietly welcome the demise of Hamas', UnHerd (3 December 2023).
93. Koelbl, *Behind the Kingdom's Veil*, p. 119.
94. Ariel Kahana, 'Senior US lawmakers review plan linking Gaza refugee resettlement to US aid to Arab countries', *Israel Hayom* (29 November 2023).

95 F. Gregory Gause, 'What the war in Gaza means for Saudi Arabia', *Foreign Affairs* (7 November 2023).
96 'Saudi Arabia's response to the Israel-Gaza war', Arab Digest (10 November 2023).
97 Gause, 'What the war in Gaza means for Saudi Arabia'.
98 Maged Mandour, 'The fracturing of the Sisi/Bibi love affair', Arab Digest (4 December 2023).
99 Helen Lackner, 'The risk of Western escalation in the Red Sea', Arab Digest (16 January 2024).
100 BBC *World at One* (16 January 2024).
101 Vijay Prasad, 'Israel's war on Palestine and the global upsurge against it', *Counterpunch* (15 January 2024).
102 Ben Farmer, 'Saudi Arabia and five countries to join China and Russia in Brics group', *Telegraph* (24 August 2023).
103 Ibid.
104 Dennis Ross, 'I might have once favored a cease-fire with Hamas, but not now', *New York Times* (27 October 2023).
105 David Rosenberg, 'Gaza war interrupts tourism recovery for Israel and neighbors', *Al-Monitor* (17 January 2024).
106 Alison Kaplan Sommer, 'Are right-wingers celebrating Palestinian deaths in Rafah the "true face" of Israel?', *Haaretz* (27 May 2024).
107 'Saudi Arabia's response to the Israel-Gaza war'.
108 Keir Simmons and Henry Austin, 'Clock ticks on US–Saudi deal as election and Gaza war threaten to derail landmark agreement', NBC News (29 May 2024).
109 Max Blumenthal, 'October 7 testimonies reveal Israel's military "shelling" Israeli citizens with tanks, missiles', *Grayzone* (27 October 2023).
110 Yaniv Kubovich, 'Israeli army probing death of 12 hostages in Kibbutz Be'eri house shelled on orders of senior officer', *Haaretz* (6 February 2024); Hilo Glazer, 'Who is Barak Hiram, the IDF general who ordered tank fire on a kibbutz home with 13 hostages inside?', *Haaretz* (31 May 2024).
111 'Hanegbi praises "crucial" Qatari diplomatic efforts', *Times of Israel* (15 October 2023).
112 Anchal Vohra, 'How Qatar became a potentially indispensable hostage mediator in Israel-Hamas War', *Times of Israel* (31 October 2023).
113 Roula Khalaf, 'Lunch with the FT: Sheikha Moza', *Financial Times* (10 July 2023).
114 Declan Walsh, 'Tiny, Wealthy Qatar goes its own way, and pays for it', *New York Times* (22 January 2018).
115 David Roberts, *Qatar: Securing Global Ambitions of a City-State*, Hurst, 2017, p. 143.
116 Ibid., p. 99.
117 Koelbl, *Behind the Kingdom's Veil*, p. 246.
118 Andrew Hammond, 'Reordering the Saudi religion: MBS is defanging Wahhabism, not dethroning it', Maydan (20 September 2021).
119 Souad Mekhennet and Greg Miller, 'Jamal Khashoggi's final months as an exile in the long shadow of Saudi Arabia', *Washington Post* (22 December 2018).
120 Ibid.

121 'Washington Post subtly admits slain Khashoggi columns were "shaped" by Qatar', *Arab News*, (23 December 2018).
122 Ibid.
123 Ibid.
124 Koelbl, *Behind the Kingdom's Veil*, pp. 43–5.
125 Martin Chulov, 'Saudi aide accused of directing Khashoggi murder edges back to power', *Guardian* (8 October 2021).
126 Aamer Madhani and Josh Boak, 'Biden gives Saudi Crown Prince Mohammed a hearty handshake', Associated Press (9 September 2023).
127 'MbS: his psychology and lifestyle', Arab Digest (29 September 2023).
128 John Hudson and Claire Parker, 'Blinken meets resistance in courtship of Egypt and Saudi Arabia on Gaza war', *Washington Post* (15 October 2023).

Index

Aarts, Paul, 194
abangan, 142
Abbas, Mahmoud, 256, 257, 309
Abd al-Aziz bin Muhammad (d. 1803), 55
Abd al-Aziz, Omar, 247–8
Abd al-Latif. *See* Latif, Abd-al
Abd al-Rahman bin Faisal, 58, 62, 67, 71, 72, 74, 85
Abdessalem, Rafik, 325
Abdin, Muhammad Surur Zayn al-, 185
Abdullah ibn Abd al-Aziz Al Saud (king), 83, 87, 116–18, 119, 191, 196–9, 203, 208, 235, 292
Abdullah ibn Abd al-Rahman (Ibn Saud brother), 100
Abdullah ibn Faisal (Saudi emir), 60–2
Abdullah ibn Hussein (emir of Transjordan), 84
Abdullah, Muhammad bin, 122
Abdurahman, Aman, 166
Abraham Accords, 42, 255, 309, 310, 311, 323, 331
Abrahamic peace, 317
Abrams, Elliott, 210
Abu Dawud, 60
Abu Saud, Mawlana, 161
Abu Zubaydah, 204
Acheson, Dean, 101
Adam, Jafar, 171
Adham, Kamal, 106

Afary, Janet, 308
AFC Energy, 282
Aga Khan Academies, 183
aghal (headrope), 79, 86
Ahl al-Sunnah ('People of the Sunnah'), 171
Ahl-e-Hadith, 141, 161, 177, 178
Ahmad, Talmiz, 26
Ahmadiyya, 141
Ahmed, Akbar, 92
Ahmed ibn Abd al-Aziz (prince), 36–7, 41, 262
Akar, Hulusi, 5
Aktay, Yasin, 2
Akyol, Mustafa, 133, 134
al-amn al-fikri ('ideological security'), 326
al-Arab (TV station), 33
al-Ahsa (region), 57, 83
Al ash-Sheikh (House of the Sheikh), 59, 60
Albanese, Catherine, 301–2
Albani, Muhammad Nasir al-Din al-, 28
Alexiev, Alex, 160
Al Fahd, 203–4, 208
Al-Haramain Islamic Foundation, 164–5
al-hay'a (the 'Committee'), 147
Alhokair, Fawaz, 198–9
Ali, Hamid bin Abdullah al-, 300
Al-Ittihad, 298
Al Jazeera, 3, 33–4, 35, 39, 150, 324, 325

al-Khalifas, 192
al-kuhul al-watani ('national alcohol'), 253
Allegiance Council, 36
al-Murrah, 58, 67, 68
al-mutawi'a (or *mutaween*), 77, 147
al-Qaeda, 25, 32, 34, 36, 145, 165–6, 175, 185, 187, 204, 207, 209–10, 212, 254
Al Sabah family, 58, 68
al-Sahwa, 138
Al Saud, Abd al-Aziz. *See* Ibn Saud
Al Saud family, 21, 22, 31, 32, 39–40, 57, 59, 68–9, 125, 163, 217, 230, 233–6
al-Shubuk ('the fences'), 253
al-tadamun al-islami ('Islamic solidarity'), 167
AlUla Oasis, 283–4, 288, 290–1
al-wala' wa'l-bara' (loyalty and disassociation), 60, 121, 182
Alwaleed bin Talal (prince), 33, 197–8, 281
al-Wefaq, 33
al-Yamamah ('The Dove') arms deal, 217–18, 222
Amnesty International, 169, 245, 297, 306
Angawi, Sami, 135–6, 137
Ansari, Hind al-, 309
antisemitism, 148–50, 151, 153–4, 155, 316
anti-Shia, 26, 34, 40, 126, 161, 165, 173, 190, 211, 213, 245, 254
anti-Sufi, 165, 168
'Aqab, Wadhah bint Muhammad bin, 104
Aqil, Aqil ibn Abd al-Aziz al- (Sheikh), 165
Arab D (hydrocarbon source), 96
Arab Democracy Foundation, 324
Arab Digest, on pro-Palestinian sentiment, 319
Arab Human Development Report (UN), 228
Arabia, map of (18th century CE), viii
Arab–Israeli dispute, 57, 97, 323. *See also* Arab–Israel peace negotiations; Middle East peace process
Arab–Israeli War
  1948, 120, 147
  1973, 120
Arab–Israel peace negotiations, 14, 318
Arab Spring, 20, 21, 28, 32, 39, 40, 191, 192, 209, 210, 213, 245, 286, 298, 326
Arafat, Yasser, 147

Aramco, 97, 101, 106, 110, 112–13, 126
Architects Climate Action Network (ACAN), 278
Arnold, Michael, 20, 26
art patronage, 295
asabiyya (group feeling, social solidarity, clannism), 78, 79
Asad, Muhammad (formerly Leopold Weiss), 72, 107
Asaker, Badr al-, 8
Asharite, 133–4, 158
ashraf (Prophet's lineage), 122
Asir (region), 90–2
Assad, Bashar al-, 213–16
Assiri, Ahmed al-, 8
Atar, Dan, 305
At-Turaif, 280
Austin, Lloyd, 320
Awdah, Salman al-, 28–9, 138, 185, 188, 189, 326
Awlaki, Anwar al-, 181–2
'Axis of Resistance,' 255, 313
Aziz, Abd al- (d. 1803), 55
Aziz, Sultan bin Abdal-, 196, 201
Aziz, Talal bin Abd al-, 33, 35, 197
Azmeh, Aziz al-, 130
Azzam, Abdullah, 27–8
Azzam, Abdullah al-, 144–5
Azzam, Selim, 144

Ba'asyir, Abu Bakr, 166
BAE (British Aerospace), 217, 218, 219, 221
Baghdadi, Abu Bakr al-, 23, 124, 189
Bakish, Bob, 12
Balad (Jeddah), 281
Bandar ibn Abd al-Aziz, 126
Bandar bin Aziz Bilila, 138
Bandar bin Sultan (prince), 14, 22, 201–19, 221–3, 260–1
Banga, Ajay, 12
banlieus, 142
Banna, Hasan al-, 142, 143, 146, 185
Banu Qurayzah, 148
Bar'el, Zvi, 310
Barelwi, 161
Barr, James, 101
Barrett, Devlin, 206
Barril, Paul, 124
Barton, Dominic, 285

Basic Law of Government, 230–1
Bassnan, Osama, 205
Battle of Mulayda (1891), 62
Battle of Plassey (1757), 69
Battle of Qusayr (2013), 32
Battle of Sibila (1929), 89, 119
Battle of the Ditch, 148
Bauchi State Shariah Commission, 169
baya (allegiance), 230, 262
baya (fealty), 104
Bayoumi, Mrs, 205, 206
Bayoumi, Omar al-, 205
Beddoes, Zanny Minton, 12
Behind the Kingdom's Veil (Koelbl), 268
Bell, Gertrude, 82–3, 85
Bello, Ahmadu, 167
Ben Ali regime, 191–2
Ben-Gvir, Itamar, 333
Benjamin of Tudela, 148
Benzema, Karim, 296, 299
Berkowitz, Ari, 42
Bhutto, Benazir, 174
bidah (unnecessary innovations), 167
Biden, Joe, 17, 29, 42–3, 206, 255, 310–11, 314, 317, 329, 332
Bill and Melinda Gates Foundation, 12
Bin Laden, Bakr, 281
Bin Laden, Mohammed, 92
Bin Laden, Osama, 25, 92, 144, 145, 150, 166, 175, 176, 208
Binladen Group, 122, 133, 135
Blair, Tony, 219, 221
Blazwick, Iwona, 290, 291
Blinken, Antony, 311, 316, 331
Blumenthal, Max, 321, 322
Board of Senior Ulama, 129
Bofill, Ricardo, 280
Bogdanich, Walt, 13, 284
Boko Haram, 34, 170–1, 172
Bolton, John, 17–18, 258
Book of God's Unity (Wahhab), 128
Bostani, Meshal Saad al-, 7–8
Boston Consulting Group (BCG), 9, 265, 273, 284, 286
Bradley, John, 130–2, 187
Bremer, Louis, 9
BRICS, 317
British Aerospace (BAE), 217, 218, 219, 221
Brookfield Asset Management, 15

Brown, Marshall, 274
Bullitt, William, 97
Burton, Elise K., 157–8
Bush, George W., 14, 203, 209, 210
buyas, 239

Callahan, David, 12
Callamard, Agnes, 19–20
Calosci, Loup, 271
Cameron, David, 13
Carnegie Endowment for International Peace, 305, 308, 309
CASOC (California-Arabian Standard Oil Company), 96
caste-prejudice, 201
Cengiz, Hatice, 1
Center for Religious Freedom (CRF), 180
Central Intelligence Agency (CIA) (US), 16, 17, 31, 36, 43, 170
Cerberus Capital Management, 9
charitable organizations, 236–42
Charles (British king), 329
Cheney, Dick, 14, 209, 210
Cherkaoui, Tarek, 20, 26
Chronicle of a Death Foretold (Cherkaoui and Arnold), 20
Churchill, Winston, 99, 100
Cities of Salt (Munif), 108–10
Clapper, James, 6
Clayton, Gilbert, 87
Clinton, Bill, 202, 307
Clinton, Hillary, 212
Coates, Dan, 6–7
Cockburn, Patrick, 211–13
Collective Retreats, 276–7
Commins, David, 48–9, 63, 64, 79–80, 81–2, 87, 128, 129, 130
Committee for the Defence of Legitimate Rights, 127, 191
Committee for the Promotion of Virtue and Prohibition of Vice, 147
Constitution of Medina, 148
consultancies, political role of Western consultancies, 287–8
Cook, Peter, 268–9, 272, 277
Cook Haffner, 268
copper mines, 282
Cordesman, Anthony, 234
Corker, Bob, 18

corruption
  acknowledgement of, 223
  allegations of, 198
  arrests for, 197, 281
  attack of, 132
  campaign against, 200–1, 221
  crackdown on, 200
  as culturally loaded, 223
  grand corruption, 222–3
  House of Saud and, 122
  investigation into, 218–19, 220
  Jews and, 102
  moral corruption, 146
  Muslims and, 121
  Sardar on Meccan real-estate corruption, 137
  spreading of, 130
  use of term, 224
Covid-19 pandemic (2020), response to, 134–5
Cowper-Poles, Sherard, 219
Cox, Percy, 75, 84, 85
creationism, 155
culture, use of to wean Saudi society off oil, 292
Cupitt, Don, 240–1

Daesh, 124, 254; *see also* ISIS
Daily Sabah, on Saudi hit squad, 8
Dajjal, 123–4
Dakhil, Turki al-, 19
Dallal, Ahmad, 63, 66
Dammam Dome, 94
Dammam no. 7, 95
Dan Fodio, Usman, 65, 66
Dantas, Marcello, 291
Dar al-Ifta, 140, 288, 289
Darwin, Charles, 157
Davis, Ian, 285
da'wa (call/mission/evangelism), 52, 62, 159, 163, 164, 172, 177, 178, 179
dawla (state/dynasty), 226, 231
'Day of Rage' (2011), 192
Dearlove, Richard, 211, 212
Dembélé, Moussa, 299
Denes, Agnes, 291
Deobandis, 141, 147, 159, 160, 161, 164, 175, 177, 178
Depani, Alpa, 267

de Pimodan, Quentin, 246–7
Derbal, Nora, 236–7, 238, 239, 240, 241
Dercon, Chris, 292
desert agriculture, 252–3
Desert X, 291
Devaney, Thomas, 105
Dezeen, Tarek Quddumi interview, 269
D. G. Schofield (tanker), 96
Dha'l Khilsa, 46
Dickson, Harold, 83, 88
Dimon, James, 12, 313
diwaniyyat (receptions), 232
Dobzhansky, Theodosius, 156
Don, Caisin bin, 206
Dorsey, James, 164, 172–3, 175, 177, 299, 302
Dostum, Uzbek Abdul Rashid, 176
Doumato, Eleanor, 180–1
Dowayan, Manal al-, 291
Durand Line, 178
Durkheim, Emile, 152–3, 301
Duwaish, Faisal al-, 76, 88

ecological disaster, 251–3, 279–80
Economist
  MBS interview, 228
  on overall proportion of Christians and Muslims, 170
  on programme of reforms, 9
Edge of Arabia, 290
education, gender parity in, 108, 114
Edwards, Harry, 301
11 September 2001 attacks on US, 92, 175–6, 182, 205–6, 207–8, 209
El-Fadl, Khaled Abou, 22–3, 137–9
Elhadj, Elie, 251, 252
Elixir (consulting company), 285
Eltahawy, Mona, 250
Erdogan, Recep Tayyip, 41
evangelism, 166, 254. See also da'wa (call/mission/evangelism)
Evans, Tom, 294
evolution, study and teaching of, 156–8
executions, 244–5
extremism, 254
Exxon, 94

Facebook, 22, 286, 287
Fahd ibn Abd al-Aziz (king), 61, 117, 133, 162, 185, 208, 298

Fahd, Nasr al-, 188
Faisal (crown prince), 105
Faisal (Ibn Saud son), 103
Faisal ibn Abd al-Aziz (king), 26, 27, 34, 67, 83, 88, 91, 92, 102–6, 117, 135, 140, 144, 167, 205, 210, 323
Faisal (prince), 91
Faisal, Haifa al- (princess), 204–5
Faisal, Nawaf bin (prince), 298
Faisal bin Abdullah (prince), 199
Faisal ibn Hussein (king of Iraq), 83
Faisal ibn Musaid (assassin of King Faisal), 140
Faisal ibn Turki (d. 1865), 57, 58
Faisal bin Turki, 298–9
family values, 230–62
Faqih, Sa'ad al-, 191
Faqih, Wilayit al-, 193
fard ayn (individual duty), 145, 188
Farhan, Badr bin Abdullah bin Mohammed bin (prince), 295
Farouk (king), 68
Fassi, Hatun al-, 241–2
fatwas, 127, 129, 132, 140, 160, 184, 188, 288–9, 300
fear, climate of, 243, 287
Federally Administered Tribal Areas (FATA), 178
FIFA World Cup. *See* World Cup
Financial Times
  on Cameron's employment by Greensill Capital, 13
  on PIF of MBS, 9
  on Sahel, 172
Fink, Larry, 11, 12
firqat al-namir (leopard squad), 7, 8
Fleming, Carol, 250
Fofana, Seko, 299
Ford, Bill, 12
Foreign Affairs, on information technologies, 248
Forsythe, Michael, 13, 284
fossil fuels, 293, 294
Foster, Lord, 278
Fowler, Wyche, 234, 235
Fraser, Jane, 313
Freeman, Chas, 217–18
Freud, Sigmund, 152–3
Frontline, Bandar interview, 222

Fulani, 170
Future Investment Initiative conference
  2017, 11
  2018, 12
  2023, 312–13

Gall, Carlotta, 179
Gallant, Yoav, 315
Garangawa, Abdullahi (Sheikh), 168
Gause, Gregory, 312
gay rights, 308
Gaza, crisis in/war in, 38, 257, 306, 312, 313–19, 320, 321, 323, 332, 333, 334
George Tenet medal, 36
Gerges, Fawaz, 261
Ghamdi, Mohammed al-, 245
Ghani, Ashraf, 176
Ghannouchi, Rachid al-, 31, 40–1, 325
Gharem, Abdulnasser, 289–90, 295, 334
Ghawar Field, 96
'giga-projects', 278–9
GIGN (Groupe d'Intervention de la Gendarmerie Nationale), 124
GMP Architekten, 281
Goldsmith, Lord, 219, 220–1
golf, 303
Golyer, Everette, 98
Gormez, Mehmet, 134
Grafftey-Smith, Laurence, 68, 100
Graham, Bob, 204
Gray, John, 286
Greenfield, Adam, 275
Greensill, Lex, 13
Guardian, on conversation between MBS and Macron, 258
Gulf (oil company), 94
Gumi, Abubakar, 167, 168
Guriev, Sergei, 287
Guterres, António, 195

Haaretz, on NSO, 248
Hadi, Abdrabbuh Mansour, 38
Hafter, Khalifa, 37
Hajj, 59, 85, 86, 96, 98, 103, 133, 167, 179
Hajj Research Centre, 135
halal, 99
Hamas, 24, 38, 150, 255, 257, 309–10, 311, 317, 320, 321, 322, 323, 326, 331, 332, 333, 334

Hamid, Abdullah al-, 29
Hammond, Andrew, 115, 326
Hanbali school of law, 59, 133–4, 158, 326
Hanbali–Wahhabi, 118
Hanegbi, Tzachi, 323
Haq, Sami ul-, 175
Haqqani, Jalaluddin, 177
Haram area, Mecca, 133
haram (forbidden), 140
Harbi, Ahmed Eid al-, 298
Harbi, Thaer al-, 8
Hariri, Saad, 256, 257
Harnischfeger, Johannes, 169, 170
Harris, Kamala, 332
Hasafiyya, 143
Hasawi, Abd al-Aziz al-, 8
Haspel, Gina, 16, 257
Hausa, 65, 167, 170, 171
hawala, 165
Hawali, Safar al-, 29–30, 127, 185, 190, 326
Hawsawi, 298
Hawwa, Sa'id, 145
Hazaras, 174
Hazmi, Nawaf al-, 182, 205
Headscarves and Hymens (Eltahawy), 250
Hegghammer, Thomas, 121
Heizer, Michael, 291
Hejaz, 55, 56, 57, 58, 60, 72, 83, 84, 85, 86, 87, 90, 111, 133, 163
Henderson, Jordan, 296
Henry IV of Castile, 104–5
Hersh, Seymour, 214, 215
Hezbollah, 14, 24, 25, 254, 255, 256, 310, 313, 319
Higher Judicial Council, 140
hijra/hijras/hujar (emigration), 65, 76, 77, 80, 81, 86, 87
hijri (century), 122
Hikers, 237–8
Hill, Christopher, 173
himaya (protection), 53, 81
Hiram, Barak, 322
hisba ('commanding the good and forbidding the evil'), 146–7
Hithlain, Fahdah bint Falah al-, 263
Hitler, Adolph, 24, 27, 150, 151, 152
HOK (architects), 268
Holden, David, 105, 106, 107
Hollingsworth, Mark, 217, 218

homosexuality (*liwat*), 308
Hope, Bradley, 263–4
Hoskins, Harold, 98
House, Karen Elliott, 43–4, 113, 114–15, 227, 235–6, 250
The House of Saud (Holden and Johns), 105
Houthis, 24–5, 38–9, 194, 255, 313, 314
huddud, 129
Huffington, Arianna, 12
human rights, 7, 9, 44, 126, 169, 242, 243, 247, 260, 272, 278, 297, 304, 306–7
Human Rights Watch, 244, 297, 306
Hunt, Bryan, 177–8
Hunt, Jeremy, 195
Hussa bint Ahmed Al Sudairi, 36, 201, 203, 204
Hussain, Safiyya, 169
Hussein (king), 84–6
Hussein (Sharif), 83, 84
Hussein, Saddam, 132, 184, 186, 203, 209
husseiniyas (halls), 125
Huwaitat, 273–4
Huwaiti, Abdal Rahim al-, 274

Ibn Abdal-Latif, Abdallah, 62
Ibn Abdullah, Sulayman, 60
Ibn Ajlan, Muhammad, 61–2
Ibn al-Arabi, 64
Ibn al-Farid, 48
Ibn Ali, Hassan, 90–1
Ibn Ali, Huysayn, 46
Ibn Amr, Abdullah, 63
Ibn Arabi, 48
Ibn Arabi, Muhyi'l din, 50
Ibn Baz, Abd al-Aziz (grand mufti), 61, 119–21, 132, 141, 156, 160, 166, 184, 185, 288, 289, 300, 302
Ibn Bijad, 88
Ibn Ghanam, Husayn, 47
Ibn Hanbal, Ahmed 50
Ibn Hithlain, Dhaidhan, 88
Ibn Hussein, Ali, 85, 86
Ibn Jibrin, Abdullah (Sheikh), 127
Ibn Khaldun, 77–9, 82
Ibn Musa'id, Khalid, 140
Ibn Rashid, Muhammad, 58, 62
Ibn Saud, ix, 35, 67–93, 94, 95, 96, 97, 98, 99, 103, 104, 129, 227

Ibn Sihman, 87
Ibn Suhaym, Sulayman, 48–9
Ibn Taymiyya, 46, 50, 51, 128, 171
Ibn Thunayan, Abdullah, 57–8
Ibrahim Pasha, 56, 60
Ickes, Harold, 98
Idris, Ismail, 167
Idrisi, Sayyed Muhammad al-, 90
Iffat bint Mohammed Al Thunayan (wife of King Faisal), 106
Ignatius, David, 327
ikhtilaf (differences), 162
Ikhwan, 79, 80–1, 82, 85, 86–8, 89–90, 91, 119
Ilyas, Maulana Muhammad, 159
immigrant workers, deaths of in work-related accidents, 304–6
Indyk, Martin, 14
'in-marriage,' 233
Instagram, 22, 286, 287
interfaith dialogue, 116, 117
International Islamic Relief Organization, 164
Iraqi Petroleum Company, 94, 95
ISIS, 24, 25, 34, 124, 170, 210, 211, 213; see also Daesh
islahhiyun ('reformists'), 194
Islamic centres, 163
Islamic State, 174, 254
IslamQA, 288
Ismailism, 141
Israel. See also Netanyahu, Benjamin
  normalization with, 311, 319
  settlement expansion in West Bank, 13–14, 147, 257, 310, 313, 314, 315, 320, 332
  two-state solution in Israel–Palestine, 311, 321
Israel Defense Forces (IDF), 219, 309, 312, 313, 321, 322
Israel–Palestinian peace process, 14, 17, 216, 312. See also Middle East peace process
Issa, Muhammad bin Abdul-Karim al-, 30
Izala, 167, 168, 171

Jabarti, Abd al-Rahman al-, 59
Jabhat al-Nusra, 214, 254
jahiliyya (ignorance), 52, 145

jama'a al-Islamiyya (Islamic associations), 146
Jama'a al-Salafiyya al-Muhtasiba (JSM), 119
Jamaah Ansharut Daulah, 166
Jama'at Ahl-Als" Sunnah li-Dawa wa'l Jihad ('Group of the People of the Sunnah for Preaching and Jihad'), 170
Jama'at al-Sunna al-muhammadiyya, 147
Jamaati Islami, 141
Jama'atu Nasril Islam (Society for the Support of Islam), 167
JCPOA (Joint Comprehensive Plan of Action), 43, 191, 255, 282
Jeddah, 280–1
Jeddah Tower, 281
Jemaah Islamiyah, 165
Jews, 13–14, 24, 47, 97, 98, 99, 102, 124, 147–55, 207, 211, 254, 311, 320
jihad, 52, 55, 65, 145, 166, 172, 173, 175, 176, 184, 188, 302
John Paul II (Pope), 156
Johns, Richard, 105, 106, 107
Jones, Toby, 184, 186, 188–9
Joyriding in Riyadh (Menoret), 243
Juhayman al-Utaybi, 119–21, 122, 124, 137, 187
Junaibi, Ahmad Abdal Aziz al-, 4
Jundullah, 174–5
Jungers, Frank, 110–12

Kaeser, Joe, 12
kafala (foreign businesses/sponsorship), 81, 227
kafir (unbeliever), 50
kalima (Islamic credo), 334
Kamel, Salah, 199
Kanté, N'Golo, 296, 299
Kantorowicz, Ernst, 226–7, 228
Karoui, Hakim al-, 40
Karzai, Hamid, 176
Kennedy, Helena, 5
Kerry, John, 255
Khadija, 135
Khalaf (Sheikh), 273
Khaled, 57, 58, 198
Khalid ibn Abd al-Aziz (king), 76
Khalid ibn Musa'id, 140
Khalid ibn Salman Al Saud (brother of MBS), 260

Khalidi, Ahmed al-, 188
Khalifa, Hamad bin Isa al-, 32
Khalifa, Hamad bin (Sheikh), 325
Khamenei, Ali, 24, 255
Khan, Imran, 258
Kharaji, Qadi Abdullah al-, 69
Kharijites, 50–1
Khashoggi, Jamal, 1–9, 12, 15–16, 17, 19–20, 23, 30–3, 34, 40, 41, 43, 132, 138, 194, 208, 246, 247, 257, 261, 303, 312, 319, 327–8, 329, 330, 331, 334
Khashoggi, Salah, 2, 5, 328
Khattab, Umar ibn al-, 23, 47–8
Khattab, Zayd ibn al-, 47
khawarij (heretics), 190
Khilewi, Mohammed Abdullah, 223
Khomeni, Ayatollah, 125
Khosrowshahi, Dara, 12
khuba (Friday sermon), 180
Khudayr, Ali al-, 188
khuwwa (tribute), 52, 53, 81
Kim, Jim Yong, 12
King Abdulaziz Center for World Culture (Ithra), 292–3
King Abdullah charitable foundation, 199, 201
King Abdullah Economic City, 246
The Kingdom (Lacey), 113
King Fahd Academy, 154, 182, 183
King Faisal International Prize (1994), 34, 35
King Salman's Park (Riyadh), 280
The King's Two Bodies (Kantorowicz), 226
Koelbl, Susanne, 202, 215–16, 246, 268, 287, 312, 327
Koulibaly, Kalidou, 299
Kramer, Martin, 148–9, 153–4
Kristof, Nicholas, 15
kufr (disbelief), 65–6
Kushner, Charles, 15
Kushner, Jared, 13–14, 15, 16, 18, 42, 256, 257

Lacey, Robert, 89, 113
Lacroix, Stéphane, 30, 121, 144, 145
Lagarde, Christine, 11
Landler, Mark, 17
Larsen, Henning, 281
Lashkar-e-Jhangvi, 174

Latif, Abd al-, 60, 61, 62
Latif, Muhammad ibn Ibrahim ibn Abd-al, 140–1
Lawrence, T. E. ('Lawrence of Arabia'), 83
LGBTQ+, 306–7, 308
The Line, 265–77, 289, 291
LIPIA, 166
LIV Golf, 303
liwat (homosexuality), 308
Lloyd, Richard, 215
Ludwig II (King of Bavaria), 270–1
Lush Gardens, 293

Maas, Wilhelmus, 274–5
MacEoin, Denis, 160–1, 182
Macron, Emmanuel, 257–8, 329
Mada'in Saleh (al-Hijr), 283, 288
Madani, Mustafa Mohammed al-, 8
madhhab (law school), 55, 59
madrasas (religious schools), 161, 162, 175
Mahdi (Islamic Messiah), 121, 122, 123
Mahrez, Riyad, 299
Maier, Karl, 282
majalis (pl., traditional meetings), 236
majlis (singular, assembly), 70
Maktab al-Khidamat (Office of Services), 145
Malihi, Abdullah al-, 248
'mallam' (*alim*), 65
Mané, Sadio, 296
manhaj (revolutionary programme), 189
Mansour (Ibn Saud son), 98, 103
Mansur, Abu Jafar al-, 266
Maritime Truces, 70
marja ('source of emulation'), 194
Markazi Masjid, 160
marriage, 104, 106, 108, 114, 127, 169, 231, 232–5, 237, 239, 250, 306
Marx, Karl, 153
Marxism, 152
Marzouq, Khalil al-, 33
Masoud, Tajik Ahmed Shah, 176
Mater, Ahmed, 289–90, 291
Matthiesen, Toby, 112, 127
Maududi, Abu Ala al-, 145, 177
mawlid (Prophet's birthday), 46, 181
May, Theresa, 258
Mayne, Thom, 265–6, 268, 275
MBC (media company), 200

Index

MBN. *See* Nayef, Muhammad bin (MBN)
MBS, 2, 5, 6, 9, 11, 13, 14, 15, 16, 18, 19, 24, 26, 27, 28, 29, 30, 34, 35, 36, 37–8, 40, 43, 44, 137, 138, 196, 200–1, 208, 228, 246, 255–60, 272, 284, 287, 312, 313, 326
MBZ. *See* Zayed, Mohamed bin (MBZ)
McGuinness, Martin, 329
McIlroy, Rory, 303
McKinsey and Company, 9, 12–13, 246, 265, 273, 284–6
McLoughlin, Leslie, 73, 80, 104
MDPTU (molecular diagnostics and personalized therapeutics unit), 155
Mecca, 21, 22, 26, 55, 56, 59–60, 65, 76, 85, 86, 113, 119, 125, 132, 133, 134, 135–7, 139, 142, 162, 234, 235, 267, 299
Medina, 26, 55, 56, 60, 65, 76, 86, 133, 134, 139, 151, 234, 235, 299
Mehmet Ali, 56, 60
Meijer, Roel, 141, 142, 162
Mein Kampf (Hitler), 150, 152
Menon, Shivshankar, 332, 333
Menoret, Pascal, 243, 249, 250, 253, 254
Meos (Indian community), 159
Meshari, Badr al- (Sheikh), 289
Messi, Lionel, 296–7
Metcalf, Barbara, 160
Meulen, Daniel van der, 72
Middle East Eye, on death squad, 7
Middle East peace process, 256–7
Mihdhar, Khalid al-, 182, 205
Miller, Aaron David, 39
Ministry of Defence (MoD) (Britain), 221
Minority Rights Group, on killing of Shia, 174
Mishaal bin Abdullah (prince), 199
Mishari (Ibn Saud son), 103
MiSK Foundation, 12, 286
Miteb bin Abdullah (prince), 197, 199
Mnuchin, Steven, 11, 12
Modi, Narendra, 258, 259
Montagu, Caroline, 232, 236, 241, 242
Moosa, Ebrahim, 161–2
Morsi, Mohamed, 21, 210, 312, 324
Mossad, 333
Movement for Islamic Reform, 191
Movement of Vanguards' Missionaries (MVM), 125
Moza bint Nasser, Sheikha, 324, 327

Mu'ammar, Uthman ibn, 47
Muasher, Marwan, 229
Mubarak (Sheikh), 69, 70, 71, 72, 75
muftis (scholars authorized to issue fatwas), 289
muhaddith (modernizer), 326
Muhamad Belo, 65
Muhammad (Ibn Saud brother), 75
Muhammad (Ibn Saud son), 98
Muhammad (Sheikh), 69
Muhammad Ahmad, 123
Muhammed Abduh, 142
Muhanna, Muhammad, 207
Muharram, 125
Muhiuddin Chisti, 65
mujaddid (renewer), 47, 122, 137, 326
mujahidin, 153
Mujtahid (Interpreter) (blogger), 44, 330–1
Munajjid, Muhammad Saleh al- (Sheikh), 288, 289
Munif, Abdul Rahman, 108–10
Munthohir, Saiful, 166
Muqadimma (Introduction) (Ibn Khaldun), 78
Muqrin, Mansour bin, 7
Musaid, Jawhara bint, 76, 107
Mushaikhass, Yussuf al-, 245
Musk, Elon, 285
Muslim Brotherhood, 21, 24, 25–6, 27, 28, 31, 34–5, 37, 40, 41, 119, 142, 143, 144, 145–6, 147, 210, 311–12, 323–4, 325–6, 327
Muslim World League, 30, 164, 167
Mutair, 88
mutaween (or *al-mutawi'a*) (religious police), 77, 228. *See also* religious police
Mu'tazilism, 134, 158
Mutreb, Maher Abdulaziz, 2, 8, 17
muwahhidun ('unitarians'), 54

Na'imi, Ali al-, 126
nakba (the 'catastrophe'), 147, 312
Namias, Olivier, 271
Nasi, Margherita, 264
nasiha, 29
Nasr, Vali, 41, 179
Nasrallah, Hasan, 319
Nasser, Abd-al, 144
Nasser, Gamal Abdel, 105, 141

National Security Agency (NSA) (US), 6
Navarra, Blanca da, 104
Nawwaf bin Abd al-Aziz, 212
Nayef (prince), 196
Nayef ibn Abd al-Aziz, 34, 187
Nayef, Muhammad bin (MBN), 35–6, 37
Nazis, 97, 99, 150, 151, 152, 155, 211
Nejd, 45, 46, 48, 51–2, 55, 56, 57, 60, 62, 63, 74, 80, 83, 85, 88, 91, 111
Nejdi, Abdullah ibn Ibrahim al-, 46
Neom, 264–78, 279, 286, 289
Netanyahu, Benjamin, 13, 42, 309, 310, 314, 333
Nettler, Ronald, 150
Net Zero, 293
New York Times
  on elevation of MBS, 35
  on Khashoggi killing, 8–9, 18
  on McKinsey tracking dissidents, 12
  on Mideast peace process, 256–7
Nielsen, Rasmus, 156, 157, 158
Nimr, Nimr al-, 31, 193, 194, 244
niqab (full facial veil), 92
Nizamuddin, 65
Nizari Ismaili, 174
normalization, 308–9, 310–11, 319, 320, 323, 331
Noura, 222
NSO (software company), 247

Obama, Barack, 43, 181, 215, 255
O'Conor, Nicholas, 75–6
Oldfield, Philip, 274
Oliver Wyman (consulting company), 265, 273
Omar, Mullah, 176, 177
Oppenheimer, J. Robert, 275, 276
Organisation of Economic Co-operation and Development (OECD)
  Convention on Combating Bribery, 219–20
  Financial Action Task Force, 241
Oslo Accords, 309–10
Ottaway, David, 202
Our Struggle with the Jews (S. Qutb), 149–50
'out-marriage,' 233
Oxagon, 279–80
Oxford Business Group, 155

Palestine
  Anglo-American commission on, 101
  Jews preference to go to, 99, 101
  opposition to Jewish settlement in, 147
Palestinian Authority (PA), 309, 310
Palestinians
  defense of rights for, 257
  peace process, 14, 17, 216, 312
  pro-Palestinian sentiment, 147, 151, 309, 312, 317, 318–19, 323
  state for, 256
  two-state solution in Israel–Palestine, 311, 321
panis et circenses (bread and circuses), 130
Panorama, on BAE Systems, 219
Pashtun, 175, 176, 178
patriarchy
  petroleum and, 94–115
  structures of tribal patriarchy, 232
Payette, Tom, 266
pederasty, 308
Pegasus (malware), 247
Pellegrino, Chiara, 27, 28
Pence, Mike, 14
Peston, Maurice, 220
petroleum, and patriarchy, 94–115
Pew Research, on Muslims residing in US, 181
Philby, Harry St John, 94, 95, 98, 101, 105, 107, 108, 291
Piano, Renzo, 281
PIF (public investment fund). *See* public investment fund (PIF)
PII, 207
Policy Exchange, 160, 183
Politico, Sokolsky and Miller article, 39
polygamous marriage, 231
polygyny, 232
Porat, Yasmin, 321, 322
Postol, Theodore, 214–15
Prasad, Vijay, 315, 316
Proctor, Rebecca Anne, 290, 291–2, 294–5
Project MAPS (Muslim Americans in the Public Square), 180
Pron, Olivier, 264
pro-Palestinian sentiment, 147, 151, 309, 312, 317, 318–19, 323
Protocols of the Learned Elders of Zion, 24, 150, 152–5

public investment fund (PIF), 9–11, 272, 273–4, 277, 278, 281, 282–3, 296
Putin, Vladimir, 258

Qadhafy, Muammar al-, 172, 325
Qadiri, Monira al-, 291
Qadiryya, 167
qadis (judges), 59, 63, 69, 85, 128, 129, 130
Qahtani, Ali al-, 197
Qahtani, Muhammad al-, 122, 137
Qahtani, Nasser al-, 248
Qahtani, Saud al-, 8, 16, 17, 246, 319, 328–9
Qaradawi, Yousuf al-, 34, 35, 40, 324
qaris (Quran reciters), 69
Qatar Foundation, 327
Qatari Youth Opposed to Normalization, 308
qibla (direction of Mecca), 99
Qidiyya, 280
Quddumi, Tarek, 269
Questions of the Revolution (Awdah), 28
Qutb, Muhammad, 27, 144, 145
Qutb, Sayyid, 24, 27, 144, 145, 149–53, 177, 184, 325

Rahman, Umar Abd al- (Sheikh), 145–6
Raisi, Ebrahim, 255
Rakkabi, Zayn al-Din al-, 150
Rasheed, Madawi al-, 5–6, 10, 52, 53, 90, 93, 127, 185, 191, 192–3, 226–7, 230, 231, 256
Rashid, Ubayd al-, 74
Rashids, 63, 68, 71, 72, 73, 74
rationalism, 134, 158
rawafid ('rejectionists'), 188
Reagan, Ronald, 202, 217
Red Line Agreement, 94, 95
Red Sea Project, 289
Reema bint Bandar (princess), 201, 260–1
Reidel, Bruce, 202
religious pluralism, 30, 39, 117
religious police, 77, 147, 228, 238, 256, 326
religious supremacism, 148, 149
repression, 244, 287
restoration programmes, 280
Rida, Rashid, 142–3
Riedel, Bruce, 7, 18
Rihani, Ameen, 74, 107
Rivellino, Roberto, 298

Roberts, David, 324
Robinson, Mary, 293, 294
Roelants, Carolien, 194
Ronaldo, Cristiano, 296, 297
Roosevelt, Franklin D., 97, 98, 99
Roshn (branch of Saudi PIF), 277–8
Ross, Dennis, 317
Rouhani, Hassan, 255
Roy, Olivier, 153, 160
Royal Institute of British Architects (RIBA), Professional Code of Practice, 278
Royal United Services Institute, 212
Rugman, Jonathan, 2, 3, 4, 5
Rumsfeld, Donald, 209
Rundell, David, 311, 317

Saad, 75
Sabah, Mubarak al- (Mubarak the Great), 69
Sadat, Anwar, 146
Sahel, 172
Sahwa (awakening) movement, 132, 184, 186, 188, 189, 326
Salafism, 21, 63, 141–2, 145, 164, 170, 171, 254
salam aleikum ('peace be upon you'), 141
Saleh, Ali Abdullah, 38–9
Salem, Maggie Mitchell, 327
Salman ibn Abd al-Aziz (king), 3, 43, 134, 191, 196–8, 203, 241, 256, 261–4, 280
Salman, Abdulaziz bin (prince), 262, 282, 294, 317
Salman, Khalid bin, 16
Salman, Mashhoor bin Hasan, al- (Sheikh), 300
Salman, Mohammed bin (MBS). *See* MBS
Samin, Nadav, 231
Sampson, Anthony, 100, 101–2
santris, 142
Sanusiyya, 90
Sardar, Ziauddin, 136, 137
Sartre, Jean Paul, 153
Saud al-Faisal (prince), 58, 60–2, 118
Saud ibn Abd al-Aziz (king), 103, 104, 105–8
Saudi Arabia
    'coming out party,' 11
    founder of, 67
    identity of, 21

Saudi Arabia (cont'd)
  internet penetration in, 22
  path to modernity, 140
  United States relations with, 101
Saudi Arabia Exposed (Bradley), 130–2
Saudi Arabian National Guard (SANG), 199
Saudi Aramco, 114, 126, 132
Saudi Center for International Strategic Partnerships, 285
Saudi Civil and Political Rights Association, 244
Saudi Electricity Company, 281
Saudi Football Association, 298
Saudi Ministry of Islamic Affairs, Dawah and Guidance, 164
Saudi Pro League, 296
Saudi Publications on Hate Ideology Invade American Mosques (CRF), 180
Sayf, Muhammad bin, 119
Sayyid al-Qahtani, 122
sayyids, 48
Scheck, Justin, 263–4
Schindler, John R., 6
Schumer, Chuck, 311
Schwarzman, Stephen, 12
SCL Group (Cambridge Analytica), 286
Scramble for Arabia, 284
Senussi, Alia al-, 290, 291–2, 294–5
7 October 2023 (Hamas attack on Israel), 38, 310, 311, 313, 321, 322, 323, 331
Shabbab, 34
Shaikh, Aal al-, 302
Shalit, Gilad, 333
Sharia and Life (TV show), 34
Shea, Nina, 180, 182
Sheikh, Muhammad ibn Ibrahim al-, 299
Shekau, Abu Bakr, 171
Shertock, Moshe, 98
shirk (polytheism/idolatry), 65, 167, 181
Shuaibah (solar power plant), 282
Singh, Manmohan, 332
Sipah-e-Sahaba, 173
sirat, 69
Sisi, Abd al-Fattah al-, 21, 210, 262, 312, 314
Sky, Emma, 213
Smotrich, Bezalel, 333
Snøhetta (architect firm), 292
Socal, 94, 95, 96–7, 110

soccer (football), 296–302
Society of Removal of Innovation and Re-establishment of the Sunnah, 167
Sokolsky, Richard, 39
Soldiers of God: Culture and Morals (Hawwa), 145–6
SOM (architecture studio), 281
Son, Masayoshi, 11
Soon-Shiong, Patrick, 12
Sorkin, Andrew Ross, 12
Specialized Criminal Court, 244, 245
Spin Dictators (Guriev and Treisman), 287
sports, 296–304
sportswashing, 297, 298, 304, 307
Stalin, Joseph, 331
Stapleton, Stephen, 289–90
Stevens, J. Christopher, 210
Strada, Terry, 208
Sudairi, Ahmed Al, 203
Sudairi, Fahd Al, 203
Sudairi, Hussa bint Ahmed Al. *See* Hussa bint Ahmed Al Sudairi
Sudairi family, 203–4, 262
Sudais, Abdulrahman al-, 22, 23, 137, 138
Sufism, 64, 90, 141, 143, 167, 173
Sulaiman, Abdullah, 100, 101
Sultan bin Salman (prince), 119–20
Sunday Club, 241–2
Sungkar, Abdullah, 166
sustainability, 293–4
Sustainability Studio, 293

Tablighi Jamat (TJ), 142, 159–60
takfir/takfirism, 50
takfir/takfirism (infidelity), 51, 64, 121, 142, 145, 168, 188
Talal, Alwaleed bin. *See* Alwaleed bin Talal
Talib, Saleh al- (Sheikh), 138
Taliban, 34, 175–6, 177, 178, 179
Tamgo, 282
Tantawi, Ali, 35
tawhid (divine unicity), 46, 52, 54, 62, 64, 77
Tawijeri, Khaled al-, 198
Tayi, Auda Abu (Sheikh), 273
ta'zir, 130
Tehrik Taliban Pakistan, 174
Tenth Protocol of the Elders of Zion. See Protocols of the Learned Elders of Zion.
Texaco, 96

Thani, Tamim bin Hamad al-, 306, 323
Thani, Mohammed bin Abdul Rahman al-, 307, 314
Thanis, 324
Thatcher, Margaret, 217
Thiel, Peter, 285–6
Thumayri, Fahad al-, 206–7
Thuniyan, Suliman Abdul Rahman al-, 7
Tijaniyya, 167, 168
Tillerson, Rex, 15
Tillich, Paul, 301
Tonet, Aureliano, 264
Transparency International, 222–3
Treatise on God's Unity (monotheist manifesto), 46
Treaty of London (1840), 57
Treisman, Daniel, 287
Trofimov, Yaroslav, 122–3, 125, 126
Trucial States, 70
Truman, Harry, 99, 101
Trump, Donald, 13, 15–16, 17, 40, 41–2, 43, 182, 191, 195, 197, 200, 254–5, 257, 258, 303, 311, 332
Tuastad, Dag Henrik, 298
Tubaigy, Salah al-, 2, 3, 8
Turki bin Abd al-Aziz, 107
Turki bin Abdullah (d. 1834), 57,
Turki bin Abdullah (prince), 197, 199
Turki al-Faisal (prince), 31, 41, 179, 189–90, 205, 248
Turki bin Nasser, 222, 223
Turkish Petroleum Company, 94
Turner, Ashley, 288
Turrell, James, 291
Twitchell, Karl, 94
Twitter/X, 22, 28, 197, 198, 242, 245–6, 247, 286, 287, 289, 321, 330
two-state solution in Israel–Palestine, 311, 321

ulama ('the learned men'), 45, 85, 88, 140
Umm Mansour, 106
United Nations
    Arab Human Development Report, 228
    King Abdullah's visit to (2008), 116–18
uranium, 282
Utaiba, 85, 88, 119, 124
Utaybi, Juhayman al-. *See* Juhayman al-Utaybi

Uthman (caliph), 152
Uyairi, Yousuf al-, 189

Valentine, Simon, 243
Varagur, Krithika, 164, 165, 166, 167–8, 170, 172
Vinnell Corporation, 186
virginity, 250
virility, 104, 105, 106
Vision 2030, 9, 11, 246, 254, 279, 281, 286, 289, 297
visionary projects, 276

Wahba, Hafiz, 82
Wahhab, Muhammad ibn Abd al-, 30, 45–66, 128, 326
Wahhabi-Salafism, 21, 22, 24, 26, 61, 91, 160
Wahhabi/Wahhabism, 21, 30, 32, 39–40, 45–66, 71, 76–7, 81, 114, 115, 118–19, 141, 146, 164, 254, 326
wala wa'l-bara ('loyalty and disavowal'), 141
wali al-amr (Islamic guardian of the state), 326–7
Wali Allah (Shah), 64
Wall Street Journal, on The Line, 272
Wardle, Robert, 219
Warren, Elizabeth, 303
Weber, Max, 226
Weimann, Gunnar, 169
Weizmann, Chaim, 98
West, John Carl, 124
WhatsApp, 16, 242
Whitson, Sarah Leah, 303
Williamson, Chris, 278, 279
Winship, Tony, 222
Woods, Tiger, 303
World Assembly of Muslim Youth, 141, 143, 164
World Christian Encyclopedia, on overall proportion of Christians and Muslims, 170
World Cup
    1978, 298
    2022, 275, 308, 309
    2034, 296
World Muslim League, 141, 143
Wright, Nicholas, 248–9
Wyden, Ron, 303

Xi Jinping, 258, 259, 287, 316

Yamasaki, Minoru, 271
Yang Jiechi, 260
YIG (Young Initiative Group), 238
yoga, 288, 289
Young Turks, 262
Yousuf, Muhammad, 171
YouTube, 1, 22, 23, 242, 244, 299

Zahrani, Khaled Yahya al-, 4
Zaidi, Akbar, 177
zakat (purifying dues), 54, 55, 81, 238
Zarqawi, Abu Musa al-, 189
Zayed, Mohamed bin (MBZ), 25, 37, 38, 323
Zia-ul-Haq, Muhammad, 147, 173, 176
zina (crime), 239
Zionism, 98, 102, 151, 153, 154
Zirkili, Khair al-Din, 107
Zogby International, 180